MODERN RHETORICAL CRITICISM

THIRD EDITION

Roderick P. Hart

University of Texas at Austin

Suzanne M. Daughton

Southern Illinois University at Carbondale

PEARSON

Boston   New York   San Francisco
Mexico City   Montreal   Toronto   London   Madrid   Munich   Paris
Hong Kong   Singapore   Tokyo   Cape Town   Sydney

Executive Editor: Karon Bowers
Series Editor: Brian Wheel
Series Editorial Assistant: Jennifer Trebby
Marketing Manager: Mandee Eckersley
Composition and Prepress Buyer: Linda Cox
Manufacturing Buyer: JoAnne Sweeney
Cover Coordinator: Joel Gendron
Editorial-Production Coordinator: Mary Beth Finch
Editorial-Production Service: Omegatype Typography, Inc.
Electronic Composition: Omegatype Typography, Inc.

For related titles and support materials, visit our online catalog at www.ablongman.com

Between the time Website information is gathered and then published, it is not unusual for some sites to have closed. Also, the transcription of URLs can result in unintended typographical errors. The publisher would appreciate notification where these errors occur so that they may be corrected in subsequent editions.

Library of Congress Cataloging-in-Publication Data

Hart, Roderick P.
    Modern rhetorical criticism / Roderick P. Hart and Suzanne M. Daughton.—3rd ed.
        p. cm.
    Includes bibliographical references and index.
    ISBN 0-205-37799-8
    1. Rhetoric. 2. Criticism. 3. Persuasion (Rhetoric) 4. Literature—History and criticism—Theory, etc. I. Daughton, Suzanne M. II. Title.

PN175.H37   2004
808—dc22

2004053156

Printed in the United States of America.

10   9   8   7   6   5   4   3   2   1   09   08   07   06   05   04

CONTENTS

Unit III
SPECIALIZED FORMS OF CRITICISM

PREFACE

The study of rhetoric is an old one. It was studied by the ancient Greeks and Romans, by medieval courtiers, by Renaissance theologians, and by political thinkers in the emerging democracies of the eighteenth century. Each sensed that something special, something powerful, happened when a firebrand mounted a political platform or entered a church pulpit or hand-delivered a scathing editorial. This power continues to be unleashed today, and so rhetoric is once again being studied with gusto. Here's why: "fair and balanced" news coverage, twenty-second radio commercials, Internet political campaigns, televised evangelism, *The West Wing*, the resurgence of state militias, reality TV, AIDS awareness campaigns, La Leche League International, welfare reform, poetry slams, Adolph Hitler's Big Lie, and Arnold Schwarzenegger. All of these characters and events collect in the rhetorical arena. All of them change people's lives. To ignore them is to risk one's political, moral, and financial security.

Modern Rhetorical Criticism is a comprehensive, up-to-date guidebook to public rhetoric. It is written for those taking coursework in rhetorical criticism and for students of literary criticism interested in rhetorical approaches to ideas. Its goals are threefold: (1) to broaden the reader's conception of persuasion so that its uses in law, politics, religion, and commerce are seen as different species—rather than different genuses—when compared to its less obvious uses in literature, science, education, and entertainment; (2) to sample critical studies of rhetoric produced in the United States the past thirty years; and (3) to equip the reader with the critical tools and attitudes needed to see how rhetoric works its magic.

Any book is necessarily selective. The reader will not find in *Modern Rhetorical Criticism* a complete history of rhetorical thought or of the rival schools of criticism making up that history. Rather, we emphasize primarily the U.S. tradition of critical inquiry. Historically, this tradition has featured public debate and the spoken word. More contemporary studies have branched out into various media, and the book takes those persuasive forms into account as well. In an era of electronic media, rhetoric—whether oral, written, visual, or nonverbal—has taken on a power and a reach never before witnessed in human history. Each day, after all, the mass media entice us to remember some things and not others, to spend money on this product and not that one, to grieve about these circumstances and to ignore those. Such enticements lie at the heart of rhetoric. We ignore them at our peril.

The book begins with two overview chapters, one on the nature of rhetoric and one on the nature of criticism. These introductory discussions present the basic terminology of rhetorical study and show why criticism is so central to the intellectual life. Unit II pushes deeper into rhetorical artifacts themselves by providing the basic tools needed to understand the situations, ideas, arguments, structure, and style making up rhetorical exchanges and to see how the electronic media have fundamentally altered those exchanges during the last half century. Finally, Unit III treats more ambitious forms of analysis—those dealing with role, culture, and drama—and also shows why certain contemporary schools of ideological criticism—feminist, Marxist, and poststructuralist approaches—must be understood by anyone hoping to produce intelligent criticism today.

The third edition of *Modern Rhetorical Criticism* differs from the second in several ways. It includes completely new coverage of the rhetoric of the Internet, exploring the ways in which the rhetoric of news, narrative, advertising, visual imagery, and entertainment combine in this newest mass medium. An entirely new section on postcolonial criticism concludes the final chapter, highlighting the ways in which multicultural concerns have led to the interrogation and opening up of traditional texts and forms of criticism. Also, the latest edition of *Modern Rhetorical Criticism* updates the critical research, as well as provides new tools and practical advice for dissecting messages. In addition, new examples of criticism are provided so that theory is continually made practical for the reader.

Several features make this book unique. For example, besides presenting a wide array of critical techniques and summarizing hundreds of critical studies, the book contains numerous pieces of original criticism. Sometimes, the texts analyzed are masterworks—patriotic oratory, Orwell's *Animal Farm*, Shakespeare's *King Lear*—and sometimes they are more practical—Army recruitment literature, newspaper editorials, love letters. These sample analyses are intended to show how genuinely creative criticism "opens up" a text that the persuader has, consciously or unconsciously, wrapped up tightly.

Three other features make *Modern Rhetorical Criticism* distinctive:

Critical probes. Designated by the ◈ icon, and now in every chapter in Units II and III, are specific questions critics can use in analyzing rhetorical artifacts. These probes are the critic's tools. When used insightfully—which is to say, when used carefully, patiently, and imaginatively—these questions shed light on textual and contextual matters often ignored by the average listener or reader.

Chapter headnotes. Each chapter begins with a sample persuasive message that graphically previews the chapter's content. These headnotes range from Broadway lyrics to contemporary funeral prayers, from news magazine covers to Internet-circulated jokes, from social protest rhetoric to cosmetics advertisements.

Tips for the Practicing Critic. New with this edition, all fourteen chapters conclude with concrete, practical suggestions and advice for critics interested in practicing these forms of analysis. Suitable for beginners as well as more advanced critics, these tips make rhetorical criticism accessible, in all its varieties.

The very existence of *Modern Rhetorical Criticism* shows how important rhetorical inquiry has become during the past forty years. In colleges and universities, more and more academic courses are devoted to rhetorical matters. When taught in academic departments of speech or communication, they bear such titles as Rhetoric and Media, Speech Criticism, Contemporary Public Address, Political Communication, Persuasion and Propaganda, or Historical/ Critical Research Methods. In departments of English, they fall under such headings as Rhetoric and Literature, Text and Language, Stylistics, Rhetoric and Genre, or Advanced Composition and Exposition. Moreover, sociologists, anthropologists, political scientists, historians, and religious scholars have all demonstrated increasing interest in rhetorical issues. But no matter what such courses are called, they tend to tell the same tale: Rhetoric has always been with us and always will be. The aim of *Modern Rhetorical Criticism* is to help the reader become not just a critical consumer, but a critical connoisseur of rhetoric's daily offerings.

ACKNOWLEDGMENTS

Although writing is an isolated task, communities usually deserve credit for its success. We are grateful to the many individuals who have generously shared their thoughts, time, and talents in the making of this third edition. We would like to express our thanks to those who reviewed the book: Ronald H. Carpenter, University of Florida; Terence Morrow, Gustavus Adolphus College; and David Olsen, California State University, L.A. Students—especially Scott Carnes, Kristin Banning Glenn, Alex Kment, Sarah McNeece, Matt Mitroff, Twilla Sawyer, and Chuck Walts—provided valuable feedback, suggestions, and reality checks. Swetha Basani, Nicole L. Defenbaugh, Lesli K. Pace, Sarah McNeece, and Dr. Kevin Clark helped make the nettlesome aspects of writing this book less nettlesome. Professors Nilanjana Bardhan, Vanessa Beasley, Craig Gingrich-Philbrook, Carol Jablonski, Deborah Smith-Howell, Donna Strickland, Nathan Stucky, and Anita Vangelisti read portions of the manuscript and offered well-timed support in addition to sage advice and counsel. Professors David Payne and Joanne Gilbert made essential contributions to earlier versions of Chapters 12 and 13, respectively. Professors Lisa Brooten, Jonathan Gray, Maurice Hall, Kim Kline, John Llewellyn, and James Mackin provided critical technical and cultural expertise. Finally, special thanks to Sirriya Din, Leigh Wolf, Jeannine Banning, Jane Steinhouse, and the Hart, Daughton, Gunning, and Stucky clans—especially Eileen Morley, Jack and Paula Daughton, and Nathan and Michael Stucky—for helping shape these pages through their insight, faith, support, encouragement, and love.

Chapter 1

THE RHETORICAL PERSPECTIVE

Because as they cut it was that special green, they decided
To make a woman of the fresh hay. They wished to lie in green, to wrap
Themselves in it, light but not pale, silvered but not grey.
Green and ample, big enough so both of them could shelter together
In any of her crevices, the armpit, the join
Of hip and groin. They—who knew what there was to know about baling
The modern way with hay so you rolled it up like a carpet,
Rather than those loose stacks—they packed the green body tight
So she wouldn't fray. Each day they moulted her to keep her
Green and soft. Only her hair was allowed to ripen into yellow tousle.

The next weeks whenever they stopped cutting they lay with her.
She was always there, waiting, reliable, their green woman.
She gathered them in, yes she did,
Into the folds of herself, like the mother they hadn't had.
Like the women they had had, only more pliant, more graceful,
Welcoming in a way you never just found.
They not only had the awe of taking her,
But the awe of having made her. They drank beer
Leaning against the pillow of her belly
And one would tell the other, "Like two Adams creating."

And they marveled as they placed
The cans at her ankles, at her neck, at her wrists so she
Glittered gold and silver. They adorned what they'd made.
After harrowing they'd come to her, drawing
The fountains of the Plains, the long line
Of irrigating spray and moisten her up.
And lean against her tight, green thighs to watch buzzards
Circle black against the pink stain of the sunset.

What time she began to smolder they never knew—
Sometime between night when they'd left her
And evening when they returned. Wet, green hay
Can go a long time smoldering before you notice.
           It has a way
Of catching itself, of asserting that
There is no dominion over it but the air. And it flares suddenly
Like a red head losing her temper, and allows its long bright hair
To tangle in the air, letting you know again
That what shelters you can turn incendiary in a flash.
And then there is only the space of what has been,
An absence in the field, memory in the shape of a woman.
      [Macdonald, 1985:75–6]

This is not, mainly, a book about poems. It is a book about rhetoric and the rhetors who create it, as well as criticism and the critics who perform it. It is a book that invites careful attention to the messages of daily life. This book encourages us to pick and probe at messages designed to influence human thoughts and actions. It invites careful attention to such **rhetorical artifacts,** that is, the leftovers of rhetorical acts: the records that remain and can be re-examined after the speech, letter, debate, editorial, or performance has been created and in some cases, ended. Because it is a book about **rhetoric,** it is a book about the art of using language to help people narrow their choices among specifiable, if not specified, policy options. Not a very sophisticated definition, perhaps, but one that has its intuitive attractions. For example, we know, intuitively, that the poem above involves a special use of language. But is it language designed to *narrow* the choices of other people? Not in an obvious sense. Our day-to-day experience with obvious forms of rhetoric — advertising, political speeches, televised evangelism—tells us that if poet Cynthia Macdonald is attempting to persuade us of something specific, she has chosen a strange tack indeed.

Admittedly, Macdonald uses language well—beautifully, in fact. She paints her pictures with dexterity, creating for us the simple beauty of the bountiful pasture she describes, allowing us to hear the casual conversations of the laboring brothers, inviting us to feel the alternating softness and hardness of the carefully baled hay. Poet Macdonald also evokes rich feeling states: the brothers' feelings of entitlement, sensual comfort, and loss; the wonder of watching nature's earthen blackness blend into the "pink stain" of her sunsets; the catch in the breath as the brothers realize that their feelings of control were illusory. Macdonald, then, gives us precisely what a good poet often gives us—old thoughts thought anew, old feelings felt anew—but does she give us rhetoric?

Many scholars have argued in the affirmative. Any use of language, Richard Weaver claims, is sermonic. "We are all of us preachers in private or public capacities. We have no sooner uttered words than we have given impulse to other people to look at the world, or some small part of it, in our way" [2001:1360]. Influential literary critic and rhetorical theorist Kenneth Burke told us that "effective literature could be nothing else but rhetoric" [1931:210]. Literary scholar Wayne C. Booth authored a germinal text entitled *The Rhetoric of Fiction* [1961] that presumed the persuasiveness of literature. And in their encyclopedic anthology of Western rhetorical theory, *The Rhetorical Tradition*, Patricia Bizzell and Bruce Herzberg [2001] note that disagreement over the proper description of the relationship between what the Ancient Greeks called rhetoric and poetic has been going on since, well, the time of the Ancient Greeks. "Even if, as many critics have argued, there is a distinction between the 'contemplative' goal of literature and the 'active' goal of rhetoric, literature frequently uses persuasion and argumentation. . . . [Throughout history,] the independence of rhetoric and poetic has been asserted and defended just as frequently as their interrelatedness" [Bizzell & Herzberg, 2001: 1193].

So it seems that poetry may be rhetorical, and rhetoric may be poetic. But does that mean that poetry should be subjected to rhetorical criticism? Some of it certainly would yield rich insights. A careful reading of "Two Brothers in a Field of Absence," for example, could note the shift to the second-person form of address in the final stanza: "before you notice," "letting you know again / That what shelters you can turn incendiary in a flash." Such changes, in which the reader is suddenly placed in the role of an eyewitness, signal a subtle but powerful turn toward the rhetorical. This use of "you" implies that although the brothers had mistakenly tried to assert dominion over a woman, the reader can be expected to know better—or at least, to learn from their example. Another clue that could support such an interpretation is the poem's title, "Two Brothers in a Field of Absence." French feminists and others, following the work of Sigmund Freud and Jacques Lacan, have noted that in Western patriarchal culture, "woman" has often been (mis)understood to be symbolic of a castrated man (and therefore less than a man), because of her "absence" of male genitalia [Bizzell & Herzberg, 2001:1225]. But here, the "absence" or loss is caused by the woman's refusal to live under male domination, which essentially negates male power. Macdonald thus removes the "castration" from "castration anxiety," pointing toward the real prize: "dominion." (Most women don't want male anatomy, they want self-determination.)

But our interpretation of Macdonald's poem offers arguable implications rather than clearly specified policy options. We take the position here that poetry, while at times highly rhetorical, can differ from rhetoric. As with any other medium of communication, several of which we will explore in this book, certain examples or artifacts will be more likely to reward a careful look than others. In its written form at least, poetry often assumes a contemplative reader, one who has time to reread and rethink. Rhetoric is an active art; it cannot trust its audience to mull over its meaning long after the message has been delivered. Poetry may thus have the luxury of being elliptical and enigmatic, at times challenging even basic understanding. Rhetoric takes no such chances.

Certainly, any given message or artifact can be highly poetic or highly rhetorical, or both at once. The two are not mutually exclusive, nor are they even different ends of the same continuum. As meteorologists tell us, temperature and humidity combine to create our physical experience of heat or cold. Likewise, the degrees of rhetorical and poetic artistry in a message combine to create our experience of memorable and moving discourse. Shakespeare's version of Marc Antony's famous speech ("I come to bury Caesar, not to praise him . . .") is clearly high on both scales, since it remains a classic example of gorgeous prose that, just incidentally, uses irony so masterfully as to incite a riot. On the other hand, the listings in the residential phone book are comparatively low on both measures. The following speech, while obviously an example of what the Greeks called *epideictic* rhetoric (ceremonial speech that praises or blames), would score lower on the poetry index.

> Mr. Speaker, I rise to celebrate a victorious day for West Genessee High School as both the men's and women's lacrosse teams captured the New York State Lacrosse Division 1, Class A Championship titles. It was a memorable day that will go down in history for the Wildcats, as both teams soared triumphantly to the top.
>
> The day began as the women's team traveled to Cortland, New York to defend their state title, and this is exactly what they accomplished. . . . Later that afternoon at Hofstra University, the men's lacrosse team regained the State title with an exciting 10–9 victory. As Coach Mike Messere stated "It was one of the most exciting games I've seen."
>
> West Genessee Lacrosse has always had the reputation for a stellar program, and as displayed this past weekend, the program continues to generate gifted athletes. These students work hard year-round to master the sport, and because of their relentless hard work, dedication, and passion for the game, they came out true champions.
>
> I am proud of these devoted athletes, and I commend the coaching staff, parents, and entourage of supporters who traveled this long road with them. This type of outcome does not happen overnight, nor is it the result of just one season. It takes years of dedication to get such results, and this entire team should be proud of their accomplishments. [Walsh, 2002: E1055]

Any person of aesthetic sensibility will be almost embarrassed by the stark contrast between Cynthia Macdonald's mellifluous lines and Representative James Walsh's banal sports reporting in the halls of the U.S. Congress. In contrast to Macdonald, who demands thoughtful reconsideration from her readers,

Walsh makes us squirm with his tedious pontificating ("The day began . . ."), his tiresome clichés ("both teams soared triumphantly to the top . . ."), and his ponderous overstatements ("It was a memorable day that will go down in history . . ."). Unrequired pontificating, tiresome clichés, ponderous over-statements. This is rhetoric. Or at least some of it. The worst of it, perhaps. But every day, in every profession, people like James T. Walsh produce rhetoric, much of it trivial, some of it important, all of it purporting to help others sort through their choices.

Modern Rhetorical Criticism invites us to study why the *Congressional Record* is filled with such stuff, why Representative Walsh's constituents were flattered by his blandishments, and why his colleagues in the House smiled be-nignly when he read his remarks into the *Record*. Because he operates as some-thing of a classic persuader here, Walsh tries to "cut off" the many options for response available to his audience. Walsh's **policy options** are clearly specified ("let's congratulate the Wildcats"), whereas Cynthia Macdonald never tells her audience exactly what she expects them to *do* as a result of reading her poem. This lack of specificity is what makes reading verse such a pleasure: It gives us room to wander; it permits a vacation from choosing between this concrete possibility and that concrete probability. Representative Walsh, in contrast, is all business.

But must all rhetoric be as pedestrian and self-serving as James Walsh's? Clearly not. Human history has been written by great people creating great messages for social betterment. Often, these great statements have seemed more poetic than pragmatic, as satisfying to the heart as to the head. Consider, for example, the following artifact. The exiled Tibetan Buddhist leader, His Holiness the Dalai Lama, wrote an essay for the British-based magazine, *Ca-duceus*. In that essay, he asks,

> How are we to achieve world peace? Through anger, hatred, the arms race? No. True world peace can be achieved only through mental peace. And mental peace is based on the understanding of or conviction in the importance of compassion and the concept of impermanence. Through such an understanding or conviction one can then genuinely practice tolerance and respect for others and recognize that all human beings are brothers and sisters, even though we may be different in terms of our ideological, political or economic system. These are secondary issues. The most important thing is that we are all the same human beings wishing for happiness and seeking to avoid suffering. We are interdependent because we need each other for our very survival. . . . In order to achieve genuine, lasting world peace, we must first develop peaceful relations with others, and I believe we can only achieve that if we have inner peace within ourselves. . . .
>
> Our ultimate goal should be the demilitarization of the entire planet, but to achieve that, first some kind of inner disarmament is necessary. The key . . . is inner peace and the foundation of that is a sense of understanding and respect for each other as human beings, based on compassion and love. Some may dismiss compassion and love as impractical and unrealistic, but I believe their practice is the true source of success. Compassion is, by nature, peaceful and gentle, but it is

also very powerful. It is a sign of true inner strength. To achieve it we do not need to become religious, nor do we need any ideology. All that is necessary is for us to develop our basic human qualities. [Dalai Lama, 2002:10]

This is hardly Walsh-like discourse. A great man, not an average man, is expressing himself. And he is writing of great matters, not of expedient matters. Like poet Macdonald, the Dalai Lama draws on our most basic human commonalities, and uses simple language with elegance. But there is an awkwardness to his language also. He repeats himself, at times using more words than he really needs. The Dalai Lama's message could use a little editing: smoother flow, less redundancy.

But to call for such changes would be to miss the point of this rhetorical artifact, for the Dalai Lama had no intention of producing poetry. In the context of war and terrorism, he wanted one thing: to communicate his simple truth about the most profound bedevilment of the human condition. His eloquence derived from the emotional investment he made in his message, from his personal experiences as a refugee, and from the powerful simplicity of his logic. All of this made for an *artistry* not seen in Representative Walsh's celebration of high school lacrosse but it also made for an *insistence* not apparent in Cynthia Macdonald's poem. In short, the Dalai Lama mustered as much artistry as his insistence would allow.

Modern Rhetorical Criticism will probe these subtleties of human interaction. The book presents practical techniques for uncovering the wishes and schemes hidden in public discourse and shows how important answers arise when one asks the right questions. It details a number of theoretical perspectives for "taking apart" the messages we hear each day so that we can better appreciate why, rightly or wrongly, the James Walshs of the world far outnumber the Dalai Lamas and the Cynthia Macdonalds. But before considering these perspectives, let us consider what rhetoric is and what it is not.

THE ARTS OF RHETORIC

The premises in this chapter are threefold: (1) Rhetoric is a special sort of human activity; (2) it takes a special kind of practice to understand it; and (3) by understanding it, one acquires a special perspective on the world itself. We can get some sense of the special nature of rhetoric by contrasting the messages above. After reading Macdonald's poem, for example, each reader has a unique set of feelings and expectations. Macdonald develops many images, trips off many associations. She seems to demand nothing in particular from us as readers. Walsh, in contrast, clearly seeks universal agreement from his audience about a narrowed set of choices. He takes pains to provide background for his audience, uses language in highly conventional ways, mentions specific names and dates and places, is obvious when identifying good (victory) and evil (failure), and tells his audience what he wishes them to do next (applaud).

There is also a purposiveness in Walsh's remarks that is missing in Macdonald's poem. Walsh seems less patient than Macdonald; he is almost boorish in his concern that we get his story straight. Macdonald, in contrast, seems more willing to let us find our own story within her story. She wants us to be different after reading her poem but she seems content to let *us* explore the dimensions of that difference. Both rhetoric and poetry tell a story, but the rhetor (that is, the one who uses rhetoric) takes special pains to be sure that the moral of the story is clear to the audience.

But what is the moral of Cynthia Macdonald's story? Some might be unconvinced by the feminist reading we offer above, and see this poem as a naturalistic foray into the primitive connections between humans and their agricultural products. Others might see Macdonald as a retrograde sexist, celebrating a masculine world of physical dominance in which woman becomes a pliable object to be freely manipulated by men.

Any of these interpretations are possible, and they are the sorts of things that critics debate about. But the important thing to note here is that *the poet herself does not resolve these disputes.* All critics need to offer textual evidence to support their claims. Apart from providing clues in the poem that support one interpretation more than another, the poet keeps her own counsel, content to provoke questions in her readers but not to answer them.

Like poetry, rhetoric is an art. Like poetry, rhetoric creates a story out of nothing, using words to bring to life feelings we may have forgotten, plans we may not have considered. As we see in Walsh's speech, rhetoric uses common ideas, conventional language, and specific information to influence audiences' feelings and behaviors. The story rhetoric tells is always a story with a purpose; it is never told for its own sake.

Given our definition of rhetoric above, every rhetorical task involves five basic moves: (1) the rhetor tries to exert change by using **symbols** (verbal and nonverbal communication) rather than non-symbolic forces (like guns or torture); (2) the rhetor must come to be regarded as a **helper** rather than an exploiter; (3) the rhetor must convince the audience that new **choices** be made; (4) the rhetor must **narrow** the audience's options for making these choices, even though (5) the rhetor may become subtle by not **specifying** the details of the policies advocated.

Thus, the user of rhetoric peddles choices, even though most people naturally resist making choices unless forced to do so. And if forced to do so, people also naturally resist having their search for a solution prematurely constrained by someone else. So persuasion takes work: The rhetor must "help" without appearing gauche or paternalistic and the rhetor must establish that the world is not yet fundamentally right (hence requiring new choice-making by the audience) but that it can soon be set right by making the (narrowed) choice the rhetor endorses.

The average TV commercial tells this tale a thousand times daily, with Young Heterosexual being driven to insecurity (and choice) by the desire to make the Best First Impression on Ideal Romantic Partner. Knowing Voice-over arrives on the scene with the perfect answer in a pack of new Narrowed Choice gum. Lust proceeds on its merry course, we are led to believe, and choice-making recedes into the background until Unmanageable Hair strikes fifteen minutes later. Not all persuasion is this predictable, of course, but all of it involves the art of managing choices.

If rhetoric is an art, it is an art that sometimes differs from the arts of poetry and painting. It is an art with these characteristics:

1. *A cooperative art.* Rhetoric is an art that brings rhetors and audiences together. It cannot be done in solitude. To speak by oneself in a closet is of course possible but hardly normal. Rhetoric makes little sense unless it is made for others. After all, the reactions of other people will be its measure: their votes, their purchases, their conversions, their affection. And so rhetoric is a transactive art because it brings two or more people together in an atmosphere of potential change.

By sharing communication, both rhetors and audiences open themselves up to each other's influence. In that sense, communication is not something that is *done* to others. Rather, it is something that people choose to do to themselves by consenting to communicative contact. By agreeing to rhetorical exchange, says Arnold [1972:16], people acknowledge their dependence upon one another. In the world of rhetoric, a rhetor succeeds only when he or she can induce an audience to "contribute" their knowledge, feelings, and experiences about the matter in question. The rhetorical critic studies such invitations to cooperate.

2. *A people's art.* Rhetoric is an ordinary art. Its standards of excellence are the standards of ordinary people. Rhetoric is rarely as graceful or as lilting as poetry because the people for whom it is made are too busy to bother with grace and lilt. Rhetoric works within the constraints of everyday logic. The heroes in rhetorical history are people like Louisiana populist Huey Long, who severely mangled the King's English whenever he spoke but who was loved by his constituents because of it, not in spite of it. Rhetoric is often neither pretty nor fetching, although it can be both. At times it is even heavy-handed, although it tries never to be seen as such. At its best, rhetoric is ordinary language done extraordinarily.

3. *A temporary art.* Normally, rhetoric is rooted in the age of its creation. The people who create rhetoric speak today's language, not yesterday's. Such rhetors use time-bound examples, time-bound statistics, time-bound jargon, caring little how it will sound tomorrow. That is why most of the rhetoric we hear each day sounds more like James Walsh's than Abraham Lincoln's. Or, more precisely, that is why only one or two of Lincoln's speeches continue to be re-read today. The remainder of his speeches dealt with issues and personalities that no longer concern us. Only on a few occasions did he turn rhetoric

into poetry. Like the Dalai Lama, Lincoln knew that most rhetoric was meant to be consumed, not savored.

4. *A limited art.* As Bitzer [1968] reminds us, rhetoric is only deployed when it can make a difference. Rhetoric cannot really move mountains, which is why so few people stand at the bases of mountains to orate. Similarly, for years Palestinians could not move Israelis by speaking to them and that is why, sadly, they often did not try. Neither of these situations was "rhetorical" in Bitzer's sense because human discourse could not seem to change them. Rhetoric can do much, but it cannot do everything.

5. *A frustrating art.* There are no laws of rhetoric. There are important guidelines but little else. To be effective in persuasion one must cultivate a sensitivity to what the ancient Greeks called *kairos:* the ability to use the right argument and the deft phrase at precisely the right time. As Miller [2002:xii] notes, *kairos* is the principle of timely, creative response to the particular situation as well as "adaptation and accommodation to convention, expectation and predictability." When deciding what to say, the rhetor always swims in a sea of uncertainty because (1) people normally argue only about uncertain matters (e.g., Should gay marriage be permitted?) rather than about that which is fixed (e.g., the inevitability of death) and because (2) people are so complex, so changeful, and so ornery about so many matters. Thus, when thumping for more funding for the space shuttle, a NASA spokesperson must often leave the best scientific arguments at home because it is ordinary citizens and their representatives, not scientists, who fund space missions. Rhetoric, then, deals with the probable, the best case that can be made under limited circumstances. It is used to decide the undecided question and to solve the unsolved problem [Bryant, 1972:20–1]. People talk when they can think of nothing else to do but feel that they must do something.

6. *A generative art.* Contemporary writers [e.g., Cherwitz and Darwin, 1995] tell us that rhetoric produces most of what passes for everyday knowledge. They claim that rhetoric helps us learn what other people think (e.g., whether or not space funding should be increased) and also to learn our *own* minds about things (e.g., the old saying that one never really knows something until one can teach it to someone else). By arguing with one another we produce what is called social knowledge, which determines much in human affairs.

Today in the United States, for example, witches are no longer burned, African Americans are no longer limited to plantation employment, and Japanese Americans are no longer interned. But in other eras, *when other arguments prevailed,* such "truths" were taken for granted and, more important, were used as the basis for social policy. So rhetoric never produces True Truth. It produces partial truth, truth for these times and these people. As Johnstone [1969:408] says, "the only way to tell whether what I have is a truth or a falsehood is to contemplate its evocative power," that is, its power to secure the agreement of others. And lest we think that such social knowledge is not really knowledge, we need only reflect upon the comparatively recent history of witches, African Americans, and Japanese Americans.

THE RANGE OF RHETORIC

One way of understanding rhetoric is to consider what it is and what it is not or, better, *how much* of a thing it is and *how much* of another thing it is not. In Figure 1.1, "the rhetorical" is depicted as an area bordering on other domains but one that is nonetheless special. For example, rhetoric resembles science in that both the scientist and the rhetor want to be taken seriously. The persuader wants the audience to believe that calamity will in fact strike unless the rhetor's warnings are heeded. Like the scientist, the persuader marshalls evidence (e.g., the testimony of experts, certain statistical trends, etc.), uses this evidence to comment upon some real, not imagined, feature of the observable world (e.g., "overpopulation will inundate the infrastructure of this city"), and then employs this package of arguments to support a policy recommendation (e.g., "we must put an immediate moratorium on building permits"). But even though both the scientist and the persuader seek to make things demonstrably true, the persuader is willing to treat the perceptions of *ordinary people* as the acid test of demonstratedness. The scientist, in contrast, normally is expected to meet a more exacting standard of truth (empirical verifiability, the judgments of experts, experimental replication, etc.), while the persuader's truth is

FIGURE 1.1 Realm of the Rhetorical

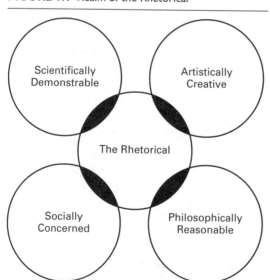

often fifty-one percent truth: the majority judgment of ordinary citizens. For most persuaders on most issues, fifty-one percent truth is sufficient.

As we have mentioned above, the persuader, like the poet, is artistically creative. Both use symbols to breathe life into ideas. Neither uses tangible tools (like pick axes) to change tangible phenomena (like rocks). Rather, both the artist and the persuader use their imaginations to engage their audience's imaginations. But as we have noted before, the persuader's creativity is often exercised in behalf of decidedly short-term gains (i.e., assent on the particular issue at hand) and the persuader, because he or she is a "narrower," is unlikely to give an audience the intellectual freedom normally permitted them by the artist. It is also true that the imagination of the persuader is not likely to be as uncontrolled as that of the traditional artist because, as we have said, rhetoric is a *social* art. It does little good for the rhetor to take flights of fancy unless the audience can come along as well.

The persuader also tries to be philosophically reasonable, to insure that an argument makes the kind of *patterned* sense that will be understood by others. The rhetor typically avoids the incomplete mental image, the sudden self-interruption, or the discordant use of language that lends excitement to more purely artistic endeavors. It is also true, however, that the persuader typically uses what works and is less scrupulous in argumentation than the philosopher. The rhetor uses, in Aristotle's terms, all the means of argument available, not just those recommended in the logic books.

As we shall see in Chapter 5, there is a special logic to persuasion, a psycho-logic, and it is to these informal methods of reasoning that the practical rhetor most often pays homage. Thus, as Morrison [1992] points out, it even makes "sense" at times for rhetors (e.g., GLBT, or Gay/Lesbian/Bisexual/Transgendered folks) to challenge accepted categories of sexual identity in order to shock audiences into "queer" ways of seeing and being. The logic of persuasion is sometimes a curious logic.

Finally, the persuader is socially concerned, at least in part. The persuader is a public person, seeking to change not just one life but many lives. When abandoning solitude, the persuader promises that many people's lives will be improved in some important way. But the persuader is not a social worker. As McGee [1975] says, persuaders present *their* versions of what "the people" believe, often taking great liberties with public opinion when doing so. Thus, the persuader's social concern is limited to his or her private version of the ideal life, a life in which everyone owns a Dodge truck or votes a straight Socialist ticket. The persuader wants to make a particular kind of change, a public change. Those who dream social dreams need the aid of others.

Because it borders on so many worlds, the realm of rhetoric is powerful. The rhetor draws upon each of these worlds and yet steps back from each simultaneously, seeking to become a poet, but a poet of practical consequences, a scientist, but a scientist unencumbered by footnotes. The persuader also becomes an easygoing logician and a social worker with an eye on the bottom line. By blending these roles skillfully as, say, Hillary Rodham Clinton did when serving as First Lady, persuaders become highly influential. For this reason alone they bear watching. Watching them is the job of the rhetorical critic.

The definition of rhetoric provided above is obviously a generous definition, one designed to encompass a variety of messages. Included within this broad definition would be the television docudrama, the cooing of lovers on a park bench, the scientific treatise, the invocation at the City Council meeting, the reprimand from the boss at work, the presidential address, the college lecture, the adolescent's whining during dinner, the blockbuster movie, the top sergeant's welcome to boot camp, the sermon from the pulpit, the Diet Coke commercial, the psychiatrist's counseling session, and much else.

All of these situations require the use of language and all of them can result in both obvious and nonobvious forms of influence. Indeed, it is a hallmark of the critical perspective that all messages be examined carefully, *especially* those that seem to lie outside the realm of rhetoric. The most basic job of the rhetorical critic is to be able to discover *when* rhetoric is being used in the first place. Persuaders, after all, do not always own up to their profession. Often, they would like to be mistaken for a scientist or a poet or a philosopher. By keeping a sharp eye peeled for the essential features of rhetoric, however, the critic can discover when rhetoric has come to call.

Normally, three features make a message rhetorical: (1) **delineations of the good,** (2) **resonance for a particular audience,** and (3) **clear or clearly implied policy recommendations.** (We conceive "policy" here in its broadest sense, including proposals of marriage, requests for repentance, voter solicitations, and much else.)

For example, Table 1.1 presents three similar-yet-different lists of events ranging from the obviously rhetorical to the less obviously rhetorical. As one moves from right to left, notice how the events change in subtle yet important ways, increasingly lending themselves to more immediate and powerful rhetorical uses. In the case of the photographs, for example, it is not hard to imagine how the picture of an Appalachian shack could be used in the hands of a community activist seeking federal funding. Such a picture presents a special invitation to the viewer to think *now* about matters of right and wrong. The fact that this is an "American" shack makes Americans especially uncomfortable because it calls into question certain aspects of the national dream. Perhaps because of this audience resonance, policy recommendations seem to jump out of the picture for many Americans ("Let us put a stop to this kind of poverty" or "Why don't those people get a job and live better?").

The picture of the White House is more ambiguous. One can imagine the photograph being used in patriotic ways in the United States ("the seat of our democracy") and quite differently by hardliners in Iran ("lair of the Great Satan"). It could be used for comedic effect on Comedy Central ("The Prez's house") or for purely crass boosterism on a multicolored flyer ("Bring your convention to Washington. Hotel rates have never been lower").

TABLE 1.1 Types of Rhetorical Events

Messages	More Obviously Rhetorical	Ambiguous	Less Obviously Rhetorical
Photographs	An Appalachian shack	The White House	A South Sea hut
Telephone call	From Handicapped Workers of America	From a son at college	From a rich friend
Drama	Guerrilla theatre	Off-Broadway drama	Broadway musical
Signs	On a highway billboard	At an hourly parking lot	On a restroom door
Commercials	About hamburgers from Wendy's Restaurants	About drugs from the National Basketball Association	About Picasso from the National Museum of Art
Magazines	*Michigan Militia Report*	*Harper's*	*Time*
Guided tours	At Budweiser plant	At Lincoln Memorial	At Yellowstone National Park
Humor	Political jokes	Ethnic jokes	Animal jokes
Poetry	Langston Hughes	Wallace Stevens	E.E. Cummings
Trip directions	From Big Al to his car lot	From a new boyfriend to his lake cabin	From Rand McNally to Salt Lake City
Statistics	From International Association of Oil Producers	From Mobil Oil Corp.	From U.S. Department of Energy
Music	Folk songs	Church hymns	Rhythm and blues
Football	Halftime pep talk	TV color commentary	Cheerleaders' cheers
Storytelling	Religious testimonials	Folklore	Fairy tales

The South Sea hut, in contrast, might lend itself to any number of case-makings. Previous rhetoric in the U.S. culture, at least, seems not to have marked it yet for special use and hence the image makes fewer immediate and specific demands on us. (Should it be used for a travel brochure? In connection with religious missionary work? As a symbol of exploitation in the developing world?)

As one moves from right to left in Table 1.1, one gets the feeling that (1) the rhetor's exact purposes for persuasion become less ambiguous, (2) perhaps as a result, the emotions of the rhetor lie increasingly close to the surface, (3) increasingly specific "policies" are being recommended to the audience or at least broadly hinted at ("Give now," "Follow the Word"), (4) the question of essential good and evil has become less of a question, and (5) finding an "ideal audience" for the message would become easier because fewer and fewer people can fill the bill as the rhetoric heats up. In short, as we move from right to left, things become more rhetorical.

This is not to say, of course, that we should turn our backs on less obvious rhetoric. Indeed, critics have become increasingly interested in these subtler messages precisely because most people (that is, most potential audience members) are oblivious to the *hints* of good and evil or *implied* policy recommendations buried within them. Thus, for example, critics have looked at painting as rhetorical action [Helmers, 2001], at sanitized racism in letters-to-the-editor [Lacy, 1992], and at U.S. memorial sites as evidence that rhetoric requires material form [Blair, 1999]. Throughout this book, we will look for rhetoric in all of its haunts and hideaways.

THE FUNCTIONS OF RHETORIC

Thus far, we have discussed what rhetoric is and what it is not, where it can be found, and what shapes it takes. It now remains for us to examine what rhetoric *does,* how it functions in human society. Of course, we will be studying the uses of rhetoric throughout this book but here, briefly, we can examine some of its less frequently noticed uses.

1. *Rhetoric unburdens.* People make rhetoric because they must get something off their chests, because the cause they champion overwhelms their natural reticence. Rhetors refuse to let history take its slow, evolutionary course and instead try to become part of history themselves. The history they make may be quite local in character (e.g., picketing a neighborhood abortion clinic), but rhetorical people typically do not hang back. They sense that the world around them is not yet set and so they approach it aggressively, often convinced that they can make a difference, always convinced that they must try.

Savoy magazine, which caters to an upscale African American readership, recently added activist/comedian/entrepreneur/actor Dick Gregory to its "Hall of Fame," citing the following rationale:

> Because he's the only man we know who has run for president *and* shined shoes. . . . Because when he got his girlfriend Lil pregnant, he married her because his mama said he should, and he has stayed married for 43 years. Because he made white folks laugh at their own foibles and prejudices until their sides ached. Because he lived by his beliefs, even when the price was his freedom. . . . Because his failed campaign for mayor of Chicago paved the way for a young Carl Stokes, the nation's first black mayor of a major city. . . . Because he had the audacity to name his book *Nigger* and then invited white folks to "take a *Nigger* home tonight." Because he embodied The Movement. [2001–2002: 34]

This list catalogues a range of historical and contemporary values of African American culture. The rhetor is confident that readers will respond to the familial appeal, addressing African Americans as an extended family in need of preservation ("mama said he should," "white folks" as outsiders). Politically, the rhetor takes for granted a shared commitment to uplifting the race (paving the way for a black mayor) and achieving social justice (being imprisoned for one's beliefs, "The Movement"). The conservative emphasis on marriage is contrasted with the belief that at times, one should behave audaciously in order to shock and draw attention to oppression ("take a *Nigger* home tonight"). Different as they are, however, each sentence asserts without qualification or apology. In order to see oneself in this target audience, the reader is expected, even required, to approve of each item listed.

In a sense, then, communication is a kind of presumptuous imposition on other people. When A tries to persuade B, for example, A affirms that (1) something is wrong in B's world and (2) that A can fix it. Thus, if it is true that the poet is an escapist, it is also true that the rhetor is an infiltrator. Naturally, the arrogance of the rhetorical act is normally well disguised by the practicing persuader who is, after all, only there to "help" ("You owe it to *yourself* to sign this contract," "The *disabled* do indeed appreciate your contribution"). Still, a rhetorical engagement is no less intrusive just because its intrusions have been camouflaged.

2. *Rhetoric distracts.* When speaking, a rhetor wants to have all, not just some, of our attention. To get that attention, the rhetor must so fill up our minds that we forget, temporarily at least, the other ideas, people, and policies important to us. Naturally, we do not give our attention freely, so it takes rhetoric at its best to sidetrack us. One way of doing so is for the rhetor to control the premises of a discussion. As McCombs and Shaw [1972] demonstrated some years ago, the power of the mass media derives not so much from their ability to tell us what to think but what to think about. When choosing to report on industrial lead poisoning, for example, a local T.V. station simultaneously chooses *not* to cover the crowning of the Peach Queen or the win-loss record of the local Double A farm club. By "setting the agenda" in this fashion, by controlling the premises pertaining to newsworthiness, the media can thus influence any conclusions drawn from those premises.

Similarly, in his study of military training camp "jodies," or work songs, Knight [1990] discovered that they did more than simply help the time pass on a long march. By examining jodies as a rhetorical performance, Knight illustrated that these deceptively simple songs served to socialize young men to kill without hesitation or remorse. So the rhetor asks the audience to think about this topic, not that one, to try out this solution, not that endorsed by the rhetor's opponent. In this sense, rhetoric operates like a good map. Maps, after all, have a distinctive point of view: They "favor" interstate highways (by coloring them a bright red) over rural roads (often a pale blue); they emphasize urban areas (blotched in yellow) over small towns (tiny dots); they adapt their appeals to vacationers (by highlighting Yosemite) rather than to truckers (no diners are listed). Like the rhetor, the roadmap bristles with integrity, implying by the precision of its drawings that it provides the complete story: all the highway news that's fit to print.

Rhetoric, too, tries to narrow our latitudes of choice without giving us the feeling that we are being thereby hemmed in. Rhetoric tries to control the *definition* we provide for a given activity ("Your church offering isn't a monetary loss; it's a down payment on heaven") as well as the *criteria* we employ to solve a problem ("Abortion is not a religious issue; it's a legal one"). By also emphasizing one rhetor *category* over another (e.g., George W. Bush as commander-in-chief vs. George W. Bush as failed entrepreneur), persuaders invite us to focus on this and not that, on here and not there, on now and not then.

3. *Rhetoric enlarges.* In some senses, modern persuaders are like the heralds of old. They move among us singing the siren song of change, asking us to consider a new solution to an old problem (or an old solution to a problem of which we were unaware). Rhetoric operates, then, like a kind of intellectual algebra, asking us to equate things we had never before considered equatable. Thus, for example, Adolph Hitler rose to fame (and infamy) by linking German nationalism with increased militarism and Germany's economic woes with Jewish clannishness. These were corrupt equations but for him they were useful ones.

Often, the **associations** encouraged by rhetoric are no less sophisticated, or honorable, than those created by Adolph Hitler. Nevertheless, these linkages are the workhorses of persuasion. So, for example, some manufacturers of personal computers now virtually assure unwary parents that computing skills will translate instantly into educational achievement for their children. It is interesting to note that persuaders rarely ask for major expansion of their audiences' worldviews. They imply that only a slight modification is in order. Persuasion moves by increments of inches.

Often, persuaders **disassociate** ideas in order to expand the viewpoints of their audiences. So, for example, Bankamericard changed its name to Visa in the early 1970s so that the more international flavor of the new name would offset the growing anti-Americanism found in Western Europe at the time. Similarly, American Indian writers have used what Powell [2002] calls "rhetorics of survivance" (a combination of survival and resistance). Such writers adopt the contemporary ways of speaking about Indian-ness and yet respond to those ideas critically, in order to "reimagine what it could mean to be Indian" [p. 396]. It becomes the persuader's task to demonstrate that any such alterations are a natural extension of thoughts and feelings the audience *already* possesses and that any such new notions can be easily accommodated within the audience's *existing* repertoire of ideas. That is why rhetoric is called an art.

4. *Rhetoric names.* To understand the power of rhetoric we must remember that creatures and non-creatures alike (people, frogs, rocks, bicycles) are born without labels. People are, as best we know, nature's only namers. And they name things with a vengeance: Newman's Own Spaghetti Sauce; Sri Lanka; black holes; the Utah Jazz; Nirvana. People take their naming seriously: Newly enfranchised Americans have anglicized their names to ward off discrimination; professional women have retained their original surnames to avoid being seen as the property of their mates; and the fate of captured Taliban and Al Qaeda "detainees" hung on whether they were considered "prisoners of war" and therefore protected under international law.

No doubt, naming is as important as it is because meaning is such a variable thing. A tornado-ravaged town, after all, is but wind and torment until it is publicly labeled by the appropriate official as a "Federal Disaster Area." Some executions spawn massive religious movements (e.g., the death of Jesus Christ) or excite political passions (e.g., that of Oklahoma City bomber Timothy McVeigh), while other executions are met with mere curiosity (e.g., that of Gary Gillmore, the first person to be executed in recent times). The facts in each of these capital punishment cases were different, of course, but so too was the rhetorical skill of the partisans who labeled the executions.

The naming function of rhetoric helps audiences become comfortable with new ideas and provides audiences with an acceptable vocabulary for talking about these ideas. Through rhetoric, "white flight schools" are transformed into "independent academies," "labor-baiting" becomes the "right-to-work," a "fetus" is seen as an "unborn child," "suicide" is replaced by "death with dignity," and a vague assemblage of disconnected thoughts and random social trends is decried as "secular humanism." A major challenge for the rhetorical critic, then, is to study how namers name things and how audiences respond to the names they hear.

5. *Rhetoric empowers.* Whom does it empower? Traditionally, the answer to this question has been "public speakers." Western rhetors, those with the political power in their culture, have often tended to be already privileged in a variety of ways by virtue of being white, heterosexual, male, and economically secure. As a result, rhetoric (especially public address) has been blamed for the oppression of women and poor people of all races, and men of color as well. This led to dialogue among several feminist rhetoricians. Condit [1997], Foss, Griffin, and Foss [1997], and Downey [1997] articulated and disputed claims about the extent to which rhetoric requires cooperation (a value often identified with feminism), whether definitions of "eloquence" needed broadening, and the centrality of interdependence to our understandings of rhetoric, gender, and feminism.

Those who decry the art of rhetoric sometimes do so because its users embrace many truths, not just one. Traditionally, teachers of rhetoric have encouraged us to consider alternative modes of expressing ourselves and not to just settle on the first thought that comes to mind. This attitude sometimes brings censure to rhetoric. Those who embrace absolute standards of right and wrong have always had problems with rhetoric because, above all, rhetoric encourages flexibility. Flexibility, in turn, provides options: to address one audience or several; to mention an idea or avoid it; to say something this way, not that way; to tell all one knows or only just a bit; to repeat oneself or to vary one's response. Rhetoric encourages flexibility because it is based on a kind of symbolic Darwinism: (1) rhetors who do not adapt to their surroundings quickly become irrelevant; (2) ideas that become frozen soon die for want of social usefulness.

Such flexibility, in turn, permits continual growth, for the individual as well as for society. Rhetorical theorists contend that the possible ways of making an idea clear are as numerous as the potential audiences to receive them

[Hart and Burks, 1972]. Moreover, because it encourages adaptability, rhetoric permits personal evolution for rhetors as well. Both 1960s feminist Gloria Steinem and consumer advocate Ralph Nader continued to be prominent in later decades not because they changed their beliefs fundamentally, but because they found new *ways* of telling their truths as they matured.

Social power, then, often derives from rhetorical strength. Grand ideas, deeply felt beliefs, and unsullied ideologies are sources of power too but, as Plato told us, none of these factors can be influential without a delivery system, without rhetoric. Purity of heart and a spotless record for integrity are assets to a political rhetor but they are hardly enough to sustain a campaign unless those qualities are *shared* with the voters. As Bryant [1972:23] remarks, if they are to be used with confidence "a bridge or an automobile or a clothesline must not only *be* strong but must *appear* to be."

6. *Rhetoric elongates.* What does rhetoric make longer? Time. Time, that most precious of all substances, can be extended—or, more accurately, seems to be extended—when rhetoric is put to use. Consider the Reverend Martin Luther King, Jr. When he spoke at the March on Washington in 1963, King certainly knew that civil rights laws would not be enacted just because he mounted the public platform. *But King succeeded in making the future seem to be the present* because his appeals reached so deeply into people's souls and because his futuristic images were painted so vividly: "I have a dream . . . that one day, right here in Alabama, little black boys and black girls will be able to join hands with little white boys and white girls as sisters and brothers. I have a dream today!" [King, 1964:374].

Naturally, King's speeches did not cause immediate legal and social changes. But for his followers, the devastations of the past commanded less of their attention when they listened to him describe future possibilities. In his presence, audiences lingered in the future and felt better because of it. As Hart [1984a:764] says, rhetoric can become a "way station for the patient."

Most persuaders sell the future when trying to move audiences to a better place, a happier circumstance. Whether it is robust health through Herbalife, a slimmer figure with Healthy Choice, or tax cuts with George W. Bush, rhetoric transports us, momentarily at least, across the boundaries of time. Admittedly, this is a kind of surrogate or false reality. But genuinely effective rhetoric makes such criticisms of literal falseness seem small-minded. When tempted with visions of untold wealth via Amway or a glorious afterlife via Jesus, many people relax their guards.

It is also true that rhetoric can be used to appropriate the *past*. When doing so, of course, skilled persuaders do some historical housecleaning. Thus, as Warner [1976] tells us, most patriotic celebrations in the United States omit from their oratory stories of ethnic or religious persecution. Rhetors on such occasions steer clear of these unquestionable historical facts because ceremonial rhetoric has its own upbeat story to tell. Rhetoric tells a *selective* history, taking us back in time for a brief, heavily edited tour of that which was. But as the good eulogist knows, not everything about the dearly departed needs to be told at the funeral. The eulogist reminds us of the deceased's grandest virtues, his or her most endearing qualities, because only the best of the past can make the present seem less tragic. So, while rhetoric often tells literal lies, most of us would have it no other way.

CONCLUSION

In this chapter, we have covered the essentials of rhetoric. We have seen that rhetoric has a combination of features not found in other creative arts like painting and music and poetry. Rhetoric's creations are practical creations and because they are the creations of real people living in the real world, rhetoric is a controversial thing to study. Many people do not like rhetoric, which is to say, they like their own rhetoric best. But human beings have little choice but to use and respond to rhetoric if they wish the world to be different than it is. Jonas Salk may have invented a vaccine for polio but no further vaccines will be discovered at the Salk Institute unless its fundraising goes well. Neal Armstrong may have set foot on the moon but he was permitted to do so only because congressional arms were twisted by the space lobby in the United States. Similarly, those Americans who enjoy riding on an interstate highway system or watching rock videos should thank the structural and acoustic engineers who made such marvels possible but they should thank, too, the rhetorical engineers whose persuasive appeals generated the funding needed to nurture those inventions along.

So rhetoric is with us, for both good and ill. It is with us because most worthwhile ideas come from groups of people working in concert. For religions to thrive there must be apostles. For ideas to be understood there must be teachers. For justice to be served there must be lawyers. To turn our backs on rhetoric would be to turn our backs on the sharing of ideas and hence any practical notion of human community. So rhetoric is with us because it must be with us.

But just because rhetoric exists and just because we must use it does not mean that it is easily understood. This book is dedicated to the proposition that rhetoric can and must be understood. The assumption here is that the more lenses available for viewing rhetoric, the greater our understanding. Thus, each chapter of this book will dissect persuasive messages. In some chapters, we will use wide-angled lenses to examine such broad features as setting and role and purpose, and in other chapters we will use more refined lenses when viewing argument, form, structure and language. We will consider what various schools of criticism have to say about persuasion and then look at some of the fascinating things scholars have found about the many forms of rhetoric. But we should do none of that until we have an instrument for doing so. And so we will now examine a microscope suitable for examining rhetorical exchange: the critical perspective.

TIPS FOR THE PRACTICING CRITIC

1. Although some argue that "everything is rhetorical," a definition that excludes nothing is useless. Certainly, every message has some element(s) that may be interpreted as rhetorical. But in early critical work, it will be best to use the lists of characteristics provided in Chapter 1 (especially the "five basic moves" and "three features" that make a message rhetorical) to determine whether the message in question fits our working definition.

2. After determining that the piece of discourse meets these definitional standards, try to isolate elements in the text (specific words and phrases, structural placement/order of ideas, ways of referring to self and intended audience, etc.) that illustrate the rhetor's purpose and/or bias.

3. Note that in the analysis of the Dalai Lama's message, we focused on what was most important *in this situation and at this time*. Rather than *simply* reading the text, noting its flaws, and concluding that it "needs editing," the critic takes into account the emotional power of the essay. This far outweighed any minor editorial problems, which were probably not even noticeable to its intended readers. Keep in mind that close reading of the text is necessary, but not sufficient, for good criticism. Be sure to "step back" and look at the different situational elements of the message. At different times, different features of the message and its environment carry more persuasive force. Later chapters will address individual features in depth (see especially Part II: "General Forms of Criticism").

Chapter 2

THE CRITICAL
PERSPECTIVE

As our coaches used to say, "OK, people, settle down and listen up." We have been enjoying a lovely little spate of French-bashing here lately. Jonah Goldberg of *The National Review*, who admits that French-bashing is "shtick"—as it is to many American comedians—has popularized the phrase "cheese-eating surrender monkeys" to describe the French. It gets a lot less attractive than that.

George Will saw fit to include in his latest *Newsweek* column this joke: "How many Frenchmen does it take to defend Paris? No one knows, it's never been tried." That was certainly amusing. One million, four hundred thousand French soldiers were killed during World War I. As a result, there weren't many Frenchmen left to fight in World War II. Nevertheless, 100,000 French soldiers lost their lives trying to stop Hitler.

On behalf of every one of those 100,000 men, I would like to thank Mr. Will for his clever joke. They were out-manned, out-gunned, out-generaled and, above all, out-tanked. They got slaughtered, but they stood and they fought. Ha-ha, how funny. In the few places where they had tanks, they held splendidly. . . .[Ivins, 2003]

Texas-based syndicated political columnist Molly Ivins penned these words in early 2003 in response to the anti-French sentiment then sweeping the United States. Although the French were not alone in criticizing what they saw as an American rush to war against Iraq, they had become the primary target for American contempt. Americans were boycotting French wine and cheese and renaming their favorite reconstituted-potato-based fast-food "Freedom Fries."

Into this rhetorical environment, Molly Ivins issued this wake-up call. Her column begins with a direct, almost confrontational address to her readers, self-consciously borrowing an all-American (and typically male) mode of commanding our attention with coachly authority. Then her tone immediately turns ironic as she reports on the social climate as if it were a season of holiday parties ("we have been enjoying a lovely little spate"). She names two conservative fellow columnists and quotes their anti-French jokes, glossing them with the label of "shtick," implying a flaccid and facile humor beneath the dignity of these otherwise cogent thinkers. By quoting their put-downs rather than simply glossing them as "French-bashing," Ivins invites readers to laugh or groan, if they are so inclined. But after mentioning "cheese-eating surrender monkeys," she conveys her disapproval, forecasting more serious trouble ahead with the assessment "It gets a lot less attractive than that." And then she brings in the heavy weaponry, both literal and rhetorical. Immediately after quoting Will, Ivins provides a sad, cold accounting of a literal answer to his question ("How many Frenchmen . . . ?"): either 1.4 million or 100,000, depending on when the historical accounting begins.

Sarcasm, according to Harris, is irony with an added dash of critical contempt [2003:22]. Ivins's next sentence ("On behalf of . . . those . . . men, I would like to thank Mr. Will for his clever joke") uses sarcasm to invite chagrin, ashamed regret, on the part of readers who may initially have laughed at Will's line. How risky is Ivins's strategy here? Is she setting her audience up to laugh, and then chiding them, "Shame on you!"? Aren't readers likely to be angry at her, for making them feel foolish or berated? After all, such jokes are merely for entertainment, or at most, designed to arouse patriotic sentiments. Or is Ivins really playing it safe? The answer will differ depending on the audience presumed to be reading. Some readers no doubt reacted defensively to her message. But one could argue that her regular readers would have expected her to take strong, unapologetic stands, as she is wont to do. Rhetoric can be complicated stuff indeed.

Rhetorical criticism is the business of identifying the complications of rhetoric and then unpacking or explaining them in a comprehensive and efficient manner. This definition implies several things: Rhetorical texts are complicated; there is an orderly way of describing these complications; and the best criticism describes them elegantly. So when confronting messages, the critic examines such factors as role, language, arguments, ideas, and medium to navigate the complications and reduce the confusion persuaders intentionally or unintentionally create.

Thus, *Modern Rhetorical Criticism* is a guide to insightful interpretation. The book outlines methods for inspecting persuasive messages in order to see what insights about people they might contain. Before considering critical techniques, however, we need to know about the critical enterprise itself, an enterprise designed to expose the clever rhetoric of clever writers like Molly Ivins. This chapter offers such a perspective.

THE PURPOSES OF CRITICISM

In the passage above, Molly Ivins operates as both persuader and critic. As a critic, she dissects Jonah Goldberg's and George Will's messages with care and, as a persuader, she accuses them of forgetting history and unjustly maligning old allies. In her column, Ivins did what good critics do: She examined rhetorical texts to account for all of their important meanings, not just those the persuader featured.

Naturally, another critic might argue that Ivins acted disingenuously when transforming simple witticisms into something sordid. In either case, the critic would be doing what good critics do: building an argument about social conditions by observing what people say. Naturally, only a community of informed persons could judge whether Ivins was the rhetorical criminal or hero here. This community of critics would listen to the contrasting arguments, examine the evidence each offered, and then render its judgment. So that is what rhetorical critics do. But why do they do it? There are several reasons:

1. *Rhetorical criticism documents social trends.* Rosenfield [1972:133] sees the critic as a sort of sports analyst who takes part in the swirl of life but who also has perspective on it. Rosenfield distinguishes between the fan who enjoys the game of persuasion and the expert commentator who both appreciates and comments knowingly upon it. Criticism therefore requires special discernment: the ability to stand simultaneously in the midst of and apart from the events experienced. Like the sports commentator, the critic provides an instant replay of the event, pointing out features that the too-involved fan was unable to see because of the immediacy and excitement of the event itself. The critic re-views the scene of the action, calling attention to features of persuasion that the audience saw but did not notice.

The good critic magnifies without distorting, focusing upon rhetorical characteristics that, while humble, may nevertheless be important. Thus, for example, Daughton [1995] noticed that Angelina Grimké, an influential nineteenth-century abolitionist, both enacted her controversial message of female empowerment and reinforced it for her audience in the very sentence structures of her speech. Late in her Pennsylvania Hall address, Grimké specifically turned to her female listeners with the words, "Women of Philadelphia! Allow me as a Southern woman, with much attachment to the land of my birth, to entreat you to come up to this work" [36]. Daughton noted that Grimké's direct address to the women in her audience, women who could never vote in their lifetimes, was strategically located at the end of the address, where it dignified and defined women as citizens of a particular place, apart from their relationships to men. Daughton argued that Grimké was able to invite these women to join her in working for abolition only *after* she had demonstrated by her own living example that women's public arguments could have powerful effects.

The good critic notices verbal trends, features that are too regularized to be accidental and too suggestive to be unimportant. According to Farrell [1980], the critic thereby treats messages as symptoms of some larger social fact. The critic says: "I see a bit of *X* here and am willing to bet that there is more *X* to be found in society at large." Marback [2001], for example, studied the impassioned debate surrounding the Oakland, California, school board's adoption of the "ebonics" resolution in late 1996. The resolution granted first-class status (and classroom use) to what had been called Black English, often previously assumed to be a defective form of Standard (= White) English. The purpose of the resolution was to help inner-city African American students learn in all subjects, not to prevent them from mastering the dominant code of Standard English. Despite good intentions, the resolution sparked a national uproar, outraging critics on both the right and the left. Marback analyzed the arguments of supporters and opponents of the measure. Blaming African American teachers and students for poor achievement, he argued, effectively directs public attention away from the ways in which our attitudes about literacy help maintain, rather than change, the unequal economic status quo. Thus, the critic acts as society's vanguard, spotting in today's rhetoric the smoke that becomes tomorrow's fires.

As Brockriede [1974] has said, all rhetorical critics are arguers. Antismoking activists, for example, argue that cigarette advertisements encourage teenage addiction. Many critics thus argue that *regularized* features of rhetoric have become dangerous to society. In other circumstances, it is the absence of regularity that causes alarm: Appeals to national unity drop off in political campaigns and letters to the editor become self-centered rather than community-centered. Combining these perceptions, the critic might posit the rise of a New Narcissism and then speculate about its consequences for society at large. In short, the critic's job is to discover trends and then see where they lead.

2. Rhetorical criticism provides general understandings via the case study method. By scrutinizing a small number of texts, the critic restricts the range of available insights. Even if a thousand televangelized sermons were collected for study, the critic would still be examining messages rooted in a peculiar political circumstance, in a specialized medium, and in a unique cultural backdrop. Even with such a large sample, the critic would still only have a sample, a mere whisper of history's religious utterances. Because the critic's focus is therefore tight, the critic's challenge is to tell the largest story possible given the necessarily limited evidence available.

So the critic is a sampler, and samplers must be both modest and cautious. But what the critic gives up in *scope* is offset by the *power* of insight made available. What insures this power? Choosing a provocative text for study, asking important questions of that text, and drawing intriguing conclusions. The critic is indeed a sampler, but that which is sampled—human discourse—is hardly trivial since people embed in their talk some of their most complicated motivations. It is the critic's job to sort through these embeddings, finding evidence of the universal in the particular and yet, as Leff [1992] cautions, respecting the integrity and particularity of each message/event.

The critic therefore operates like the anthropologist who finds in the smallest ritual a complete depiction of tribal history and culture. The good critic never studies a particular text simply because it exists but because it promises to tell a story larger than itself. This means that no message is too modest for careful inspection. If human brutality is indeed on the rise, it might as well be evidenced in the interviewing styles of late-night radio commentators as in the rhetoric of the Ku Klux Klan.

Like all research activities, criticism requires that one (a) *isolate* a phenomenon for special study (e.g., the rhetoric of U.S. space exploration), (b) *describe* special aspects of that phenomenon (e.g., that rhetoric's heavy reliance on metaphors), (c) *classify* features of that phenomenon (e.g., its dependence on frontier metaphors vs. temporal metaphors), (d) *interpret* the patterns noticed (e.g., "the American people are still not capable of thinking in terms of fixed borders"), and (e) *evaluate* the phenomenon (e.g., "Will the U.S. become extra-terrestrial imperialists?"). These five intellectual skills are, of course, central to all forms of disciplined inquiry but they constrain the critic in particular ways, as we will see throughout this book.

3. *Rhetorical criticism produces metaknowledge* (that is, explicit understanding of implicit realizations). There are many similarities between literary and rhetorical criticism. Both require acuteness of perception, both demand textual exploration, and both expose human wants and desires as expressed in symbols. But there is also a difference: While few of us speak poetry in the day to day, all of us, as Moliere reminded us, speak prose. We are all persuaders of a sort, even if our rhetorical successes never partake of literary greatness. Rhetorical criticism therefore broadens the range of what can be studied. Rhetorical criticism is criticism of social life itself.

And so everyone is capable of doing rhetorical criticism without ever reading *Modern Rhetorical Criticism*. By having lived, talked, and listened for years, all of us have done the homework necessary to do criticism. Consider, for example, the following rather ordinary message:

> COM 390R. *Seminar in Contemporary Rhetorical Criticism.* May be repeated for credit when topics vary. Semester topics have included dramatistic criticism, content analysis, and methodologies for movement studies. Prerequisite: Upper-division standing.

What sort of message do we have here? Without question, a course description from a college catalog. But how is it possible for a reader who has never opened the course catalog of the University of Texas at Austin to make such a perception? And why do we have such *confidence* in that perception? Why could we not possibly mistake this message for a chili recipe or a page from Fodor's latest guide to Austria? Wherein lies the "implicit knowledge" necessary to identify this textual fragment? If we know this much about rhetoric, what else do we know that we don't know we know? And how do we know such things?

Last question first. We know such things because we are members of life's audience. We know it because each day, without effort or conscious attention, we are voracious consumers of messages. Each day, we swim in a sea of rhetoric: commercials for underarm deodorants, letters from loved ones, *People* magazine. Each year, we process, discard, and reprocess a virtual blizzard of discourse. As we go, we add to our extraordinary catalog of messages, constantly increasing the complexity and subtlety of our rhetorical knowledge. There is not a course description alive that could escape our detection.

Alas, the knowledge just described, although useful, is normally inert. While most people can identify messages accurately enough, few are able to explain *how we know what we know*. Few people pay attention to the details of their rhetorical experience. Upon critical reflection, however, almost everyone can do so. For example, the form of our course description is revealing: incomplete sentences, abnormal punctuation patterns, and inconsistent italicizing all suggest a hurried, businesslike tone, a message uninterested in wooing its reader. In addition, its reasoning patterns are telegraphic. Concepts like "prerequisite" are never explained, creating a heavy demand on the reader to supply the ideas necessary to make sense of the message. The language is also formidable: excessive use of jargon, polysyllabic words, and opaque phrases (e.g., COM 390R).

Also revealing is what is not found in the text. Nobody runs or feels here. No *doing* is being done. This absence of verbs suggests institutionalization, hardly what one would expect from what is essentially a piece of advertising. But this is a special sort of advertising, advertising without adjectives. The topics mentioned are not "new and improved," just topics. And much else is missing. There are no extended examples to help the reader see what the course will be like, no powerful imagery to sustain the student's sense of wonder while standing in the registration line, no personal disclosure by the author to build identification with the reader. It is as if this message did not care about its reader or even itself. It does nothing to invite or entice or intrigue. It does not unburden itself.

Most students know that such course descriptions cannot be "trusted." Students know that they are approved by committees and therefore do not bear the marks of the instructor's personality. Students know that such descriptions are processed by a bureaucracy that impresses its rigidities onto them. Students know that they must sample the rhetoric of their peers and professors before signing up. These latter rhetorics, students reason, will have the detail and humanity necessary for proper decision making. And so course descriptions dutifully sit in college catalogs: unread, unrespected, unloved. A hard life.

Frequently, then, criticism reminds us of what we already know about the world. It asks us to compare each new message to the data bank of messages already accumulated over a lifetime of audiencing. Criticism asks us to make our implicit knowledge explicit because only explicit knowledge can be used in practical ways. So rhetorical criticism is quite ecological: It invites us to become more active in retaining each day's messages so that they can later be recycled for use in understanding new messages.

4. *Rhetorical criticism invites radical confrontation with others and their cultures.* Perhaps this phrasing is a bit melodramatic, but criticism is a wonderful way to get outside ourselves. Naturally, most of us resist leaving our own perfect worlds to enter the strange, dark habitats of others. Our worlds are orderly, theirs chaotic; ours enlightened, theirs bizarre. But we also have wanderlust, a curiosity about the not-us, which is why vacationing in strange lands is such a prized experience. Rhetorical criticism can be a kind of vacationing, a way of visiting the not-us by examining what they have to say. As with all vacationing, though, criticism requires preparation—attitudinal preparation. We must remember that all persons have reasons for doing what they do (even if their reasons are not our reasons) and that we cannot understand others unless we are willing to leave our own tastes and prejudices at home. And if we are unable to leave them at home, we should at least leave them in our suitcases while exploring.

This is not a moral injunction (criticize others as you would have them criticize you). It is an intellectual injunction: One cannot *understand* others unless one appreciates how they reason and behave. But this injunction is not easy to follow. Consider, for example, the following materials distributed daily on city streetcorners:

- *Jesus and Mary Speak to the World through Veronica Luken*
  (Our Lady of Roses Shrine, Bayside, New York)
- *Heard any Good Fag Jokes Lately?*
  (National Gay Task Force)
- *Fight Forced Busing*
  (National Socialist White People's Party)
- *Smoking in Public: Let's Separate Fact from Friction*
  (R. J. Reynolds Tobacco Co.)
- *Dear Recreational Vehicle Owner*
  (The Good Sam Club)

Many people's first response to this smorgasbord of texts is: "Only in America!" From the standpoint of criticism, this is a healthy response. At least initially, the good critic examines all rhetoric in a spirit of wonder rather than one of censure: What do RV owners have to say to one another? How does a tobacco company conceal its self-interest in a public service announcement? And who, pray tell, is Veronica Luken?

Questions like these pull us into rhetoric and thereby pull us toward people, people who experience the world in special ways. If done well, criticism forces us outside the comfort of how we think and feel. It asks, for example, why racists are racists. What experiences have shaped them? Why are they so afraid of integration? What *really* threatens them? Bus-riding? Dark skin? Inferior education? Perhaps. But could it also be rapid change or social mobility or perhaps just life-in-general? All of these are possibilities, and only careful, critical inspection of *Fight Forced Busing* could help us sort through them.

Because the rhetorical critic examines messages meant for other people at other times, it is hard to do criticism and remain provincial. Rhetoric brings us face-to-face with otherness. Thus, when examining texts the critic is almost always an uninvited guest. The good critic remembers this and offers explanations of rhetoric as it was created, not as he or she would have had it created. The critic operates in this fashion not because it is nicer to do so but because it is smarter.

It is often not easy to be a good guest at someone else's party. Critics are people too, after all, who often feel strongly about the public matters they study. So it is useful to remember certain ground rules.

GROUND RULES FOR DOING CRITICISM

(a) *All public messages make sense to someone.* Because rhetoric is a people's art, it is sometimes easy to feel superior to it. Despite their noxious appeals, however, someone must like the collection of once-athletic men shown congregating in bars during beer advertisements. Someone must appreciate their swagger and love them despite their mangled grammar. It is the critic's job to presume such attractiveness and to discover the basis of its appeal.

(b) *All criticism is autobiography.* George Bernard Shaw's famous phrase is as true today as it was at the turn of the twentieth century. As hard as they try, critics can never be completely objective about rhetoric. Nor should they be. But they should at least be *conscious of their subjectivity,* aware of the biases they bring to their task and willing to explain those biases when sharing their observations with others.

(c) *Description before evaluation.* The critical instinct—I like it/I hate it—is a powerful instinct and it rears up in us frequently. But to make sense out of something that is radically other, the critic must first get the lay of the land. Thus, the ultimate challenge is to explain rhetoric with which we disagree or to find flaws in rhetoric to which we are instinctively attracted. The good critic therefore tries to understand the message in its original context before asking: What does this message do for me?

Although these attitudes cannot solve all critical problems, they can be helpful guidelines. Rhetorical criticism puts us in direct touch with humanity because it examines what humans do most artfully—write—and most instinctively—talk. The critic of rhetoric therefore stands in a privileged place.

QUALITIES OF THE IDEAL CRITIC

Not all critics are born equal. There is no Declaration of Critical Independence to insure that each critic will be perceptive. Even when examining a rich, suggestive piece of rhetoric, some fail to appreciate its nuances. The gifted critic, on the other hand, can build a provocative story out of the humblest message. So, for example, Davis [1998] noted that "the rhetorical lives of the 'everyday' masses of Black women are neglected" in contemporary scholarship [78]. She argued that "A Black feminist approach to rhetorical criticism celebrates the theoretical significance of the 'ordinariness of everyday life' to reveal Black women's ways of crafting identities within an oppressive [society]" [77]. Because the rhetoric upon which Davis built her case was quite ordinary, she had to be especially creative to find the truths hidden in its informality. But perceptiveness and creativity are not completely inherited. They can be nurtured. It is possible to become more perceptive critics if we (1) adopt a useful set of attitudes and (2) ask the right sorts of questions. Later chapters will suggest some of these questions but first we will examine the characteristics of the ideal critic.

1. *The good critic is skeptical.* The good critic does not take life at face value. Skeptics treat life on their terms, not on life's terms, and most assuredly, not on the persuader's terms. The good critic is one who stands back and watches, who will not be drawn into the pyrotechnics of rhetoric until fundamental questions about the rhetor's motives have been resolved. Skepticism, however, need not lead to cynicism. The skeptic is one who insists on taking a second look at everything simply because there is always more to a story than first meets the eye. The cynic, on the other hand, is a skeptic gone sour, one who refuses to take even a first look because of past disappointments.

Two key presuppositions of the skeptic are that all rhetoric denies itself and that good rhetoric denies itself completely. There are, of course, a few forthright persuaders to be found—the used car dealer, the streetcorner evangelist—who tacitly admit to their status as persuaders. But even here there is sleight-of-hand. The used car dealer agrees to take less for the automobile because he "was young once too and remembers his first car." And the evangelist is never motivated by personal ego when buttonholing passersby but is "compelled from afar to do the work of the Lord." These people do not wish to be seen only as persuaders; they wish to be seen as something more exalted in addition.

Still others deny the rhetorical function entirely. Adams [1986] tells us that newscasters, for example, look to a geographical region's popularity with American tourists before deciding which natural disasters to report. These reporters-turned-persuaders seek direct, but unacknowledged, influence. They use their supposed objectivity to escape critical detection by holding up signs emblazoned with the statement "No persuasion here. Look elsewhere for objects of criticism." The good critic does not look elsewhere. The good critic does not even blink.

As Fisher [1989] and others explain, persuaders often use narratives to throw critics off the persuasive scent. Storytelling, as Ronald Reagan well understood, signals a time-out: "Listen to this story as a story. You need not worry about argumentative propositions being advanced here." Most of us relax in the presence of narratives. Thus a "mere" story, *Uncle Tom's Cabin,* became one of the most potent pieces of civil rights rhetoric the United States has known. And thus business executives sell stock options during cocktail parties, those "time-out" events that advance rhetoric by denying its possibility. In some senses, then, the nonpersuader is the best persuader and the non-appeal the ultimate appeal.

2. *The good critic is discerning.* One need not be a genius to be discerning. Sherlock Holmes was not brilliant but he was discerning. He knew when to pay attention (when others were not around), how to pay attention (by looking to the left when others looked to the right), and where to pay attention (by looking in the kitchen rather than in the formal dining room). Holmes's eyes took in no more information than did those of the local constable. But unlike the local constable, Holmes had better categories for sorting and storing the information he collected. Both noticed the brown shoes on the body of the deceased but Holmes also noticed the absence of scuff marks.

Holmes did so because he had a theory of scuff marks. To the constable, shoes were shoes, but to Holmes the way people scuffed their shoes was a function of the purposiveness of their walk, which was a function of their life-style, which in turn was a function of their social habits and, ultimately, their mental habits. And that is why a man wearing unscuffed shoes would never have died a natural death while roaming through the moors. *That* sort of person detests moors.

Like Holmes, the good critic is hard to distract. Concentration is a precious gift for a critic since persuaders try so hard to divert their audiences' attention. As a result, the good critic pays attention to textual details that most audiences ignore. Thus, by simply noticing the raw frequency of certain word choices, Hart [1986] concluded that Ronald Reagan's first inaugural address was more ideological than was normal for a ceremony, a kind of rhetorical hangover from a very ideological campaign. Of course, Ronald Reagan himself did not assume that his choice of individual words would be of much interest to his audience. He no doubt presumed that his lectern-thumping would be muffled by the pleasant stories he told. That is why, when examining the Reagan speech, it proved useful to look elsewhere.

Most good critics look elsewhere. To understand the routines of social power in the United States, for example, Whittenberger-Keith [1989] inspected neither economic charts nor voting patterns but manners books. To determine the extent of contemporary racism, Rainville and McCormick [1977] looked not at open-housing laws but at the descriptions of black and white athletes provided by sports commentators. In both cases, the critics assumed that: (1) All texts are filled with data, even if some of these data seem irrelevant at first blush; (2) what is not present in a message is often more important than what is present; and (3) how an idea is phrased may sometimes be less important than the fact that the idea is mentioned at all. The good critic therefore asks questions of texts that audiences and poor critics rarely ask. But discernment should not be confused with eccentricity. Few critics ask how often the letter "E" is used in a passage because nobody has yet generated a *good reason* for doing so. Rather, the good critic has a sense for significance, a sense that matures as more and more discourse is examined. This was Sherlock Holmes's kind of sense.

3. *The good critic is imaginative.* Almost anyone can gather facts about a message. But it takes a good critic to know what to do with them. For example, most people in the 1970s had seen the late night public service announcements urging safe driving. Murray Edelman [1977] had observed them, too. But because he was skeptical, discerning, and imaginative, Edelman thought harder than most people about this ostensibly innocent rhetoric. Although controversial, his conclusion about the safe-driving advertisements was provocative: Such campaigns place responsibility for highway safety completely *on the driver* and therefore deflect attention from a major source of highway carnage—automobile manufacturers. Not only did Edelman see rhetoric where there appeared to be none, and not only was he able to zero-in on just the right features of the texts he analyzed, but he was also able to link his observations to a larger story about how entrenched economic interests use persuasion to maintain positions of privilege.

One need not be a leftist to appreciate how Edelman operated here. The larger story he told—his theory—enriched his inquiries. He did not investigate public service advertisements because he enjoyed them (who does?) but because when watching them late one night he was struck with a general idea about how political pressure operates in the United States. Naturally, this one analysis by Edelman could not establish some grand new law of political influence, but his case study did raise several general questions that he, and others, could try to answer by collecting more evidence. But it was the imaginative leap from data to theory that made Edelman's observation such an important one.

4. *The good critic is not timid.* Nothstine, Blair, and Copeland [1994] remind us that, because rhetoric is so powerful, the good critic cannot shrink from judgment. That is, good critics form authoritative assessments based on evidence in the artifact. Each day, powerful individuals use rhetoric to feather their nests and to deny others their rights. There are, to be sure, countervailing rhetorics but it takes a critic to know one from the other. Gaining such knowledge transforms criticism from an intellectual game to an engaged lifestyle and the student of rhetoric into a footsoldier in an age-old political battle. To engage in this battle, we must be able to think like the enemy.

THE REASONS FOR CRITICISM

A message is worth analyzing if it tells a story larger than itself. This means that the good critic always has a rationale for examining a text. These rationales take many forms: (1) the study may be worth doing because the rhetor has dealt with a **classic dilemma** (e.g., How can a president apologize for backing misguided legislation without losing his authority?); (2) the rhetor may have dealt imaginatively with **unresolved tensions** (e.g., How can a president appeal to the farmers without losing the urban vote?); (3) the rhetor may have addressed **projected problems** (e.g., How can a president make the nation comfortable with life in a financially uncertain world?); (4) the rhetor's situation may be a **parallel instance** of a continuing one (e.g., How did early presidents change citizens' health habits?); or (5) the rhetor may have been the first to confront some **unique circumstance** (e.g., What persuasive tools can a president use during an impeachment trial?).

There are, of course, countless such good reasons for doing rhetorical criticism. Notice that in all of the above instances, however, the critic has addressed issues of general interest. Concern for the larger story, therefore, should animate each piece of criticism written.

GUIDELINES FOR DEVELOPING A CRITICAL RATIONALE

(a) *No message is inherently worthy of study.* Just because a given text fascinates the critic does not mean that studying it will be worthwhile. Often, criticism becomes eccentric and too specialized because the critic fails to develop a clear reason for doing criticism. This produces scholarship-by-whim. Thus, when picking a text, the critic should be asking: *Why* does this message intrigue me? "Just because" is not a sufficient answer.

(b) *The past speaks to us constantly.* Examining the rhetoric of the past, even the distant past, can be quite useful because it gives us perspective on the lives we live today. Naturally, as Wichelns [1972:43] reminds us, all rhetoric is "rooted in immediacy" and we therefore must be careful not to distort the past in a headlong rush to find within it contemporary relevance. But people are people. Cultures are cultures. And rhetoric is rhetoric. The past has much to teach us if we but open our ears to its voices.

(c) *People who are larger than life may not be life-like.* "Tabloid scholarship" [Hart, 1986a:293] presumes that persuasion by "great" persons will be especially worthy of study. This is a poor assumption. It is easy to become distracted by high profile rhetors like presidents and popes, people who say interesting things but are far removed from the lives most people lead. The good critic remembers that the messages of ordinary people are often highly suggestive because they better represent how persuasion-in-general functions.

(d) *Imitation is not the sincerest form of flattery.* All too often, critics fail to go far enough in their analysis because they merely "translate" a message rather than explain it. This is especially true for the beginning critic who is tempted to latch onto an existing critical system and then superimpose it on an unsuspecting piece of rhetoric. The result is criticism that succeeds only in finding new examples of old persuasive strategies.

No set of guidelines will ensure brilliant criticism. But the guidelines above will ensure that we ask *why* criticism is being done in the first place. Skepticism and discernment are central to good criticism, but unless the critic makes an imaginative leap from text to idea, and then to judgment, criticism becomes wasted time and wasted paper. Persuasion is too interesting and criticism too productive to be overturned by unasked and unanswered whys.

THE STANDARDS OF CRITICISM

Evaluation seems to leap out of a word like criticism. Most people are critics in this sense when they complain about the local transit system or the tardiness of mail delivery. Normally, however, these everyday evaluations are not reflective. Few people are willing to actually visit the offices of the transit company, do a time-and-motion study of its operations, interview its personnel, pore over maps of urban geography, calculate the economies of scale produced by different routings, and then do the massive data synthesis necessary to determine whether there is, in fact, sufficient reason to be perturbed by the late bus at the corner of Maple and First. So it is important to distinguish between general complaining and *reflective complaining,* better known as criticism. Equally, it is important to distinguish between the knee-jerk compliment and the *reflective compliment,* which is also criticism. The judicious critic is therefore one who knows when and how to render an evaluation.

Most faulty critical statements result from premature evaluation, from judging the goodness of a rhetorical message before having carefully inspected its parts, before having collected data sufficient to sustain the critical judgment. Another type of faulty evaluation occurs when the critic fails to specify the standards used in the evaluation. We react differently to a critic who says "My mother is a terrific cook because she only buys food in yellow containers" than we do to one who argues "My mother is a good cook because she prepares tasty foods low in cholesterol." The first critic seems to be using absurd standards for judgment while the second seems more reasonable— reasonable, that is, in the eyes of other, reasonable people. In this connection, Black [1978a:7] makes the critic's obligations clear:

> The person who hears a speech and says, "I like it," is not making a critical statement. [That person] is reporting the state of his [or her] glands; [s/he] is speaking autobiographically. If we happen to like the person or if we are curious about the state of his [or her] glands, we may be interested in [this] report. Certainly his [or her] psychoanalyst would be interested in it. But neither the analyst nor we should confuse the statement with criticism. It is not criticism because, although it may be stimulated by an object, it is not *about* an object; it is a statement about the rhetor's own feelings, and nothing more.

Rhetorical critics have used quite a variety of critical standards to evaluate the rhetoric they have studied. Debate over the proper role of politics, activism, and theory in rhetorical criticism has enlivened many a journal [Darsey, 1994; Hart, 1994a; McGee, 2001; Kuypers, 2000b; Cloud, 2001; Black, 2002; Campbell, 2002]. Although we shall not detail every conceivable standard here, it is interesting to note their variety, any one of which can be used intelligently or foolishly. The judicious critic is one who knows which standard to use and why. And the exceptionally judicious critic is one who gives fair attention to the many alternative standards by which persuasion may be evaluated, some of which are:

1. *The Utilitarian Standard.* Given the limitations of the situation, did the message do what it was intended to do? Did people react as the rhetor hoped? Compared to other rhetors on this topic in situations like this, did this rhetor do as well as could be expected?

2. The Artistic Standard. Was the use of language or other symbols exceptional? Did the artifact meet the highest standards of beauty and formation? Did it so stimulate the imagination that it brought new ideas to life?

3. *The Moral Standard.* Did the message advance "the good" and encourage public virtue? Did the rhetor provide sufficient moral instruction to move the audience toward worthy, not just convenient, goals? Did the artifact meet acceptable standards of right and wrong?

4. *The Scientific Standard.* Did the message represent reality fairly? Did the rhetor's arguments have a factual base and did conclusions follow directly from the evidence presented? Could the claims in the message be independently verified?

5. *The Historical Standard.* Is it likely that the ideas presented and the values endorsed will outlast the rhetor? Did the message set processes in motion that resulted in major social changes?

6. *The Psychological Standard.* Did the message purge the emotions of the rhetor? the audience? Did it calm important fears? Were people so motivated by the message that social energy and personal commitments were renewed?

7. *The Political Standard.* Did the message advance the goals of the social groups the critic endorses? Will the "right" sort of people be advantaged by it? Will any harm be done to the most deserving people in society because this message was created?

Two things should be clear about this list of standards. First, it is no doubt incomplete—each critic can, and should, freely supplement the list. But whichever standard the critic selects should be defensible as "appropriate." A second important point is that messages which meet one standard may fail miserably in light of another. So, for example, a speech at a religious revival may succeed in increasing donations to the church (utilitarian standard) and, because its description of the afterlife is so masterful (artistic standard), the congregation's guilt over their indulgent life-styles may be relieved (psychological standard).

On the other hand, in describing sin the revivalist may have grossly distorted the extent of the national drug problem (scientific standard) by making it seem as if it were only a problem for minority groups (political standard), thereby making it unlikely that anyone in the future would have much respect for the remarks he made (historical standard). Clearly, one must operate thoughtfully when choosing critical standards as well as when deploying them. Rarely do we have trouble deciding whether we like a thing or dislike it. Explaining why we feel this way takes something else. It takes a judicious critic.

CONCLUSION

Criticism is complicated, yes, but also highly rewarding. To look carefully at what people say and how they say it is to take the human enterprise seriously. Rhetoric is an attempt to build community by exchanging symbols, and since the building of community is what makes us most human, listening to what people have to say is to pay them the ultimate compliment. This is true even if we, as critics, sometimes listen more carefully than is normally expected—or desired. And in paying this much attention to what people say, we also pay attention to ourselves, which makes criticism a journey of self-discovery as well.

There is nothing magical about good criticism. Good criticism is the art of developing and then using **critical probes:** specific, intelligent questions to be asked of a given text. Dozens of these **critical probes** are distributed throughout this book. By using them in criticism, the critic cannot help but become more discerning. Also, because the subject matter here is rhetoric, this book will no doubt add to the reader's supply of skepticism. And because the work of professional critics will be examined throughout, the reader will be presented with many examples of judiciousness. It is our hope that the variety of subjects and methods presented here will spark the imagination of the next generation of critics.

TIPS FOR THE PRACTICING CRITIC

1. Use the discussion of Ivins's column as a model for attempts to be "very hard to distract" as a critic. Do not look elsewhere for persuasive messages simply because Ivins seems "merely" to present a history lesson. Just as no message is inherently worthy (or unworthy) of analysis, no *genre* of messages is inherently worthy or unworthy of critical attention. If a piece of discourse calls itself "harmless," all the more reason to pay attention. Do not let the creator of a message dictate how to "read" that message; the

motives or reasons for speaking that the rhetor gives are hardly ever the *only* motives behind the communicative act.

2. Do not be discouraged if you are at first unable to do more than say "I like it/I hate it." Ask *why* you are reacting this way to this message in particular. Do specific words or phrases trigger certain positive or negative associations? If unable to immediately identify a single feature of the message that prompts this reaction, the critic is probably reacting to a combination of subtle elements, such as the tone of the message. Try rewording part of the message to see the effect. For instance, if a politician says, "My fellow Americans, I come before you today with a heavy heart. . . ." imagine instead, "I want to talk with you today about a very important problem. . . ." The first version may sound pompous, formal, or melodramatic, while the second may seem direct, informal, and down-to-earth. Why? What makes the first sound pompous and self-important? How does the simple and immediate language ("I want to talk with you") in the second manage to change the rhetor's image? Do this several times throughout the message. Gradually, you will be able to discover what it is about the organization and presentation of the rhetor's ideas that invites a particular response ("I like it/I hate it/It's funny/It's boring," and so on). Keep track of answers to the question "Why do I feel this way about this message?" and you will soon have a set of notes about the message. You will have made your implicit knowledge explicit. Now you can start to use it.

Chapter 3

ANALYZING SITUATIONS

[I wish I could sing!] I speak to you as an American Jew. As Americans we share the profound concern of millions of people about the shame and disgrace of inequality and injustice which make a mockery of the great American idea. As Jews we bring to [this] great demonstration, in which thousands of us proudly participate, a two-fold experience—one of the spirit and one of our history.

In the realm of the spirit, our fathers taught us thousands of years ago that when God created man, he created him as everybody's neighbor. "Neighbor" is not a geographic term; it is a moral concept. It means our collective responsibility for the preservation of man's dignity and integrity.

From our Jewish historic experience of three and a half thousand years we say: Our ancient history began with slavery and the yearning for freedom. During the Middle Ages my people lived for a thousand years in the ghettos of Europe. Our modern history begins with a proclamation of emancipation.

It is for these reasons that it is not merely sympathy and compassion for the Black people of America that motivates us. It is above all and beyond all such sympathies and emotions a sense of complete identification and solidarity born of our own historic experience.

[Friends], When I was . . . [in] . . . the Jewish community in Berlin under the Hitler regime, I learned many things. The most important thing that I learned in my life, and under those tragic circumstances, is that bigotry and hatred are not the most urgent problem. The most urgent, the most disgraceful, the most shameful, and the most tragic problem is *silence*. A great people which had created a great civilization had become a nation of silent onlookers. They remained silent in the face of hate, in the face of brutality, and in the face of mass murder.

America must not become a nation of onlookers. America must not remain silent—not merely Black America, but all of America. It must speak up and act from the President down to the humblest of us, and not for the sake of the Negro, not for the sake of the Black community, but for the sake of the image, [the dream], the idea, and the aspiration of America itself.

Our children, yours and mine, in every school across the land, every morning pledge allegiance to the flag of the United States and to the Republic for which it stands, and then they, the children, speak fervently and innocently of this land as the land of "liberty and justice for all."

The time, I believe, has come for us to work together, for it is not enough to hope together—for it is not enough to pray together—to work together, that this children's oath—pronounced every morning from Maine to California, from North and South—that this oath will become a glorious, unshakable reality in a morally renewed and united America. [Thank you.]

This chapter begins with a question: Who gave this speech? Here are several more: Can we be sure that this was, in fact, a speech and not an essay? If a speech, when and where was it given? Under what social and psychological circumstances? Was the audience wealthy, middle-class, or poor? Were they Jewish like the speaker or perhaps religiously and ethnically diverse? How did they feel about the topic? Was the speaker male, female, or transgendered? What about the speaker's education, status, age and occupation?

Such questions may seem bizarre. Few people, after all, must deal with mystery messages. Most texts come prepackaged, replete with the information needed to make sense out of them. Most messages are understandable because we confront them in their natural habitats: in a particular place and time. Besides, if we ever did happen upon a mystery message, surely we could quickly identify its origins via Internet search engines.

This chapter will presume that no such search engines exist. It will also presume that most persuasive messages contain information that normally slips past the unperceptive observer, but still influences that observer. We will see here that every message contains "genetic markers" that reveal much about its parentage—where it came from and why. We will discover that since each persuasive message is produced in a unique rhetorical situation, it therefore does something unique, thereby constituting a unique speech-act. We will also discover that the situation itself can make a statement apart from the statements contained in the words of the message.

In a sense, all criticism is a kind of guessing game, with the critic trying to shed light on the rhetorical shadows of a text. By inspecting a message carefully the critic turns presumed knowledge into tested knowledge. So, for example, how do we know that the artifact above was, in fact, a speech? The clues are several. For instance, it would be presumptuous for a writer to pen the first sentence since these remarks seem part of a *continuing* dialogue with somebody the speaker never identifies. While writers sometimes start in the middle of things, they rarely leave their readers without background clues for long, certainly not forever. But a speaker talking to a live audience could make such a reference if they had just shared some sort of musical experience, which seems to be the case here.

Also, the language in the message does not seem quite smooth enough for written composition. The sentences are frequently short—simple, declarative—and they contain few of the embedded clauses common to essay or textbook writing. The rhetor often engages in direct address here ("we share," "our fathers taught us"), a feature often found in personal correspondence. But the rhetor also uses *formal* direct address here ("Friends . . .") that would be off-putting if found, say, in a loved one's postcard from Tahiti. The words in the passage are common ones, so the message could be a popular editorial, but the speaker ends by thanking the audience for their attention, something that writers never do. After all, while a writer can presume that time is being freely provided by readers (who can pick up or put down the printed matter at their leisure), the speaker is always aware that attention is a gift that busy and easily bored listeners give to speakers. And so we have a speech.

A contemporary speech? Possibly, although one gets very little flavor of today's hard-nosed pragmatism and political action committee-controlled politics here. There is no talk of funding possibilities, enactable legislation, or factual precedent. Rather, the speech seems to be a *beginning* ("The time . . . has come"). We hear of plans being made, not of victories being savored. Moreover, the speaker attempts to turn his individual listeners into some sort of collective ("our children, yours and mine"), as if he could not presume that they already shared the same priorities.

What else do we have? We have singing, Jews, Blacks, collective responsibility, repudiation of silence, pledges of allegiance from North to South, a post-World War II time frame, and, most pregnantly, the Emancipation Proclamation. This is also a short speech, perhaps one of many given that day. Moreover, the speaker is either rudely ignoring local personalities and local conditions or is reaching out to a *national* constituency ("from Maine to California"). All in all, this sounds like the language of the 1960s, an era in which even political rhetoric sounded religious and in which a term like "great demonstration" had an ideological rather than a mercantile meaning. This sounds like the era of the gospel-singing Mahalia Jackson, who preceded our speaker, and of Martin Luther King, Jr., who spoke just after our speaker. The place: Washington, D.C. The scene: the Lincoln Memorial. The audience: some 200,000 civil rights marchers. The date: August 28, 1963.

And our speaker? What does the message/situation tell us? A male, no doubt, for few women addressed such large crowds in the United States in 1963. The mere *act* of speaking at a massive demonstration like this was an outward sign of power and the roots of sexism held fast in 1963, even within the then-forming civil rights establishment. The language, too, is full of male forcefulness (e.g., when the speaker sets his own scene: "I speak to you as an American Jew"). Also, the gentle paternalism (" 'Neighbor' is not a geographic term; it is a moral concept") and historic persona ("During the Middle Ages my people . . .") clearly suggest the thoughts of an older speaker (or a self-important younger one). Finally, even though the phrase "a rabbi" was removed in the first line of the fifth paragraph, the speaker himself signals his occupation with his scholarly distinctions ("not for the sake of the Black community, but for the sake of . . ."), his spiritual exhortations ("a glorious, unshakable reality in a morally renewed and united America"), and his sermonic style ("in the face of hate, in the face of brutality, and in the face of mass murder . . ."). The speaker was Rabbi Joachim Prinz [1963], then national president of the American Jewish Congress and one of several speakers who shared the platform with Dr. King on that historic day in 1963.

So our critical work is done. But was it worth it? Would it not have been easier to simply look up the required information? Easier, yes. More informative? Decidedly not. In the language of Chapter 2, looking it up would not have explained **how** we knew that we knew important distinctions between contemporary and noncontemporary speech, between male and female speech, between religious and secular speech, between private and public speech, between mature and immature speech, between formal and informal speech, and between speech and nonspeech.

In this chapter, we will come to understand that all messages "do" as well as say and that all messages bear the imprints of the social situations that produced them, thereby making rhetoric a situated art that can only be understood when text and context are considered simultaneously. In this chapter, we will see that the best reference work of all is that housed in the critic's personal library of rhetorical knowledge.

THE MEANINGS OF SPEECH-ACTS

A basic fact about speaking often goes unnoticed: It is an activity. That is, by addressing another, a speaker both says something **and does something.** Many critics miss this "doing" function in their headlong rush to study words. But as Hart [1987:xxi] has said, "by choosing to utter words to another, a speaker makes at least these decisions—to speak to A and not to B; to speak now and not then or never; to speak here and not there; to speak for this period of time, not longer or shorter. These rhetorical decisions contain 'information' for us as observers if we are wise enough and patient enough to track these decisions."

Daily life often teaches these lessons about speech-acts. Sometimes painfully: Despite his gift for storytelling, a guest overstays his welcome at a party; despite her good intentions, a young executive is fired for sharing classified information with a colleague in a public restaurant; despite their affability, a married couple insults their new neighbors by greeting them with a wave instead of an extended conversation. In each of these cases, the messages exchanged were innocent enough, but matters of place, timing, and relationship undid them.

Philosopher J. L. Austin [1970] has labeled this "extra" dimension of persuasion its **performative** character. Austin himself was particularly intrigued by situations whose performative features dominated its message features (e.g., if said in the right context, "I do" both communicates loving sentiments *and* gets one married). But as Benjamin [1976] has observed, not only speeches, but all rhetorical messages probably have important performative aspects to them, which is why the critic should calculate a message's performative features *before* doing any sort of careful textual analysis.

Consider, for example, the furor aroused when a physician published a brief column in the illustrious *Journal of the American Medical Association*. The piece was entitled "It's Over, Debbie" and vividly detailed a case of euthanasia performed by the author-doctor. Hyde [1993] has analyzed this letter and argues that its importance lay not in what it said but in *what the act of publishing it did*. Many doctors, after all, have done mercy killings but few have acknowledged doing so and fewer still have done so in print. Some journals had discussed euthanasia but not the most prestigious medical publication in the United States. In other words, "It's Over, Debbie" caused a ruckus in the medical community, even among physicians who never actually read the article.

All of this happened because rhetoric acts. It does so because it contains, according to Arnold [1974:38–43] and Hart et al. [1983:13–14], any number of "implicit understandings." That is, the decision to communicate with another means at least these things:

1. *The rhetor feels something is wrong.* This wrong thing may not be a calamity but even a friendly greeting to a passerby can be seen as an attempt to ward off alienation and increase goodwill in society. Preachers preach and teachers teach because of the sin and ignorance they hope to offset. Politicians speak politics when they envision that their legislative mandates are in trouble. Indeed, politics is inevitably rancorous because it focuses upon the most persistent of problems: poverty, disease, war, natural disaster. Even a speech at a happy event, such as a toast at a wedding, is designed to wave away nonhappiness for the couple. People talk when they are troubled and during all other moments they are quiet. The first question the critic must ask, therefore, is: What's wrong?

2. *The rhetor is not yet desperate.* Rhetors are optimists; they believe that communication can change human affairs. By sharing symbols, people convey hope. Total desperation, in contrast, drives people away from rhetorical solutions and toward more "transcendent" remedies such as contemplation, substance abuse, or violence. So where there is rhetoric there is hope, or so implies the person who takes the trouble to speak or write. It is for these reasons that peace talks between rival powers always make front-page headlines. The mere agreement-to-talk proves that hope abides.

3. *The rhetor is committed.* To something. Perhaps just to him- or herself, perhaps to the proposal being advocated. But communication, especially in

public, implies a dramatic commitment primarily because of the substantial risks attendant to it. Often, these commitments are emotional (e.g., for a social activist) and often they cost us time (e.g., a campaigning politician), money (e.g., a poorly paid campus evangelist), relationships (e.g., a lecturer traveling the country without her family), or sleep (e.g., a late-night television commentator). In each case, the speaker signals that speaking is worth the cost.

4. *The audience is open to change.* Audiencing, too, is a commitment, a tacit acknowledgement that we are not set in our ways. To attend a live event, after all, is to interrupt what one is doing, to don coat or dodge raindrops, sometimes to stand in line for tickets, occasionally to be seated in uncomfortable surroundings, often to be confronted with strange thoughts and uncomfortable emotions. Satisfied teenagers have no need for education, satisfied citizens have no need for politics, satisfied people have no need for rhetoric.

Thus, a key question for the rhetorical critic is this: By communicating on this topic to this audience in this setting at this time, what "news" is the rhetor making? Sometimes, the "news" lies in the **rhetor-topic** relationship, as when reports that poets were planning to protest the war on Iraq prompted First Lady Laura Bush to cancel a scheduled White House symposium on "Poetry and the American Voice." At other times, the news lies in the **rhetor-setting** relationship, as when President George W. Bush addressed the nation on Iraq from the deck of an aircraft carrier. Or the story could lie in the **rhetor-audience** relationship, as when Dixie Chicks' lead singer Natalie Maines criticized Bush and was promptly boycotted by country-music fans and DJs. In each of these situations, both a statement and a metastatement was made by the rhetor. It is this larger statement that the critic must examine in each instance of persuasion.

It would matter little, for example, what the pope said about papal infallibility should he ever agree to discuss it. The mere *fact* of his doing so would send an important message. Similarly, when the rap group Public Enemy retracted anti-Semitic statements made by their own Professor Griff they silently acknowledged, according to Sloop [1994], the power of the liberal consensus in the United States. And as Brydon [1985:148] observed, the mere agreement of a political incumbent to debate a challenger can send a message of great strength or great weakness to voters, media personnel, and challenger alike. At times, not to speak is to say a good deal.

THE FUNCTIONS OF SPEECH-ACTS

Because the natural tendency of the critic is to be fascinated with words and their meanings, it is not always easy to focus on the "action" of a speech-act. This was less of a problem for Maurice Bloch [1975] and his colleagues who studied the speaking activities of people in nontechnological societies. Because they were strangers to the tribes they studied, the researchers could shift their attention from the words spoken to the speaking activities *as activities.* In his book, Bloch presents the work of ten different anthropologists who fanned out all over the world to study what speechmaking "did" for the societies they studied.

One of these researchers studied the Merina of Madagascar and found the oratory to be depersonalized, bearing no distinctive stamp of the speaker. Indeed, even the orator's intonation patterns had been fixed by tradition, suggesting that for the Merina the act of speaking was automatically an act of tribal submission. In another case, among the Tikopia of the Solomon Islands, the chief of the tribe rarely showed up for the activities, thereby insuring that his authority could never be directly questioned by those in attendance. In the speeches of the Kaoleni of Kenya, researchers found few references to hierarchy or leadership since to mention such matters would have been to call attention to sharp economic cleavages in that society.

The impression one gets from such oratory is one of *constraint*. Political speaking in such societies seems more a display than a problem-solving process. Speaking generally about such cultures, Bloch [1975:8] observes that "the orator's words are almost entirely not his own [because] he sees them as handed down from the ancestors. He will have learned all the proverbs, stories and speech forms and his main aim is to repeat them as closely as possible." Bloch [p. 9] goes on to say that listeners in these societies also make clear social statements when they take part in such speaking events: "On these occasions if you have allowed somebody to speak in an oratorical manner you have practically accepted his proposal . . . When someone speaks to you in this way there quite simply seems to be no easy way of saying 'no' or commenting on the substance of what is said." In short, Bloch and his colleagues found that such speech-acts were symbolic tokens of basic political structures. For them, speaking *was* political action.

Closer to home, Hart [1987] conducted a comprehensive study of the basic rhetorical decisions made by recent American chief executives. Rather than examine the texts of presidential messages, Hart simply recorded the date, place of delivery, occasion, topic, audience, and political circumstance of each of the presidential speeches delivered from 1945 onward. This amounted to a database of some 10,000 speech events. By looking at the pattern of speech decisions— whom presidents talked to, about what, when and where—he hoped to catalog the most basic functions of presidential discourse. The question Hart asked— what does speech do?—focuses on a fundamental set of metamessages and therefore should be asked during any rhetorical inquiry. Although Hart focused on public speech, these remain profitable questions for any rhetorical event.

1. *Speech situations index power.* Hart observed that the first audience addressed by Ronald Reagan after his assassination attempt consisted exclusively of press correspondents, suggesting how central the media now are to a president's image of strength.

2. *Speech situations index ego needs.* For example, Hart discovered that Lyndon Johnson gave an unusually large number of speeches in his home state,

probably because Texas audiences confirmed for him that he had finally "made it" as a national figure (something he never seemed quite sure of himself).

3. *Speech situations index social obstacles.* Hart concluded that the presidency is becoming more difficult since chief executives are increasingly delivering preplanned speeches to preselected audiences instead of putting up with the give-and-take of press conferences (the first President Bush was particularly fond of this tack).

4. *Speech situations reveal speaker priorities.* Unlike any of the other chief executives, Jimmy Carter continued to speak extensively in the two months *following* his 1980 defeat for reelection. Why? He was a dogged individual strongly committed to the policies the electorate had just repudiated.

5. *Speech situations reveal audience priorities.* Presidential speaking has now become a full-time business. Presidents speak extensively, even during summers and nonelection years. For whatever reason, the American people seem to have developed an insatiable appetite for presidential oratory.

6. *Speech situations reveal speaker/audience relationships.* Presidents are now spending more time speaking to private groups than to ordinary citizens. No doubt, such changes have been occasioned by alterations in patterns of political fund-raising, a fact also reflected in increased speaking activities in the Sun Belt, a part of the country undergoing great surges in population (and infusions of capital). In short, presidents use speech to flatter the people they must flatter.

Our concern in this section has been with *pre*-rhetorical analysis, not with words but with word-using. Because rhetoric is always a situated activity, rhetors must structure the right "configuration" of elements—audience, topic, setting, and so on—for maximum impact. Shortly, we shall turn to more detailed analyses of these elements, but before doing so let us consider the first question to be asked of any rhetorical event: *What **act** is being performed here?*

This is a simple question, but answers to it are normally complex. An elementary way of answering this question is to reduce the speech activity to one "ing" word, a gerund. Admittedly, such an approach is simplistic, but that is precisely its value: It reduces the speech-act to its most basic performative feature. Although the critic is free to choose any characterizing term for this purpose, Table 3.1 presents a starter's list, borrowing from the work of Gaines [1979] and supplemented by other suggestions as well.

The key move here is to describe, not to evaluate, the speech-act. Naturally, as with all criticism, the critic must be able to defend the term chosen to categorize the rhetorical act in question. No doubt, different critics analyzing the same event would spot different "performances." That is appropriate, since this exercise provides only a first, quite partial, glimpse of the event in question. But there is real utility in attempting this critical procedure, not for the answers derived but for the questions raised. It seems clear, for example, that our Rabbi at the Lincoln Memorial was not attempting to amuse or sur-

TABLE 3.1 Available Terms for Characterizing Speech-Acts

activating	disputing	ordering
amusing	distracting	placating
angering	diverting	praising
announcing	edifying	promising
avoiding	enacting	refuting
calming	encouraging	reminding
challenging	enlightening	reporting
commencing	entertaining	requesting
confusing	escalating	retracting
consecrating	finishing	rousing
continuing	frightening	shocking
deceiving	humiliating	soothing
delaying	inciting	startling
demanding	inspiring	surprising
deterring	insulting	teaching
displaying	intimidating	warning
disposing	leading	

prise. But was he commencing something or continuing something? Was he warning or encouraging his television audience? Was he soothing or challenging the tired civil rights workers? And what was he doing most often? Questions like these focus on the most general terrain of a speech-act and help orient any subsequent textual analysis. They also throw light on the architecture of the rhetorical act—who said what to whom and why—and thereby raise valuable questions that are often overlooked.

THE COMPONENTS OF SPEECH-ACTS

This section will consider how a critic can better understand a message by reckoning with its larger social situation. According to Bitzer [1968], a number of situational factors operate to suggest what can and cannot be said by a person in a given instance. Some of these suggestive factors lie within the speaker (e.g., knowledge, experience, psychological state) while others are external (e.g., the time of day, what others are saying, etc.). In either case, a message becomes a public record of how the speaker coped with the suggestions built into the rhetorical situation. Figure 3.1 captures the most basic of such factors. Several features of the model are worth noting:

1. *The model situates the message within an array of social forces.* No piece of discourse can be understood outside of its natural habitat. While an ancient poem or painting may delight persons living generations later, that is rarely the case with more overtly persuasive rhetoric. Old rhetorical messages seem to chide subsequent readers: "You really should have been there." Thus, Arnold

FIGURE 3.1 Elements of a Rhetorical Situation

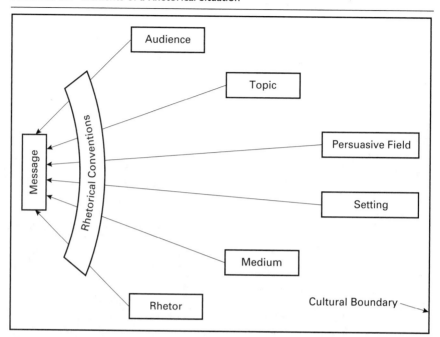

[1968] notes that when the parliamentary speeches of William Butler Yeats were anthologized, the editor provided the situational details necessary to makes sense out of the speeches. In contrast, collections of Yeats's poems rarely contained such situational markers.

2. *The model describes a system of elements.* Any speech-act is always more than the sum of its parts; to change one element is to change the whole. Anyone who has seen the "same" *Dateline* audience put to sleep by a discussion of the national deficit and electrified one week later by a Ben Affleck/Jennifer Lopez interview knows that changing one element of a rhetorical system can produce changes throughout that system.

3. *All situational elements operate within a unique cultural boundary.* It is often hard to see the effects of culture upon human interaction. Nevertheless, the critic must try to do so since culture penetrates all message-sending and all message-receiving. To an uncritical American moviegoer, the latest action flick about fictional CIA agent Jack Ryan may seem to consist of universal themes, but it takes only the slightest cultural sensitivity to be able to trace its sexism and nationalism to a long cultural history of conservative U.S. values.

4. *An artifact is the visible record of a complex interaction.* The critic focuses heavily on the artifact because that is all that is left after a dynamic human encounter has occurred. One way of tracking this complexity is to compare two versions of the "same" text. For example, McMullen and Solomon [1994]

found that the feminist themes in Alice Walker's book, *The Color Purple,* were replaced by a more general, and hence lucrative, American dream emphasis by director Stephen Spielberg when the book was turned into a movie.

5. *The artifact is the rhetorical critic's touchstone.* Anthropologists may study social settings, sociologists may study audiences, psychologists may study media effects, and historians may recount the careers of great speakers. But it is the rhetorical critic who uniquely examines the marks left on messages by these various forces.

Our model, then, conceives of artifacts as repositories of information about situational elements. Morris [1996] studied a commencement address *Peter Pan* author and closeted homosexual J. M. Barrie delivered in England in 1922. While the speech was not a "coming out" narrative by today's standards, it still revealed a great deal. As Barrie's contemporary Sir Hugh Walpole observed: "[A]lthough he meant all that he said, he meant also a great deal more than he said" [Morris, 1996: 208]. As Morris observes, any artifact (or text) always provides the critic with clues to its context, even context the rhetor may have wished to hide. One way of discovering the context within the text is to inquire into the **intertextual** aspects of a message— the bits and pieces of previous texts "deposited" into a new text. So, for example, Taylor [1992] reports that the *Letters and Recollections* of physicist Robert Oppenheimer (who helped invent the atomic bomb) were often "re-used" by other persuaders for their own purposes as they selectively drew upon, and re-formatted, Oppenheimer's original thoughts.

To get an idea of how this configuration of factors can operate in the complex world of human persuasion let us consider some critical probes for the situational analyst:

RHETOR VARIABLES
- Besides discussing a particular topic in a particular location, is the rhetor making some sort of *social statement* by speaking or writing?
- Does the audience have first-hand knowledge of the rhetor that he or she can draw upon rhetorically?
- Is the rhetor "sainted" or "victimized" by stereotypes listeners have of "people like this"?
- Is the rhetor free to specify his or her motives for communicating?
- Has the rhetor subscribed to a particular ideology or doctrine that expands or limits what can be said?
- Does the rhetor possess any unique assets or liabilities when speaking on this topic?
- *What textual evidence shows that the rhetor considered these factors when framing the message in question?*

These questions deal with how social role, personal ideology, and public image constrain, sometimes dictate, what a rhetor says. On occasion, for example, a college teacher may struggle to keep a lecture free of personal bias in order to keep students from questioning everything the teacher has to say (about this, and all other, topics). In such cases, Personal Ideology wages a war with Social Role in the presence of Public Image. The message produced—the lecture itself—often carries the battle scars.

In other instances, the mere fact of speaking can carry the most important message. Logue and Miller [1995], for example, tell the story of a rural Georgia mayor who began to lose power in the community when he chose to debate, rather than reason with, two elderly women who protested their water bill. After months of publicity, the mayor very much regretted his decision. He severely underestimated the staying power of his two angry constituents as they constantly made him look the fool, eventually even appearing on the *Tonight Show*.

Rhetoric changes audiences but it can also change speakers as well. Jamieson [1988b] notes, for example, that the advantage of modern presidential debating lies not in the political information provided the citizenry but in the debates' abilities to insure that the candidates themselves become informed on the issues! Speakers may create messages but, often, messages recreate speakers as well.

AUDIENCE VARIABLES

- Regardless of the practical outcome of the interaction, has the audience made any significant *social statement* by choosing to listen, read, or watch?
- To what extent is this audience a "rhetorical audience," that is, one that can directly implement the change the rhetor is requesting?
- Can the rhetor capitalize on existing common ties with the audience?
- What previous personal or philosophical commitments (e.g., group memberships) has the audience made that may affect their responses?
- What contrary information or attitudes does the audience have that can inhibit the rhetor's success?
- What recent experiences has the audience had that may affect their responsiveness?
- *What textual evidence shows that the rhetor considered these factors when framing the message in question?*

Simply agreeing to become part of an audience can constitute a major social statement. As Meyer [1995] notes, when the Establishment begins to listen to the strident cries of social movement activists, change is surely in the wind. Meyer found that "elite" speakers even began to re-produce movement refrains themselves, dramatic evidence of their having listened to their opponents.

Beasley [2001] studied over a century of local addresses by U.S. presidents, speeches that could presumably center on particular concerns of relatively homogeneous groups. However, she found that even here, presidents seek to "manage American pluralism" by inviting listeners to identify themselves based on their occupations, locations, and party affiliations (rather than race, class, or other potentially divisive and hence troublesome characteristics) [p. 25]. In so doing, these speakers capitalized on what was "built into" their audiences demographically.

TOPIC VARIABLES

- Is this topic socially acceptable? Is the fact that it is being discussed a significant *social statement?*
- Is the topic either volatile or innocuous? Is public opinion highly polarized on this matter?
- How complex is the topic? Can it be reasonably discussed with this audience in this setting?
- Because of how this topic has been discussed before, must the rhetor deal with it in a certain way?
- Does the topic have any special features that make its discussion via this medium advantageous or risky?
- *What textual evidence shows that the rhetor considered these factors when framing the message in question?*

Each speech topic has a "range of discussability." Some topics (e.g., the Golden Gate Bridge) let a speaker roam freely when discussing them, while others tightly rein one in (e.g., sexual harassment). It is difficult for many Americans to talk about such indelicate matters as hemorrhoid treatments or funeral arrangements, products and services requiring advertisers to be especially inventive rhetorically. The range of discussability for a topic may also be constricted by its complexity. For example, years ago the Mathematical Association of America opened its annual meetings to the press in order to gain wider public understanding of the important work that mathematicians do. Alas, the experiment failed: Only four of the eighty invited reporters bothered to attend [Kolata, 1975:732].

At other times, linking a speaker (say, a prominent Roman Catholic) to a topic (say, cover-ups of child sexual abuse by American priests) within a particular medium (say, television news and talk shows) can create enormous difficulties—if you are Boston Cardinal Bernard Law, a man some saw as the next pope, but who instead resigned in scandal. In short, any one element in the configuration of elements can create topical difficulties. Several operating at the same time can create rhetorical nightmares.

PERSUASIVE FIELD

- Taken as a whole, can this situation be seen as a *counterstatement* to some other set of messages?
- Have the rhetor's previous communications to this audience expanded or limited current persuasive possibilities?
- What statements have other people made in the past that constrain what can be said now?
- What sort of immediate "verbal competition" (e.g., heckling, rebuttal) is the rhetor being subjected to?

- Can future rhetorical messages be envisioned that require anticipatory strategies now?
- *What textual evidence shows that the rhetor considered these factors when framing the message in question?*

The persuasive field consists of all other messages impinging upon an audience in a given rhetorical situation. These messages could have been authored by the rhetor previously, by other members of the audience, or by persons not present. During a news conference, for example, a president often must cope with rumors that have been circulating in the newspapers, with recent Congressional attacks on his administration, or with the complaints of protestors outside the White House. All of these forces are added to the mix when the president approaches the microphone for the first question.

At times, the persuasive field will be unusually message-filled as, for example, during controversy about the causes of a pandemic such as AIDS. Reeves [1998:4] studied the rhetoric of rival French and American scientists seeking to isolate causes amidst a flood of "ridiculous theories." She concluded that the two groups' competing rhetorics offer competing lessons: American researchers attracted first praise, then censure for their bold approach to marketing their theory, while the French team's prudent reluctance to offer overtly persuasive discourse initially hid the novel contributions of their work.

For these and other reasons, savvy rhetors seek to set and limit their own agendas, knowing that with so many intertextual forces now at work in an age of mass media, all messages contain the ghosts of other messages. Thus it was not surprising when Gilberg et al. [1980] found that a presidential speech given today often tracks last week's newspaper. Public persuaders must be responsive to an ever-changing persuasive field.

SETTING VARIABLES

- Is any *social statement* being made by the rhetor by communicating at this time in this place?
- Is there a special kind of "history" attached to where the message is being delivered? Does that place affect what can be said?
- Do any nonverbal events (e.g., aspects of sight, sound, feeling, etc.) affect the rhetor's plan?
- What events are likely to occur in the future that will affect what can be said now by this rhetor?
- *What textual evidence shows that the rhetor considered these factors when framing the message in question?*

Over time, some physical locations take on special social (and rhetorical) significance. When announcing his bid for the 1996 presidential campaign, for example, Senator Phil Gramm stood in front of the Texas A&M University military cadets, thereby declaring himself, both verbally and nonverbally, a man of conservative values. Other settings permit other options. Queen Elizabeth II made history by celebrating her Golden Jubilee with a "Party at the Palace," at which musical artists such as Atomic Kitten, Blue, and former Spice Girl Emma Bunton performed. In so doing, she enlivened the staid image of Buckingham Palace and the Royal Family it symbolizes.

Because we cannot visualize time, a setting like Buckingham Palace tends to stand for history. Setting thus can function in complicated ways; for example, it can both contribute to human alienation and market a remedy for it. Dickinson [1997:1] sees a rise of "memory places" in contemporary America. He notes that uncertain times encourage nostalgia for a past when social identity and behavior (class, race, gender) seemed clear and predictable. This yearning is heightened in urban centers where the fast pace and juxtaposition of cultures and values lead to an almost dizzying splintering of self and community. Sites such as Old Pasadena in Los Angeles are carefully structured to create a comforting, if illusory, sense of leisure and order, offering consumers the ability to perform a desirable identity through their purchasing choices. The place itself invests those identities with "historical" validity.

Aspects of time (the hour of the day) and timing (when an event occurs relative to other events) are also important factors. As Gronbeck [1974:86] says, a persuasive message may fail because the speaker is the wrong person for the moment, because the audience is not yet "primed" to take the appeal seriously, or because the message is presented too soon or too late. So, for example, the nation was primed for a heartfelt apology from Bill Clinton immediately after the sex scandal involving White House intern Monica Lewinsky became public, but it was only his second apology, a month later, that fulfilled that function. The first address was legalistic and evasive. Had he delivered the second apology first, the impeachment hearings against him might never have gone forward. Timing is also important in the business world where product-messages are carefully adapted to the entertainment schedule. This is why beer is advertised during football telecasts and why soap is advertised during, well, soap operas.

MEDIA VARIABLES

- Is the rhetor making any important *social statement* by delivering a message via this medium?
- Does the modality chosen (i.e., spoken or written) enhance or detract from the rhetor's message?
- Does the size of the audience the medium can reach present or deny any important rhetorical possibilities?
- Are there any important "sponsorship effects" associated with messages presented via this medium?
- Does the medium chosen permit the rhetor's personality to become an important force of persuasion?
- Do subaudiences exist because of the medium chosen for the message?
- *Is there textual evidence that the speaker considered these factors when framing the message in question?*

A medium is that which "carries" a message. At the simplest level, for example, we are aware of the very different rhetorical possibilities of speaking versus writing. Normally, marriage is proposed in person—while speaking—rather than by telegram because speech is personal and intimate while telegrams are both too cold and too terse for something as complicated as love. On the other hand, "Dear John" is more likely to receive a breakup letter than a phone call because writing helps one focus one's thoughts, craft one's arguments and, above all, circumvent the emotionalism of the moment.

The Dear John letter, of course, is one of the most hated messages ever devised because its sender makes such a powerful social statement by choosing a distanced medium for a former intimate. It is likely, therefore, that many such letters are destroyed before they are read through. No matter how carefully the words may be phrased, the rhetorical *act* is a fundamentally alienating one.

As we will see in Chapter 9, persuasion has changed dramatically with the advent of the mass media. Before, when speakers addressed throngs of listeners face to face, the speaker's message could not be dispersed widely but the speaker could see and touch the immediate audience. Radio and television reach many more listeners but they are now presented with "images" rather than with live speakers in close proximity.

Scholars continue to sort out the complexities of the mass media. But some things we know. For example, the mass media create "sponsorship effects," with listeners now having built-in expectations for *any* televised message. That is, TV viewers have come to expect informality rather than formality, personalized rather than impersonal arguments, visual rather than bland supporting materials, interactive rather than lecture formats, and much else. Also, because so many persons can be reached at the same time via television, rhetorical messages are becoming increasingly complex, as speakers adjust different parts of the same message to the different subaudiences they face simultaneously.

So, for example, Rosteck [1994] found that the Democrats' 1992 convention film, *The Man from Hope,* succeeded because it managed (by using a variety of mythic appeals) to appeal to both the partisan convention-goers as well as to the less partisan, more easily distracted viewers at home. On another front, Wander [1984] has shown that any presidential foreign policy address must now speak directly to the voters, as well as to their journalistic overhearers, and to friendly and unfriendly members of Congress as well. It gets more complicated: At the same time, the president must send careful signals to rival powers without missending signals to American allies. This overlapping of audiences may account for the sometimes bizarre sound of contemporary politics.

RHETORICAL CONVENTIONS

- Has this configuration of elements come together before?
- If so, are there rules of interaction that must be followed by the rhetor?
- If this rhetorical situation is a new one, must any general rhetorical guidelines be honored here?

- Does any *one* element (rhetor, audience, topic, etc.) have special weight?
- *What textual evidence shows that the rhetor considered these factors when framing the message in question?*

Without question, people are efficient. Rather than invent a completely new message for each new social event, they formulate rhetorical guidelines to deal with stock situations. The first moment or two of the ordinary street-corner conversation, for example, is highly predictable. We discuss health, the weather, sports, and little else.

Although seemingly insignificant, such standardized locutions tell a good deal about cultural assumptions. For example, it is noteworthy that even on a comparatively bawdy program like *The Bernie Mac Show,* indiscriminate adultery, personal arrogance, and corporate rapaciousness are—in virtually every instance—ultimately punished. Admittedly, compared to television dramas of the 1950s, it now takes longer for transgressions to be discovered and transgressors disciplined. But it has long been part of the American Code that such behaviors deserve censure, so we have developed formulas for discussing such things. Colonial values are still powerful in the United States and, were he to return, Puritan preacher Jonathan Edwards might be able to guest-direct an episode of *Bernie Mac,* so well does he know the story line of American morality.

At times, configurational elements go together so often that rituals of interaction develop. In such instances, speakers become tightly constrained in what they can say and listeners learn to appreciate the sameness of rhetorical exchange. So, marriage ceremonies, eulogies, Bar/Bat Mitzvahs—all these are heavily constrained by rhetorical conventions, signaling that standard problems (i.e., transitional moments) persist and that they are so important that public solutions must be found for dealing with them.

Even when full-blown rituals are not present, one can spot conventions at work. One can discuss athletics in mixed company but not athletic supporters. The term African American is now acceptable but the term Negro is not. The careful critic will spot such rhetorical rules and then ask *why* they exist, largely because these verbal habits so often point up a society's special preferences as well as its special vulnerabilities.

CONCLUSION

This chapter has emphasized two things: (1) the very *decision* to communicate can be an important kind of social action and (2) the various elements of a rhetorical situation often become *imprinted* upon the message, thereby becoming a valuable source of insight for the critic. Let us conclude our discussion with an example. The case in point is a piece of rhetoric portrayed in the movie *Patton,* based on a real speech given in July of 1944 by General George S. Patton [1946] prior to crossing the English Channel for an assault on the

German armies in France. Even a brief excerpt from Patton's speech reveals its distinctive tones:

> Men, this stuff you hear about Americans wanting to stay out of this war is a lot of b___s___! Americans love to fight, traditionally. All real Americans love the sting of battle. When you were kids, you all admired the champion marble player, the fastest runner, the big league ball player, the toughest boxer. The Americans love a winner, and cannot tolerate a loser. Americans despise cowards. Americans play to win; all the time. I wouldn't give a hoot for a man who lost and laughed. That's why Americans have never lost, and will never lose a war. The very thought of losing is hateful to an American. . . .
>
> You are not all going to die. Only two percent of you here would die in a major battle. Death must not be feared. Every man is frightened at first in battle. If he says he isn't he's a goddam liar. Some men are cowards, yes. But they will fight just the same, or get the hell scared out of them watching men who do fight, who are as scared as they. The real hero is the man who fights even though he is scared. Some get over their fright in a few minutes under fire; some take hours; for some it takes days. The real man never lets fear of death overpower his honor, his duty to his country, and his innate manhood. . . .
>
> An Army is a team: It lives, sleeps, eats, fights as a team. This individual heroic stuff is a lot of crap. The bilious bastards who wrote that kind of stuff for the *Saturday Evening Post* don't know any more about real battle than they do about f_____!. . . . We have the finest food, the best equipment, the finest spirit and men in the world. . . . Why, by God, I actually pity those sonsofbitches we are going up against: by God, I do! . . .
>
> My men don't surrender. I don't want to hear of a soldier under my command getting captured unless he is hit. Even if you are, you can still fight back. This is not b___s___, either. The kind of man I want is like the lieutenant in Libya who, with a Luger against his chest, jerked his helmet off, swept the gun aside with the other hand, and busted hell out of the Boche with his helmet. Then he jumped on the Hun and went out and killed another German. By this time, the lieutenant had a bullet through his chest. Now, that is a MAN for you . . . . [Patton, 1946: 2–5]

Even a cursory look at Patton's remarks will reveal some of the major **social statements** here: a great general taking the time to talk to raw recruits; the soldiers seated together, building esprit de corps prior to an important battle; the general dealing candidly with such topics as courage, self-image, mortality, and immortality, signaling with this choice of topics that the moment was important to him. The clear sense of counterstatement is also obvious, with Patton using the speech-act to argue that the rumormongers, Tokyo Roses, and *Saturday Evening Posts* were wrong in every detail. By meeting with the men (on their turf) so soon before battle, Patton no doubt sent them an important message of solidarity, as he did by giving a live speech rather than a radio address.

The imprints of the various situational elements are also unmistakable. The speech is Pattonesque: coarse, crude, unyielding, defiant, a clear indication of a **rhetor variable** at work. In some senses, Patton's reputation was so much larger than life that he even may have had to overstate his positions in order to meet the men's exalted expectations of him, which may be why the text combines both superpatriotism with a faint sort of anarchism. Evident here too is the everyday talk of the everyday soldier, a hint of the **audience variables** with which Patton had to deal. Patton's images are earthy and his language colorful because earthiness is the constant companion of the foot soldier and colorfulness his only respite.

In some senses, the speech treats the individual **topic variables** in conventional ways but by *combining* deeply philosophical topics (e.g., the purpose of life) with brutishly practical matters (e.g., getting fed), Patton gives his listeners an exhilarating rhetorical ride. In some senses, the structure of the speech is conventional (one is reminded of football coaches at halftime) but the language used—imperative rather than declarative sentences, contrast devices rather than comparison devices—is unmistakably Patton's.

A comparison of Patton's speech with the trimmed-down version delivered by George C. Scott in the movie *Patton* (made some thirty years later) shows how **media variables** can change things considerably. In the original, for example, Patton spent a good deal of time talking about the importance of the hard training his men had recently experienced, something omitted in the movie speech because the popcorn-eaters had no doubt been otherwise employed in recent weeks. The original speech also spends more time talking about the reality of death, giving it a kind of authenticity missing in Scott's speech. There is also a depth of detail in the original speech missing in the movie version (e.g., of a soldier near Tunis fixing a telephone wire in the thick of battle). Comments like these possess a real-world integrity demanded by the **setting variables** impinging on a real general speaking only moments before a real battle.

Moviemakers have their own rhetorical challenges, however. For example, they deleted Patton's careful instructions to his men not to mention that they had seen him (a security measure) since the average theater patron would hardly have understood the historical context for these remarks. Also, the movie version is only half the length of the original speech and has none of the internal repetition found in Patton's version.

Very tight **rhetorical conventions** affect filmmaking, conventions dictated by the fast pace expected in the war film genre. Whereas George Patton had to reach real soldiers experiencing real fears, George C. Scott needed only to make a quick and dramatic impression on his listeners so that they would be set up to enjoy the next two hours in the darkened theater. In a sense, then, neither George Patton nor George Scott owned their speeches. Their audiences did.

For the student of rhetoric, situational analysis must be the first procedure in any critical operation. Getting a broad perspective on the speech-act is important because rhetoric torn from its context makes, at best, distorted sense. Later chapters in this book delve deeper into the sinews of messages. These anatomical excursions are important because in detail lies precision. But the good surgeon reaches for the scalpel only after having done an overall physical workup of the patient. The critic should do likewise by treating rhetorical situations in all of their complexity. To do less would be a kind of critical malpractice.

TIPS FOR THE PRACTICING CRITIC

1. Use the message variables presented in Figure 3.1 and amplified in the following pages (and the list of critical probes) as a checklist when beginning analysis. In preliminary efforts, attempt to account for the effects of each of these elements of the rhetorical situation on the artifact. Then choose the questions that have yielded the richest answers for further development. These can form the core of the critical essay.
2. Make sure to present both conclusions *and the reasons* for asserting such claims, as in the analyses of the Rabbi Prinz and Patton speeches. This allows readers to judge the arguments fairly. Even as you strive to show how this artifact can teach critics something about a "larger story," be sure that the evidence will support every claim you make. Good rhetorical criticism is an art. For each artifact, try to strike a balance between discovering and reporting new and interesting principles of persuasion and making sure that the proof backs up the findings.

Chapter 4

ANALYZING IDEAS

A pool table; don't you understand? Friend, either you're closing your eyes to a situation you do not wish to acknowledge, or you are not aware of the calibre of disaster indicated by the presence of a pool table in your community.

Well, you got trouble, my friend. Right here, I say, trouble right here in River City. Why, sure, I'm a billiard player; certainly mighty proud to say, I'm always mighty proud to say it. I consider that the hours I spend with a cue in my hand are golden. Help you cultivate horse-sense, and a cool head, and a keen eye. Did you ever take and try to give an iron-clad leave for yourself from a three-rail billiard shot? But just as I say it takes judgment, brains, and maturity to score in a balk-line game, I say that any boob can take and shove a ball in a pocket.

And I call that sloth, the first big step on the road to the depths of degradation. I say, first, medicinal wine from a teaspoon—then beer from a bottle. And the next thing you know your son is playing for money in a pinched-back suit, and listenin' to some big out of town jasper hearin' him tell about horse-race gamblin'. Not a wholesome trottin' race. No! But a race where they set down right on the horse. Like to see some stuck up jockey-boy settin' on Dan Patch? Make your blood boil? Well, I should say.

Friends let me tell you what I mean: You got one, two, three, four, five, six pockets in a table, pockets that mark the difference between a gentleman and a bum, with a capital "B" and that rhymes with "P" and that stands for "POOL."

And all week long your River City youth will be a fritterin' away; I say your young men will be fritterin'. Fritterin' away their noontime, suppertime, chore-time, too. Get the ball in the pocket—never mind gettin' dandelions pulled or the screen door patched or the beef steak pounded; and never mind pumpin' any water 'til your parents are caught with the cistern empty on a Saturday night. And that's trouble!

Yes, you've got lots and lots of trouble. I'm thinking of the kids in the knicker-bockers, shirttailed young ones, peekin' in the pool hall window after school. You got trouble, folks, right here in River City. Trouble, with a capital "T" and that rhymes with "P" and that stands for "POOL." [Willson, 1958]

Professor Harold Hill, that consummate salesperson-*cum*-shyster depicted in the musical comedy *The Music Man,* is a man of ideas. He borrows old ideas (loving hard work, avoiding sin) and new ideas (music as salvation) to form the best idea of all: combining old and new to make a profit. Those familiar with the play or film know that Hill's method was to sell instruments and uniforms for a boys' band, promising to teach the children to play. The hitch that made him less-than-honest was that when the uniforms arrived, Hill uniformly departed because, in the words of a rival, "He don't know one note from another!" But when he spoke, Professor Hill showed that he was a fine student of American culture, which is of course a complex amalgamation of old and new ideas.

In fashioning his sermon/advertisement, Hill focused not on the particular ideas the residents of River City, Iowa, favored in 1912. Rather, he concentrated on the enduring ideas their forebears respected at the close of the last century and that their great-grandchildren would also appreciate toward the turn of the next. In doing so, Hill proved himself an adept intellectual historian of the United States; he proved, too, that good rhetors must first be good listeners.

And Harold Hill was a fine listener. His constant sales trips through the Midwest taught him much about the plain-speaking, plain-thinking Middle Americans who were his customers. Before he set foot on the sidewalks of River City he knew the people he would pass. He knew, for example, that the neatly trimmed lawns were maintained by people who respected Western rationality and orderliness, ideas having their presuppositions in the Enlightenment and their implications in getting the dandelions pulled. He knew that country folks at the turn of the century in the United States had been raised on a stern diet of Calvinism (regardless of religious denomination) and on conceptions of incremental spirituality ("And I call that sloth, the first big step on the road to the depths of degradation").

For such people, sin was not only progressive but also concrete. Theirs was a Christian worldview, not a Platonic one, and so unpounded beefsteak could stand as a sign of perdition just as surely as the death of Jesus Christ had stood as rejection of pagan philosophizing. Their life was also a life of immediacy, of planting and tending and harvesting, of coping with Nature. Thus, they distrusted foolishness—"boobs" and the like—favoring instead "horse-sense" since animals were so central to their material survival and since material survival was tied up in complicated ways with moral matters.

Also, because rural life makes land and its care the measure of the individual, and because the greater the expanse of one's land the greater one's personal risk, there was also a self-imposed provincialism to Harold Hill's customers that made them instinctively wary of "out of town jaspers." At the same time,

River City residents were heirs to American pluralism. Their resulting friendliness made it possible for them to be seduced by an out-of-towner even as they were being warned of one.

In other words, Harold Hill had to be as much a philosopher as a peddler of slide-trombones. For him, persuasion involved understanding people's first premises, their base-assumptions. The study of philosophy is the study of these first premises and **the study of rhetoric is the study of first premises-in-use.**

Harold Hill was not a self-conscious philosopher. He knew things in the way practical people know things: by imitation and observation. But unlike most, Hill had an ability to ground persuasion in people's basic thoughts. Hill's artfulness is that his rhetoric did not sound "philosophical" at all. It sounded practical and cozy, not abstract and antiseptic. Miss Marian, River City's resident rhetorical critic (and later Hill's inamorata) quickly saw through his rhetoric. She did what the best critics do: She traced the ideas Hill used to their first assumptions and reasoned that these were probably *not* the assumptions held by the average cosmopolitan professor of musicology. Miss Marian tracked Hill's ideas to their roots and found them lying in River City and not in Harold Hill. Smart woman, Miss Marian.

In a sense, Harold Hill made something out of nothing when he contrasted godlessness with euphonic piety. Neither euphony nor piety invited this linkage but Hill linked them anyway. It took rhetorical imagination to do so. But persuaders have always been opportunistic in these ways, a fact that produces horror, admiration, or bemusement in critics. Miss Marian, a librarian and hence one sensitive to texts and the cataloging of ideas, reacted in all three ways from time to time. These will be our options as well, and Miss Marian will be our inspiration as we consider how persuaders use ideas and how critics can catch them doing so.

THE STUDY OF IDEAS

In a way, all rhetorical critics study ideas. And likewise each chapter in this book focuses upon the rhetorical uses of ideas. But this chapter focuses on the basics, on how persuasive appeals come to be. Here, we emphasize gathering elementary rhetorical facts in order to describe phenomena in detail and with precision. Careful, systematic description is especially important in rhetorical criticism since rhetoric is such an emotional thing to study. That is, if the rhetoric being studied is powerful, the natural tendency is to applaud it or decry it. The descriptive impulse arrests this very natural, but critically dangerous, inclination by asking what we know for sure about the message in question.

Good description requires gathering facts before doing interpretation or evaluation. But description itself is not simple. For instance, for some observers the essential fact about the statue of a Confederate general in a town square is that that person fought for the Confederacy. To others, the statue symbolizes general (not Southern) leadership or loyalty. To a Leftist, the statue is an abomination because it glorifies war; to a Rightist the statue is an abomination because it is covered with pigeon droppings. A teenager tuned into a Sony Walkman may find the statue dull because its inscription is too flowery, while the geologist standing next to her may be fascinated by the volcanic traces in the rock quarried for the statue. Thus, if we can be unsure what a thing (like a statue) is or what its most central feature is (its Southernness? its geological qualities?), then finding the essential nature of anything as dynamic as a rhetorical exchange becomes even more daunting.

Because of the complexity of rhetoric, it makes sense to initially (1) isolate and (2) list a message's main ideas. This chapter will present two techniques for doing so, each of which has these benefits:

1. *Analyzing ideas tells what is present and what is not.* A strange proposition, at first, but an important one. By examining a persuasive text, after all, we confront the rhetor's final set of ideas, the rhetor's best guess of what could be said in the situation at hand. But the ideas *not* chosen can also be informative, even though this presents something of a dilemma for the critic: Whereas the message itself records what was said, what was not said obviously includes everything else potentially sayable. Harold Hill talked of pool tables, but not inflation or virtual reality or plane geometry. The solution to the critic's dilemma is to discover what **relevant and important** things Harold Hill did not say. Accordingly, this chapter includes a "universal" list of idea types for critical use. This is not a perfect solution, since no list of anything human can be exhaustive and any list can become artificial. But the benefits outweigh the liabilities and the list will be a good starting point.

2. *Analyzing ideas alerts us to rhetorical patterns.* Throughout this book, we urge critics to pay special attention to patterns of ideas. Even though exceptions to patterns can be important, the concept of exception makes no sense apart from the concept of pattern. So there is a sense in which all critics are mathematicians because, whether they are aware of it or not, they count things when making discriminations. For example, a critic may say, "The rhetor's use of language was brilliant." (Translation: "Compared to a group of rhetors, this rhetor deviated substantially from the mean on a number of language variables.")

The point here is not to make critics sound like crazed scientists but to dramatize how critics depend on perceptions of rhetorical pattern and how often, knowingly or not, critics make statements of proportion: for example, "I was surprised that the rhetor ignored the budgetary argument." (Translation: "Given the amount of time most people spend talking about money, spending this much time on aesthetics seems out of the norm.") But even though critics depend on rhetorical patterns, they do not always acknowledge this dependence or document their claims about matters of proportion. The critical techniques in this chapter can rectify that.

3. *Analyzing ideas helps to explain rhetorical "tone."* Tone is something that all persons feel but that few have been trained to describe with precision. Tone

FIGURE 4.1 Scales for Describing Rhetorical Tone

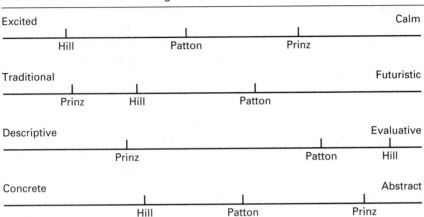

refs to the emotion, manner or attitude conveyed in a message. Even though the tone of a message can be hard to describe, it may be easy to identify. For example, when students of criticism were asked to describe the Hill speech as well as the Prinz and Patton speeches discussed in Chapter 3, they did so with ease and with impressive unanimity. When asked to position these speeches on the scales presented in Figure 4.1, their agreement approached 90 percent.

As is often the case with tone, the students could not be shaken in their judgments of these speeches but, equally, they were hard pressed to state explicitly how they knew what they knew. However, by stepping back a bit, taking the time to sketch the flow of ideas, using standard idea lists to describe the messages being examined, and constantly asking "What, specifically, is telling me what I know to be the case?" the students became more precise.

One ancient, simple technique they used was to translate the texts into their own language via outlining, thereby de-rhetoricalizing what the rhetor had made rhetorical. This chapter will present more ambitious techniques, thereby giving the critic a **technical language** for discussing the hard-to-discuss. Such techniques are no cure-all but they can advance the scholarly discussion. In that spirit, we offer them here.

A TOPICAL APPROACH TO IDEAS

Nobody knows precisely where ideas come from or why some ideas bubble to the surface of public discussion more often than others. And yet our daily experiences require us to establish priorities about ideas. Someone with a "personality problem," for example, often just has an "idea problem"—that is, he or she thinks differently than we do. Travel to a foreign country can be difficult for the same reason. The impatient American who drums her fingers on the table of the Roman cafe while waiting for service learns that some ideas (like efficiency) are not equally revered in all cultures. Indeed, the concept of "culture" is shorthand for "groups of people who prefer the same kinds of ideas and go to the same sorts of places to find new ones."

At times, it seems as if there are as many ideas in the world as there are people. The proof of this is found each day in the pages of the *National Enquirer*, a tabloid that specializes in the idiosyncratic ("Boy marries great aunt," "Honor student dismembers algebra teacher"). But there is a predictable idiosyncrasy to the stories published in the *National Enquirer*, as if the editors rewrote the same stories each week, changing only the names and locations of the aunts and algebra teachers. Such constancy implies that the millions of individual stories in the world derive from a limited number of "master stories." This chapter presents sixteen places from which such stories are drawn, in the belief that knowing about these ideational places increases one's sensitivity to rhetorical ideas.

Students of persuasion have always been interested in the common themes of public discourse. The ancient Greeks thought these traditional themes (*topoi*, or "topics") underlaid all ideas; similarly, the ancient Romans conceived of a limited set of commonplaces capable of "housing" all conceivable arguments. Two thousand years ago, training in persuasion taught rhetors to fashion arguments from these ideas-behind-all-ideas. More recently, Wilson and Arnold [1974] identified a list of **Universal Topics** from which most ideas derive. They claim that some variation on these themes can be found in any message, public or private. Say Wilson and Arnold [p. 76]:

> For a good many centuries scholars argued that people talk on a fairly limited number of themes, that they vary the treatments of basic ideas but not the basic ideas themselves. You need not hear or read many speeches or essays to see that these thinkers were right. We all discuss the same general types of ideas over and over. This is not a sign of laziness, it is the natural result of the kinds of things people feel they need to talk to each other about. We all discuss and argue chiefly about human affairs, and the ways you can think about human affairs are limited within any culture. The result is that we can actually predict in advance many of the categories of thought any talker will use . . .

Throughout history, topical systems like Wilson and Arnold's have been used as brainstorming devices to help students invent ideas for speaking or writing. Rather than being asked to "just think" about a given subject matter, for example, students have been given a list of topics to help stimulate their imaginations. But systematic use of these universal topics in criticism has not been as common, even though such a system can be helpful to the critic for these reasons: (1) It is a reasonably *complete* way of categorizing persuasive arguments; (2) it is a simple and efficient method of *reducing* a message to its essential rhetorical character; (3) because it is a fixed system, it can reveal *patterns* of argument that might not have been noticed otherwise; and (4) it allows the critic to make *proportional* statements about the themes of a given message.

Listed below are the sixteen universal topics Wilson and Arnold have isolated in their studies. Next to each are examples (from Hart et al. [1983:52–3]) of how the topic might be developed in an argument by a surgeon general discussing the common problem of hearing disorders:

1. EXISTENCE or nonexistence of things (e.g., "over 50 percent of the elderly have hearing disorders");
2. DEGREE or quantity of things, forces, and so on (e.g., "hearing problems can range from mild ringing in the ears to total deafness and even death");
3. SPATIAL attributes, including adjacency, distribution, place (e.g., "the ear covers only a small area of the body but magnifies sound incredibly");
4. TEMPORAL attributes, including hour, day, year, era (e.g., "one can lose hearing overnight");
5. MOTION or activity (e.g., "fast movement can cause dizziness because of inner ear problems");
6. FORM, either physical shape or abstract categories (e.g., "some hearing losses result from outer ear problems");
7. SUBSTANCE: physical or abstract; the fundamental nature of a thing, often signaled by definitions (e.g., "the roots of hearing loss sometimes lie in basic, psychological trauma");
8. CAPACITY TO CHANGE, including predictability (e.g., "the inner ear can improve itself");
9. POTENCY: power or energy, including capacity to further or hinder something (e.g., "hearing problems can make us unable to discriminate any sort of speech");
10. DESIRABILITY, in terms of rewards or punishments (e.g., "such difficulties hinder social interactions and can adversely affect employment opportunities");
11. FEASIBILITY: workability or practicability (e.g., "lip reading training is possible in some cases");
12. CAUSALITY: the relationship of causes to effects, effect to effects, adequacy of causes, and so on (e.g., "abnormal growths in the ear cause problems");
13. CORRELATION, coexistence or coordination of things, forces, and so on (e.g., "hearing difficulties can be related to viral diseases");
14. GENUS-SPECIES relationships (e.g., "hearing specialists are an important part of the larger medical community");
15. SIMILARITY or dissimilarity (e.g., "the hearing problems of older people and those that affect children may be different");
16. POSSIBILITY or impossibility (e.g., "the inner ear cannot be corrected by surgery but hearing aids can provide some relief").

GUIDELINES FOR USING THE UNIVERSAL TOPICS

Students have found the following suggestions useful.

1. Work with two or three other critics, designating each member of the team a "specialist" on four or five of the universal topics.

2. Proceed through the message statement by statement, with relevant members of the critical team making "bids" for "ownership" of individual statements.
3. Assign each statement to no more than two categories. Delay resolving any uncertainties until the entire message has been inspected.
4. If disagreement persists after discussion, assign the statement to multiple categories on a proportional basis.

Classroom experience has shown that these categories are easy to learn. After only a few group experiences students can master the system and use it in their own critical projects. The goal here is *not* to develop scientific precision but to provide a rough "topical translation" of the artifact.

The worth of any critical system lies in its utility. Accordingly, Table 4.1 presents the topical sketches that student critics developed of the Prinz, Patton, and Hill speeches. When doing their work, the students focused on three basic critical probes:

- Which topics were used?
- Which were not?
- How were audiences invited to respond as a result of this distribution of topics?

Clearly, these passages present very different profiles. But first we should note the similarities, the most dramatic of which is that all three rhetors used Correlation quite often. Given the different situations they faced, what could such a finding mean? Most likely, it suggests that each rhetor felt the need to build bridges, perhaps because each was in some sense an outsider. Harold Hill's case is an obvious one. He first works insistently to link pool halls and sin

TABLE 4.1 Comparative Use of Universal Topics

Universal Topics	Rabbi Prinz	Harold Hill	George Patton
Existence	2	14	5
Degree	9	7	6
Spatial	6	9	3
Temporal	10	11	2
Motion	5	11	5
Form	0	0	2
Substance	18	0	13
Capacity to change	5	2	4
Potency	8	7	6
Desirability	7	28	7
Feasibility	0	1	9
Causality	4	7	13
Correlation	9	8	13
Genus-species	5	0	0
Similarity/dissimilarity	8	1	4
Possibility/impossibility	4	1	9

and later links musical instruments with virtue. The strain of these linkages makes us smile as we easily recognize Hill's subterfuge. We see that Hill is using these good Iowans by appropriating their values and anxieties for his mercantile purposes. But it is also true that Hill's status as a geographical outsider left him with little choice other than to build bridges. Sloth and degradation, frittering and corruption—disingenuous correlations for a seller of band instruments, but not unlike those used weekly at a Billy Graham Crusade.

Rabbi Prinz was a cultural rather than a geographical outsider, and so he too offered equations: Jewish and Black ghettos, Jewish and Christian morality, Old World and New World dreams. His correlations are more uplifting than Hill's but similar in that both took the "high road" morally: Prinz because he was a cleric, Hill because he was a conniver.

And George Patton's exalted status made him an outsider as well, someone removed from the life of the everyday soldier. As a general among generals, Patton had to demonstrate clear relationships between the war he was fighting and the war he expected his men to fight. His equations were graphic in their simplicity: the Army life and the sporting life; dehumanization and German militarization; American virtue and all virtue.

To a lesser extent, all three rhetors made use of Potency, Motion, Degree, and Desirability. They did so because each in their own way was a highly energized persuader with a grand new world to describe. Harold Hill's world included virtuous and energetic young people marching toward the Good (and carrying his band instruments). General Patton, too, paints a vibrant picture of strong, active soldiers overcoming a feckless and morally bankrupt enemy. Although he is less histrionic than either Hill or Patton, Rabbi Prinz takes pains to link Degree ("the most urgent, [. . .] the most tragic problem") with Potency ("a glorious, unshakable reality in a morally united America") in order to pound home his themes of justice and equality for all.

All three rhetors were therefore activists and their rhetoric reflects that fact. But none was a college lecturer and hence none spent time detailing abstract, structural relationships (e.g., Form or Genus-Species relationships). Also, because each meant to begin dialogue rather than nail down practical policies, they generally avoided such sticky issues as how and when change would be implemented, and at what price. Other rhetors on other occasions could tackle these details.

In this sense, Harold Hill was the classic salesperson: long on promises and short on application. Notice that he develops a 28:1 ratio of Desirability to Feasibility, not at all unlike the sales pitch for the lawn tractor delivered weekly in the Sears Garden Shop. In his rousing conclusion, for example, Hill links the soon-to-be River City Boys Band to Maine, Plymouth Rock, and the Golden Rule but never mentions the price of a piccolo.

Hill also spends considerably more time on the topic of Existence than the other rhetors, perhaps because he had a problem: He had no problem. That is, there was no compelling reason for the quiet folks in River City to have their collective ears assaulted by adolescent music-making (and to pay good money for the privilege of doing so). Harold Hill knew this, and he also knew that the motivating "problem" had to be a major one. So he used what he had—a pool hall—and he willed that shameful instance to a universal sin. His speech is thus really two speeches, with Existence dominating the first and Desirability the second.

Rabbi Prinz made the bravest attempt of all three rhetors at Capacity to Change ("America must speak up and act from the President down to the humblest of us"), but his attempt is still modest, perhaps because his primary rhetorical purpose was to set up the magnificent oration of Martin Luther King, Jr., immediately following, an address that would amply discuss such themes. It is also noteworthy that the Rabbi completely eschewed Feasibility, perhaps for reasons of time or a perceived lack of fitness with the ceremonial occasion, or perhaps because the civil rights movement was then in its infancy and nobody knew exactly *how* human justice could be achieved.

Given such limitations, the Rabbi was wise to stick with Substance. He spent most of his time defining key concepts: silence, hatred, morality. Such a scholarly (Talmudic?) approach cost the Rabbi Harold Hill's energy and George Patton's assuredness but it no doubt helped him play the part he was intended to play at the March on Washington.

A different tone emerges in the Patton speech. Patton used Feasibility and Possibility, no doubt because a Desirable but Impossible speech would hardly have been motivating to men about to enter battle. More subtly, however, he also stressed Causality, explicitly telling his men which actions would produce which effects (e.g., "Every man in the mess hall, even the one who heats the water to keep us from getting diarrhea, has a job to do"). A causally driven speech like Patton's is indeed heartening. It is clear, pragmatic, and thoroughly Western in its philosophical orientation. Such a speech raises no question (e.g., cowardice, defeat) that it does not also answer. Patton begins with causal patterns (hard work produces athletic success) and ends in the same way (bravery under fire insures immortal glory).

Equally interesting is Patton's use of Substance. It is this topic that distinguishes his remarks from messages heralding sure-fire success or a money-back guarantee. The substances that concern him are bravery and patriotism. By themselves, such matters could have produced empty abstractions. And, indeed, there is a sermonic quality to Patton's statement, with only Rabbi Prinz (at 18 percent) surpassing him on Substance. Patton's speech is interesting because he capitalizes on both theoretical *and* practical themes, with the former whetting listeners' appetites while the latter insured them sustenance. The result is tremendous rhetorical energy, perhaps explaining why students were so ambivalent when describing the tone of Patton's speech (see Figure 4.1).

As we mentioned, the statements in an artifact indicate where a rhetor *ended* thought about the subject at hand. But it is also important to know where a rhetor *began* looking for thoughts. Topical analysis leads the critic to the essential places from which those words emanated. Because it focuses on such basic matters, topical analysis is particularly useful for examining public controversies, arenas in which people often talk past one another precisely because they have *begun* their arguments in different places.

Imagine, for example, how rancorous discussion could become between a rhetor who operated from Feasibility ("let's do this because it will work") and another who operated from Substance ("let's do this because people must be protected from their baser natures"). According to Einhorn [1981], that is precisely the situation in which James Madison and Patrick Henry found themselves during the Virginia Ratification Debates, with Madison arguing on the basis of practicality and Henry arguing philosophically.

Studies can use ideational analysis to explain the success or failure of individual rhetors or movements. Sarch [1997] studied birth control advertisements in the 1920s and 1930s. Although at that time birth control was considered obscene and therefore illegal, advocates used Genus-species and Substance arguments to transform public understanding of birth control into an aspect of medical science. In another study, Mackin [1991] warns that an attempt to build community on the basis of people's Dissimilarity from their rivals may work in the short run but will ultimately destroy the "ecology" of the larger human community. Similarly, Lucaites and Condit [1995] analyzed the rhetoric of martyred civil rights activists Martin Luther King, Jr., and Malcolm X. They found that, while both men relied on "equality" as a rhetorical touchstone, King argued for a transcendent human Similarity, while Malcolm constructed the Substance of equality as that of balance between antagonistic powers. And as Zyskind [1968] has shown, Desirability and Feasibility are the hardiest rhetorical topics in American cultural history. Any movement that cannot deploy such arguments must probably resign itself to marginal status.

The topical approach is only one among many ways of examining ideas. And because it is so general, it only begins the process of criticism. But a systematic approach has its uses. After all, one of the most perplexing decisions about doing criticism is where to start. Topical analysis allows critics to start their criticism where persuaders start their persuasion.

A JUDGMENTAL APPROACH TO IDEAS

The topical approach for describing ideas tends to be rhetor-oriented. A second approach is Arnold's [1974], which focuses on the judgments *listeners* are asked to make during persuasion. Arnold's approach, derived from the work of Aristotle, is based on these assumptions: (1) when rhetors speak, they assume that listeners will make judgments about their remarks; (2) a verbal text is a record of the kinds of judgments audiences are being asked to make; (3) a text records only the *potential,* not the actual, judgments listeners make; (4) because rhetorical occasions are often standardized, there are a limited number of *classic* judgmental requests.

In building his system, Arnold catalogued these standard rhetorical occasions and concluded that four arguments predominate in the social world: What is empirically true? What makes us happy? What is legally or morally correct? How should we proceed? Arnold reasoned further that most rhetorical statements reflect one or more of these "stock issues" and thus that all statements radiate from one of four classic judgmental requests. Modified a bit they are:

1. *Factual.* Some statements ask listeners to consult the world around them and consider what is true. Such consultations can be focused on the past ("Suicide bombings disrupted progress toward peace"), the present ("Flight Club is an online service that pairs young, single travelers in airports"), or the future ("I'll pick you up after soccer practice"). Because these statements occur in rhetorical texts, they often do not meet a scientist's rigorous standards of factuality. Rather, they are treated as commonsense facts. Thus, even a controversial statement like "This tax cut will bankrupt Social Security" is treated as a Factual request because the listener is being encouraged to consult real-world conditions when judging the rhetor's assertion.

2. *Desirable.* Other statements ask listeners to consult their own general wishes and preferences (or those of their social group) and consider what makes them happy (or unhappy). Unlike factual statements, desirable requests have a clearly evaluative flavor. (Arnold calls these "optatives.") The values undergirding them include taste, efficiency, beauty, or practicality. John F. Kennedy's famous quip about Washington, D.C. ("a city that epitomizes the best of Northern hospitality and Southern efficiency"), utilizes several of these for humorous effect.

3. *Adjudicative.* These statements, akin to Aristotle's notion of "forensic" rhetoric, ask listeners to consult some formal code of behavior and consider how a particular behavior measures up. Like Desirables, Adjudicatives are evaluative. But Adjudicative requests ask that formal, institutional (often written) standards be consulted mentally before passing judgment. Such codes are normally more specific and rigid than the more general Desirable standards. The specifications they make can include law ("The accused has committed a heinous crime, your Honor"), religion ("The Bible fully endorses tithing, my children"), etiquette ("First dates should end before dawn"), or political ideology ("Good Republicans support welfare reform"). Intriguingly, Arnold [1974:93] notes this distinction between Desirables and Adjudicatives: "One need not like the standards to apply them."

Over time, groups of people often transform general, Desirable standards into Adjudicative ones so that dogma results. For example, the "Miss America Code" replaces for beauty contestants the standards of propriety the rest of us use. The "Scientific Method" is ingrained in young chemists, replacing their earlier standards of ordinary carefulness. To become indoctrinated is to learn to use such codes when making decisions. Knowing such things, and knowing that code-based judgments are often more reliable than more general wishes and preferences, persuaders are strongly attracted to Adjudicative statements.

4. *Directive.* Some statements, which Aristotle [2001:185] called "deliberative," ask listeners to consider "the expediency or harmfulness of a proposed course of action." Whereas Desirables invite us to think about what we want (the end or goal), Directives ask us to approve a particular method of getting there (the means). Directive statements (or, as Arnold calls them, Predictive of Desirability statements) explicitly or implicitly detail the positive consequences of adopting a new attitude or standard of behavior. Rhetorical messages differ dramatically in how clearly they explicate the good that will result from rhetor/audience agreement. In some persuasion, for example, the promises are bold and unmistakable but fairly sketchy ("One oil rig, 14 showers and the soapy scum of 127 sweaty men, for over a month. Let's hope someone brought the Tilex" [2003]) while other forms of persuasion (e.g., a brochure for a resort hotel) detail the wonders that await the tourist. In still other cases (e.g., perfume advertising), Factuals and Desirables provide verbal text while pictures (e.g., a wind-swept beach in Bermuda) are used to hint at promises for how to attain the good life. Normally, then, "hard-sell" and "soft-sell" can be measured by calculating the (1) frequency, (2) explicitness, and (3) detail of the *verbal* promises made.

A helpful way of employing the judgmental approach is to catalog the artifact's individual statements, using the definitions and examples above as a guide. In addition to the four "pure" types of judgments, most rhetorical messages will contain mixed statements as well. Often, it is the critic's ability to account for these mixed perceptions that makes Arnold's system especially useful. That is, while a statement like "I joined Bruno's Health Spa" clearly makes a Factual request of the listener ("you believe me, don't you?"), a statement like "I joined Bruno's Health Spa and lost 75 pounds in only one month" operates very differently. In the second (Factual/Directive) statement, the rhetor clearly implies "And you can too!" even though this statement never appears in the text itself. Intuitively, we "know" that the second statement differs markedly from the first but it is initially hard to say exactly how the two statements differ. Arnold's system gives us a technical language for talking about such subtle-but-important differences in rhetorical texture.

Table 4.2 presents the eight most common types of judgmental requests along with brief commentary on their likely uses in persuasion. While not exhaustive, this list should be sufficient for most purposes. As with the topical system, critics analyze the artifact statement by statement, asking and answering the following critical probes:

- Which judgmental clusters are developed in this message?
- Where do they occur in the message?
- Which judgments are conspicuously absent or underrepresented?
- What are the implications of these clusters and their positioning?
- How do they invite audiences to respond to the artifact?

When first learning, it is useful to work in teams with other critics. Ideally, however, the critic makes these judgmental discriminations alone and only

TABLE 4.2 Some Common Types of Judgmental Requests

Judgment Type	Example	Use
1. Factual	"You can't get to Boise by airplane."	A workhorse strategy in persuasion. Used to establish substantiveness.
2. Desirable	"It's not worth the paper it's written on."	Used to establish the desirability or undesirability of a claim.
3. Adjudicative	"Anyone would say that is not a real American."	A "high-profile" strategy often used when the audience subscribes to a clear-cut code of right and wrong.
4. Directive	"With Smith in our camp, we can't help but win the election."	A very obvious "pitch" in which a speaker delineates the forthcoming benefits of a proposal.
5. Factual/desirable	"Ms. Jones told me that your work has been unsatisfactory lately."	Usually appears as (formal or informal) testimony. Used to substantiate evaluations offered.
6. Factual/adjudicative	"If you pursue this course of action, the Church will roundly condemn you."	A strategy that borrows the credibility of another code or institution in order to heighten the acceptability or unacceptability of a policy.
7. Desirable/directive	"Anyone as sweet as you will go places in this world."	Often used in "hard-sell" persuasion. Shows that the evaluation given means something (that is, it has observable consequences).
8. Factual/directive	"Rita's high IQ will make her a great deal of money later in life."	A narrative approach that hopes that the listener will make a subtle transference to his or her life. Hints that if good things happened in Case A, they will also happen in Case B.

later compare notes with others. In that way, the perception of the individual analyst is buttressed by the breadth of group vision.

Students of criticism using the judgmental system have made several interesting points about the three speeches mentioned earlier. For example, they noted that the "military code" produced a number of Adjudicative requests from Patton (e.g., "this individuality stuff is a bunch of crap") but that he warmed up his audience first by making a number of culturally sanctioned, Desirable requests (e.g., "Americans traditionally love to fight"). Students who compared the real Patton speech to the movie version found 50 percent fewer Factual requests in the latter, indicating that real soldiers need hard data but that movie audiences are primarily interested in "color" (i.e., in Patton's undeniably evaluative language).

Reliance on Directive judgments differed radically from speech to speech: The latter half of Patton's speech was composed almost entirely of Directives, but Prinz's speech used almost none. Indeed, roughly 90 percent of Prinz's speech consisted of Factuals and Adjudicatives. Apparently, the Rabbi saw his job as one of establishing the similarity between Jewish and Black experience and then Adjudicatively aligning the goals of the civil rights movement with religious and constitutional mandates. The result is a somber tone (no Desirables) as well as a sober tone (no Directives), both of which contrast sharply with Harold Hill's message.

The first third of Hill's speech (quoted above) is a salad of Desirable judgments based on pleasure ("the hours I spend with a cue in my hand are golden") or means of relaxation ("Not a wholesome trottin' race. No!"). As Hill warms to his subject, the second third of his speech is heavy on Adjudicatives, closing with this stark admonition: "That game with the fifteen numbered balls is the Devil's tool." The irony of the speech, of course, lies in the riotous *mixing* of Desirables and Adjudicatives as well as in Hill's presumptuous use of sacred codes for the selling of band instruments.

Having made these observations, however, does the judgmental system promise more than critical jargon? We find at least six major advantages to this approach:

1. *The system highlights rhetor/audience relationships.* One of the first studies to use this system [Douglass and Arnold, 1970] found it to be much less sterile than other critical procedures because it forces the critic to pay attention to *social* realities and not just to the verbal eccentricities of a given message. By conceiving of a rhetor as one who constantly makes requests of listeners, the critic is reminded that communication must be cooperative to succeed. Kuypers [2000a] studied a public letter from James Dobson, leader of the conservative group Focus on the Family, and found that Dobson used a sophisticated combination of judgment requests for different audience types: Adjudicatives and Desirables to appeal to his constituents, and Factuals and Adjudicatives to avoid dismissal by those outside the group. He also found that Dobson used a ninth type of request: Adjudicative/Directive, as in statements that implied that the United States would risk the wrath of God for conducting fetal-tissue research. The judgmental system thus highlights the ways in which rhetors may be addressing more than one audience at a time, a phenomenon increasingly likely in the mass media age.

2. *The system exposes patterns of rhetoric.* In Chapter 6, we will discuss generic studies of rhetoric, studies focusing on how certain messages can be grouped together in distinctive classes. Most of us are aware of these classes. Using such information, we sort each day's mail: personal letters, bills, charitable solicitations, junk mail. But what rhetorical markers help us do the sorting? How, exactly, does a letter from Uncle Steve differ from a letter from Uncle Sam? Most likely, Uncle Steve loads his letter with Factuals and Desirables ("had a lovely time at the show last week with your cousin, Hannah") whereas Uncle Sam tends more toward Adjudicatives and Directives ("the penalty for not replying to this notice within 30 days is . . .").

Often, clever persuaders try to transport the tone of one rhetorical class (e.g., a revival meeting) to another situation (e.g., setting the stage for a pitch for band instruments) so as to disguise their persuasive intentions. Using the judgmental system, the critic becomes sensitive to the tonal features of these different rhetorical classes.

3. *The system identifies influential situational factors.* Most people know that the mass media have changed how persuasion operates, but what do those changes look like? What adaptations must a reporter make, for example, when relating a story to a television audience rather than writing it for the local paper? (More detailed Factuals in the latter?) What is the essential rhetorical difference between a legal drama on television and an actual trial in the county courthouse? (Fewer dull Adjudicatives in the former?) How have members of Congress changed their styles now that C-SPAN carries their spoken remarks live? (More lively Desirables?) Now that even out-of-the-way speeches by a presidential candidate can be videotaped and replayed for a national audience, how will campaign speeches change? (Less obvious Directives?) Because the judgmental system is so sensitive to changes in rhetorical tone, the system holds real promise for monitoring situational influences.

4. *The system increases sensitivity to ideology.* A real advantage of the Arnold system is that it distinguishes between Desirables and Adjudicatives, that is, between informal and institutionalized beliefs. As Hart [1971] and Clark [1977] found, religious and secular discourse often differs sharply, with the former depending on Adjudicatives and the latter having to settle for Desirables. Along a different line, Jablonski [1979a] discovered that even though many sociological changes swept through the Roman Catholic church in the 1960s, the judgmental patterns in its rhetoric did not change, suggesting that *rhetorical* conservatism may inhibit philosophical radicalism. By comparing the use of formal and informal evaluations, then, the critic can often make uncommon discoveries about public discourse.

5. *The system helps explain rhetorical momentum.* Some messages seem to trudge along slowly, making their cases with deadly precision while others fly by, dazzling the eye with rhetorical fireworks. Often, this latter effect is generated by linking one Directive statement after another, as we see in the following rather breathless piece of advertising:

> Ski. Mix. Meet. Vail is tall and tan and single and every night's like Friday. It's a swift track down an alpine bowl in tandem with that Austrian accent who rode up in the gondola with you. And helped with your bindings and gave you goose bumps.
>
> Vail is wineskins at noon at a romantic level called timberline. It's gaslight, fondue, and accordions. Discovery in a boutique. Youth. And experience that ages well. There's even a trail called Swingsville. . . . [Vail Resort, n.d.]

This excerpt might serve as a baseline against which all messages could be judged for momentum! Most texts do not contain such energy. According to the studies done thus far, Directive statements comprise about 10 percent of the average public speech; normally, such statements are found in conclusions.

The proportion in advertising is probably much higher; the ad from which the passage above was extracted approached 80 percent Directive statements. Often, the proportion of Directive statements in a message will be a good indicator of rhetorical subtlety, so the critic should be especially attentive to both the number and placement of these judgments. Developing sensitivity to rhetorical momentum can be the best ally of the critic interested in consumer protection.

6. *The system can be used to index cultural change.* Because the judgmental system is simple and yet comprehensive, it helps detect alterations in rhetorical fashion. As we shall see in Chapter 11, changing cultural values, attitudes, or knowledge are often reflected in popular rhetoric. Clark [1999], for example, found that in the early stages of the AIDS scare, Factual/Directives issued by medical scientists falsely reassured the heterosexual population by bolstering their sense that AIDS was a "gay" disease. However, with the knowledge that AIDS could be blood-borne, the cultural discourse reverted to long-standing myths about easy, almost magical pollution of the common blood supply. Factual/Desirable statements about "undeserving" victims of AIDS laid implicit or explicit blame for the epidemic at the doorstep of its first identified hosts, creating public hysteria and ratifying homophobia. These superstitious fears could not be soothed by rationality, despite the medical community's updated Factual/Directive attempts to prevent further infection through public education about how the disease was spread. Judgmental analysis thus provides explanations for the power and limits of such rhetorical attempts at crisis management.

CONCLUSION

In this chapter we have explored two major ways of examining ideational content. Although the topical and judgmental approaches are only two among many, both are good places for a critic to start. Both systems take some getting used to but they give the critic a fairly precise way of talking about an art—the art of rhetoric—that is so often imprecise. Both systems urge the critic to "violate" the natural structure of a message by reducing it to its most basic ideational units. In so doing, the critic runs the risk of somewhat distorting the rhetorical experience listeners themselves underwent. But this seems to be a risk worth running, especially if it helps the critic discuss the audiencing experience in ways that audiences themselves might find strange but which they could not disavow.

Persuaders, of course, do not encourage such dismantling of their arguments. That is why the critic must attempt it. In many ways, the simple act of recategorizing a rhetor's ideas is a fundamentally revolutionary act for it means that *the critic's system,* not the rhetor's system, will guide the critic's perceptions. In this sense, rhetorical criticism is a game of cat-and-mouse played by critic and rhetor. While the rhetor gets a head start, the topical and judgmental systems of analysis give the critic an extra advantage.

TIPS FOR THE PRACTICING CRITIC

1. Chapter 4's sample analyses of the ideas behind the Hill, Prinz, and Patton speeches demonstrate how to practice "description before evaluation." Ideational analysis jumpstarts the critical process by providing ways to describe what the critic sees going on in the text. Ideally, someone unfamiliar with the message should be able to understand the resulting analysis as a fair, reasoned piece of discourse about an artifact. Although all words arguably contain evaluative connotations (positive and/or negative), *first* try to describe precisely what ideas the rhetor used (or did not use) and how they were used, without divulging any evaluations of the speech, and *then* judge their probable effectiveness on an audience.

   If the rhetor is advocating a position with which you violently disagree (or just as vehemently support), it may be necessary to first let yourself use loaded language to describe and illustrate the persuasive attempts of the rhetor. Then, force yourself to describe the same message in terms that have the opposite connotations. Support each argument with evidence from the text you are examining. Pretend that you agree with the rhetor, or that you are the rhetor. What prompted you to deliver this message in this fashion? Then put yourself in the position of a strong opponent of the rhetor. What are the rhetor's motives now?

2. Since people in the same culture go to the same places to get their ideas, it is essential for critics to achieve some understanding of the culture of the rhetor and the audience for each message they examine. This does not mean that one cannot study messages which were intended for an unfamiliar audience, but it does mean that research into the historical, social, and political context is necessary. This is true even for a speech delivered in the critic's hometown and is especially true for texts from other countries and other eras.

3. Remember that ideational analysis—breaking the speech down into individual sentences and assigning those segments to categories based on the rhetor's topic or the judgment s/he is asking listeners to make—is approximate and should be used as a starting point for rhetorical criticism. Ideational analysis, since it deals with human symbol use, is not something that critics can practice with scientific accuracy and should not be considered the "final word" on any speech. Rather, ideational analysis allows the critic to begin his or her analysis where the rhetor began his or her work on the speech: with the ideas themselves. With this beginning, the critic can proceed from the "what" through the "how" and the "why" of the message and begin to answer the implications or significance question, which editors and teachers sometimes offer in a colloquially phrased challenge: "So what?"

Chapter 5

ANALYZING ARGUMENT

In 1973, feminist scholars Ehrenreich and English published a slim volume entitled *Witches, Midwives, and Nurses: A History of Women Healers.* They began as follows:

Women have always been healers. They were the unlicensed doctors and anatomists of western history. They were abortionists, nurses and counsellors. They were pharmacists, cultivating healing herbs and exchanging the secrets of their uses. They were midwives, travelling from home to home and village to village. For centuries women were doctors without degrees, barred from books and lectures, learning from each other, and passing on experience from neighbor to neighbor and mother to daughter. They were called "wise women" by the people, witches or charlatans by the authorities. Medicine is part of our heritage as women, our history, our birthright.

Today, however, health care is the property of male professionals. Ninety-three percent of the doctors in the US are men; and almost all the top directors and administrators of health institutions. Women are still in the overall majority—70 percent of health care workers are women—but we have been incorporated as *workers* into an industry where the bosses are men. We are no longer independent practitioners, known by our own names, for our own work. We are, for the most part, institutional fixtures, filling faceless job slots: clerk, dietary aide, technician, maid.

When we are allowed to participate in the healing process, we can do so only as nurses. . . . Our subservience is reinforced by our ignorance, and our ignorance is *enforced*. Nurses are taught not to question, not to challenge. "The doctor knows best". . . .

Our position in the health system today is not "natural." It is a condition which has to be explained. In this pamphlet we have asked: How did we arrive at our present position of subservience from our former position of leadership?

We learned this much: That the suppression of women health workers and the rise to dominance of male professionals was not a "natural" process, resulting automatically from changes in medical science, nor was it the result of women's failure to take on healing work. It was an active *takeover* by male professionals. . . .

The suppression of female healers by the medical establishment was a political struggle, . . . part of the history of sex struggle . . . [and] . . . part of a *class* struggle. Women healers were [the] people's doctors. . . . Male professionals, on the other hand, served the ruling class. . . . They owe their victory—not so much to their own efforts—but to the intervention of the ruling class they served. . . .

To know our history is to begin to see how to take up the struggle again.

***

WITCHCRAFT AND MEDICINE IN THE MIDDLE AGES

Witches lived and were burned long before the development of modern medical technology. The great majority of them were lay healers serving the peasant population, and their suppression marks one of the opening struggles in the history of man's suppression of women as healers.

The other side of the suppression of witches as healers was the creation of a new male medical profession, under the protection and patronage of the ruling classes. This new European medical profession played an important role in the witch-hunts, supporting the witches' persecutors with "medical" reasoning:

> . . . . Because the Medieval Church, with the support of kings, princes and secular authorities, controlled medical education and practice, the Inquisition [witch-hunts] constitutes, among other things, an early instance of the "professional" repudiating the skills and interfering with the rights of the "nonprofessional" to minister to the poor. (Thomas Szasz, *The Manufacture of Madness*)

The witch-hunts left a lasting effect: An aspect of the female has ever since been associated with the witch, and an aura of contamination has remained—especially around the midwife and other women healers. This early and devastating exclusion of women from independent healing roles was a violent precedent and a warning: It was to become a theme of our history. The women's health movement of today has ancient roots in the medieval covens, and its opponents have as their ancestors those who ruthlessly forced the elimination of witches.

The age of witch-hunting spanned more than four centuries (from the 14th to the 17th century) in its sweep from Germany to England. . . . The witch-craze took different forms at different times and places, but never lost its essential character: that of a ruling class campaign of terror directed against the female peasant population. Witches represented a political, religious and sexual threat to the Protestant and Catholic churches alike, as well as to the state. . . .

The extent of the witch-craze is startling: In the late fifteenth and early sixteenth centuries there were thousands upon thousands of executions—usually live burnings at the stake—in Germany, Italy and other countries. In the mid-sixteenth century the terror spread to France, and finally to England. One writer has estimated the number of executions at an average of 600 a year for certain German cities—or two a day, "leaving out Sundays." Nine-hundred witches were destroyed in a single year in the Wertzberg area, and 1000 in and around Como. At Toulouse, four-hundred were put to death in a day. In the Bishopric of Trier, in 1585, two villages were left with only one female inhabitant each. Many writers have estimated the total number killed to have been in the millions. Women made up some 85 percent of those executed—old women, young women and children. . . .

. . . Undoubtedly, over the centuries of witch hunting, the charge of "witchcraft" came to cover a multitude of sins ranging from political subversion and religious heresy to lewdness and blasphemy. But three central accusations emerge repeatedly in the history of witchcraft throughout northern Europe: First, witches are accused of every conceivable sexual crime against men. Quite simply, they are "accused" of female sexuality. Second, they are accused of being organized. Third, they are accused of having magical powers affecting health—of harming, but also of healing. They were often charged specifically with possessing medical and obstetrical skills. . . .

The Church associated women with sex, and all pleasure in sex was condemned, because it could only come from the devil. . . . Lust in either man or wife, then, was blamed on the female. . . . On the other hand, witches were accused of making men impotent and of causing their penises to disappear. . . .

Not only were the witches women—they were women who seemed to be organized into an enormous secret society. . . . The witch-hunting literature is obsessed with the question of what went on at the witches' "Sabbaths." (Eating of unbaptised babies? Bestialism and mass orgies? So went their lurid speculations . . .)

. . . As a leading English witch-hunter put it: "It were a thousand times better for the land if all Witches, but especially the blessing Witch, might suffer death". . . . Witch-healers were often the only general medical practitioners for a people who had no doctors and no hospitals and who were bitterly afflicted with poverty and disease. In particular, the association of the witch and the midwife was strong: "No one does more harm to the Catholic Church than midwives," wrote witch-hunters Kramer and Sprenger. [Ehrenreich and English, 1973: 3,4,6,7,8,10,11,12,13]

Witches, Midwives, and Nurses was published during the "second wave" of American feminism in the 1960s and 1970s. (The "first wave," of course, was the fight for suffrage.) This artifact from the Women's Liberation movement provides a glimpse into women's history not found in traditional history texts. Decades after its original publication, the claims it makes remain startling, its rhetoric remains confrontational. During a moment when women were beginning to reclaim power in many aspects of their lives (the women's health classic, *Our Bodies, Ourselves,* appeared the same year), this little pamphlet exposed and critiqued the ways in which female healers had been the target of organized, sanctioned abuse for centuries. This is history that makes its politics clear. And so it is unquestionably rhetoric.

There are many interesting features of *Witches, Midwives, and Nurses.* Barbara Ehrenreich and Deirdre English understood that the best defense (against the erasure of women from the history of medicine, and against charges that women, especially power-hungry feminists, were witches) was a good offense.

Rather than assume the stance of "objective, neutral reporting" adopted by many journalists, biographers, and historians, Ehrenreich and English wear their activism on their collective sleeve. They argue that the "witch" label has been used for centuries to punish women who overstep the bounds of their prescribed role, they condemn this practice, and they advocate social change. Although today witchcraft has been playfully domesticated by novels and films such as *Practical Magic*, television shows like *Sabrina the Teenage Witch*, and bumper stickers that read "My other car is a broom," in 1973 taking witchcraft seriously enough to investigate it—in all of its aspects, allegations, and consequences—was unheard of.

In the language of Chapter 3, Ehrenreich and English's speech-act was it-self fascinating. The message stood as bravery incarnate: embattled women unfairly attacked by powerful men and institutions, finally breaking silence on behalf of millions of their oppressed and murdered sisters. Of course as women, their right to participate in even a metaphorical "battle" was itself controversial, since women were supposed to be passive and gentle by nature. Such challenges to traditional views of women encourage the audience to view the artifact as an Action (and a call to further Action) rather than a Reaction. Ironically, by speaking out so forcefully and discussing in detail what these wise women did, Ehrenreich and English risk that resistant readers will reject their message, perhaps even reading it as confirmation of damaging stereo-types about witches in particular, and strong women in general.

In the language of Chapter 4, *Witches, Midwives and Nurses* combines three of the four judgmental types: a Factual listing of women's representation in medicine, past and present; Desirable appeals to values such as justice, fair-ness and equal opportunity; and even some Directive advice ("To know our history is to begin to see how to take up the struggle again"). Noticeably ab-sent are Adjudicative appeals to formal codes and laws. This makes sense when we consider that the pamphlet's rhetorical purpose is one of debunking such codes and demonstrating how they have historically been used to rob women of power, dignity, even life itself.

In this chapter, we will examine argument—the linking of ideas in support of identifiable propositions. We will track how rhetors move their listeners from one assertion to the next and, ultimately, to some overriding assertion. In analyzing argument and reasoning, we must rethink what we know about them, for the logic of persuasion is a *human logic* in which reasoners are able to build bridges between ideas that professional logicians would find flimsy. Because the logic of persuasion is also an *informal logic,* the critic must be re-minded that listeners' reasoning standards are looser than those used by sci-entists in the laboratory or by judges in court. It is a logic based as much on feeling as on thinking or, more accurately, it is a logic that presumes that all feelers think and that all thinkers feel. Thus, Ehrenreich and English's emo-tional pamphlet "made sense" to a great many of their readers even though it relied heavily on sources that were admittedly "sketchy and often biased"

[1973:5]. Here, we will try to discover what sort of sense Ehrenreich and English made and for whom they made it.

And it is important to view "sense" as something that is indeed *made*. In persuasion, sense is negotiated by people who use their beliefs, hopes, fears, and experiences to guide them. Audiences never start from scratch. They encounter each message in the context of everything they have heard previously. Clever rhetors like Ehrenreich and English understand this and hence build "reasoning aids" into their messages. In this chapter, we will use three different tools to examine how such rhetors reason and we will see that each model tells us something different about Ehrenreich and English's argument.

But perhaps the most important thing that can be learned about reasoning is taught by Ehrenreich and English themselves. Immediately after their recitation of the casualties of hundreds of years of witchhunts, the authors present an italicized aside, which acts almost like the chorus, directly addressing the audience, in a Shakespearean drama: *"There is fragmentary evidence—which feminists ought to follow up—suggesting that in some areas witchcraft represented a female-led peasant rebellion. Here we can't attempt to explore the historical context of the witch-hunts in any depth. But we do have to get beyond some common myths about the witch-craze—myths which rob the "witch" of any dignity and put the blame on her and the peasants she served"* [1973:8]. The sense of "what we must do" is only compelling to the extent that the readers trust the writers and share their viewpoint as feminists. In persuasion, audiences never separate a rhetor's reasoning from his or her credibility. Critics may wish it otherwise, but it is never otherwise. It is this fact that will begin our discussion of argument.

THE LOGIC OF PERSUASION

Many people become frustrated by what passes for logic in the practical world. Oliver North, who lied under oath to a Senate investigating committee during the 1980s, almost wins a Virginia Senate seat in 1994. One of Mr. North's neighbors, Gordon Liddy, a convicted felon because of the 1970s Watergate affair, is given a Freedom of Speech Award by an association of talk show hosts even though he had used his show to patiently instruct his listeners on where to aim when trying to shoot federal drug agents (the groin area, he decided).

This makes sense? Has the public gone mad? Is nothing constant? Are people without memory? Has logic lost its logic? Questions like these can be maddening, but the rhetorical critic cannot indulge them. To understand persuasion is to understand a new kind of logic.

Traditional logic—the logic of the scientist, the judge, and the philosopher—has always stood as Grade A, approved logic, as well it should. Traditional logic, or technical logic, posits certain rigid rules of reasoning (e.g., syllogistic forms), emphasizes certain modes of fact-gathering (e.g., the scientific method), promotes certain modes of inference (e.g., arguing from legal precedent), and preaches the gospel of exhaustive research and rigorous testing of propositions. These intellectual tendencies are said to best distinguish humankind from lower animals and to undergird the most important human discoveries. When the space shuttle Challenger disaster occurred in the late 1980s, for example, evidence indicated that scientists had reasoned poorly when designing the crucial O-rings for the rocket boosters, leading to the fatal explosion seconds after takeoff. The postdisaster hearings conducted by the military and Congressional bodies often were models of traditional logic, as computer printouts, weather charts, and laboratory reports were examined in microscopic detail.

But the public hearings were often something else as well. With the astronauts blaming the scientists and the scientists blaming the military and the military blaming the manufacturers and the manufacturers blaming the politicians and the politicians blaming the gods, the hearings were a field day for name-calling, flag-waving, question-begging, back-stabbing, rank-pulling, obfuscating and every other brand of argument known to civilization.

But the astronauts and the scientists and the military and the manufacturers and the politicians could not be blamed entirely for reasoning in these ways for they all shared one damnable trait: They were human. As humans, they were imperfect logicians. As humans, they had anxieties, memory lapses, biases, and worries about job security that clouded their thinking. As humans, they could reason like machines only so long before reaching for more shameless rhetorical materials. And those charged with deciding the truth in the case—the American people—had to fight through their own prejudices to make sense of a senseless tragedy.

So the logic of persuasion is neither tidy nor pretty. What passes for sense-making in everyday rhetoric stretches the boundaries of traditional logic. In persuasion, the guidebooks of technical or scientific reasoning must be set aside and a new, more indulgent, standard employed, a standard that looks more generously on people—both rhetors and audiences—and their curious ways of reasoning. Admittedly, the critic can forsake these standards and use the dictates of traditional logic to censure informal arguers. But the critic who wishes to understand how *people* reason will make assumptions like these:

1. *In persuasion, every act is rational (to the actor) at the time.* This means that both rhetors and audiences always have "good reasons" for doing what they do. Even though these reasons may not meet the critic's personal standards of goodness, this proposition suggests that any message that becomes popular will have a powerful logic to it. The advertiser who creates (and the consumer who responds to) a computer-generated advertisement featuring an SUV in wilderness accessible only by helicopter should perhaps be censured for environmental indifference and naïveté, respectively. But the critic's job is to discover why this message works: **What unspoken needs does it meet for consumers? What fantasies does it trip off? What values does it herald?** Rhetorical criticism is the study of *other people's* sense-makings; it is the critic's

job to re-present such sense-makings faithfully. To do less would be to miss an important part of the human story.

2. *The logic of persuasion is always credibility-driven.* Persuasion comes to us embodied: Most people cannot separate the substance of a message from its author. This is especially true in spoken persuasion where the rhetor's attitudes, voice, and personal appearance interact constantly with what the rhetor says. While the examples of reasoning found in formal logic books are often unattributed (i.e., *Who* was it exactly who first claimed, "All human beings are mortal. Socrates is a human being. Therefore . . . ?"), examples in rhetoric books almost always have a name attached. Thus, the genetic research of a neo-Nazi scientist has no chance of being taken seriously by the scholarly community, no matter what its inherent scientific worth. In persuasion, inherency lies *within people,* not within ideas.

This is why small children are in danger of accepting rides from strangers: they have been taught that adults are authoritative and well-intentioned. Rhetors with high credibility are thus allowed to ramble, to become patently unclear, or to present distressing evidence and yet retain their appeal. Under such conditions, listeners themselves seem somehow willing to fill-in the logical gaps. Thus, as Maranhão [1990] reports, the very possibility of achieving health via the psychoanalytic method rests on the kind of *authority* the analyst has for the client. Maranhão adds that it is the psychiatrist's job to work to increase such credibility during therapy sessions. In persuasion, rhetor and message are always wed, as are reasoning and feeling states.

3. *The logic of persuasion is always saliency-driven.* Saliency is the other great law of persuasion. It states: The listener will virtually always find the *important* and the *immediate* to be most reasonable. In a technical logic designed to test universal facts and establish enduring truths, this proposition would make no sense. But in the world of people, logic is a sometimes thing. Needs and experience, not abstract truths, guide human decision making. It is one thing to discuss the clinical utility of euthanasia and quite another to remove the life support system *from one's own mother.* During such moments, medical charts and sociological abstractions become dry as dust as the immediacy and importance of such a decision become overwhelming. On a less momentous front, the old advice not to grocery shop while hungry is wise since the law of saliency decrees that people never decide in the abstract even when they think they do.

4. *The logic of persuasion is audience-dependent.* The logic of persuasion is a "weak" rather than a "strong" logic. Its standards of reasonability vary sharply from audience to audience. This is what makes criticism such a fascinating enterprise: It opens up for inspection an endless variety of reasonings. The rhetoric of skin color, for example, will sound different at a conference of dermatologists than it will at the annual meetings of the National Basketball Association, different still at a gathering of the Ku Klux Klan. Each group will reason about skin color differently and thus it becomes the critic's job to understand

the "local logics" at work in each instance. So, for example, after Black [1970] found an excessive number of cancer metaphors in the rhetoric of the radical right, he traced these metaphors to the group's central reasoning process: (1) that they felt on the brink of ruin, (2) that they felt deceived from within, but (3) also that they were willing to fight to the death. In other words, the good critic finds logic wherever rhetoric is found.

5. *The logic of persuasion is a logic of association.* While technical logic focuses on causality, rhetoric is guided by the weaker dictates of association. A smear campaign in politics is often fueled by associations. Although it makes no causal sense to launch a federal investigation merely because of one's work history or ethnicity, it can make *associative* sense to do so. So when a Congressional committee looked into his former business dealings, one-time U.S. Labor Secretary Raymond Donovan charged that former building contractors (like himself) always seem worthy of federal investigation, that former building contractors from New Jersey seem automatically indictable, and that former New Jersey building contractors who also happen to be Italian seem automatically guilty.

Because determining true causality is so rare in human affairs, ordinary arguments rarely prove things with scientific certainty. Rather, they trade on the logically weaker but psycho-logically attractive standards of plausibility, rationalization, and current biases. So, for example, Mechling and Mechling [1992] report that contemporary Quaker rhetoric came to endorse peace on psychological rather than religious grounds. This happened, the authors argue, because potential converts to the peace movement were increasingly becoming part of a "New Class" (they were more affluent, more worldly, and more middle-class than their forebears) and, hence, the Quakers began to frame their arguments in more bourgeois, less theological, ways.

6. *The logic of persuasion is often a logic of emotion.* The old Western dichotomy between the heart and the head makes little sense in the world of rhetoric. Most students of persuasion now agree that to contrast people's "logical" and "emotional" tendencies is wrongheaded. When they react to persuasion people react with all of themselves. To describe some rhetorical appeals as logical in nature (e.g., monetary arguments) and others as emotional (e.g., patriotic arguments) is therefore to deal artificially with a complex process of thinking/feeling. During each moment of each day, people think/feel. Rhetors think/feel when they speak and listeners think/feel when they listen. The fact of the matter is that some people get quite emotional about their tax returns while others become rather cold-blooded when justifying military actions.

When studying persuasion, therefore, the critic must be primarily concerned with the **emotional authenticity** of a rhetor (i.e., Does the rhetor really seem to be experiencing the emotion she claims to be experiencing?), with the **emotional integrity** of a performance (i.e., Does the rhetor's background give him the "right" to be this emotional on this matter?), or the **emotional register** of an argument (i.e., Is the rhetor's state of arousal too high or too low for the matters being discussed?). And it must be remembered that questions of this sort are questions about *reasoning,* about how packages of emotions and ideas serve as arguments in the ordinary world.

Given the six features above, the logic of persuasion may seem a completely dishonorable logic: an advertiser convinces us that we need clothing we do not need, a lawyer encourages clients to cry on the witness stand to win jurors' sympathies, a preacher claims he will go without food if church donations don't increase by 200 percent. In persuasion, these claims stand as argument. Shame on persuasion.

In light of these features, the critic has two choices: (1) to honor traditional logic by ignoring persuasion completely or (2) to study how and why such appeals work and then to warn others about the logic of everyday rhetoric. This second option seems most sensible. After all, the first is defeatist, not to mention elitist. But the second option encourages closer study of people, a fundamentally humane act indeed.

EVIDENCE AND REASONING

The success of a persuasive argument is often determined not by notions of formal validity but by questions of *sufficiency:* **Is there enough to go on here? Is more support required? Is the case overstated?** A good approach for the critic, then, is to examine the weight of the arguments offered in a given message. By contrasting heavily documented propositions to those mentioned in passing, the critic can detect the rhetor's areas of confidence and also the rhetorical trouble spots. Naturally, the evidence used in public arguments rarely meets rigorous standards of empirical testing. Although Ehrenreich and English presented many definitions in their historical account, they were hardly definitions that would sit well with antifeminist readers. Rather, their redefinitions of previous understandings of witchcraft and its relation to the male-dominated medical profession gave sympathetic readers the sense that Ehrenreich and English were slashing through centuries of sexist programming to reveal women's illustrious history in the healing arts. On many occasions for many listeners, some evidence is enough evidence.

When inspecting arguments, the critic asks questions like these:

- Generally speaking, does the message make use of much supporting material or is it flatly assertive?
- Does the rhetor use a large number of sketchy arguments or build a tighter case with few propositions but more evidence?
- Which arguments have ample supporting materials, which are given short shrift, and why?
- What *kinds* of evidence does the rhetor use? Do they change from point to point in the message?

Table 5.1 presents standard kinds of rhetorical evidence and critical probes to reveal how a given message functioned and how its author perceived the

TABLE 5.1 Analyzing Clarification Devices

Type	Functions	Example*	❓ Critical Probes
Serial examples	Adds totality to a speaker's remarks by presenting, in scattered fashion, numerous instances of the same phenomenon.	"Parents can act as our reference groups, as can friends, political groups, religious organizations, social fraternities, and so on."	How frequently are groups of examples found in the message? Is there any overall logic to the types of illustrations chosen? Which arguments are devoid of examples? Why?
Extended example	Adds vivacity to a speaker's remarks by presenting a detailed picture of a single event or concept.	"Let's consider what happened to John Jones, a college undergraduate who has had trouble 'sorting out' his reference groups. John started school like most people, and so on. . . ."	How many different extended examples are used? How much detail is provided within them? Are "story qualities" clearly apparent in the examples? Are the examples real or hypothetical? Is the narrative interrupted at any point? Why?
Quantification	Adds a feeling of substantiveness to a speaker's remarks by concrete enumerations.	"Some experts estimate 70 percent of our decisions are affected by our reference groups, and that one out of every three people experiences tensions in relation to reference group choice."	How often are dates, sums, and quantities provided in the message? When are they used? What sorts of arguments do they support? Which arguments that could be quantified are not quantified? Why?
Isolated comparisons	Adds realism to a speaker's remarks by drawing analogically on a listener's past experiences	"Reference groups are like partners—you can't live without them, but sometimes it's darn hard to live with them!"	What sorts of "equations" are set up by the speaker? Do the two elements of an equation "naturally" go together or is the equation novel? In offering the comparisons offered, what assumptions about the audience does the rhetor seem to be making? Are the assumptions justified?
Extended comparison	Adds psychological reference points to a rhetor's remarks by successively structuring his or her perceptions along familiar lines.	"A reference group is similar to a mother—it nurtures our feelings when we are hurt; it disciplines us for violating its norms; it helps us mature by. . . ."	Are extended comparisons extensively or infrequently used? What sorts of arguments are developed with this device? Is the "known" half of the comparison well adapted to the audience so that they can appreciate the "unknown" half?

*Example: A sociology lecture on the topic of "reference groups."

TABLE 5.1 *(continued)*

Type	Functions	Example	⟨?⟩ Critical Probes
Testimony	Adds to the inclusiveness of a rhetor's remarks by quoting appreciatively from known or respected sources or depreciatively from sources of ill-regard.	"Sociologist Carolyn Sherif has said that none of us can really escape the influence of the groups we identify with—our reference groups."	What sorts of persons/ sources does the rhetor depend on? How often is this dependency manifested? Is there an obvious logic to the persons/sources chosen for support? How careful is the rhetor's documentation of the sources quoted? What types of persons/sources are never quoted?
Definition	Adds to the specificity of a rhetor's remarks by depicting opposed elements.	"Let's consider what is not meant by a reference group. It is not just any group we belong to, nor is it always identifiable. Rather it is . . ."	Is any major attempt made here to define important concepts? Which terms/ ideas are defined fully? Which key terms/ideas are presented without definition? At what point in the message are definitions offered?
Contrast	Adds a dramatic quality to a rhetor's remarks by depicting opposed elements.	"Those who identify with many groups have very different attitudes from those who are more individualistic."	What sort of "reverse equations" are presented by the rhetor? Are both elements of the contrasts drawn from audience experiences? Is dependence on contrasts heavy, moderate, or light? Do contrasts overshadow comparisons and is it significant that they do?

rhetorical circumstances. Because evidence forms the foundation and supporting walls of discourse, the critic who uses these critical probes becomes something of a building inspector, prowling around in the basement and walking amidst the scaffolding to see whether the rhetorical structure is as good as it should be and, if not, why nobody noticed.

Table 5.2 presents a rough estimation of how frequently the various clarification devices have been used in the Ehrenreich and English text and in some of the speeches examined previously. A quick inspection shows that each artifact presents a different picture, with some messages resembling others on some dimensions but none being duplicates. This makes sense, since one of the speeches was purely fictional (Harold Hill) while another was quite real (Patton). One message was religious with a political tone (Rabbi Prinz) while

TABLE 5.2 Comparative Use of Clarification Devices*

Clarification Devices	Rabbi Prinz	Harold Hill	George Patton	Ehrenreich & English
Serial examples	0	11	18	23
Extended examples	14	50	30	17
Quantification	0	11	2	18
Isolated comparisons	17	15	14	0
Extended comparisons	37	0	0	0
Testimony	8	0	4	7
Definition	6	7	17	23
Contrast	17	6	16	12

*Numbers indicate percentages of message using the devices listed

another was political and historical (Ehrenreich and English). It is little wonder that the evidentiary profiles are distinctive.

These clarification devices can be thought of as reasoning aids, as argumentative promises to listeners: "If you don't like my comparative argument, here's one with contrast." "If these serial examples make an idea clear for you, this extended example will make it even clearer." "If you're having trouble moving from Proposition A to Proposition B, listen to how a respected source made that same intellectual movement." Some rhetors choose poorly when selecting evidence: They choose the wrong device; choose the right device but then develop it poorly; or overlook an argument needing support while providing unneeded attention to a self-evident argument. Making wise choices about such matters is what rhetorical excellence is all about.

The evidentiary choices made by our four rhetors seem sensible. General Patton saw his job as one of giving his men a clear sense of purpose. His heavy use of Definition shows that. In his speech, he explains the real-life meanings of teamwork and patriotism and does little else. Since his time before battle was short, Patton chose a streamlined argument, hoping that his men would at least take away a fresh understanding of these two concepts. Patton also uses a good deal of Contrast, distinguishing the fighting ability and moral superiority of the American troops from their German counterparts. Fairly heavy use of Contrast creates "division"—sharp distinctions, opposed viewpoints, observable differences—the kind of black-and-white thinking that keeps confusion to a minimum during battle. All in all, then, a good day's work for Patton or, more precisely, a good five minutes' work.

Harold Hill's speech could not be more different. He defines very little, makes no Extended Comparisons, offers no Testimony. Such devices would have slowed his speech to a crawl. Playwright Meredith Willson wanted something snappy and hence wrote only a patina of support into Hill's script. So Hill tries primarily to generate initial shock and concern in his listeners, followed by a grand enthusiasm for band instruments. Hill bases most of his speech on the Extended Example of the pool table, figuring that this speech would be but the first in an extended campaign to separate the good folks of River City from their currency.

Like Patton, Hill sought simplicity. But unlike Patton, Hill hoped to build intensity of motivation, which might have been dissipated if spread over a wide range of arguments in behalf of tuba playing. Hill's Extended Example thus became what debaters call a need case, a kind of problem-stating that ultimately invites a "plan," which Harold Hill just happened to have handy in his display case.

Rabbi Prinz's speech resembled Hill's, in part, because he too needed a streamlined performance. Rather than use examples, however, the Rabbi made dramatic use of the Extended Comparison, showing how the experiences of Jews in Nazi Germany paralleled those of African Americans in the United States. This heavy use of comparison springs directly from the very speech-act in which Prinz participated: His physical presence at the March on Washington said "We Jews stand with you Blacks on this matter." So the social action of the *event* neatly parallels the rhetorical action of the *text*.

Comparisons, however, have their rhetorical costs. They tend to be listlike and, when used in great profusion, better suited to lectures or scientific reports than to halftime speeches or advertising copy. Moreover, unlike serial examples (which the Rabbi almost never uses), comparisons can put audiences to sleep. But given the Rabbi's role—that of rhetorical helpmate to Dr. King—he apparently felt it was enough to take his stand on the right side of the issue, make a simple, unembellished statement, and then quit the scene. He did so movingly.

Compared to the other rhetors, Ehrenreich and English's heavy use of Quantification is significant. Because they were making the case that women's circumscribed roles in contemporary American medicine were the result of a centuries-old, politically and economically-motivated campaign, Ehrenreich and English went to great lengths to detail the scope and breadth of women's persecution as witches and midwives, and their consequent sidelining as nurses. Their even heavier use of serial examples served this purpose as well, establishing the multiplicity of roles formerly open to women in the healing arts ("doctors, anatomists, nurses, counsellors, pharmacists, midwives") and the ways those opportunities have been replaced by less respected service positions ("clerk, dietary aide, technician, maid"). Their significant use of extended examples ("Witch-healers were often the only general medical practitioners for a people who had no doctors [or] hospitals and who were bitterly afflicted with poverty and disease") provide depth to complement the breadth of the statistical evidence they cite. Together, quantification, serial and extended examples make up well over half the message, reflecting the fact that a large part of Ehrenreich and English's rhetorical task was to convince the reader of the extent of the problem.

Before they could convince their audience of the extent of the problem, however, Ehrenreich and English first needed to establish its existence. Definition and contrast provide most of the rest of the evidence in the opening of

Witches, Midwives, and Nurses. Definition (of women as healers, contemporary doctors as the descendents of the inquisitors) serves to identify the problem, and contrast helps the reader understand the oppositional nature of the forces at work, and imagine other possibilities: "Women healers were [the] people's doctors. . . . Male professionals, on the other hand, served the ruling class."

Although it is a humble type of analysis, examining argumentative support reveals how rhetors work their minds rhetorically. For example, Dow and Tonn [1993] found that a key difference between Texas governor Ann Richards's style and that of previous (white male) politicians is that she used far more Extended Examples and Serial Examples than her male counterparts, thereby bringing more "humanity" to public discourse. On a very different front, Katriel [1994] studied the rhetoric used by tour guides in Israeli settlement museums. She found that Zionist ideology was being subtly woven into these presentations by a preponderance of Isolated Comparisons which favored Jewish, not Arab, readings of history as well as by pieces of biblical Testimony used to explain contemporary phenomena. In other words, Katriel found propagandistic elements by examining some of the most elementary, and most often overlooked, rhetorical devices available.

Naturally, examining evidence patterns of this sort cannot tell us everything that needs to be known about persuasion. But these patterns can often point up what is *at issue* in discourse. However, reasoning involves more than the marshalling of evidence. Important as evidence patterns are, sometimes rhetors' arguments gain momentum from what may seem an unlikely source: the stories they tell.

NARRATIVE AND REASONING

At first, narrative and reasoning might seem antithetical. "Poets tell stories," is our initial response, "scientists reason." But a growing number of scholars believe that there is a logic to storytelling, a logic the rhetorical critic must understand. These scholars argue that public policy is often determined by the stories persuaders tell. Sometimes, these stories are complex, springing from deep cultural roots; often, stories told today are but updated versions of century-old tales. Because they are practical people, persuaders do not tell these stories with the novelist's richness of detail or sense of abandon.

And overt persuaders normally tell only snippets of stories, an anecdote here, an abbreviated fable there, always moving listeners forward to some propositional conclusion. But narratives do advance persuasion because (1) they disarm audiences by enchanting them, (2) they awaken within audiences dormant experiences and feelings, and (3) they thereby expose, subtly, some sort of propositional argument. Recent studies have shown that people reason differently in the presence of narrative. Its native features suggest why:

1. *Narrative occurs in a natural timeline.* There are beginnings, middles, and endings to narrative. Once we start on a narrative, we feel compelled to

follow it through to its conclusion. All stories, even bad stories, inspire the desire to see how it turns out. Narratives tempt us with closure.

2. *Narrative includes characterization.* People are interested in people. Narratives are the stories of what people do. Often, narratives introduce interesting people, sometimes grand people, to an audience. When we encounter such narratives, our natural sense of identification makes us want to find out more about their lives.

3. *Narrative presents detail.* A good story, such as a fine novel, transports us to another time or place by offering fine-grained treatments. When the narrator describes the clothes people wear or the customs they follow or the dialect they speak, we come to know that time and place as if it were our own. Details captivate.

4. *Narrative is primitive.* No culture exists without narrative. Most cultures celebrate their sacred narratives on a regular basis (e.g., a Fourth of July celebration) and most cultures indoctrinate their young by means of narrative (e.g., fairy tales). Narrative appeals to the child in us because, unlike life, it contains a complete story with certain consequences.

5. *Narrative doesn't argue . . . obviously.* If a narrator tries to make a point too forcefully, we feel cheated. Good narrative holds open the promise that we—as audience—help to determine its meaning. Narrative can appear to be proposition-free argument, or argument with a hidden bottom line. Narrators charm because they promise a story well told. But every such story encourages particular reactions from its audience.

These propositions apply to all narratives, but strongly rhetorical narratives have special features, special obligations, in addition. For example, because rhetorical narrative is *narrative,* opponents find it hard to attack ("it's only a story, after all"). But because rhetorical narrative is also *rhetorical,* because it is storytelling-with-a-purpose, it must also abide by certain rules of purposiveness. Thus, rhetorical narratives are (1) normally brief, (2) often repetitious, (3) sketchy in characterization, (4) frequently interrupted, and (5) rarely exotic.

In the middle of *Witches, Midwives, and Nurses,* for example, Ehrenreich and English launched into just such a narrative. They did not produce great poetry at that time but they did produce good rhetoric, especially for the educated, middle-class, feminist women that they especially wanted to reach:

THE SUPPRESSION OF WOMEN HEALERS

The establishment of medicine as a profession, requiring university training, made it easy to bar women legally from practice. With few exceptions, the universities were closed to women (even to upper class women who could afford them), and licensing laws were established to prohibit all but university-trained doctors from practice . . . [But] the laws [were] used selectively. Their first target was not the peasant healer, but the better off, literate woman healer who competed for the same urban clientele as that of the university-trained doctors.

Take, for example, the case of Jacoba Felicie, brought to trial in 1322 by the Faculty of Medicine at the University of Paris, on charges of illegal practice. Jacoba was literate and had received some unspecified "special training" in medicine. That her patients were well off is evident from the fact that (as they testified in court) they had consulted well-known university-trained physicians before turning to her. The primary accusations brought against her were that

> . . . she would cure her patient of internal illness and wounds or of external abscesses. She would visit the sick assiduously and continue to examine the urine in the manner of physicians, feel the pulse, and touch the body and limbs.

> Six witnesses affirmed that Jacoba had cured them, even after numerous doctors had given up, and one patient declared that she was wiser in the art of surgery and medicine than any master physician or surgeon in Paris. But these testimonials were used against her, for the charge was not that she was incompetent, but that—as a woman—she dared to cure at all. [Ehrenreich and English, 1973:17–19]

There are many appealing aspects of Ehrenreich and English's narrative. By first relating the history of the legal obstacles to women in medicine, they establish how the university-trained doctors identified and prosecuted their major economic competitors. When they then promise an example, Ehrenreich and English allow the reader to experience a brief period of **suspense.** As they tell the story of Jacoba Felicie, her skill and dedication to her clients create admiration and **concern for the protagonist,** perhaps even **identification.** The **familiar character types** and **storyline** are (perversely) comforting: the underdog (a selfless woman devoted to helping others) is unjustly persecuted by the powerful (male legal and medical professionals). Characters and plots like these can be found nightly in almost any television drama and they serve to commit the audience to the argument as only storytelling can.

According to Mader [1973], a narrative must also have **rhetorical presence,** a vividness of detail that brings to life the ideas advanced. Ehrenreich and English achieve this by weaving in specific places (Paris), numbers and dates (six witnesses, 1322), quotations ("she would examine the urine in the manner of physicians") and, most important, people (Jacoba Felicie and the Faculty of Medicine). Ehrenreich and English also play on the understandings contemporary audiences would have of malpractice litigation, using those presumptions to produce a **dramatic twist** ("But these testimonials were used against her, for the charge was not that she was incompetent, but that—as a woman—she dared to cure at all"). The finality of those words "she dared to cure at all" brings a sense of tragic **closure** to the narrative, although the details of Felicie's punishment are never specified. Through these narrative techniques, the audience is invited to dwell in outrage and indignation over the gross injustice visited upon a woman who lived and died seven centuries ago.

Scholars who have investigated the rhetorical uses of narratives seem both fascinated and alarmed by what they find. Black [1992:147–170], for example, explains that the narrator's role is extraordinarily powerful, a role whose innocence inhibits listeners from thinking about the arguments embedded in the tales being told them. Black concludes, therefore, that narratives often tell the simplest and most comforting story possible, which is ample reason to keep an eye on them since life itself is normally neither simple nor comforting.

For a number of reasons, then, it is useful for the critic to scrutinize narratives carefully. The following critical probes seem especially suited to doing so:

 1. Does the narrative spring from a Master Narrative? If so, what tradition forms the basis for the appeal? How is the narrative adapted to its new context? Hillbruner [1960] notes that many contemporary narratives have their roots in older narratives and that the critic who is sensitive to such parentage can discover the new implications of these old stories. For example, Motion [1999] examined the narratives that female politicians in New Zealand used to justify their entrance into public life. In order to validate such "nontraditional" choices for women, these candidates drew on powerful old stories of heroes fighting for ideals such as justice and patriotism, and grafting onto them culturally "feminine" ideals of loyalty to family.

Olson and Goodnight [1994] found a fascinating shift in the overall storyline used by those who wish to continue to wear fur. In earlier times, fur was justified on the basis of fashion alone. More recently, fur fanciers have attached themselves to the old cultural narratives of capitalism (in this case, the subnarrative of consumers' rights). In doing so, they have given their cause *political* weight and thereby circumvented the more constraining, self-serving, and ephemeral narratives of "moving up" or "getting a piece of the dream."

 2. What propositional content is the narrative designed to reveal? Although narratives do not argue explicitly, they do indeed argue. Their style of argument is devastatingly natural because it uses a realistic timeline to tell who did what when. But behind any narrative lie primitive rhetorical decisions for the rhetor: Which facts to stress and which to ignore? Which characters to mention, which to amplify? When to start the story, when to stop it? By making each of these decisions and dozens more like them, the persuader/narrator is also deciding which *ideas* to amplify and which to thrust into the background.

Miller [1999], for example, studied Native American protests over the use of Indians as mascots for sports teams. He concluded that one primary rhetorical obstacle the protestors face is that "entire generations of fans grew up playing 'cowboys and Indians.' To these fans, performing 'Indian' is as harmless childhood play. Letting go of Native American symbols in our sports arenas . . . means letting go of precious myths about how the American West was won" [p. 200]. By framing the tomahawk chop as harmless play, sports fans cling to the idea of a conquered wilderness, civilized by settlers of European ancestry. Such a seductive story—and the privilege that enables it—are difficult to relinquish.

 3. What propositional content is the narrative designed to mask? This probe encourages the critic to inquire into the underlying purpose of the narrative at hand. When telling a story, after all, the persuader operates preemptively by *not*

doing something else. For example, Triece [1999] found that popular mail-order magazines of the early twentieth century appealed to working-class women by promising them the ideals of True Womanhood (purity, piety, submissiveness, domesticity) associated with women of wealth. But these appeals could only work by negating the existence of "thousands of women and girls outside the pages of the magazines who were publicly calling attention to, and challenging the inhumanities of, the factory system through strikes, walk outs, and parades" [p. 44].

Kirkwood [1983] comments on the mood-changing power of narrative (it comforts and relaxes us), observing how fiction or a shocking tale suspends "ordinary rationality" and places it in the service of escapist visions. He notes that the humble parable, for example, is really a very powerful form of argument because it (1) shifts the discussion from actual fact to imagined or recreated fact, (2) subsumes the discussion of principle to the discussion of narrative detail, and (3) reduces the listener to childlike (i.e., story-loving) status. Because the narrator takes on a "mantle of spiritual parenthood" [p. 72], says Kirkwood, narrative is not a small matter. When narrative is onstage, then, the critic is wise to look offstage.

Some critics would have us add a fourth, less descriptive, question about narrative: How effectively and how faithfully does the narrative deal with its subject matter? This, of course, is the evaluative question and it is important to ask because storytelling seems so innocent. Fisher [1987] argues that any narrative will have varying amounts of both **narrative probability** (i.e., good story qualities: followability, completeness, believability) and **narrative fidelity** (reliability and truthfulness) and that the critic should inspect narrative closely for both features. General guidelines for effective rhetoric can help the critic judge narrative probability but we do not yet have clear standards for measuring either truthfulness or reliability. As for fidelity—the extent to which the narrative matches the reality it purports to describe—individual critics will have to use their own judgment by determining (1) what was knowable in a given case, (2) what was knowable by the rhetor in particular, and (3) how faithfully the resulting narrative captures what was known.

Ultimately, of course, there can be no final determination on such matters, for accuracy and goodness often exist in the eye of the beholder. But it seems clear that critics must inspect narrative carefully. Narrative can seem to be merely diverting, and its rhetorical invitations to the reader harmless. But especially when introduced into discussions of public policy, its diversions must be studied for a basic reason: Rhetorical stories have entailments; they imply consequences. Narrative demands vigilance because the reasoning it encourages is often as facile as the stories themselves are compelling.

TOULMIN AND REASONING

A useful method for understanding reasoning is based on the work of Stephen Toulmin [1958] who many years ago outlined a new way of thinking about informal human argument. Toulmin's approach was a reaction to the models of formal logic then popular in philosophical circles. He believed that such models were too static to deal with something as dynamic as human thought and so he proposed a system better adapted to the actual logics used by actual people. Toulmin did not prescribe how people ought to reason; instead, he tried to describe how they actually behaved. Toulmin's approach was quickly seized upon by rhetorical scholars. One such application was that of Hart [1973] who inspected some fifty-four different messages using a modified version of Toulmin's approach. We present this modified version here.

Toulmin's system reduces arguments to a kind of outline so as to establish their overall logical movement. By collapsing a text to its skeletal structure, the critic becomes less encumbered by the great amounts of diversionary or supporting material normally contained in a message. Used in this rough fashion, the Toulmin system is more robust than precise, but it provides an economical way of talking about large quantities of discourse.

At the simplest level, the critic using the Toulmin system "translates" a message into Toulminian terminology. At a more ambitious level, the system allows the critic to (1) make patterned sense out of discourse by focusing on its most essential logical movements; (2) use the Toulmin layout of a message as a general starting point for later, more fine-grained, analyses; and (3) employ a standard system so that many different kinds of discourse can be compared on the same basis.

In modified form, the Toulmin system asks the critic to isolate in a given message three key features:

1. *Major Claims [MC]* (a) are the broadest, most encompassing, statements made by the rhetor, (b) lie at a level of abstraction higher than all other statements the rhetor makes, (c) represent what the rhetor hopes will become the "residual message" in listeners' minds (i.e., the main thoughts remembered when the details of a message have been forgotten), and (d) are frequently repeated or restated in the message.

2. *Major Data [MD]* lie at a level of abstraction immediately beneath that of the Major Claim. Major Data are the supporting structures of discourse, statements answering the listener's questions: What makes you say that? What do you have to go on? Major data themselves subsume what might be thought of as Sub-Data: facts, illustrations, bits of evidence, and other clarifying devices used to ground the rhetor's assertions.

3. *Warrants [W]* are the keys to the Toulmin approach. They make the "movement" from Major Data to Major Claim possible. Toulmin [1958:98] described warrants as "general, hypothetical statements which can act as bridges and authorize the sort of step to which our particular argument commits us." So, for example, if a rhetor makes the assertion that "Ransom money should never be paid to free U.S. hostages seized abroad" (Major Claim) because "you can't deal with terrorists" (Major Data), the "missing" part of the argument is something of the sort: "Only terrorists would seize an airplane" (Warrant).

Ehninger and Brockriede [1963] describe three types of warrants commonly found in public argument: (1) **Substantive warrants [SW]**—ideas based on what is thought to be actual fact (such as the terrorists-are-irresponsible notion used above); (2) **Motivational warrants [MW]**—ideas suggesting that some desirable end must be achieved or that some desirable condition is being endangered (e.g., The argument "We must pay the ransom money" [MC] because "the people will crucify us in the upcoming elections if we don't" [MD] somehow depends for its reasonability on the notion that "getting re-elected is a good thing" [W]; (3) **Authoritative warrants [AW]**—ideas based on the credibility of the rhetor or on the source of testimony offered by the rhetor (e.g., To warrant the argument "We can't pay the ransom" [MC] because "I've told the people in the past I wouldn't do so" [MD], a rhetor would be depending on some such notion as "inconsistent people are crucified in politics" or "this ransom issue isn't worth my political scalp" [W].

In laying out a given message, the critic answers some fairly simple critical probes:

1. What are the Major Claims being offered by the rhetor? (Attend particularly to repeated or reparaphrased statements.)
2. What are the Major Data presented? (Many, but not all, of these will be found contiguous to the Major Claims made.)
3. What are the range of warrants that could reasonably authorize such Data-Claim movements?(Answer this without consulting the message directly.)
4. Into which category (substantive, motivational, authoritative) would each of these potential warrants fall?
5. Which of these warrants were explicitly supplied by the rhetor and which were left unspoken?

Step #5 is especially crucial in criticism. Most discourse, if not all, depends heavily on the cooperation of listeners to complete the reasoning circuit begun by the rhetor. A streetcorner shout to "get out of the street [MC], a bus is coming [MD]" hardly needs to be attended by the warrant "buses can make mincemeat out of you." Our reactions to such a cry of warning are instinctual: We quickly help the argument along by supplying from our knowledge (e.g., of physics) and our biases (e.g., self-preservation) the missing pieces and parts needed to make sense out of the warner's "argument."

Thus, most persuaders rarely say everything that could be said, trusting that if the correct data are chosen for the correct claim, the audience will allow the argumentative movement, if not propel it. From such a perspective, the persuader becomes a solicitor, one who uses language to entice listeners to participate silently in an argumentative exchange. The Toulmin system encourages us to search for such "missing" elements since examining the *unstated* in discourse provides the most subtle understanding of rhetor-audience relationships.

FIGURE 5.1 Toulmin Layout of Letter to the Editor

Major claims	Warrants	Major Data
	A = authoritative M = motivational S = substantive 0 = suppressed ** = supplied	† = subdata provided 0 = subdata omitted
1. Anderson is a Democrat.	(None)	(None)
2. He's running for office.	(None)	(None)
3. Let's vote for him.	3-1. Christians make good officials. (M/0)	He's a Christian. (0)
	3-2. Honesty is important in government. (M/0)	He's honest. (0)
	3-3. Trust is important in government. (M/0)	You can trust him. (0)
	3-4. You can rely on my judgment. (A/0)	I've known him for a long time. (0)
4. We need good men.	(None)	(None)
5. Let's vote for Anderson.	(None)	(None)

To understand the value of the Toulmin system, let us consider a simple example, a letter to the editor in a small-town, Midwestern newspaper that is neither subtle nor argumentatively complex:

> On the Democratic ticket you see Ben Anderson's name. He is a good Christian man. He is an honest man, and you can trust him.
>
> Let us all go to the polls and vote for Mr. Anderson. I've known him for a long time.
>
> We need good men in our offices and more like him. Let's you and I go and vote for Mr. Anderson.

Figure 5.1 lays out the letter's argument. Several things are striking: (1) Three of the claims are simply asserted. No data are supplied to establish their validity. This gives the message its choppy, telegraphic feeling; (2) the central argument—that Anderson should be elected—is supported by four different pieces of data, none of which has subdata. This gives the message its confident and businesslike tone; (3) none of the data-claim movements is explicitly warranted.

The three needed motivational warrants (i.e., that Christianity, honesty and trustworthiness are desirable) are omitted as is the one authoritative warrant (i.e., that the writer is credible). These missing warrants give the message its homey, emotional touches. Neighbors speaking over the back fence do not need to supply warrants and people who are sounding off often do not supply them either.

As a result, this message is "presumptuous." The argument demands a good deal from the newspaper reader because of its sketchiness, a feature somewhat required by the enforced brevity of these letters but also expected from anybody letting off steam. These distinctive, often charming, qualities make letters to the editor the most popular feature in almost any local newspaper.

The Toulmin approach can also describe more complex discourse—like that of Ehrenreich and English—and so Figure 5.2 presents a Toulmin layout of the early portion of *Witches, Midwives, and Nurses*. One of the real advantages of the Toulmin system is that by outlining a message skeletally, it emphasizes a message's value appeals and deemphasizes its beguiling use of language. A Toulmin sketch tells us, for example, that Ehrenreich and English had a sympathetic but largely uninformed audience in mind. They were trying to revise received historical understandings. They had a relatively complicated case to make, with eight major claims presented in quick succession. The startling nature of their news explains why they provided detailed evidence for almost every claim. (The exception is major claim #4: Readers unlikely to supply the suppressed motivational warrant themselves probably would not have read this far into the document.) Similarly, the authors count on readers to share their political viewpoint: All but one of the warrants are suppressed. Also, substantive warrants occur early in the document to provide "factual" grounding, and authoritative warrants dominate the latter section, after the authors have presumably convinced the readers that they know whereof they speak.

The Toulmin system is useful for several reasons. For one thing, it helps explain tone. For example, the boldness of the Patton speech probably resulted from his rapid transition from major data to major data, all in the service of one major claim ("We will be victorious") but none developed via subdata. In contrast, the frivolous tone of Harold Hill's speech results from his dependence upon sacred warrants (the wages of sin, the importance of industry, communal obligations, etc.) for profane purposes (the selling of band instruments).

Tone is also an important factor at the end of the semester when college professors get to hear The Student Lament—"I simply must have an 'A' in this course." Many professors regard this as a presumptuous argument, perhaps because it depends heavily on highly questionable warrants to legitimize the movement from data to claim. These warrants include: *The Puritan Ethic* ("I've worked really hard in here"), *Ego Unbounded* ("I've really liked your course"), *In Loco Parentis* ("I'll flunk out of school unless you help me out"), or *Capitalism Incorporated* ("A lesser grade will hurt me on the job market").

FIGURE 5.2 Toulmin Layout of Ehrenreich and English's Argument

Major claims	Warrants	Major data
	A = authoritative	+ = subdata provided
	M = motivational	0 = subdata omitted
	S = substantive	
	0 = suppressed	
	** = supplied	
1. Women have always been healers.	A license is not a prerequisite to healing. (A/0)	Women were the unlicensed doctors of Western history. (+)
2. Today, health care is the property of male professionals.	Doctors and administrators, rather than nurses, control the medical profession. (S/0)	In medicine today, men are bosses, women are workers. (+)
3. Women's subordinate position is not "natural," but was the result of an active "takeover."	Divisions in society are the result of the subordination of women and the poor. (S/0)	Women healers served the people, while male professionals served the ruling class. (+)
4. To know our history is to see how to take up the struggle again.	It is necessary to struggle to regain the power we lost. (M/0)	(None)
5. Witchburning was an early battle in men's fight to suppress women healers.	The scope of the witch-hunts proves the seriousness of the threat witches posed to the male institutions. (A/0)	The age of witch-hunting spanned more than four centuries and several countries. (+)
6. As a result of the witch-hunts, women, especially women healers such as mid-wives, continue to be associated with the negative image of the witch.	This exclusion of women from independent healing roles was a violent precedent and a warning, and would become a theme of our history. (A/**)	Today's women's health movement harkens back to witches' covens, and its opponents are the rhetorical descendents of those who hunted them. (+)
7. The corresponding rise of the male medical profession was subsidized by the ruling classes.	Powerful institutions seek to maintain power in the hands of those they deem worthy. (A/0)	The Inquisition was an early case of the "professional" repudiating the skills and interfering with the rights of the "nonprofessional" to minister to the poor. (+)
8. The charge of "witch-craft" came to cover a multitude of sins.	8.1 Female sexuality was a threat to men. (A/0)	Women were blamed for every sexual problem. (+)
	8.2 Women joining together for their mutual interest was a threat to men. (A/0)	Women were accused of being organized. (+)
	8.3 Any sort of women's power regarding health was a threat to men. (A/0)	Women were accused of both harming and healing. (+)

Because these values are so deeply ingrained in U.S. culture, students using them are bewildered (not to mention irritated) when instructors call attention to these warranting structures. The professor who responds to such a request with the faintly European assertion, "Excellence, not character, is rewarded here," comes across as a cultural alien.

Finally, the Toulmin approach equips the critic with a system that may explain why a given message failed to persuade. Like other critical tools, the Toulmin approach provides the critic with a technical language for describing rhetorical trends which cannot easily be described in lay language. So, for example, a message may fail because its Major Claims are too disparate (e.g., the rhetor rambles), because claims are offered without data (e.g., the rhetor rants), because Major Data are offered but not linked to any obvious claim (e.g., the rhetor becomes anecdotal), because there are no culturally available warrants for the data chosen (e.g., the rhetor seems irrelevant), or because the rhetor explicates warrants too insistently (e.g., the rhetor pontificates). Thus, the Toulmin system is one of the best available methods for explaining that curious brand of thinking/feeling known as human reasoning.

CONCLUSION

For many years, the study of reasoning was the sole province of the philosopher. Later, the children of philosophers, psychologists, began to explore the workings of the human mind. Whereas the philosopher treated ideas in their pure forms (which is to say, in their most abstract forms), the psychologist investigated what people felt when thinking about ideas. More recently, rhetorical critics have set out to discover how persuasive messages mediate human reasoning. Such critics have not become as abstract as the philosopher nor as individualistic as the psychologist. Instead, they have searched for evidence of *social reasoning* by looking "through" messages to the human beings producing and receiving them. In that sense, the study of public argument is the study of how minds meet.

This chapter has championed a psycho-logical model of argument, taking the position that reasoning is more than computing. This model purposively abandons the thinking/feeling dualism so often found in Western culture and the elitism found in technical or idealist models. It urges the critic to study the rules of *ordinary* reasoning, even if those rules spring from the humble advice found in everyday proverbs and folktales. It urges the critic to study the rhetoric of "peculiar" people because learning about strangers so often translates into genuine self-knowledge. It urges the critic to study the "intuitive validity" a message has for listeners, even if the listeners' standards for validity are not the critic's. Finally, it reminds the critic that reasoning is something that people do in their own marvelously complicated ways. May that ever be the case.

TIPS FOR THE PRACTICING CRITIC

1. Use the probes in this chapter as a checklist or starting point in examining the logic behind the messages we analyze.
2. Refer to Table 5.1 for examples of clarifying devices rhetors may use, and refer to the sample discussion of the work of Prinz, Patton, Hill, and Ehrenreich and English as a model. Try to show what overall effect is likely to result from this particular combination of elements. (Did the rhetor bring in lots of evidence from other sources? Did the rhetor rely mainly on extended examples to prove the point? What does this tell us about the response the rhetor desired from the audience?)
3. Use the three approaches presented here as guidelines and use them in conjunction with the other strategies for doing criticism presented in previous chapters. Just as no one persuasive technique will be appropriate for every situation, no one critical approach is appropriate for every message. Ideally, messages should be examined from several different angles before the critic settles on the most important perspective(s) from which to work. Take this as challenging rather than discouraging; it means that growth and increased flexibility as a critic is a lifetime learning process. We can learn something new about ourselves and the world with each message we examine; our potential need only be limited by our openness to new ideas and approaches.

Chapter 6

ANALYZING FORM

LEAR: Attend the lords of France and Burgundy, Gloucester.
GLOUCESTER: I shall, my liege. [Exeunt Gloucester and Edmund.]
LEAR: Meantime we shall express our darker purpose.
Give me the map there. Know that we have divided
In three our kingdom: and 'tis our fast intent
To shake all cares and business from our age;
Conferring them on younger strengths, while we
Unburthen'd crawl toward death. Our son of Cornwall,
And you, our no less loving son of Albany,
We have this hour a constant will to publish
Our daughters' several dowers, that future strife
May be prevented now. The princes, France and Burgundy,
Great rivals in our youngest daughter's love,
Long in our court have made their amorous sojourn,
And here are to be answer'd. Tell me, my daughters,
(Since now we will divest us, both of rule,
Interest of territory, cares of state),
Which of you shall we say doth love us most?
That we our largest bounty may extend
Where nature doth merit challenge. Goneril,
Our eldest-born, speak first.
GONERIL: Sir, I love you more than words can wield the matter;
Dearer than eye-sight, space, and liberty;
Beyond what can be valued, rich or rare;
No less than life, with grace, health, beauty, honour;
As much as child e'er loved, or father found;

            A love that makes breath poor, and speech unable;
            Beyond all manner of "so much" I love you.

CORDELIA: [Aside] What shall Cordelia do? Love, and be silent.

LEAR: Of all these bounds, even from this line to this,
            With shadowy forests and with champains rich'd,
            With plenteous rivers and wide-skirted meads,
            We make thee lady: to thine and Albany's issue
            Be this perpetual. What says our second daughter,
            Our dearest Regan, wife to Cornwall? Speak.

REGAN: Sir, I am made
            Of the self-same metal that my sister is,
            And prize me at her worth. In my true heart
            I find she names my very deed of love;
            Only she comes too short: that I profess
            Myself as enemy to all other joys,
            Which the most precious square of sense possesses;
            And find I am alone felicitate
            In your dear Highness' love.

CORDELIA: [Aside] Then poor Cordelia! And yet not so;
            since, I am sure, my love's
            More richer than my tongue.

LEAR: To thee and thine, hereditary ever,
            Remain this ample third of our fair kingdom;
            No less in space, validity, and pleasure,
            Than that conferr'd on Goneril. Now, our joy,
            Although the last, not least; to whose young love
            The vines of France and milk of Burgundy
            Strive to be interess'd; what can you say to draw
            A third more opulent than your sisters? Speak.

CORDELIA: Nothing, my lord.

LEAR: Nothing.

CORDELIA: Nothing.

LEAR: Nothing will come of nothing: speak again.

CORDELIA: Unhappy that I am, I cannot heave
            My heart into my mouth: I love your majesty
            According to my bond; nor more nor less.

LEAR: How, how, Cordelia! mend your speech a little,
            Lest it may mar your fortunes.

CORDELIA: Good my lord,
            You have begot me, bred me, loved me: I
            Return those duties back as are right fit,
            Obey you, love you, and most honour you.
            Why have my sisters husbands, if they say
            They love you all? Haply, when I shall wed,
            That lord whose hand must take my plight shall carry
            Half my love with him, half my care and duty:
            Sure, I shall never marry like my sisters,
            To love my father all.

> LEAR: But goest thy heart with this?
> CORDELIA: Ay, good my lord.
> LEAR: So young, and so untender?
> CORDELIA: So young, my lord, and true.
> LEAR: Let it be so; thy truth, then, be thy dower . . .
>   [Shakespeare, 1603:983–4]

"Thy truth, then, be thy dower." Not a happy epitaph for a would-be heiress. And not a very rhetorical epitaph either. Young Cordelia, faithful daughter of her aging and self-indulgent father, need only have uttered sweet nothings to inherit a kingdom. Cordelia's sisters, Goneril and Regan, surely had no trouble meeting Lear's challenge. They understood the speech-act implicitly: Tell him you love him and make him forget that he forced you to say so. When in human history have such riches hung upon the mere saying of a speech?

And Lear was hardly choosy here. Were he our contemporary, the lyrics to any Top 40 love ballad would have sufficed. So what's wrong, Cordelia? Why not "mend your speech" for a moment? Why let your audience confuse your integrity with a lack of tenderness? Why get philosophical when the situation so clearly invites you to be mercenary?

Cordelia's defense of her actions is hardly compelling. She pleads lack of rhetorical competence: a love "richer than her tongue." She stands on personal principle: an unwillingness to "heave her heart into her mouth." But Cordelia's outrage seems even more basic: She resents using a standard rhetorical form to show unstandard love of a parent. She resents being trooped across Lear's stage, the third in a line of singing princesses, forced to mimic speech that is neither exalted nor subtle. Cordelia was not unloving nor was she unwilling to discuss her love. Rather, she felt that love has its own timetable and that it is diminished when employed suddenly and unfeelingly. Above all, Cordelia resents the formulas of love, formulas repeated daily to her father by courtiers, formulas her sisters have turned into parodies of devotion. In rejecting these formulas, Cordelia became less a persuader than a critic. Sadly, critics almost never please kings.

This chapter discusses forms and formulas. It is concerned with three things. First is **structure**—the apportionment and sequencing of message elements. Structural decisions are decisions about which ideas should be given what amount of attention and how ideas should be arranged for maximum impact. So, for example, an important structural feature of Cordelia's speech is the balance she strikes between discussions of her love for her father and the love she someday expects to have for a husband. This equivalence made little sense: Lear was clearly not interested in sharing the rhetorical spotlight, especially not with a nonexistent son-in-law. Cordelia's sisters, on the other hand, were highly conventional. Their rhetoric placed Lear on stage by himself. They did not confuse their father, covering less ground in their speeches but with greater impact. Cordelia's rhetorical ambition, in contrast, prompted only scorn.

This chapter is also concerned with **form**—the patterns of meaning audiences generate when they take in a message. Form refers to the "shape" of meaning, how ideas are linked together by audiences. Some ideas (e.g., inflationary spirals) sit in an audience's mind alone and unloved, associated only with abstruse economic principles, boring political editorials, and a vague sense of unpleasantness. Other ideas (say, a county fair) instantly generate a host of associations: cotton candy, Ferris wheels, games of chance, the Fun House, popcorn, prize-winning livestock, and memories of childhood. Thinking of a county fair fills up the mind in ways that inflationary spirals cannot. If it has been a long time since our last fair, the smells of food and animals will immediately help to "fill out" our mental form, making us properly anticipatory as fair-goers.

Implicitly knowing such things, Goneril tells Lear that her love surpasses those things her father already prizes ("eye-sight, space, and liberty"). Her speech asks Lear to think of life's most precious qualities ("grace, health, beauty, honour") and then to round out this mental picture by adding her love to the concoction. Cordelia, in contrast, runs competition with herself, asking her father to ponder her affection in the company of such unpleasant things as contracts ("I return those duties back as are right fit") and jealousy ("that lord whose hand must take my plight"). Law, envy, and love—hardly a comfortable mixture of ideas for a defensive old man.

Finally, this chapter treats **genre**—a class of messages sharing important structural and content features and which, as a class, creates special expectations in an audience. Genres exist because rhetors are imitative, borrowing from yesterday when deciding what to say today. Genres like the political commercial on television and the gold-watch speech at the retirement dinner develop because people's life experiences are so similar: They are born, they grow up, they fall in love, and they die. They always have, and they always have needed to speak of these experiences, resulting in pink and blue birth announcements, motivational commencement addresses, marriage proposals under the stars, and moving funeral orations. Each of these messages echoes its forebears, at least in part.

Naturally, history can be a tyrant. Utilizing the formulas of rhetoric requires a Faustian bargain: guaranteed social acceptability in exchange for independence of thought. Lear's daughter, Regan, opted for this deal, drawing upon a rich tradition of courtly love ("I profess myself an enemy to all other joys"), thereby anticipating her father's anticipations. Cordelia, in contrast, intentionally violated the generic rules. She combined biology ("you begot me") with sociology ([you] bred me") and delivered herself of a dispassionate, intellectually balanced college lecture. Good genre. Wrong audience.

This chapter probes how message structure interacts with expected patterns of meaning (form) to produce persuasion. Structure and form are a complex business, but examining rule following and rule violating is almost always profitable. This chapter's thesis is that by knowing who follows rhetorical rules and who does not, the critic can learn much about the whys and wherefores of these rules. Perhaps this is why Shakespeare opened his great tragedy with the generic struggle presented above. Perhaps he sensed that an important moral lesson could be taught by depicting who used rhetoric and who was used by it. With Shakespeare as our first teacher, then, let us become better students of structure and form.

STRUCTURE AND FORM IN RHETORIC

The key distinction between structure and form is this: Structure is something that rhetors do and form is something that audiences do. Structures are identifiable in artifacts; forms emerge in audience's minds. Figure 6.1 provides a clear, albeit elementary, example of this distinction. If asked the question "Which picture has the *clearest* meaning?" most people would pick Figure 6.1A. If then asked "Which picture has *special* meaning?" the same answer would be given. Figure 6.1A symbolizes the United States of America. Versions of it have been planted on the moon, on a statue of Saddam Hussein, on Olympic team jackets, on car antennae, and on the coffins of heroes in Arlington National Cemetery. Figure 6.1A has also been worn on the backsides of student protestors in the 1970s, burned in the streets of Baghdad in the 1980s,

FIGURE 6.1 Relationships between Content and Structure

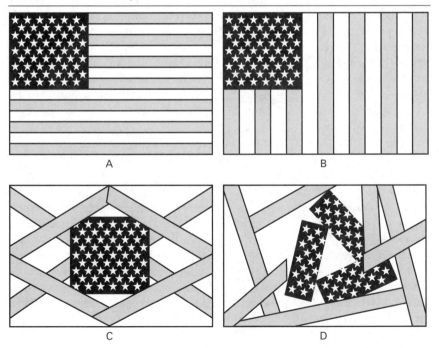

and displayed during Fourth of July automobile sales for decades. Figure 6.1A inspires many, infuriates others. It is drenched in meaning.

But Figures 6.1B, C, and D show that Figure 6.1A's content is not exceptional. Figure 6.1A is merely a special arrangement of iconic characters: stars, bars, and backgrounds. Its meaning, the form it takes in the perceiver's mind, is heavily dependent upon its basic *structural* elements. Even a slight rearrangement of these elements (Figure 6.1B) changes the evocative power of the symbol completely. A more ambitious rearrangement (Figure 6.1C) removes virtually all of its "Americanicity." While Figure 6.1C possesses a certain raciness not present in Old Glory, it is still unlikely to draw a salute.

Figure 6.1D seems so distorted as to be sacrilegious. It takes perceptual gymnastics to see that its content is identical to that of Figure 6.1A. Upon viewing it, schoolchildren would wonder and patriots would quake, both assuming that there is only one "right" way to assemble such elements. They would resist *any* arbitrary arrangement of these features, sensing that even the slightest variation on the "true" optical theme would steal its formal meaning. When it comes to Figure 6.1A, most Americans are visual fundamentalists.

Figure 6.1 teaches an important lesson: Structure and content cannot be separated easily. As we moved from Figure 6.1A to Figure 6.1D, the contents of the messages became increasingly radical. *Only* Figure 6.1A is acceptable if conventional meanings are to be shared. Figure 6.1D therefore meant nothing to us. We were incapable of forming its elements into something sensible, never mind into something important, never mind into something motivating. That is, certain message structures arouse particularized expectations within perceivers, who are often unwilling to change those expectations—or forms—once they have been aroused (e.g., once stars and bars have been presented in the same visual field). Thus, formulating rhetoric involves selecting and arranging message elements and predicting how audiences will react to these elements additively. As Arnold [1974:137] notes, audiences *will* generate forms in their heads constantly. The rhetor uses structural devices to guide this process of forming.

The centrality of structure to content is best seen when structure is missing (as in Figure 6.1D) or misappropriated. For example, if a preacher somehow forgot to ask the bride and groom to exchange vows during a wedding, the event would not be "formed" as a proper ceremony by those in the church pews. Upon first noticing the omission, the wedding guests might well treat the experience as a novelty, as a preacher's ritualistic experiment. As the ceremony progressed, they would try to re-form this newly evolving reality into traditional meanings ("perhaps the vows will be exchanged just before the recessional"). Normally, a rhetor would help relieve such ambiguities by giving the audience clues on how to interpret these unexpected and discordant data. Should the rhetor fail to do so, audiences will take over the task themselves: "Poor Pastor Inqvist has become addle-brained" or "maybe Kelly and Dan are putting us all on."

Critics have often treated structure formalistically by applying a set of prescriptive laws to message organization. Research by Douglass and Arnold [1970], however, shows that few real-life messages fit these standard patterns. A more promising line of inquiry, they suggest, is to treat structure as a psychological, not as a linguistic, process, and to examine an artifact not as a set of self-contained statements but as a *stimulus to reasoning* for audiences. They warn critics that while structure can be found in messages, the more important element, form, is found in audiences' reactions to these structures.

So, for example, Douglass and Arnold urge critics to search for the kinds of "organizational help" a rhetor provides and for the inferences audiences are likely to draw as a result. By asking which ideas were emphasized and which were not, which came first and which last, which were interrupted and which were not, a critic begins to learn what audiences "did" with the rhetorical materials they were asked to process. Thus, a rhetor who tells a pointless, long-winded story or relates facts in reverse chronological order is likely to frustrate audiences' forming instincts. Ideally, then, a critic looks through message to audience, through structure to form, to find potential rhetorical effect.

A useful way of examining message structure is to question how rhetorical materials have been arranged in a given case. The following critical probes deal with **message design** (the use of standard structural devices), **message emphasis** (the comparative treatment of individual ideas), **message density** (the depth of coverage of individual ideas), and **message pacing** (the distribution of ideas through time). In each case, the critic looks for the effects message patterns have within audiences. The first of these probes has to do with message design:

Does the rhetor use an *identifiable* traditional message structure? Is this approach used throughout or only from time to time?

Here, the critic inspects a text's overall architecture to see whether it conforms to a classic pattern of message structure. Table 6.1 presents those patterns, although we emphasize that only rarely will textbook examples of these patterns appear in real-life persuasion (since rhetors often take shortcuts). Also, merely identifying these patterns is of little use unless they can also shed light on the overall rhetorical situation being studied. Since message structure relates so closely to how people think, it can tell much about a rhetor's mental habits or an audience's operating hierarchy of beliefs.

Structural cues are suggestive because people often do not think about *how* they will present ideas but only about what they will say. Thus, asking why a rhetor's first argument came first and not last forces the critic to explain what nonarbitrary logic the rhetor used when making the always-arbitrary ordering decisions. And the fact that these decisions never *seem* arbitrary to a rhetor adds to their capacity to shed light on unstated intellectual and cultural premises.

Some of our earlier messages show the importance of message design. Harold Hill, for example, used a Causal Sequence to prove that every local sin

TABLE 6.1 Common Structural Techniques in Persuasion*

Structural Type	Rhetorical Function	Example (State Legislative Debate)	Main Advantages	Main Disadvantages	◇ ? Critical Probe
Chronological sequence	Places time relationships in the foreground so that narrative becomes clear	"In the 1970s, we tried a sales tax and that proved inadequate. We moved to sin taxes in the '80s. The '90s require something new: a tax on professional services."	Builds suspense as the past unfolds into the present (or future)	Propositions the rhetor is advocating can become subordinated to the telling of the "story"	What appears to be the rhetor's rationale for discussing the particular points in time chosen for discussion?
Spatial sequence	Shows relationships between parts and parts or between parts and wholes	"The opportunities in this state are enormous. The lake area has tourist development. The tri-city area is luring high-tech industry. And the plateau region has the new Space Command Center."	Makes ideas "visual" for audiences	Too much detail may cloud the ideas being advanced	What devices did the rhetor use to demonstrate the "adjacency" of the elements described?
Ascending/descending sequence	Ideas are arranged according to their relative importance, familiarity, or complexity	"I agree with Senator Davenport that cable regulation must be at least considered this session. And I agree with Senator Foley that the open-meeting law is important. But we can't even think about those things until we agree on funding basic state services."	Gives a sense of precision by emphasizing the relationship of one concept to another	Once begun, the sequence must be completed, with all necessary stages being discussed	What specific strategic advantage is the rhetor hoping for by emphasizing climaxes or anticlimaxes?
Causal sequence	Links observable effects to underlying factors allegedly responsible for those effects	"Ladies and gentlemen of the legislature, I ask you to reflect on industrial development in this state. What's responsible for our growth in that area? I'll tell you what: a superior educational system. Let's never forget that."	Western audiences particularly appreciate causal structures	Audiences have been taught to distrust *simple* cause-effect linkages	What steps did the rhetor take to guard the *credibility* of the causal attributions made?

Problem-solution sequence	Appropriate courses of action are endorsed on the basis of their capacity to remedy problems	"You and I both know that we need a revenue bill that's at least three things: timely, fair, and adequate. That's what my plan is about."	Builds on the common psychological need within people to overcome difficulties	If audiences are unconvinced of the seriousness of the problem, boredom results	Did the rhetor spend the most time emphasizing problems or were solutions primarily stressed?
Withheld-proposal sequence	Favorable materials are piled up and the rhetor's solution mentioned only briefly at the end	"Let's reflect for a moment on what the park system has done for this state. It's the best run system in the nation and it adds four hundred million dollars a year in tourist revenue to our budget each year. Let's keep all of that in mind when we discuss funding for the parks this year."	An ostensibly "innocent" approach and therefore especially useful for a hostile audience	Highly dependent for effectiveness on the speaker's knowledge of what the audience currently knows and feels	Does the rhetor make the *transition* from general to "preferred" material gracefully and nonmanipulatively?
Open-proposal sequence	Direct, deductive presentation of a proposal followed by support for that proposal	"You people have already heard the conservative approach to doing things. Tonight I'm going to give you another perspective. We need to raise taxes immediately. Here's why."	A simple and clear sequence that appears "forthright" as a result	Can be boring for audiences if they feel that they have "heard it all before"	How does the rhetor compensate for the lack of suspense such an approach entails?
Reflective sequence	A variation on the problem-solution sequence in which the rhetor professes no particular preference for a solution	"Quite frankly, I'm not sure how to proceed at this point in the debate. State revenues have never been lower and welfare needs have never been higher. The problems are obvious. But what are the solutions?"	Sets up an "exploratory" mood by involving audience directly in problem-solving	Can be seen as manipulative if the rhetor suddenly opts for a particular solution	Does the rhetor maintain a sense of *mutual* problem-solving by actively considering all possible alternatives?

(continued)

TABLE 6.1 (continued)

Structural Type	Rhetorical Function	Example (State Legislative Debate)	Main Advantages	Main Disadvantages	? Critical Probe
Elimination sequence	A solution-oriented approach in which all but one remedy is successively eliminated by the rhetor	"So we've looked at five different options this morning and found each of them wanting. What choice do we have other than to adopt the Harris plan forthwith?"	Highly useful when the audience readily acknowledges the relevance and importance of the problem	Can be seen as manipulative of the rhetor seems to be using a straw figure argument	What does the rhetor do to guard against audience's *impatience* with such a lockstep structure?
Motivational sequence	Rhetor follows a fixed pattern of attention, need, satisfaction, visualization, and action	"Ten thousand. That's the number of state-funded abortions performed last year. Without more money, pretty soon only rich women will be able to afford abortions and the welfare rolls will swell. We simply must pass H.B. 21 and we must do it *today*."	Parallels what is thought to be a universally attractive and psychologically "whole" sequence of thought	A fairly vague series of steps that are not always easily distinguished from one another	How much time does the speaker spend on each "stage" of the sequence, and were such allocations of time justified?
Topical sequence	Breaks a subject matter into several equivalent subparts and then treats them in somewhat arbitrary order	"This has been a really productive legislative session. We've solved the budget crisis; we've tackled deregulation; and we've begun the Industrial Development Commission. I congratulate each and every one of you on a job well done."	Perhaps the simplest method available of organizing a message	Rhetors are often seduced into giving equivalent treatment to subtopics that do not merit equivalent treatment	Is there a strategically sound *ordering* to the subtopics selected for treatment by the rhetor?

*Adapted from Arnold [1974].

could be attributed to the goings-on in the pool hall. Later, Hill would present a second speech ("Seventy-six Trombones") which functioned as the conclusion to his overarching Problem-Solution strategy.

Perhaps the most interesting thing about Hill's structure is its purity. His speeches emerge in the play as set pieces, unadulterated examples of classic rhetorical design. The unerring way in which they unfold is the playwright's tip that Hill is up to no good. These structures are so pure, so self-propelling, that the theatre audience becomes enthralled with Hill-the-strategist and, at the same time, begins to feel slightly superior to him. This sense of superiority is important since if the audience could not readily discern Hill's manipulations, they would be unable to appreciate his eventual reconstruction. Thus, Hill uses the sin-then-salvation motif to perfection which, in turn, stands as evidence of his imperfection.

Things are more disorderly in real life. George Patton, for example, rambled when speaking, moving from discussion of a winning spirit, to the availability of superior equipment, to the psychology of combat, to the need for toughness, and finally to the immortality of bravery. Such a Topical structure has its advantages. Rambling gives the audience the sense that they are admitted into the rhetor's unconscious; it allows Patton to become human, even though he almost never refers to himself in the speech. Similarly, his transitions are no more elaborate than the word "now." These brief punctuations signal to the audience that something else has just occurred to Patton and that he might as well get that off his chest too. This sort of lazy structure also signals the novelty of Patton's situation: a hastily called speech by a busy general who just happened to be in the area and had no time to prepare a formal message.

This was hardly Rabbi Prinz's case, whose brief remarks were well scripted to fit into the overall scene of the March on Washington. Prinz generally followed a Chronological pattern (yesterday's Jewish ghettos, today's black ghettos, tomorrow's ghettoless America), although he is not compulsive about it. Ceremonial situations normally demand a conventional structure, which is perhaps why so many have cursed so mightily when watching the Academy Awards show each year. (Gushing nonsequiturs are occasionally charming but more often irritating.) Prinz's use of the past in service of the future was therefore sensible given his role (teacher) and status (elder). Anything more experimental on his part might have seemed out of character.

Ehrenreich and English were hardly ceremonial. Although their rhetoric was potentially motivational, they did not use the Motivational sequence. Not surprising in a broad-ranging historical analysis, they relied mostly on Chronological and Topical patterns. They used Causal and Problem-Solution structures to demonstrate the ways into and out of women's current dilemma, and Spatial sequences to illustrate how women fit into the system. They used the Open-Proposal approach ("Here's what future feminist research must do") and the Descending sequence to illustrate how the general principle of women's exclusion was enacted in the life of one woman in Paris in 1322. No Withheld proposals, no Elimination or Reflective sequences. Ehrenreich and

English aren't pretending to consider multiple options. As a result, *Witches, Midwives, and Nurses* appears straightforward. Each of its arguments and structures is designed to hammer away at the same basic points: (1) Women have been forcefully excluded from healing professions for centuries; and (2) We must halt the practices that perpetuate this shameful status quo.

A general inspection of a message's design features is useful for the overall questions it raises. Critics can also ask more specific critical probes, some of which have to deal with message emphasis:

- How rigidly does the rhetor adhere to the *topic-proper*? Does the rhetor roam widely from subject to subject or is the message highly constricted in content? Why?
- Are a great many arguments presented in scattergun fashion or just a few arguments *developed* in depth? Are interconnections of evidence and arguments clarified via previews, transitions and internal and concluding summaries? Why?
- Does an idea's *context* give it special importance or appeal? Do the statements made just before or after an idea make it more or less likely that it will be understood and accepted?

The first two sets of questions urge the critic to examine how tightly, or formally, the rhetor developed his or her case. Such inquiries help the critic examine the crucial matter of rhetorical tone. We know, for example, that an appealing thing about informal conversations is that they proceed at their own pace, with each new topic needing only a marginal relationship to the foregoing topic. At times, we prefer unstructured dialogue, which is perhaps what makes "talk radio" attractive. At other times—in a legal contract, newspaper editorial, or performance appraisal—only clear, and clearly coordinated, arguments are tolerated.

Naturally one ought not take a purist's approach to message structure since much real-life discourse does not slavishly utilize standard organizational patterns. Jamieson [1988a] extended this argument when documenting the growing disuse of formal argument during political exchanges on television. She claimed that the structural rules of everyday conversation (be interesting, be relevant, be anecdotal) best matched the structural patterns of televised speechmaking. Jamieson further claimed that because of television, traditionally "masculine" speech patterns (emphasizing classic structures) were giving way to the traditionally "feminine" qualities of personalization, ornamentation, and casual organization.

And the structure of ordinary conversation is subject to cultural pressures, as well. In Madagascar, for example, the traditional oratorical style of *kabary* "is based on the unhurried telling of ancestral proverbs, metaphors, and riddles, frequently in a dialogue using call and response" ["In *kabary*," 2002:1]. Required in ritual and often used in conversation, *kabary* emphasizes word play, with no more than 20 percent of an oration being "to the point." As singer Hanitravio Rasoanaivo says, "We are about circular movement. We are about our ancestors and their words of wisdom. We are about harmony. . . . Basically . . . we are about taking it slow" [p. 1]. And *kabary*, it turns out, is threatened by cell phone use: Speakers who do not get to the point pay extra. But speakers who get to the point quickly repudiate their cultural heritage and risk offending their conversational partners.

In a sense, both *kabary* and cell phone etiquette reinforce the point made earlier: Structure argues. They differ as to what typical cell phone conversational structure says (I'm a busy modern person looking toward the future? I'm an inconsiderate ignoramus who sees my culture as disposable?), but in both cases they show the effects produced when a message appears in one context rather than another.

- Which points are *emphasized* and which given short shrift? Does the rhetor cover the waterfront of ideas or home-in on just a few? Do these decisions expose the persuasive obstacles being faced?
- How much time is spent on the introduction of *novel* information, as opposed to recasting the familiar? Does this known/unknown ratio reveal anything important about the rhetorical situation?

These two questions relate to message density, the extent to which individual ideas are allowed to predominate in a given text. As mentioned in Chapter 1, rhetoric is often an attempt to spotlight certain ideas or to push other ideas backstage. So, for example, when partners begin househunting, they become locked in an ideational struggle with the realtor (knowingly or not). The realtor's job is to highlight the built-in curio cabinet and the hardwood floors while deflecting attention from the price of the home and the cracks in the sheetrock.

Naturally, the realtor will continually justify this rhetorical coverage during the home tour, so wary consumers must know not only their price but their topic as well. As long as the purchasing decision hinges on hardwood floors versus carpeting, the realtor is equally advantaged. And so an important rhetorical principle suggests itself: **Whoever controls the shape of the discussion controls its consequence as well.**

In confrontational situations, topical emphasis becomes especially important as the disputants try to elbow aside their rivals' topics. This is true in court where the lawyer for the defense uses the grounds of direct relevance to keep the toxicologist from testifying. It is also true in cultural critique. In an editorial in the magazine *Bitch: Feminist Response to Pop Culture*, Marisa Meltzer [2002] argues that fat suits are Hollywood's contemporary version of blackface. In her hometown San Francisco, where audiences are "notoriously politically correct," Meltzer notes that racist and sexist images in film trailers get routinely hissed at [p. 19]. But a preview for *Shallow Hal*, starring Jack Black, Gwyneth Paltrow, and a fat suit, drew no hisses, to Meltzer's dismay. *Shallow Hal* ostensibly showed the virtues of men looking to women's "inner beauty" rather than their outward appearance. But Meltzer chose to look elsewhere, and directed her readers' attention likewise. She noticed that ordinary activities are treated as hilarious cinema when artificially fat actors perform them. "With a real fat woman in the lead, the movie wouldn't be funny—it would just be uncomfortable" [p. 20]. Meltzer cites no fewer than 10 recent fat-suit-inhabitants, concluding that this formula for comedy is based "not [on] the latex suit's physical fakeness but [on] the ephemeral nature of the thin actor posing as fat. We all know that Julia, Goldie, and Gwyneth (and Martin, Mike, and Eddie) will return to their slender glory for the next part, and that's comforting—because otherwise we would have to confront the mean-spiritedness behind our giggles" [p. 20]. While her editorial could not single-handedly change the shape of Hollywood film (how many producers subscribe to *Bitch* magazine?), it does invite readers to inspect this last remaining sanctioned prejudice, to look where filmmakers would not have us look. Particularly interesting is how Meltzer justified the topical shift: She reached for overarching themes of compassion rather than competition, acceptance rather than pity. She did not let others set her rhetorical agenda.

- What is newsworthy about the *sequence* of arguments? Do first-saids and last-saids reveal anything important about the rhetor's rhetorical circumstances? What would have happened had the arguments been reversed?
- Does the rhetor alternate the *mood* of the message? Is one feature (e.g., narration, verbal intensity, itemized lists, rhetorical questions) dominant in certain portions of the message and absent in others, thereby creating peaks and valleys of rhetorical pressure on the audience?
- Does the *beginning* of the message anchor later ideas and arguments? Does the rhetor begin as if the audience already possessed common feelings on the subject, or try to disabuse the audience of current values and beliefs?
- When, if at all, are unusually *controversial* or *complex* ideas introduced in the message? Early, middle, late, never? What sort of material precedes or follows such potentially troublesome segments?

Message pacing is another important structural matter. It is concerned with *when* in time ideas are presented. Order effects are especially important in oral persuasion, because listeners (unlike readers) cannot "turn back the pages" when they miss something. For years, researchers tried to determine the most influential sequence of arguments. By using the same arguments but by varying their order for different audiences, these researchers determined that familiar ideas should be placed before unfamiliar ideas, that an attention/stress/solution pattern is especially effective, that first and last ideas are remembered better than those in the middle, that a Withheld-Proposal sequence may backfire with hostile audiences, and so on [see, for example, Bettinghaus and Cody, 1994].

But such studies offer limited generalizability; they rarely help the critic understand the nuances of a particular message. Typically, it is more useful to examine a given sequence of arguments, tracing how that rhetor approached that unique set of rhetorical problems.

An example of the importance of message pacing was the U.S. Army's pamphlet *Eleven Point Checklist for Job Hunters.* The checklist began with the statement "If you are a young man about to graduate from high school, you certainly want the best possible job you can find. To help you in accomplishing this task, we have prepared a checklist for your use. We sincerely wish you the best of luck." Having thus offered its services as guidance counselor, the Army proceeds through its checklist: (1) Pay; (2) Vacations; (3) Education; (4) Allowances; (5) Leisure time; (6) Medical care; (7) Marketing [i.e., shopping]; (8) Retirement; (9) Travel; (10) Bonuses; (11) Training.

Each point on the checklist had specific advice for the job hunter (e.g., "Travel—Your employer should agree to relocate you at your request anywhere in the U.S. or Free World at his expense. If married, this includes your family.") At the bottom of the page the audience was invited to use the checklist when weighing job offers, and then left with the preferred suggestion: "Better yet, don't waste your time, see your Army Representative today."

Several items are of structural interest here. For one thing, no item on the checklist asked the job-hunter to consider the *kind of work* he would be doing. Apparently, soldiers' day-to-day activities were not attractive enough to merit even a twelfth position on the hierarchy. And the checklist is indeed a hierarchy, with four of the first five elements relating to either money or time off. While Education is placed in third position, no details are given. In contrast, the benefits associated with most other items are amply provided: 30 days PAID vacation, a $10,000 bonus to stay more than three years, etc.

Given the age of the target audience, the authors were wise to drop Retirement to the bottom of the list with Training. Two other items at the bottom, Travel and Bonuses, are essentially restatements of Vacations and Pay and are thus filler material. Also, at no point in the sequence is the reader more than one item away from a monetary argument. The organizational pattern is thus carefully adapted to the Army's perpetual target audience: America's underprivileged. Financial opportunity reaches out from beginning to end in this message.

A number of critics have examined the effects of structural devices on persuasion. Gerland [1994], for example, did an interesting study of the first Rodney King trial in Los Angeles, the trial that resulted in the acquittal of the police officers who beat Mr. King (the acquittal was later overturned by another jury). The extraordinary thing about the first trial, according to Gerland, was that the acquittals were granted even though the jury was provided with *irrevocable visual evidence* of the beatings (via videotape). Brilliantly, however, the *lawyers for the defense* showed the jury the videotape (1) endlessly and (2) interruptedly. The former technique ultimately dulled jurors to its sensationalistic nature (we stimulus-seeking humans bore easily) while the latter technique prevented jurors from "forming" the beating as a single, coherent *statement.* In other words, the King beating became—visually—both deadening and confusing. Neither quality argues well.

Pacing and emphasis are especially important in social movement rhetoric, which, by definition, proceeds sequentially through time so as to alter beliefs and attitudes. Darsey [1991], for example, compared the rhetoric of the early gay rights movement (1948–1977) to that of its more recent manifestations (1978–1990). Intriguingly, he found that the early rhetoric focused on building the self-identity of gay members ("we're gay and we're o.k.") while the latter phase abandoned that emphasis entirely, presumably because self-esteem issues were no longer as prominent for this by now powerful minority group. In its place, however, came arguments focusing on personal security. Ironically, because gays *had* been successful in commanding public attention and securing important political gains, this increased visibility often endangered them. Clearly, political success can exact a price. Estimating that price was Darsey's job; his *structural* perceptions of the movement informed him most usefully.

GENERIC STUDIES OF FORM

As defined earlier, *a genre is a class of messages having important structural and content similarities and which, as a class, creates special expectations in an audience.* Inaugural addresses, then, constitute a genre because they share textual features and are delivered in similar circumstances every four years. Thus, when he first spoke as president, George W. Bush did not sound exactly like Ronald Reagan or Harry Truman but he did not sound completely unlike them either. Mr. Bush spoke in a 2001 sort of way because he spoke to 2001 sorts of people. But 2001 Americans were still Americans; while curious about new possibilities they were also attracted to old realities. So, when writing his inaugural address, Bush had help—the help of the ages—whether he wanted it or not. Because he was part of an historical process, he labored under generic constraints.

Generic study is the study of such constraints. It describes patterns of discourse and explains their recurrence, asking questions like these: **Why does this text seem more rule-governed than another? Why are these rules operating here rather than other rules? What happens if these rules are violated? Why do people care about rules at all?** The generic critic seeks structural and content similarities and then tries to explain them. The generic critic is therefore something like the entomologist who traces the regularities, and interesting irregularities, found in the natural world. But tucking all of life's messages into their own generic beds is hardly worthwhile if it results in nothing more than taxonomical fascination. Rather, it is *the story behind the taxonomies,* the general ideas about the natural condition, that intrigues both the entomologist and the generic critic.

Thus, when doing criticism, the generic critic operates on the following assumptions:

1. *Generic patterns necessarily develop.* Black [1992:97 ff.] demonstrates that there are a limited number of rhetorical situations and a limited number of ways of responding to these standard situations. As a result, messages form identifiable clusters over time. So, for example, when he invented the inau-

gural address, George Washington could not know that subsequent inaugurals would resemble his. But he might have guessed it, because the thoughts and feelings of a culture, if it is a culture, will be similar from age to age. Whoever addresses such people—in any era—must reckon with such constancy.

2. *Generic patterns reveal societal truths.* The generic critic examines message patterns in order to comment on the universal as manifested in the particular. Richardson [2000:611] notes that even political advertisements use the genres of popular culture because "genres are prepackaged bundles of theme, emotion, evidence, and experience—if not always action." The generic critic therefore looks for basic truths about people by examining the sometimes modest, often indistinct, trends that develop when they talk to one another. Thus, the "odd case," the text that breaks the pattern, will be of particular interest because it highlights the *rationale* behind the generic formula thereby exposed. So, if a new president fails to mention God in an inaugural address (something that has never been done), the resulting furor would call attention to the persistence of the special bond between religion and government in the United States.

3. *Knowledge of generic forces is largely implicit.* People can distinguish between a sincere and an insincere apology because they somehow understand the pure form known as "apology." Thus, when an unexpected text suddenly intrudes into a prime time show—"We interrupt this program for a special report from ABC News . . ."—viewers instinctively become alarmed even though it is hard to say precisely *why* they are alarmed or *how they know* it is time to be alarmed. The implicitness of such rules is important to the critic because the not-noticed throws light on people's first premises, beliefs so fundamental they are rarely called to conscious attention. The bulletin-within-the-show alarms viewers because it means their community has somehow been threatened, and so they sit up straighter in their chairs when hearing it. In doing so, they thereby honor their community in thought as well as action.

4. *Generic patterns stabilize social life.* Genres are conservative. They keep things in place. To speak in established ways by following the rules is to tip one's hat to the forces-that-be. For example, Murphy [1998] studied the genre of the presidential campaign history, noting its tendency to present an authoritarian reading of the election, and thus support the status quo. And we are constantly in generic training. The toddler expresses displeasure by wailing, the adolescent by sulking, but the young adult gradually learns to disagree without being disagreeable. Parents take delight in observing such maturity, in the child's growing ability to express emotion in generically sanctioned ways. Should that teenager someday become a U.S. representative, she would learn how to express contempt even more elegantly: "The honorable gentleman from Missouri must surely be mistaken." Formulas like this develop because society has decreed that talking is superior to fighting. So, even though generic formulas may appear arbitrary, careful inspection finds them perpetuating important, agreed-upon truths.

5. *Generic perceptions affect subsequent perceptions.* All critics are generic critics, whether they know it or not. That is, when approaching a text, critics bring preconceptions of generic types, comparing that text to the data bank of texts they have studied previously. Because there is no "semantic autonomy of texts," says Hirsch [1967:94], a critic's initial, categorizing judgment will color all subsequent judgments of that message. So a statement like "Tyrone, I'd like to talk to you" immediately starts the categorical search: Is this going to be a reprimand? Until that generic question is satisfactorily answered, Tyrone is unlikely to rest easy.

According to Rosenfield [1968], any message will look different alongside another message. A popular song's X-rated lyrics may seem shocking until the song is examined in the context of its genre, whereby one might conclude, "That's not unusual for hip-hop." It is also true that when viewed in isolation, any message can seem distinctive. But a careful dissection often shows that that text has borrowed some features from Category A and others from Category B when creating itself (for example, rap and hip-hop owe a great debt to street slang as well as to the blues). Finding such generic tracings in no way detracts from the brilliance of a given text. Nor does it detract from its individuality, which properly lies in the creativity of its borrowing, in the uniqueness of the rhetorical assemblage.

An interesting example of Rosenfield's observation occurred upon the death of former president Lyndon Johnson. Columnist Nicholas von Hoffman [1973:B1] penned a statement about the late president, a portion of which went like this:

> Ah, Lyndon, you're not cold yet and they're calling you great. That's what happens when one politician dies: The rest of them call him great, but, Lyndon, you deserve better than patriotic hagiography. You were better than the eulogistic junk they're saying at the memorial services.
>
> Lyndon, you got your teeth into us and we got our teeth into you. Those five years of you in the White House were a barroom brawl, and, just four years ago almost to the day, when we staggered out of the saloon, dusty and bloody, we didn't hate you anymore. We understood better how you got us into Vietnam than how Nixon got us out and we liked you more, you cussed, cussing bullheaded, impossible, roaring, wild coot.
>
> You had your credibility gaps and your silent sullennesses, but we read you. Oh, man, Lyndon, did we know you! You were the best and the worst of ourselves, the personification of our national deliriums. You were always so completely, so absolutely you. Kennedy had Pablo Casals to play for him, Nixon's got Pat Boone to pray for him, but you, Lyndon, you had Country Joe and the Fish singing songs soaked in four-letter words at you. . . .

Upon first reading von Hoffman's column, most will notice its irreverence. A more careful analysis shows that, despite its color, the editorial is also a fairly standard eulogy. Naturally, von Hoffman operates on the fringes of that genre here but he is still well within its bounds. Eulogies place one person on stage exclusively. Von Hoffman does that. Eulogies isolate the distinctive features of the deceased. Von Hoffman clearly does that. Eulogies make the dearly departed seem dearer by reframing his deficiencies and less departed by recalling his personality. Von Hoffman does both. And eulogies tell a selective history and project a diminished future because of the dead person's passing. Von Hoffman does those things as well.

Naturally, this is not a pure eulogy. Had he been asked to speak at the graveside service in the presence of President Johnson's widow, von Hoffman would have been more restrained. Equally, however, von Hoffman shows us that the eulogy and the editorial are not uncordial to one another and that his column cannot be appreciated without understanding both of its generic parents.

Rhetorical studies show that genres perform a number of important functions. For one thing, genres are *preservative;* they keep established social patterns viable. Von Hoffman, for example, did not have total license when he wrote since Lyndon Johnson was a president (and hence part of an institution) and because Johnson was dead (and hence defenseless). Similarly, Battles and Hilton-Morrow [2002] studied the popular television program featuring best friends *Will & Grace,* a gay man and straight woman. Battles and Hilton-Morrow concluded that despite the show's acclaimed advances in presenting positive gay characters, its status as a situation comedy prevents it from breaking much new ground. *Will & Grace,* they argued, relies on standard sitcom conventions such as the quasi-romantic pairing of Will and Grace and the equation of homosexuality with a lack of masculinity. This rhetorical complexity shows how the new always carries tracings of the old.

Other studies show that generic alterations proceed slowly. Projansky [2001] examined media portrayals of rape, noting that films such as *Gone with the Wind* [1939] present rape as a natural result of women's vulnerability and independence. However, toward the end of the century with the emergence of postfeminism (which posits feminism as no longer necessary), many contemporary rape narratives granted women more power, but with an unhelpful twist: They presented women, rather than society as a whole, as primarily responsible for rape prevention.

Another important feature is that genres suggest verbal *possibilities.* Because he had heard many eulogies before writing his, Nick von Hoffman did not have to start from scratch. His generic knowledge let him benefit from established patterns that had worked well previously. Analogously, Delgado [1998] showed how Chicano rap artists have borrowed and adapted the genre from African American practitioners because of its possibilities for making nationalist and critical commentary from the margins of society. And Pearce [1995] found that when radical feminists claimed the traditionally male genre of the manifesto as their own, they could use it to resist male domination.

Cherwitz and Zagacki [1986] also studied confrontational rhetoric, noting a rise in "consummatory" discourse, discourse designed to "give form to public anger" [p. 321] about international affairs without triggering nuclear holocaust. They note that when American hostages are captured or when American soldiers are attacked overseas, an American president can either fight or not fight. Consummatory rhetoric provides a third alternative: fighting with words. That is, the president can sharply denounce the incidents and place America's enemies on warning, thereby establishing "a therapeutic 'buffer' between the desire for revenge and the necessity of rational deliberation" [p. 321].

Jamieson and Campbell [1982:29] show that the **generic hybrid,** a message borrowing from two or more generic traditions, also alters standard social arrangements. So, for example, a ceremonial speaker can sometimes issue a call for political action in memory of certain age-old beliefs, thereby adding a policy-related bottom line to an otherwise solemn piece of ritual. Similarly, Jablonski [1979b] notes the creativity of **generic transference,** the substitution of one *kind of* message for another. She cites the example of Richard Nixon: Rather than hold a standard press conference to announce his replacement of Vice President Spiro Agnew (who had been forced to resign in disgrace), Nixon actually conducted a formal ceremony in the East Room of the White House. Apparently reasoning that people behave better at ceremonies than at press conferences, Nixon pulled the generic rug from beneath his detractors' feet. Jablonski [p. 171] describes his rhetorical canniness:

> . . . the East Room provided a vivid counterpoint to Nixon's earlier Watergate speeches delivered from the Oval Office. The East Room, which typically accommodates formal state affairs, was filled on this occasion with a formally attired audience of Washington dignitaries. As television cameras panned the elaborate chandeliers of the East Room, viewers at home could hear the invited guests chatting amiably, their laughter rising occasionally above the soft music played by the Marine Corps Band. Then, like bridesmaids, the majority and minority leaders of the Congress, the Cabinet, and Nixon's family filed in, processional-style. After a heightened pause, trumpets sounded the familiar "Ruffles and Flourishes" and the President and Mrs. Nixon were announced.

In a grand setting like this, it was easy indeed for the audience to forget that Mr. Nixon's first vice president was under indictment and that the president himself was currently being charged with high crimes and misdemeanors (later known as the Watergate affair).

A third function of genres is that they facilitate *listening and reading.* As Burke [1931] noted, recurring forms create "appetites" in audiences by promising, and then meeting, rhetorical expectations. People can therefore miss several days of a soap opera because its predictability (who slept with whom when and where) allows easy catch-up. But just as genre can help audiences, its misapplication can be a problem. So, for example, Jamieson [1973] notes that when the existential tragedy/farce *Waiting for Godot* first played in Miami, the audience rioted because they expected to see a Broadway comedy! This is why rhetors often provide generic clues for proper listening: "I come before you tonight with a heavy heart. . . ."

Some genres have become especially useful. One of these, the jeremiad, is a religiously tinged oration calling people back to their solemn duties under God. Johannesen [1985] reports that the jeremiad has been popular in the United States since colonial times because it gives an ultimate rationale for less-than-ultimate political activities. The jeremiad describes sin, threatens punishment, demands repentance, and promises heavenly reward for a heavenly elect. In 2000, for example, Green Party candidate Ralph Nader used this genre extensively, essentially equating his campaign—environmental protection, consumer power, corporate and governmental accountability—with the Second Coming. George H. W. Bush and later George W. Bush used this same approach to justify America's role during their respective Wars in the Gulf, as had John Kennedy when forming the Peace Corps and as had Jimmy Carter when sanctioning other nations for human rights' abuses. In the United States, at least, the Chosen People have always been very busy.

Research on genre recommends this approach to the critic for a variety of additional reasons:

1. *Generic study exposes cultural tastes.* Huspek and Kendall [1991] note, for example, that the streetcorner conversations of blue-collar workers continually reflect the essential contentiousness of the American people and their unwillingness to submit to a single, consistent ideology.

2. *Generic study explains rhetorical power.* Jamieson [1975] argues that one cannot understand why some rhetoric (e.g., the papal encyclical) has the influence it has unless one also understands its "chromosomal imprints," the rhetorical features it retains from its historical roots (in this case, the speeches of Roman emperors).

3. *Generic study reveals psychological style.* Vartabedian [1985] argues that some rhetors are "generically blind," excessively committed to one style of speech. He notes, for instance, that Richard Nixon tried to justify himself rather than his policies in Vietnam largely because self-justification had served him so well earlier in his career (e.g., his 1952 "Checkers" speech).

4. *Generic study uncovers latent trends.* Wilson [1996] argued that, rather than being merely an offshoot of detective fiction in general, the lesbian detective novel is rhetorically replacing the traditional coming-out story. Whereas coming out as a lesbian used to be seen as a revolutionary act in itself, the lesbian detective novel goes a bit further, marking efforts to work within society to change popular perceptions of homosexuality.

5. *Generic study provides evaluative standards.* Griffin [1990] has studied the rhetoric of autobiographies, particularly those written by former criminals. He notes that such books cannot be judged by the standards applied to the general biography (e.g., Did all of this really happen?) but must be evaluated by a different set of standards entirely (e.g., Does the author seem genuinely

remorseful?). Only then, says Griffin, will the critic be dealing with the text on the same basis as its intended readers.

When doing generic research, the critic uses critical probes to explain textually distinctive trends. Among the most useful of these questions are the following:

1. Do verbal *patterns* give unity to the ideas, values, language, or methods of organization employed in the text?
2. Have these patterns been observed so often that they have become *standard*?
3. Do these patterns dominate the message? That is, how *idiosyncratic* is the rhetor?
4. What *generic* label best fits this text? Is the message characterized merely by topic (e.g., a sermon) or situation (e.g., a televised sermon) or can it be described with more conceptually ambitious labels (e.g., a religious diatribe)?
5. How *tight* are the generic constraints and what accounts for their rigidity or looseness?
6. If the rhetorical situation is partly *traditional* (e.g., a western movie), does it also have *novel* rhetorical features (e.g., a Chinese cowboy in the lead)?
7. If the rhetorical situation is comparatively *unprecedented* (e.g., a televised advertisement for condoms), is any generic borrowing being done (e.g., a scientist's testimonial for the product)?
8. Does the rhetor provide generic *clues* to help the audience (e.g., "I'm your psychiatrist, not your mate. We can be candid but not lovers"). Is the specter of previous rhetorical events invoked (e.g., "Speak to me as if I were an old friend")?
9. Does the rhetor offset generic *interference* by distinguishing this message from its ancestors (e.g., "Dear Friend, this is not just another piece of junk mail. . .")?
10. Given the generic constraints in place, was the rhetor *successful* (on strategic, psychological, moral, etc., grounds)?

While generic study can be highly useful, it can also be misapplied or used excessively. There is no particular merit in classifying discourse for its own sake. Its value lies, rather, in its utility: Does it identify a rhetorical trend that might have been overlooked? Does it explain why a given rhetor failed or succeeded? Does it highlight an interesting rhetorical problem that might have been missed? In other words, the most creative generic research asks and answers important questions.

CONCLUSION

As King Lear painfully discovered, he had raised a radical for a daughter. She refused to honor the rhetorical conventions established for receiving a piece of his kingdom. Cordelia was not offended by the content of the speech Lear wanted her to give: She did love her father. But she could not separate the What of Lear's love from the How of her own. She knew that for love to be love it had to be her kind of love; it had to meet her generic expectations. She, not Lear, had to find the time and the place of love as well as its language. She understood that to use the formulas of love would be to lose love. She knew that love by generic proxy was a cheat.

Cordelia's message is thus the message of this chapter: Structure and content are siblings, form a cousin. They cannot be treated separately without fundamentally destroying the natural complexity of human communication. If it is content that gives rhetoric its substance, it is structure that gives it its variety. People become wedded to their ways of doing things (a cup of coffee with the morning paper, another while opening the mail). They come to believe that it is these patterns that make them distinctive as individuals and, in a grander sense, that make life worth living.

People also feel special about their ways of saying things. At some level, they may sense that everything worth saying has already been said at least once. But they sense that it has not yet been said *in their way* and that feeling, too, gives life meaning. Because they are social creatures, people will imitate one another. That is where genres come in. Because they are individuals, people will give speech its color by exploring its variations. That is where rhetoric comes in. And because they are complex, they will sometimes say more than they realize they are saying. That is where critics come in.

TIPS FOR THE PRACTICING CRITIC

1. Be not seduced by genre. That is, avoid the urge to classify for the sake of classifying. Make sure to have a clear purpose in mind, apart from the mere creation and labeling of categories. What larger question will generic criticism help ask and/or answer?

2. When a critic faces a rhetorical text and feels "stumped" about how its structure is working, then rearranging the message elements, or cutting or summarizing them, can help. How would playing with the message design (ordering), emphasis, density and pacing encourage an audience to react differently? When a message seems straightforward, as if there were no other possible way to say it, make it less familiar by considering possible alternatives. This allows the critic to get "inside" the logic of the message and see that, indeed, its features were not predetermined but were the result of rhetorical choices. Then the critic can begin to speculate about the influence of those choices on audiences' ways of forming messages.

Chapter 7

ANALYZING SYNTAX AND IMAGERY

[T]he scene amidst which we stand does not permit us to confine our thoughts or our sympathies to those fearless spirits who hazarded or lost their lives on this consecrated spot. We have the happiness to rejoice here in the presence of a most worthy representation of the survivors of the whole Revolutionary army.

Veterans! You are the remnant of many a well-fought field. You bring with you marks of honor from Trenton and Monmouth, from Yorktown, Camden, Bennington, and Saratoga. Veterans of half a century! When in your youthful days you put everything at hazard in your country's cause, good as that cause was, and sanguine as youth is, still your fondest hopes did not stretch onward to an hour like this! At a period to which you could not reasonably have expected to arrive, at a moment of national prosperity such as you could never have foreseen, you are now met here to enjoy the fellowship of old soldiers, and to receive the overflowings of a universal gratitude.

But your agitated countenances and your heaving breasts inform me that even this is not an unmixed joy. I perceive that a tumult of contending feelings rushes upon you. The images of the dead, as well as the persons of the living, present themselves to you. The scene overwhelms you, and I turn from it. May the Father of all mercies smile upon your declining years, and bless them! And when you shall here have exchanged your embraces, when you shall once more have pressed the hands which have been so often extended to give succor in adversity, or grasped in the exultation of victory, then look abroad upon this lovely land which your young valor defended, and mark the happiness with which it is filled: yea, look abroad upon the whole earth, and see what a name you have contributed to give to your country, and what a praise you have added to freedom, and then rejoice in the sympathy and gratitude which beam upon your last days from the improved condition of mankind! [Webster, 1825]

* * *

Throw [these enclosures] away within 24 hours. The sexual abuse of children is so ugly, so unbelievable, so Satanic that no one wants to think about it.

But someone's *got to rescue kids from incest, beatings, and rape.* "Momma, Momma, make him stop hurting me!!" they cry.

That someone's you . . . and me . . . we are the ONLY ones who can stop the incest, beatings, and rape.

An eight-month old baby rushed to the hospital with gonorrhea of the throat! How does an eight-month old baby get gonorrhea of the throat? You can figure it out. A booklet, "How to Have Sex with Kids" telling a man (1) how to penetrate the vagina of a four-year old, (2) how to keep it hush-hush so that she does not tell her parents, and (3) that, "hey . . . you're doing the kid a favor by deflowering her."

Please send a check for 1,000 dollars or 1500, or 2,000 or 20 or 100 or 50 . . . whatever.

You want to sacrifice hard and tough for this one. Sell a car, land, borrow (I did), or go to your savings account. I challenge YOU to be the one to send the $10,000 or 5,000 check.

An Ivy-League philosopher, I abandoned university teaching to work at this full time.

And I'm not alone. You're with me. We—*you and me*—stop the sexual abuse of kids.

Read the enclosed. Cry. Rage. Tell others. And rescue.

I'll send to anyone (including you) a free copy of my tape, "How to STOP the Sexual Abuse of Children." Send me names. The other side of the tape is "How to Protect You and Your Family from Attack." *Please help me to send this tape out to thousands and thousands of people . . .* [Gallagher, 1984]

These passages were authored by different persons. No surprise. In different time periods. Again no surprise. To different audiences. Obvious as well. Their genres are also different: The first passage bears the marks of the commemorative oration and the latter that of junk mail. The texts are so different that even placing them next to one another is an ironic exercise. Indeed, an admirer of the first author (Daniel Webster) might be offended by even a remote comparison between Webster's intellect and that of the second author, one W. Neil Gallagher of Tupelo, Mississippi, whose greatest distinction seems his access to a photocopier and an ample supply of stamps. So the passages are predictably different. Any fool could tell that. But it takes a special kind of fool, a stylistic critic, to tell why.

This chapter focuses on **style**, *the sum total of language habits distinguishing one text from another.* Here, we will examine language microscopically, noting which words a rhetor chooses and how they collectively produce special effects. We will investigate tone and nuance, features that audience members sense but cannot often describe. We will discover why some words provoke more intense reactions than their synonyms and why language hides meaning as well as reveals it. Mostly, we will try to become precise about imprecise things: Why does one word sound stronger than another? Why does some rhetoric seem sacred and other rhetoric profane? How does language contribute to passion? To majesty? To boredom? What makes a lawyer's language tedious when written in contracts but gripping when presented to a jury? How must the language of advertising change when new Jaguars are being sold rather than used Hyundais? Why do physicians' words insulate them from public scrutiny and why is this almost never the case with politicians?

But the most basic thing we will do in this chapter is to look closely at language. Most people do not do so. Most people pay attention to the Big Picture in persuasion: ideas, arguments, themes, examples, stories. So by looking carefully at language, the critic has a natural advantage over the casual audience. Most contemporary Americans, for example, could quickly tell that Daniel Webster's Bunker Hill Oration was alien to their era and culture. "But why?" the stylistic critic asks. To ask such a basic question is all too rare, but to ask it is to begin to find its answer.

For example, Black [1978b], a preeminent stylistic critic, explains that Webster's sentimental style is now unfashionable because people no longer respect absolute values and are therefore unwilling to surrender to Great Persons espousing Great Ideas. But for the right people, says Black, Webster's style permits an emotional "recreation under sanctioned auspices" [p. 78], a way of being shielded from unpleasant realities. To describe war veterans as the "remnant of a well-fought field" is to indulge language and thereby to indulge oneself.

This is the language of melodrama, language that elevates ordinary soldiers to "fearless spirits," that turns a battlefield into a "consecrated spot," and that transforms helpfulness into "succor in adversity." This is grand language and hence distasteful to modern Americans. A statement like "We have the happiness to rejoice here in the presence of a most worthy representation . . ." cries out for the journalist's editorial pen. Raised on a diet of glib advertising phrases, modern Americans would be asleep by the time Webster got past the dependent clauses in the sixth sentence: "At a period to which you could not reasonably have expected to arrive, at a moment of national prosperity such as you could never have foreseen. . . ."

Perhaps because they read few books and watch much television, modern Americans hate language that calls attention to itself: "May the Father of all mercies smile upon your declining years." Modern Americans also prefer verbs to adjectives, action over embellishment. In their scientific detachment, they are suspicious of "heaving" breasts, "contending" feelings, or "agitated" countenances and they are embarrassed by excessive emotionality: "The scene overwhelms you, and I turn from it." While modern Americans still remember their dead and recognize their military heroes, they are more businesslike about it. Modern Americans might therefore feel an ideological kinship with Daniel Webster but, stylistically, he alienates them.

Neil Gallagher's style alienates many of them too but for different reasons. Unlike Webster, Gallagher has plenty of verbs: "read," "cry," "tell," "rescue." Unlike Webster, Gallagher's adjectives are short, pungent: "ugly," "Satanic," "hard and tough." Unlike Webster, Gallagher does not shield his readers from reality. He pours fact upon fact ("incest, beatings, rape"), trying to impress his audience with quantitative rather than qualitative experience: "hundreds and hundreds of . . . workshops," "thousands and thousands of people." Because he is writing rather than speaking, Gallagher tries hard to address his audience personally, seeking in one brief message to both commence and consummate a relationship: "Sell a car, land, borrow—I did—or go to your savings account." While Webster's promises to his audience are philosophical, Gallagher's are concrete: "I'll send to anyone . . . a free copy of my tape." While Webster invites his audience to reach up to him, Gallagher reaches down to his.

Despite his verbal energy, Gallagher misses the mark. His words demand too much too soon ("throw this away within 24 hours") and his emotionality seems excessive for a person we hardly know. While his streamlined sentence structure is simpler than Webster's, Gallagher piles too many disjointed thoughts into too little space and hence they become a tumult: four-year olds, money, gonorrhea, the Ivy League, land sales, free tapes. While his language is informal ("kids," "hush, hush," "Momma"), its staccato pace is inelegant and emotionally abrupt. Gallagher's too-rapid treatment of the victims he claims to care for (one brief paragraph) and the speed with which he repairs to his own bottom line ("send the $10,000 or 5,000 check") make him seem a hit-and-run artist. At times, Gallagher's gracelessness makes us yearn for Webster.

To say that a nineteenth-century commemorative speech differs from a contemporary mass mailing on child abuse is hardly profound. But even our brief examination of them has exposed *two different worlds;* it is these worlds of meaning that the stylistic critic tries to understand. In making their language choices, Webster and Gallagher revealed—wittingly and unwittingly—a bit about themselves and their audiences. Webster wanted to make the world slow down in order to better savor the past; Gallagher sought a faster rotation in order to better salvage the future.

All persuaders, many unconsciously, develop a style. They do so, according to Gibson [1966:24], partly as "a matter of sheer individual will, a desire for a particular kind of self-definition." If Daniel Webster and Neil Gallagher were somehow transported to a modern cocktail party, their styles would distinguish them: Webster would hold court, Gallagher would buttonhole. But there is more to style than personality. Style is also imposed upon rhetors by time (nineteenth century versus twentieth century), by occasion (known versus unknown audiences), and by genre (eulogies, mass mailings, cocktail party chatter). As Klaus [1969:61] notes, style is important because it often "does not originate within the man; it exists apart from him, as an inheritance, a legacy, that shapes his conceptual ends as surely as he does."

Although it is intellectually promising, studying style is often a humble business. Noting that Daniel Webster habitually used the passive voice while Neil Gallagher used the active voice may seem trivial. But it is less trivial to say that Daniel Webster's world was a world in which people felt dominated by great ideas (like freedom), great myths (like heroism), great beliefs (like Christianity), great events (like Yorktown), and great people (like himself). This entire system of beliefs, this worldview, may have resulted in Webster's use of the passive since, as Milic [1971:87] says: "even some of the greatest [writers] knew very little about what they were doing when they wrote." Gallagher's breathy use of the active voice may, in contrast, have signalled the onrushing events of his times and a confusing world in which children must become warriors to protect themselves. Gallagher's language may reflect a whole way of seeing the world, a take-charge way. When choosing their verbs, then, Webster and Gallagher may have been reaffirming the times in which they lived. Equally, they may have been doing nothing more than choosing verbs.

The good critic knows that to emphasize a single stylistic feature in a text is to risk getting a hasty impression of that text. Thus, in Chapters 7 and 8 we will urge the critic to use as many tools as possible when studying language. Approaching the same message from numerous perspectives builds-in safeguards against foolishness. To appreciate the subtlety of language, one must get beyond impressionism by cataloging and counting, by gathering different kinds of linguistic data, by sorting them out in complex ways, and then by thinking some more. Language is wonderful. It charms and delights. All of us love it. But like any lover, it must not be taken for granted. The good stylistic critic never does.

EXAMINING SYNTAX

Despite centuries of interest in rhetorical style, it remains elusive. Turner [1973] notes that some would do away with the concept completely, treating it like the physicist's ether, a seemingly important but impossible-to-find phenomenon. But few have followed this lead, primarily because daily life documents the importance of style. How, for example, would historians have treated the first moon landing if Neil Armstrong had not said the perfect thing: "That's one small step for man, one giant leap for mankind"? Armstrong reportedly rehearsed his statement, knowing that he had a chance to make history a bit more eloquent with parallelism and imagery.

Other ordinary stylists also left memorable legacies. A freed-slave-turned-reform-speaker, assessing the fledgling suffrage movement, reasoned "If the first woman God ever made was strong enough to turn the world upside down, all alone, these together ought to be able to turn it back and get it right side up again." A U.S. representative, replying to the question "How can you be both a lawmaker and a mother?" quipped, "I have a brain and a uterus, and

I use both." Another member of Congress, exasperated by resistance to serious discussion of women's health issues, observed, "When I first got here, every time you'd say "breastfeeding" on the House floor there would be a snicker . . . this has been happening since creation. Can we finally get a grip on it?"

In their ordinary ways, all of these rhetors were stylists. While few scientists speak in balanced couplets, ambassadors often do and, in July of 1969, Neil Armstrong was an entire planet's ambassador. Sojourner Truth's homey Biblical allusion concluded her famous "Aren't I a Woman?" speech and envigorated a movement. Representative Patricia Schroeder's references to vital organs vividly illustrated that her different roles were simply different parts of her, organically united in the same body. And Representative Susan Molinari juxtaposed a first-hand report, a history lesson, and a bit of slang to startle her audience out of old modes of thinking.

When the individual words of such memorable phrases are viewed in isolation, they are often not impressive. As Blankenship [1968:53] notes, 195 of the 265 words spoken in Abraham Lincoln's Gettysburg Address were one-syllable words, indicating that style emerges from *word patterns*. That is, words which seem weak on their own gain strength when they come together. The genius of style is therefore the genius of architecture, not of brick making.

Pascal's famous comment on style is therefore as apt today as it was in the seventeenth century: "Words differently arranged have a different meaning, and meanings differently arranged have different effects." In other words, stylistic excellence lies in **syntax** (how words are arranged). Diagramming sentences, that dreaded activity, nonetheless highlights the crucial role syntax plays in style. Arnold [1974] urges the critic to separate the grammar of a message into its (1) **primary** and (2) **secondary** structures. (In Figure 7.1, primary structures are separated by →.) Primary structures often consist of an initial noun phrase, a verb phrase, and a final noun phrase (containing either a prepositional phrase or what was formerly called the direct object). Secondary structures include all other words in the sentence, including predicate modifiers, dependent clauses, adverbial phrases, etc. Segmenting a text in this way disrupts its natural linguistic intricacy in the service of helping the critic better appreciate its style.

Consider, for example, the humble chain letter. Rhetorically, it is completely predictable: It promises good fortune as a result of a conspiracy of letter writing. All participate, all win. Although nominally illegal in most states, chain letters will not die. Often, the impulse behind them is financial, a pyramid scheme based on people's willingness to become pests to their friends. The rhetoric of such letters mixes threats for breaking the chain with rewards for maintaining it. "Everyone an entrepreneur" goes the appeal, and the letters clog both snail and e-mail inboxes.

Given the rhetorical circumstances of chain letters—an unknown author, a questionable product, and an uncertain recipient—one might expect basic rhetoric from them. Figure 7.1 justifies those expectations. Our sample letter [Kiss, 1985] could hardly be simpler, with 13 of the 34 sentences consisting of

FIGURE 7.1   Grammatical Structure of the Chain Letter

(1) **This paper→has been sent→to you**
                                              for good luck.

(2) **The original copy→is→in New England.**

(3) **It→has been→around the world**
                                        nine times.

(4) **The luck→has   been sent→to you.**
                 now

(5) **You→will receive→good luck→within four days**
                                                      of receiving this letter, provided you, in
                                                      turn, send it back out.

(6) **This→is→no joke.**

(7) **You→will receive→it→by mail.**

(8) **Send→copies→to people.**

(9) **Do not send→money,**
                            it has no price.

(10) **Do not keep→this letter.**

(11) **It→must leave→your hands→within ninety-six hours.**

(12) **An R.A.F. officer→received→$70,000.**

(13) **Joe Elliott→received→$40,000 and lost it**
                                                  because he broke the chain.

(14)   **Gene Welch→lost→his wife→**
        While in the Phillipines   after receiving this letter.

(15) **He→failed to circulate→the letter.**

(16)   **he→received→$7,755.**
        However, before his death

(17)   **send→copies→of this letter**
        Please   and see what happens in four days.

(18) **The chain→comes→from Venezuela**
                                        and was written by Saul Anthony deCroof,
                                        a missionary from South America.

(19)   **you→must make→20 copies**
        Since the copy must make   and send them to your
        a tour of the world,   friends and acquaintances.

(20)   **you→will get→a surprise.**
        After a few days

(21) **This→is→true**
                    even if you are not superstitious.

(22) **Do note→the following.**

(23) **Constantina Dias→received→the chain→in 1983.**

(24) **He→asked→his secretary→to make 20 copies**
                                                  and send them out.

                                                              (continued)

FIGURE 7.1   (*continued*)

(25)   **he→won→a lottery→of two million dollars.**
A few days later

(26) **Eric Deddit,**   **→received→the letter**
an office employee,   and forgot it had to leave his hands
within ninety-six hours.

(27) **He→lost→his job.**

(28)   **he→mailed out→the twenty copies.**
Later, after finding the letter again,

(29)   **he→got→a better job.**
A few days later

(30) **Helen Fairchild→received→the letter**
and not believing, threw the letter away.

(31)   **she→died**
Nine days later

(32)   **send→no money.**
Remember,

(33)   **don't ignore→this.**
Please

(34) **It→works.**

---

nothing but primary structures (the elements in bold). The remaining sentences are only slightly less pure: Almost none begin with a dependent clause; only a few are compound; there are virtually no embedded constructions.

This is Dick-and-Jane language. An avalanche of simple sentences cascades on the reader, as if the slightest violations of its primary structure would ruin its persuasion. Nouns and verbs predominate, transitions are omitted, and even paragraph breaks are eschewed in the original typescript. Its basic conceptual appeal is just slightly subtler than its grammar: "Keep the letter going or you, too, might die like Helen Fairchild."

Over 59 percent of the words in the chain letter are contained in its primary structure. In contrast, General John Pershing [1919] fits only 31 percent of his remarks into the primary structure of his letter (Figure 7.2). *All but one* of his sentences are burdened by secondary structures, and the other (#4) is a compound sentence. His primary segments are weighted down in front by dependent clauses and in the rear by compound structures or series of prepositional phrases. Also, adverbs frequently peek between Pershing's verb phrases, further slowing him down. It is as if the General could not leap into a sentence without first doing calisthenics.

Statements #7 and #8 are particularly noteworthy, as Pershing gets a long running start only to step across two short primary segments. Balanced constructions ("whether keeping lonely vigil in the trenches, or . . ."), unneeded

FIGURE 7.2 Grammatical Structure of the Pershing Letter

(1) **I→cannot let you→go→**
Now that your service with the American Expeditionary Forces is about to terminate, without a personal word.

(2) **the patriotic young manhood →responded and became the formidable army**
At the call to arms, of America eagerly whose decisive victories testify to its efficiency and its valor.

(3) **our army→has executed→the will of the people**
With the support of the nation firmly united to defend the cause of liberty, with resolute purpose.

(4) **Our democracy→has been tested→and the forces of autocracy→have been defeated.**

(5) **our troops→have fulfilled→their trust and have overcome the menace to our civilization.**
To the glory of the citizen-soldier, faithfully in a succession of brilliant offensives

(6) **your part →has been→an important one→**
As an individual, in the world war in the sum total of our achievements.

(7) **each→has played→his part.**
Whether keeping lonely vigil in the trenches, or gallantly storming the enemy's stronghold; whether enduring monotonous drudgery at the rear, or sustaining the fighting line at the front, bravely and efficiently

(8) **you→inspired→the war-torn Allies→ and turned the tide→**
By willing sacrifice of personal rights; by cheerful endurance of hardship and privation; by vigor, strength and indomitable will, made effective by thorough organization and cordial cooperation, with new life of threatened defeat into overwhelming victory.

(9) **you→have served→your country.**
With a consecrated devotion to duty and a will to conquer, loyally

(10) **a standard→has been established and maintained**
By your exemplary conduct never before attained by any army.

(11) **you→are to return→to the pursuits**
With mind and body as clean and strong as the decisive blows you delivered against the foe, soon of peace.

(12) **I→ask→ you→carry home your ideals continue to live as you have served—**
In leaving the scenes of your victories, may that high and
an honor to the principles for which you have fought and to the fallen comrades you leave behind.

(13) **I→extend→to you→my thanks**
It is with pride in our success that sincere for your splendid service to the army and to the nation.

adjectives ("monotonous drudgery"), and double nouns ("its efficiency and its valor") abound here. Indeed, the chain letter managed to pack thirty-four sentences into less space than it took Pershing to lumber through thirteen (with 316 total words in the former, 357 words in the latter). Where the author of the chain letter envisioned an impatient reader, Pershing apparently anticipated the opposite.

Pershing's expectations were sensible. His letter was distributed on February 28, 1919, to all GI's returning from World War I. This was a time for reflection since, for the first time in a long time, these men had time. So the General paused and thought of grand things—valor, sacrifice, mortality—sensing that the significance of his ideas justified the grand style. The ideas he treated were timeless, ideas that would help fill the reflective moments as his men aged. The chain letter, in contrast, blows away when the next piece of junk mail is opened. Its very style invites, even demands, such treatment. But the Pershing letter issues a different invitation, which may explain why it was found, lovingly preserved, in the attic of a World War I veteran sixty-five years later.

By uncovering the grammatical structure of these two messages, we discover what Lanham [1983] calls the **Running** (or Hypotactic) style and the **Periodic** (or Paratactic) style. Each style has a special rhetorical purpose; each responds to a different human psychology. Lanham urges the critic to make an early determination of these features since they so often reveal the author's voice. The Running style, exemplified by the chain letter, and the Periodic style, exemplified by Pershing, make different commentaries about the texts that embody them. Lanham urges the critic to listen for this quiet voice to understand the subtlety of rhetoric.

The Running style is a "verb" style, not a "noun" style. It is also the most natural style because it is simplest. In a Running style, the author tells who did what to whom when, where, and how. The chain letter uses this laundry list–type of development, as fact, event, and emotion pour atop one another before finally screeching to a halt. Neil Gallagher's diatribe on child abuse is similar. In neither case is the reader given time to reflect. *Immediate* responses are the order of the day and clean, primary structures demand that that order be carried out.

Lanham identifies another feature of the Running style, offering Julius Caesar's "I came; I saw; I conquered" as its prototype. Lanham notes that this style typically suppresses information by not ordering phenomena, thereby placing responsibility on the audience's shoulders. When Caesar put coming, seeing, and conquering on the same syntactic level, says Lanham [p. 33], he left it up to the reader to determine their relative priority: "If Caesar had written instead 'Since it was I who arrived, and I who saw how the land lay, the victory followed as a matter of course,' he would have said outright what the tight-lipped 'came-saw-conquered' formula only invites us to say about him."

Similarly, because the chain letter has so few orienting devices (e.g., dependent clauses), it does not invite the reader to distinguish between the plight of Joe Elliot (who lost $40,000) and Gene Welch (who won $7,755 but who also lost his wife). Such facts merely shoot forth, propelled by the noun-verb-noun-verb syntax its excited author has chosen.

The Periodic style of Webster and Pershing operates quite differently. If the Running style is loose, the Periodic style is tight: reasoned, intricate, connected. Here, secondary structures constantly tell the audience what to do with the primary structures. Lanham [p. 77] notes that the Periodic style, "with its internal parentheses, balanced phrasing, and climactic resolution, stops time to let a reader take in the complete pattern." The Periodic style does more of the audience's work: categorizing, weighing, and qualifying.

Periodic rhetors trade (1) authority for interest and (2) spontaneous responses for delayed, but more emotionally complex, responses. Webster and Pershing willingly made such trades. Use of a more telegraphic style at such sacred moments would have seemed to them a cultural mockery. If human sacrifice did not warrant a complex style, nothing did, they may have reasoned. On the other hand, because their purposes were so practical, Neil Gallagher and the author of the chain letter also chose well. Given the enormity of the child abuse problem, Gallagher's simple, direct language stood as a stylistic signal that a solution was possible, if not imminent. Like other direct-mailers, Gallagher did not know his audience; he thus became plain in order to avoid being ignored.

Running and Periodic motifs deal solely with the structural features of language. *How* these structures are used by individuals is a very different matter. That is, not all Running styles need be tacky and not all Periodic styles produce poetry (they can as easily result in obfuscation). Former President Dwight Eisenhower offers an interesting example. As a writer, Ike had a nice, sprightly Running style and his memoirs are a pleasure to read as a result. But as a speaker, he often lost his compass amidst secondary structures. This was true even during simple ceremonial occasions as, for example, when he welcomed children to an Easter Egg roll at the White House.

This point is dramatized in Table 7.1 by contrasting what Eisenhower [1958:65] said (Hypotactically) with what he might have said (Paratactically). Clearly, Ike used twice the number of words he needed and, unlike Webster or Pershing, got no extra mileage from them. His prepositional phrases are unnecessary since his audience already knew they were standing "on the White House grounds," "on this Easter Monday." Dependent clauses in the second and third statements add neither information nor grace and his bloated syntax ("and so to them I extend my sympathies . . .") robs the message of elegance. Thus, it is not enough to determine a text's basic stylistic structure. The critic must also reckon with the *effects* achieved, or lost, by them as well.

Gibson [1966] offers a useful way of getting at these stylistic effects. He would describe Eisenhower as a **Stuffy** talker because of his lengthy clauses, avoidance of simple words, and use of the passive voice. In his system, Gibson argues that the combination of more than a dozen language variables creates

TABLE 7.1 Eisenhower's Actual versus Potential Style

Delivered Version	Potential Version
It is a privilege to welcome you once more to the annual egg-rolling contest on the White House grounds.	Welcome to our annual egg-rolling contest.
I surely hope that the weather cooperates with you properly and that you do not have the discomfort of a shower.	Let's hope it doesn't rain.
Moreover, I just learned this morning that many of the schoolchildren had to go to school on this Easter Monday . . .	I've just learned that some children had to go to school today . . .
and so to them I extend my sympathies for missing the fun of the day . . .	and I'm sorry they're going to miss the fun . . .
that I hope the rest of you will have.	that the rest of you will have.
Mrs. Eisenhower joins me in saying Happy Easter to all of you. Goodbye.	Mrs. Eisenhower joins me in saying Happy Easter to all of you. Goodbye.

distinctive styles like Eisenhower's. In addition to the Stuffy style, Gibson posits a **Tough** style (monosyllabic words, many "to be" verbs, few adjectives) and a **Sweet** style (a you-orientation, many contractions, use of the active voice). Gibson worked out specific stylistic ingredients for each style; Table 7.2 presents his recipe.

The Gibson system is useful not because it is precise (it is only a rough guide) but because it helps explain rhetorical voice. Voice is difficult to describe, but not difficult to hear. For example, John Pershing's measured voice is different from Daniel Webster's grand voice and both differ substantially from the frenetic voice of Neil Gallagher. Gibson's system helps us discuss such felt-but-unexplained phenomena. The example Gibson [p. 29–30] gives of the Tough style is especially vivid:

> In the late summer of that year we lived in a house in a village that looked across the river and the plain to the mountains. In the bed of the river there were pebbles and boulders, dry and white in the sun, and the water was clear and swiftly moving and blue in the channels. Troops went by the house and down the road and the dust they raised powdered the leaves of the trees. The trunks of the trees too were dusty and the leaves fell early that year and we saw the troops marching along the road and the dust rising and leaves, stirred by the breeze, falling and the soldiers marching and afterward the road bare and white except for the leaves.
>
> The plain was rich with crops; there were many orchards of fruit trees and beyond the plains the mountains were brown and bare. There was fighting in the mountains and at night we could see the flashes from the artillery. In the dark it was like summer lightning, but the nights were cool and there was not the feeling of a storm coming.

These are the words of Ernest Hemingway, a tough-talker if there ever was one. Gibson describes this prototypical tough-talker as an experienced,

TABLE 7.2 Criteria for Measuring Style

Variables	Tough	Sweet	Stuffy
1. Monosyllables	> 70%	61–70%	< 60%
2. Words of 3 syllables or more	< 10%	10–19%	> 20%
3. 1st & 2nd person pronouns	One "I" or "we"/100 words	Two "you" per 100 words	No 1st or 2nd person pronouns
4. Subjects (neuters versus people)	1/2 or more people	1/2 or more people	2/3 or more neuters
5. Finite verbs	> 10%	> 10%	< 10%
6. To be forms as finite verbs	> 1/3 of verbs	< 1/4	< 1/4
7. Passive verbs	< 1/20 verbs	None	> 1 in 5
8. True adjectives	< 10%	> 10%	> 8%
9. Adjectives modified	< 1 per 100 words	> 1/100	< 1/100
10. Noun adjuncts	< 2%	> 2%	> 4%
11. Average length of clauses	< 10 words	< 10 words	> 10 words
12. Clauses (percent of total words)	< 25%	< 33%	> 40%
13. "Embedded" words	< 1/2 S/V combinations	< half	> twice
14. Uses of "the"	8% or more	under 6%	6–7%
15. Contractions and fragments	> 1 per 100 words	> 2/100	None
16. Parentheses & other punctuation	None	> 2 per 100 words	None

From Gibson [1966]

close-lipped, first-hand reporter who knows what he knows and is unafraid to share it. The tough-talker is self-absorbed, sure of his footing: Hemingway sees things from *his* house, reports *his* sightings of the artillery flashes.

Gibson says there is a flatness to the narrator's voice here, a self-limiting but unquestionable sense of authority. "You would not call this man genial," says Gibson [p. 31], since "he behaves rather as if he had known us, the reader, a long time and therefore doesn't have to pay us very much attention." Instead, the voice concentrates on facts, describing things as they are, not as they seem to be. The phrases are short, the sentences compound rather than complex, and adjectives and adverbs are kept under control by nouns and predicates. This is the spare language of a clear-headed rhetor.

A second style is what Gibson calls Sweet talk. It could hardly be more different from Stuffy talk, as the language of advertising so often shows:

Have you discovered **Kathy's Kitchen Products yet?** You'll be amazed at how quick and easy they are—and how incredibly tasty as well. Wait 'til you catch the scrumptious aromas of **Kathy's** *new* frozen dinners, made as always with only the finest ingredients.

Tonight, help yourself to **Kathy's** new Chimichanga Deluxe. Loads of perfectly seasoned chicken and cheese, wrapped in a tender tortilla with all the hot sauce you'll ever need. Just add fresh sour cream and your hungry family. It's everything you need for a stay-at-home fiesta. Olé!

This voice is unquestionably more social: You and your life experiences, your tastes, and your kitchen routines are emphasized. Gibson notes that Sweet talk is filled with cliches ("the finest ingredients"), no doubt because cliches are the language of us all. There is also a more informal (Running) style here because the rhetor seeks action, not rumination, from the audience. Unstated, but very much present, is the assumption that the rhetor has the *right* to counsel the audience. This voice you have never met knows that you need something quick, easy, and tasty. This claim of unearned familiarity is the hallmark of the Sweet style, says Gibson, as is the lavish use of adjectives. The Sweet talker is a solicitor par excellence.

Gibson calls his third style Stuffy because it removes the Tough talker's sense of self and the Sweet talker's sense of other. In their place hovers a disembodied assemblage of words. Gibson [p. 93] uses a government report on smoking as his paradigm example of the Stuffy style:

Cigarette smoking is causally related to lung cancer in men; the magnitude of the effect of cigarette smoking far outweighs all other factors. The data for women, though less extensive, point in the same direction.

The risk of developing lung cancer increases with duration of smoking and the number of cigarettes smoked per day, and is diminished by discontinuing smoking.

The risk of developing cancer of the lung for the combined group of pipe smokers, cigar smokers, and pipe and cigar smokers is greater than for nonsmokers, but much less than for cigarette smokers.

The data are insufficient to warrant a conclusion for each group individually.

This is the language of the corporation, of the bureaucrat so fearful of personal exposure or, more charitably, so diligent about not misstating the truth, that he or she hides behind qualifications: "the data for women, though less extensive . . ." Stuffy talk removes passion from discourse, substituting for it a sense of detachment in which all variables (in this case, gender and smoking habits) cancel each other out. Gibson [p. 107] argues that the Stuffy talker is scared: "If this is an age of anxiety, one way we react . . . is to withdraw into omniscient and multisyllabic detachment where nobody can get us." The passive voice also helps disguise ownership of the rhetor's ideas. Thus, "smoking" and not "smokers" become the culprit of the report, and "the data," not the researcher, become responsible for the bad news about lighting up.

Gibson's system, although limited, is useful. It roughs out the stylistic terrain efficiently and gives the critic a *base point* against which to compare individual messages. Naturally, there is more to style than syntax. The statistics of grammar cannot alone explain why Webster's address seems dated or why the chain letter seems slippery. It takes richer forms of analysis to see why some discourse registers high notes and why other discourse sounds flat. It is to such aesthetic matters that we now turn.

EXAMINING IMAGERY

Both rhetorical and literary critics study imagery. But the imagery in rhetoric is often pedestrian rather than poetic. If poetic images invite tarrying, rhetorical images invite movement. Passion, not nuance, is their hallmark:

> This is God's blazing message to America in this hour—and it is without question its very last chance.
> This is the time to energize these spiritual weapons for the salvation of our land. It must be done immediately, fervently, with faith, and with tears!
> If this is done by the Christian people with all of their heart immediately, and with perseverance, this land shall not only be saved, but there shall also explode from this united prayer-power the most astounding revival in all history.
>
> MORE POWERFUL THAN TEN THOUSAND HYDROGEN BOMBS
>
> We have declared spiritual war on God's enemies and our enemies. NOW LET'S WAGE IT! [Boone, et al., 1970:30]

This passage is from a pamphlet entitled *The Solution to Crisis—America,* authored by 1950s teen-idol-turned-evangelist, Pat Boone, and two colleagues. The booklet is a forerunner of the Far Right rhetoric still in evidence today. Its imagery is neither subtle nor novel. It combines temporal metaphors ("this hour"), thermal metaphors ("blazing message"), and kinetic metaphors ("energize") to produce a sense of urgency. Metaphors of conflict ("God's enemies") add an oppositional force against which the rhetoric can struggle. The physical metaphors ("with tears") humanize the conflict and, by relating it to bodily processes, make the struggle lifelike.

Bombs falling, hearts palpitating, fires blazing—a good deal of action for a short passage. Should a literalist ask how bodily fluids ("tears") could serve as weapons, or how cerebral processes ("prayer-power") could rival atomic chain reactions ("ten thousand hydrogen bombs"), the passage would reduce to silliness. But for Pat Boone's readers, the pamphlet makes sense despite its non-sense. For them, its cacophony of images produces an integrated, emotional whole. Many of them would be willing to share their quite literal money with Mr. Boone's movement because of the factually untrue truths embedded in his imagery. Throughout history, people have marched off to literal wars because of the metaphoric battles they have already fought—and won.

Not all rhetoric is this rich with imagery. Thus, two critical probes for the critic are these:

- To what extent does a message employ nonliteral language?
- What specific purposes does such language serve?

Most people cannot speak without imagery because imagery increases the range of things that can be said and, more fundamentally, the range of things that can be thought. That is, despite his imagery, Pat Boone was hardly ready to kiss his family goodbye and march off to trench warfare. Had his family questioned his use of language, he probably would have said that the sacrifices he was willing to make for his cause *felt like* the sacrifices of troops during battle. Such martial ways of thinking perhaps freed Boone to take on challenges he would have been unwilling to accept, had he thought of his duties in less exalted terms. Even though he was, literally, only writing a cheap pamphlet for mass distribution and even though he was, literally, intending to go home after putting his printing press to bed, his wartime imagery made his job a bit grander that day. Pat Boone really meant what he unreally said.

When he wrote to thank Mr. Boone for having sent him a copy of his remarks, then-president Richard Nixon used language that was as literal as Boone's was figurative. Even though the President seemed to appreciate Boone's bequest, his rhetorical style suggested something else entirely:

The White House
Washington

Dear Pat:

I want you to know how much I appreciate your thoughtfulness in letting me have a copy of your recording, "The Solution to Crisis—America," which you gave to Secretary Romney for me at the Religious Heritage Dinner on June 18. It was especially kind of you to remember me with this meaningful and timely message, and you may be sure I am pleased to have this evidence of faith and patriotism brought to my attention.

With my best wishes,

Sincerely,

Richard Nixon [1970]

This is how presidents talk. Carefully. There are no wild flights of fancy, no embroidered stories, no riotous mixing of images here. Nixon's language is spare, precise, businesslike. While his salutation is suitably informal ("Dear Pat"), the remainder of the message is distanced: Nixon appreciates Boone's "thoughtfulness," not Boone himself; the recording was given to Romney, not to Nixon personally; Nixon is pleased to see such "evidence of faith" but he is not going to *do* anything about it. Boone's gift is described as "meaningful and timely," a phrase that could describe either the Holy Bible or *Newsweek* magazine. The passive voice ("I am pleased to have this . . . brought to my attention") places the rhetorical action in Boone's arena, not in Nixon's. Thus, while Nixon's reply is cordial on the ideational level, on the stylistic level it repudiates Boone's entire message.

By exercising stylistic restraint Nixon says, in effect, I have heard you but I am not listening to you. Because the use of imagery often signals a rhetor's heightened state of sentiment, an attempt by Nixon to match Boone's style ("You really socked it to 'em in that one, Pat"), would have joined them *emotionally* as well as argumentatively. Thus, by sending a formal, literalistic letter, Nixon's speech-act signaled he was unwilling to travel down the slippery slope of Far Right politics.

The word "imagery" derives from the same root as "imagination," a transcendence of the normal. Thus, a rhetor's relative use of imagery maps that rhetor's comfort with life-as-given. Clearly, Pat Boone is ready for a trip somewhere, while Richard Nixon is committed to staying where he is: in the middle of the political road. Of course, establishment politicians often use imagery when they speak. But they rarely do so with the sense of wild abandon displayed by Pat Boone.

Also, politicians' imagery typically throws light on specific pieces of policy ("a New Deal," "the war on drugs") and their pragmatism makes them abandon failed imagery quickly (e.g., Bill Clinton's "New Covenant" in 1995). Politicians are afraid of the world-yet-to-be; movement activists, on the other hand, embrace it willingly since it alone fully substantiates their values: saving "unborn" babies, advancing "green" politics, etc. Thus, to track the use of imagery is to track the length of a rhetor's wish list.

One standard category of imagery, the metaphor, has been the object of much scholarly inquiry. Metaphor has been variously defined but here it will be treated as a kind of depiction equating one thing with another: For example, builders of earthen dams in Kenya are likened to destroyers of dams along the Rhine in World War II and hence dubbed a Peace "Corps." Lakoff and Johnson [1980] have argued convincingly that everyday talkers would become mute without metaphor. They also write that (1) *metaphor results from thought* (e.g., if one's beliefs are unpopular, one may feel besieged, and this reflects in one's rhetoric—as in the case of Pat Boone). And (2) *metaphor stimulates thought* (e.g., if one talks of all creatures as connected by a web of life, one becomes unwilling to go to war—as in the case of the Dalai Lama). In their book, Lakoff and Johnson describe a number of functions served by metaphor, among which are the following:

1. *Metaphors selectively highlight ideas.* If an idea is important to a person or a culture, it will find its way to imagery. So, for example, Lakoff and Johnson observe that martial imagery like "I demolished his argument" or "his claims were indefensible" [p. 4] is used because some cultures treat communication as a contestable, rather than a sharable, activity. Communication can be talked about in other ways, of course, such as argument-as-journey: "We've covered a lot of ground" or "you're off in the wrong direction." Thus, the critic tracks the facts of metaphorical usage, looking for the meanings behind the meanings.

2. *Metaphors are often generative.* That is, they help people see things in a new light. So, for example, if a client thinks of love as madness ("it just happens; you

can't control it"), a marriage counselor might introduce the metaphor of love-as-labor ("marriage is something you really have to work at"), thereby calling attention to relational possibilities previously hidden by the madness metaphor. In a sense, to use metaphor is to admit a kind of defeat, to acknowledge that literal language cannot always make ideas and feelings clear. Imagery often helps to approximate what literal language cannot even estimate.

3. *Metaphors often mask ideas and values.* As metaphors become routinely used in a given language community, their implied meanings become less and less noticeable. Knowing this, the perceptive critic traces these "forgotten" meanings carefully. So, for example, Lakoff and Johnson [p. 236–7] observe that when corporate leaders treat labor as a business "resource" (for example, by placing it on a par with cheap oil), they become blind to the exploitation of workers such a metaphor encourages. As Lakoff and Johnson say [p. 237], "The blind acceptance of [this] metaphor can hide degrading realities, whether meaningless blue-collar and white-collar industrial jobs in 'advanced' societies or virtual slavery around the world."

4. *Metaphors have entailments.* That is, metaphors mean certain things but imply other things too. So, for example, a metaphor may bespeak one's personality (e.g., *sharing as a commodity:* a person who believes that "time is money"), one's intellectual worldview (e.g., *friendship as a journey:* "our relationship isn't going anywhere"), or one's cultural assumptions (e.g., *up and down:* "I'm on top of the situation" vs. "he's low man on the totem pole").

Entailments are the policy implications of metaphor. That is, if one believes that argument-is-war ("she shot down my case"), one may make certain *offensive* assumptions when speaking: (1) that people are naturally competitive, (2) that truth is less important than strategy, and (3) that short-term triumph is most important. In contrast, one who sees argument-as-a-container ("his case won't hold water") may argue *protectively,* focusing on the issue's substance rather than its personal dynamics. While people are usually unaware of their preferred images, their preferred images often expose their premises for action.

Given the rhetorical functions of metaphor, how can they best be studied? Most critics look for what Lakoff and Johnson call metaphor's **systematicity.** That is, they urge the critic to look for patterns of metaphorical usage since, while "complete consistency across metaphors is rare; coherence, on the other hand, is typical" [p. 96]. By proceeding carefully through a message, the critic can often find an underlying thematic unity to the metaphors chosen. Thus, the following are important critical probes:

- What *families of metaphors* reside in the text?
- Are they internally consistent?
- What is their cumulative effect?

Osborn [1976] provides a helpful system for examining metaphor, based on his inspections of public messages from two thousand years of various cultures. He grouped the metaphors he found into eleven metaphorical patterns, or families, that "endure in power and popularity despite time and cultural change" [p. 16] because of the almost primordial pictures they paint. While Osborn's categories may not be exhaustive, they are a good critical starting place since they touch on basic human experiences. Modified slightly, his categories include:

1. Water and the Sea (e.g., "I'm going down for the third time");
2. Light and Dark (e.g., "I'm in the dark on this issue");
3. The Human Body (e.g., "Just turn the other cheek");
4. War (e.g., "Our team was blitzed yesterday");
5. Structures (e.g., "We're operating in different frameworks");
6. Animals (e.g., "They really wolfed down that dessert");
7. The Family (e.g., "Defeat is always an orphan");
8. Above and Below (e.g., "Let's go over the top in this campaign");
9. Forward and Backward (e.g., "We're falling behind our quota for the month");
10. Natural Phenomena (e.g., "That was a peak experience for me");
11. Sexuality (e.g., "A pregnant pause followed her announcement").

The good critic will look beyond Osborn's categories since much rhetoric is specific to a culture or a sub/co-culture. A specifically Western supplement to his list, for example, might include **mechanistic** metaphors (e.g., "Is violence hardwired into humanity?"), **monetary** images (e.g., "I'm going for broke in my relationship with Amber"), **athletic** metaphors (e.g., "I'll knock this exam out of the park"), and others. But Osborn's list is a good first step because it identifies the rhetor's general mental habits and the audience's perceived motivational bases.

Dr. Martin Luther King, Jr.'s, famous "I Have a Dream" speech will help us see how powerful rhetoric works its magic. Even the most casual analysis shows that he used metaphor compellingly:

And as we walk, we must make the pledge that we shall always march ahead. We cannot turn back. There are those who are asking the devotees of civil rights, "When will you be satisfied?" We can never be satisfied as long as the Negro is the victim of the unspeakable horrors of police brutality.

We can never be satisfied as long as our bodies, heavy with the fatigue of travel, cannot gain lodging in the motels of the highways and the hotels of the cities. We cannot be satisfied as long as the Negro's mobility is from a smaller ghetto to a larger one.

We can never be satisfied as long as our children are stripped of their selfhood and robbed of their dignity by signs stating "for whites only." We cannot be satisfied as long as a Negro in Mississippi cannot vote and a Negro in New York believes he has nothing for which to vote. No, we are not satisfied, and we will not be satisfied until justice rolls down like waters and righteousness like a mighty stream.

I am not unmindful that some of you have come here out of excessive trials and tribulation. Some of you have come fresh from narrow jail cells. Some of you have come from areas where your quest for freedom left you battered by the storms of persecution and staggered by the winds of police brutality. You have been the veterans of creative suffering. Continue to work with the faith that unearned suffering is redemptive.

Go back to Mississippi; go back to Alabama; go back to South Carolina; go back to Georgia; go back to Louisiana; go back to the slums and ghettos of the Northern cities, knowing that somehow this situation can, and will be changed. Let us not wallow in the valley of despair.

So I say to you, my friends, that even though we must face the difficulties of today and tomorrow, I still have a dream. It is a dream deeply rooted in the American dream that one day this nation will rise up and live out the true meaning of its creed—we hold these truths to be self evident, that all men are created equal.

I have a dream that one day on the red hills of Georgia, sons of former slaves and sons of former slave-owners will be able to sit down together at the table of brotherhood.

I have a dream that one day, even the state of Mississippi, a state sweltering with the heat of injustice, sweltering with the heat of oppression, will be transformed into an oasis of freedom and justice.

I have a dream my four little children will one day live in a nation where they will not be judged by the color of their skin but by content of their character. I have a dream today!

I have a dream that one day, down in Alabama, with its vicious racists, with its governor having his lips dripping with the words of interposition and nullification, that one day, right there in Alabama, little black boys and black girls will be able to join hands with little white boys and white girls as sisters and brothers. I have a dream today!

I have a dream that one day every valley shall be exalted, every hill and mountain shall be made low, the rough places shall be made plane, and the crooked places shall be made straight and the glory of the Lord will be revealed and all flesh shall see it together. [King, 1964: 373–4]

King's artistry derives more from human sensitivity than from stylistic flourishes. His naturalistic imagery, for example, evokes primitive power: "storms of persecution," "winds of police brutality." Bodily processes ("all flesh shall see it") and basic social units ("sisters and brothers") also emphasize how emotionally and politically *fundamental* his argument for freedom was.

Some of King's metaphors are intentionally offensive in their roughness: lips "dripping," people "stripped." Perhaps King reasoned that more urbane language would have made him seem out-of-touch to the underprivileged and a potential object of manipulation to the overprivileged. Hence, he proposed no banquets of grandeur but just a "table of brotherhood," no captains of destiny but just "veterans of creative suffering."

King also established a sense of *forward movement* by transmuting the literal march on Washington into a symbolic march in which people "come here out of excessive trials and tribulations." He launched them on a "quest for freedom," forbidding their "turning back," commanding that they "march ahead," "facing" the difficulties of tomorrow, and moving with the swiftness of a "mighty stream." Forward motion was coupled with *ascendent movement* so that King's people could "rise up" to climb mountains "made low" by their efforts. Metaphorically, the only thing that King left standing was justice itself which was to "roll down" on his people like a cascade.

Virtually all of King's metaphors can be accommodated by the Osborn schema. This fact establishes how "primitive" King's speech was and why, as a result, it had such political and psychological power. The African American members of his audience were, after all, people who had historically worked the nation's farms, cooked the nation's meals, built the nation's buildings, and fought more than their share of the nation's wars. King concentrated on these basic images because the people he loved were so often relegated to basic pleasures. His metaphors of wind and sea and fire remind us how central the natural world is to human experience and why, since the beginning of time, people have turned their eyes skyward, looking for explanations.

King broke this naturalistic pattern only once but it was a significant departure. Early in his speech, he produced a small yet captivating cluster of **monetary** metaphors, curiously juxtaposed to his organic images. The effect is quite confrontational. King likens the Constitution and Declaration of Independence to a "promissory note" guaranteeing civil liberties. By denying these rights to African Americans, the nation has "defaulted" upon this note; it is a "bad check" which has now been returned stamped "insufficient funds." But King announces that the marchers have come to claim their rights from the nation's "vaults of opportunity." Just as quickly as King introduces this line he abandons it, returning to traditional imagery.

Although brief, these monetary images made King's speech genuinely American. Virtually everything else he said could have been said anywhere anytime. But in mimicking the language of capitalism, King staked a claim to the land on which he stood and also made an ironic commentary on his age. By allotting his audience one economic metaphor for every seven naturalistic images, King approximated the comparative economic ratio between the African Americans and European Americans of his day. In other words, only one-seventh of King's speech was fully "American," perhaps because King's people had not at that point been enfranchised in the most traditionally American way: economically. In a sense, then, Dr. King spoke in August of 1963 as something of a stranger in a strange land.

As this speech makes clear, imagery can propel rhetoric like nothing else can. It becomes a kaleidoscope for the mind's eye, allowing the audience to see ideas that otherwise would be inert. Table 7.3 goes beyond metaphor to present a more complete catalogue of images. The critic can use it to answer such questions as the following:

- How experimental is the artifact being examined (as measured by the *types* of stylistic devices used)?
- What factors explain such liberal/conservative uses of language?

TABLE 7.3 Some Common Stylistic Devices*

Device	Definition	Function	Example
Anaphora	Exactly repeating a word or phrase at the beginnings of successive clauses	Highlights the rhetor's mental grasp of a concept by displaying the *completeness* (and hence determination) of his or her thinking	"We shall not flag or fail. We shall go on to the end. We shall fight in France. . . ." (Winston Churchill)
Antithesis	Juxtaposing contrasting ideas in balanced phrases	An "argumentative" piece of imagery that *sharpens* differences significantly	"Naked came I out of my mother's womb, and naked shall I return thither." (Job, 1:21)
Hyperbole	An extravagant statement used as a figure of speech	A conscious distortion used to *describe* something that would otherwise be beyond description	"Publishing a volume of verse is like dropping a rose-petal down the Grand Canyon and waiting for an echo." (Don Marquis)
Metonymy	Using the name of one thing as the name for something else to which it has a logical relationship	Creates a new association among ideas or exploits an old association in order to add *freshness* to thought	"Agonies are one of my changes of garments. . . . I am the mashed fireman with breastbone broken." (Walt Whitman)
Oxymoron	A phrase that seems to have an internal contradiction	A contrastive device designed to, first, confuse and, then, *intrigue* audience	"That building is a little bit big and pretty ugly." (James Thurber)
Synecdoche	Identifying something by naming a part of it or identifying a part by naming the whole thing	A kind of rhetorical shorthand that provides a more *interesting* view of commonly understood objects or ideas	"Wherever wood [a ship] can swim, there I am sure to find this flag of England [the British fleet]." (Napoleon)
Irony	A statement whose "real" meaning is (recognizably) opposite of what is literally said	In-group humor used to *certify* that rhetor and audience share the same evaluative code (accomplished by either overstatement or understatement)	"Your well-known integrity has cleared you of all blame, your modesty has saved you, your past life has been your salvation." (Cicero, when attacking Clodius)
Rhetorical question	Declarative statements taking a (falsely) interrogative form	Generates a sense of *commonality* between rhetor and audience via imagined dialogue	"Are you better off now than you were four years ago?" (Ronald Reagan [Franklin Roosevelt])
Parallelism	Groupings of similarly phrased ideas presented in rapid succession	*Quickens* the rhetorical pace and therefore generates psychological momentum in audience	"We shall pay any price, bear any burden, meet any hardship, support any friend, oppose any foe in order to assure the survival and success of liberty." (John Kennedy)

*Based in part on Espy [1983], Arnold [1974], and Kaufer [1981].

Unless we are careful, stylistic analysis can become a mere exercise, cataloging for the sake of cataloging. Learning that a rhetor used three rhetorical questions and eleven hyperboles hardly advances knowledge. All rhetors use imagery and they do so all the time. The important questions about style relate to the pattern of devices used and what the rhetor gains or loses by it. The examples in Table 7.3 adequately establish what these forms of imagery are like. There is no need to do criticism solely to find new examples. Instead, the good critic concentrates on the *intellectual operations* these stylistic tokens signal.

For example, Topf [1992] studied U.S. Supreme Court opinions, noting that they have changed very little in two centuries. Topf found that the justices convey legitimacy by adopting the stylistic patterns of earlier opinions— specifically, a consistent "grammar of conflict," making Supreme Court opinions "agonistic performance utterances" [p. 20]. The opinions follow traditional patterns of recounting social dramas: breach, crisis, redress, and reintegration, with the familiarity of these narratives presumably producing comfort and reassurance. Familiar context is also important in literature, as Black [1995] argues that textual allusions can operate as metaphors, allowing both the earlier and later artifacts to modify one another in the reader's mind. In a similar vein, Kaufer [1981] urges the critic to monitor persistent use of irony because it points to the existence of a **shared code** between rhetor and audience. He asserts that irony always has evaluation built into it and that a statement like "Nice weather, huh?" made by (drenched) Person A to (drenched) Person B is an attempt to reestablish that A and B still agree on standards for evaluating weather. Irony is thus an in-joke often used by in-crowds when the pressure is off. It tends to fall flat when used in other contexts (e.g., among strangers at a funeral).

In a similar vein, Lakoff and Johnson [1980:39] have examined metonymy and note that it serves as a kind of argumentative spotlight, calling attention to one feature rather than many features. So, for example, a metonymic statement like "Osama bin Laden destroyed the World Trade Center" is a rhetorically powerful way of isolating who was responsible for a given set of actions and, consequently, who should be singled out for praise or blame. Metonymy can therefore help to determine the **intellectual focus** of a message.

But what if a text contains little imagery or "dead" imagery? Even here the critic can learn something. Arendt [1963] notes, for example, that the remarks of Adolph Eichmann, the notorious Nazi leader, typically contained only clichés, unoriginal figures of speech (e.g., "a bolt from the blue"). Arendt argues that a mind so incapable of stylistic inventiveness was a mind ideally suited to the dulling themes of Nazi orthodoxy. In Eichmann's own rhetoric, then, Arendt found traces of the rhetoric to which Eichmann himself had become addicted.

In more recent times, the horrific events of the holocaust, and even the Nazis themselves, have been used as metaphors by those wishing to evoke strong emotion. Engnell [2001:312] cautions against easy acceptance of holocaust imagery, which can "desecrate" or trivialize the events originally named by those terms, calling instead for what he terms an ethic of "creative fidelity" to guide the use of this and other highly charged, contested vocabularies.

Violent imagery is, of course, powerful, and that is what makes it so attractive to rhetors. Daughton [1993] did a close reading of the metaphors in Franklin Roosevelt's first inaugural address. In addition to the martial imagery in the speech, stemming from FDR's desire to move the country out of the Great Depression, FDR relied heavily on religious images. These two metaphoric types joined, Daughton argued, to produce an image of "holy war." The resulting combination inspired a confident **worldview:** Since God was on the country's side, failure was impossible.

Metaphor is also a good device for embodying changing **cultural trends.** Osborn [1977:359, 362–3] notes, for example, that certain metaphors diminished in popularity over time as people "conquered" the sea. Thus, whereas Edmund Burke in the eighteenth century could describe a rival as being "on a wide sea, without chart or compass . . . whirled about, the sport of every gust," such metaphors were eventually replaced by space imagery (e.g., Adlai Stevenson's "We travel together, passengers on a little space ship, dependent on its vulnerable reserves of air and soil . . ."). These alterations, says Osborn, signal more than changing rhetorical fashion. Rushing [1989] agrees, warning against the oppressive entailments of the "space as frontier" metaphor, tracing how (U.S.) Americans habitually think in terms of exploiting each new frontier. To switch from one metaphorical system to another is to switch from one style of thinking to another. So a nation that finds imminent danger lapping at the edge of its own continent may well operate with greater military and environmental caution than one brazen enough to see itself as master of the stars and beyond.

And imagery can change quickly. Hughey et al. [1987] studied alterations in the AIDS metaphors found in popular newstories, noting when AIDS was used as the tenor, or subject, of the metaphor (e.g., "AIDS is a plague") and when AIDS was the vehicle, or object, of the metaphor (e.g., "She treats me like I've got AIDS"). They found that as the AIDS story saturated American culture, there was a dramatic increase in AIDS-as-vehicle metaphors. That is, in an astonishingly short period of time, AIDS moved from the thing clarified to the thing so well understood that it explained yet other concepts. In other words, metaphor can become something of a cultural timepiece for the enterprising critic.

Imagery is important. It tells us about what motivates people (e.g., voyages, salvation), what mystifies us (e.g., oceans, birth), and what frightens us (e.g., war, disease). Rhetoric uses them all, for good and for ill. Edelman [1964] urges us to take metaphor seriously because it is so sensitive to social changes. Thus, he warns, while a phrase like "an American presence in the Middle East" may sound friendly (to a U.S. citizen), like the sort of visit one cousin might pay another, this is imagery that masks policy. It should therefore be treated with deadly seriousness by the discerning rhetorical critic.

CONCLUSION

Analyzing style is a complex business, for language will not reveal its mysteries to the casual observer. Stylistic analysis takes patience: noting metaphorical clusters, being sensitive to a special use of anaphora. Often, making such discriminations is a tedious business, yielding a handful of message facts but no obvious explanations.

But stylistic criticism can be done and done well. The critic begins, as with all worthwhile projects, patiently and sensibly: noticing an isolated phrase here, an odd colloquialism there. These thoughts percolate as the critic reads the artifact again and again, focusing on different features each time. Gradually, the critic notices more and more that was missed at first. Occasionally, critics experience dramatic epiphanies, but more often a sense of the rhetor's strategy gradually develops. The critic may notice the text's intriguing connections or differences from another text, and the message takes on new meaning with the comparison. Lanham [1983:155] likens stylistic analysis to pulling first one thread and then another until a pattern begins to unravel and the critic recognizes the rhetor's distinctive voice. It is at this special moment of familiarity that the critical task takes on steam.

Perhaps stylistic criticism seems somewhat mystical. It is. Somewhat. And it will remain somewhat mystical until people become less complicated and until language exposes its several mysteries to one and all. Such a day may arrive, but it is not here yet. And so the critic goes to work.

TIPS FOR THE PRACTICING CRITIC

1. Examining syntax via primary and secondary structures is a good starting point. Critics should also notice whether the sentence structure perhaps reinforces (or undermines) the verbal content of the message. For instance, if a supervisor sends out a lengthy memo on the need to be more efficient, employees get a mixed message.
2. A message whose style is hard to describe is probably artfully done. It may fit the circumstances of the discourse situation so well that its language seems entirely natural, leaving the critic with nothing to say! This is a signal to look more closely, to notice features of the message that seemed "obvious" or "not worth mentioning" at first. If these features succeeded in convincing a student of rhetorical criticism that they were "not rhetorical," they may be operating in subtle and significant ways.
3. Take the analysis of style, especially imagery, *very slowly*. Stop after every sentence and ask, for example, "Is this *literally* possible?" If the answer is "no," then make a note of the image. If unsure what type of device you have found, consult Table 7.3, which also lists functions of each device. Those functions are a *starting point*, rather than exhaustive. Study the device in its

context and ask what else could have fit there. It may help to restate the idea in other terms and see what changes: What is lost or gained? Many critics find it useful to mark different devices with different colored highlighters to identify patterns. For more specific guidance, refer to the critical probes.

Chapter 8

ANALYZING LEXICON

Give rest, O Christ, to thy servant(s) with thy saints, where sorrow and pain are no more, neither sighing, but life everlasting.

Thou only art immortal, the creator and maker of mankind; and we are mortal, formed of the earth, and unto earth shall we return. For so thou didst ordain when thou createdst me, saying, "Dust thou art, and unto dust shalt thou return." All we do down to the dust; yet even at the grave we make our song: Alleluia, alleluia, alleluia.

Into thy hands, O merciful Savior, we commend thy servant [Name]. Acknowledge, we humbly beseech thee, a sheep of thine own fold, a lamb of thine own flock, a sinner of thine own redeeming. Receive him/her into the arms of thy mercy, into the blessed rest of everlasting peace, and into the glorious company of the saints in light. . . .

Christ is risen from the dead, trampling down death by death, and giving life to those in the tomb.

The Sun of Righteousness is gloriously risen, giving light to those who sat in darkness and in the shadow of death.

The Lord will guide our feet into the way of peace, having taken away the world.

Christ will open the kingdom of heaven to all who believe in his Name, saying, Come, O blessed of my Father; inherit the kingdom prepared for you.

Into paradise may the angels lead thee; and at thy coming may the martyrs receive thee, and bring thee into the holy city Jerusalem. [Prayer, 1979:484–5]

These are the familiar words spoken at a traditional Christian funeral. They were taken from the *Book of Common Prayer,* an Episcopalian document, but any contemporary Christian—Baptist, Methodist, Lutheran, probably even

Mormon or Roman Catholic—could recognize and approve of them. Even though the edition cited here was dated 1979 with a first printing in 1789, few changes have been made over the years, making its style old yet ageless. While ordinary Americans do not offer formal salutations ("Come here, O Jennifer") or use antiquated tenses ("didst ordain," "createdst"), they can understand what is being said here. Also, while they now "request" rather than "beseech," "sing" a song rather than "make" one, and refer to each other as "you" instead of "thee," they can still appreciate the prayer. Its imagery is either naturalistic ("formed of the earth," "Sun of Righteousness") or corporeal ("arms of thy mercy," "guide our feet") and hence reaches across the generations. The prayer's themes—human sinfulness, the divinity of Jesus, salvation for all believers—are so well wrought and so familiar that even their archaic language cannot sap them of vitality.

No doubt, the *Book of Common Prayer* could be rewritten in contemporary language. Some denominations have done so. But for many believers, these words will do just fine, thank you very much. For them, this prayer's language is precious, in part because it is old and in part because it has brought comfort over the years to so many loved ones standing at so many gravesides. Words like these can be counted upon. Their never-changingness connects modern Christians to the first Christians and thence to not-yet-born Christians. "This is *our* language," a Christian might say, "it marks us as special. People who cannot love our language probably cannot love our beliefs."

This chapter focuses on **lexicon**, *words that are unique to a group or individual and that have special rhetorical power*. Lexicons are important to study because they set people apart. For example, even if one had never read the above prayer and was presented with a disconnected list of its constituent words, one could learn something. Even in isolation, words such as "martyrs," "humbly," "sheep," "dust," and "guide" warn a prospective group member that *submission* to something or someone is expected in the text. On the other hand, words like "redeem," "mercy," "risen," "glorious," and "kingdom" imply that personal *improvement* can be expected in return for submission. Finally, words uncommon to everyday speech like "paradise," "alleluia," "immortal," "righteousness," and "Jerusalem" add a dimension of *mystery* to the message. In effect, the very lexicon of Christianity tells its story: Repentance for sin will be rewarded eternally by God in paradise.

Lexicons make for efficiency. By using preferred words, a rhetor can establish what Aristotle called *ethos,* the rhetor's credibility or authority—the right to address an audience. Certain words can be used to cue *pathos,* emotional appeals, and *logos,* logical appeals, as well. But what happens when a rhetor does not have access to such a lexicon? What kinds of ideas are possible when certain kinds of words are unavailable? This was the situation confronting Mr. F. J. Gould [n.d.:26–8] some years ago when writing *Funeral Services without Theology* for atheists. Knowing that atheists' loved ones also needed to hear comforting words, Gould offered sample messages for the nonbeliever's funeral service. One of his remembrances was the following:

> We assemble in this place to say a kind and solemn farewell to the remains of
> _____.
>
> We come as mourners. But the act of mourning is no strange event in human life. Not only do we grieve at the passing of friends. We may often have occasion to grieve over lost opportunities, or lost wealth, or lost health. And whenever a loss brings sorrow, it is our part not simply to mourn, but also to turn the affliction to some wise purpose in our life's experience. In death, therefore, we seek to find a meaning that shall bring consolation, and enable us to draw a hidden joy from the depth of sorrow. And this joy we discover in the thought that the living and the dead make up one vast family. Memory and love unite us to the departed in sacred ties. A household may be divided among various chambers, and the members, though parted by walls, may yet dwell in real union and sympathy. And so, also, we who live in the light of the sun and stars are yet comrades of the dead, bearing their image in our thought, their names on our lips, or their influences in our very blood and ideas and habits . . .
>
> Life is but the latest note in a music that began with the birth of humanity itself. The music is a song of households knit in the bonds of mutual love; of cities and states built up by courage and self-devotion; of benefits bestowed by wit and labor for the aid of the weak and helpless; of knowledge won from nature; of precious thoughts and teachings imparted by the sages. How immense and how deep is our debt to the past! How much of thankfulness we owe to the goodness, the intelligence, and the energy of men and women who are now dead, and who toiled in faith and patience for the children of their day, and for us remoter children whom they were never to look upon! How few of these forefathers and foremothers can we know as we knew the dead to whom we here offer our parting words! Yet we derive from them our health, our stores of sustenance, our learning, our all. It is one of our profoundest joys to know that we are united to this great past. "To live with the dead is one of the most precious privileges of humanity. . . ."
>
> Each one of us can help in the glorious task of rendering some service to the family which numbers more members dead than living. Each can offer an impulse of pity, of mercy, of justice. Each can add a useful thought, a cheerful and sensible word, a happy song, an effort to express something beautiful. Each can contribute a little bravery, a little wisdom, a little aim accomplished. And, by reason of that little tribute to the general wealth, we may enroll ourselves among the influences that will pass from age to age in fruitfulness and blessing. . . .

Clearly, Gould has been creative here. Denied use of the religious lexicon, he canvases human sentiments ("joy," "grief," "courage"), human challenges ("opportunity," "affliction," "labor"), and human virtues ("bravery," "intelligence," "goodness"). These are fine words, these human words, but they are hardly special in the way that "Dust thou are and unto dust shalt thou return" is special. The metaphors Gould uses are adequate (a "family" of humankind, living in the "light" of the stars, parted at times by "walls" of separation but ultimately heartened by "stores" of sustenance), but they do not have real rhetorical punch.

Also, while the Episcopalian memorial is spare and direct, the atheists' remarks are self-consciously embellished. Each purpose is a "wise" purpose, each joy "hidden," each family "vast." Sometimes it takes double adjectives to make the point ("how immense and deep is our debt") and the use of the superlative degree ("profoundest joys," "most precious privileges") makes the passage sound almost like advertising copy. Where one noun would have sufficed, the author uses two ("precious thoughts and teachings") or even three ("the goodness, the intelligence, the energy . . .").

In short, Gould was not short. He overfills his thoughts with words. It is as if he were constantly afraid of offending some constituency and so he includes them all ("forefathers and foremothers," "cities and states," "the living and the dead"). Deprived of Biblical images of hellfire and damnation, denied the stories of saints and sinners, robbed of textured depictions of an afterlife, Gould resigned himself to abstractions. He asked his audience to enroll itself "among the influences that will pass from age to age" without specifying what such influences actually *do*. He says that in death "we seek to find a meaning that shall bring consolation" but the consolation he offers—turning the affliction "to some wise purpose"—is as gray and lifeless as death itself. Gould's abstractions are so intellectualized that at one point he even speaks of the "*impulse*" of pity, not the felt emotion itself.

In a Judeo-Christian culture, it is hard to be an atheist. It is even harder to talk like one. This is not to say that Mr. Gould has done poorly. After all, he was writing a generic eulogy, a fill-in-the-blanks address for no one in particular and hence was almost necessarily driven to the heights of abstraction. But the *Book of Common Prayer* is equally generic and yet its words seem timely as well as timeless. At least in part, this effect is produced by a lexicon whose history authorizes and whose familiarity comforts. As Chapter 7 demonstrated, effective style emerges from words well arranged, both functionally and creatively. But effective style also depends on the *types* of words a rhetor chooses. That is the topic of this chapter.

EXAMINING GROUP LEXICONS

Like people, words have histories. That is why even synonyms come to mean (and feel) differently. Blankenship [1968:59] makes this point when commenting on variations like "I am thrifty; you are stingy; he's a miser" or "I agree; you must admit; he's forced to confess." Rhetoric requires the rhetor to wander through these lexical thickets when deciding what to say. In 1995, for example, the lead singer of Blood, Sweat & Tears declared to a sweltering summertime audience that it was "as hot as the last train to Auschwitz." What is the real problem here? No doubt it was hot in that Detroit suburb on that late July afternoon. No doubt it is a good idea for a performer to try to identify with his audience, people who had been baking in the sun for many hours before the group began to play. And no doubt talking about the weather is normally a safe thing to do. But then there is that word . . . Auschwitz.

Words like "Auschwitz" are part of a disapproved lexicon, as are "fag," "genocide," and "the N-word." These words can be unnerving, whether they appear alone or in context. Other words tell a happier story, words like "integrity," "commitment," "family." In the world of politics, "safe" words like these, often accompanied by a blizzard of short, pictorial clips, now fill the televised air, often disconnected from genuine argument. It is as if the words themselves had magical power, as if by intoning words like "strong defense" and "human rights" a candidate could be assured of political worthiness. Similarly, attacking one's opponent with such words as "toxic waste" or "welfare state" makes it seem as if *the saying* of these words can alone end discussion.

Words having special evocative power for a society have been dubbed **Ultimate Terms** by Weaver [1953]. Phrases like "true American," "equal justice for all," and "scientific advancement" are what Weaver called God Terms: We mentally genuflect when hearing them. Weaver noted that much public oratory is little more than a clever interspersing of such words at appropriate times, which often turns genuine communication into mere word-saying. Weaver also noted that Devil Terms, terms like "terrorism" and "illiteracy," give us a clear picture of malevolence and are therefore also rhetorically useful.

Weaver urged critics to track uses of such language to get an early reading on emerging societal values. After the attacks of September 11, 2001, for example, the U.S. Congress passed the Patriot Act, a title that says nothing about the legislation itself and everything about the kind of unquestioning acceptance the law's sponsors wanted to promote. Using such words allows rhetors to suspend the rules of reasoning and to shift the agenda for discussion, especially if its users are specially licensed keepers of the nation's sacred terminology (as members of Congress are). Weaver himself was deeply disturbed by the potential for unscrupulous use of Ultimate Terms. Even a brief listing of their rhetorical capacities shows why:

1. *Ultimate Terms are abstract.* They normally refer to ideas (like democracy) rather than to objects (like Xbox). They normally refer to the deceased (Malcolm X) rather than the living (Al Sharpton). Because they are abstract, their meanings can be twisted (e.g., "Choose Super-Cell, the all-American Wireless"). They can also be used to encompass more than they were intended to encompass (e.g., "A good Christian should vote conservatively"). And they can appear in situations for which they were never intended (e.g., when "right to work" became a euphemism for union bashing).

2. *Ultimate Terms are efficient.* Although it only has three letters, a word like *pig* can trigger powerful emotions. Thus, when the police were called pigs in the 1960s by radical activists, this Devil Term evoked images of "filthy" individuals doing the bidding of corrupt politicians, of the police's unabated "appetite" for power, and of the monstrous "breeding" practices of

the police who, in the eyes of the Left, always appeared on the scene in excessive numbers.

3. *Ultimate Terms are hierarchial.* That is why they are called ultimate. They lie at the top of society's pantheon of values and subsume all lesser terms. For this reason, they are used to pull rank, to make an opponent's case seem small and expedient. President George W. Bush did just that when he established the Department of Homeland Security, giving it broadly defined powers to coordinate antiterror efforts. Individual rights to privacy, many argued, were a small sacrifice compared to the overarching value of security for our homeland.

4. *Ultimate Terms are pre-emptive.* They let a rhetor carve out rhetorical territory and then seal it off from others. By calling their law the Patriot Act, for example, its sponsors challenged their opponents mightily, implying: "No *real* American would oppose this." In persuasion, whoever scrambles to the high ground first can set the parameters for the debate and, often, its necessary conclusion as well. (This bears out a reputed gem from Socrates: "If you let me define the terms, I win the argument.")

5. *Ultimate Terms have unstable meanings.* This is a particularly important, and dangerous, feature. Being abstract, Ultimate Terms can change in meaning from age to age and from topic to topic but their *form* never does. In *Crafting Equality,* Condit and Lucaites [1993] present what is essentially the history of a word, the word *equality.* They argue that equality has meant different things to different people at different times in U.S. history. Sometimes it has meant "separate but equal." Sometimes it has meant legal but not economic equality. Sometimes it has meant recompense for previous inequalities. Condit and Lucaites show that the word equality is an odd one because it has always had "ultimate" meaning even though it has never meant a *single* thing. Equality, they conclude, is not a black-and-white term, precisely because it has meant one thing to Blacks and another thing to Whites throughout American history.

But persuaders often encourage us to forget this distinction between form and content. They operate as if a word is a word is a word, as if a term's final meaning is determined at its christening. Thus, when a campaigner contrasts the "economic freedom" built into the Republican platform to the "collectivist tyranny" of the Democrats, the campaigner is inviting the triangulation of colonial Boston in the 1770s, Leninist Russia in the 1920s, and contemporary conditions. Even though times, meanings, audiences, and policies change, language sometimes does not change.

At other times it does. In her analysis of Socialist and peace activist Norman Thomas's 1943 speech, "Some Wrong Roads to Peace," Whedbee [2001] lays out how Thomas attempted to redefine American attitudes in the midst of World War II. By debunking the God term "Victory" and replacing it with "Peace," Whedbee argues, Thomas invited listeners to reject the position of thrilled spectators cheering for their team, and to adopt the position of compassionate humanists, committed to alleviating all suffering.

It is easy to think of Ultimate Terms as mere semantics, as an idle game with no consequence. Nothing could be more dangerous. The loss of life and livelihood suffered by those persecuted for their race or sexuality, for example, remind us how deadly a game labeling can be. But if language is a game, Weaver would observe, the critic must become its referee. After all, God Terms like truth, justice, peace, freedom, and love really *are* worth protecting from their corrupters. Discrimination, harassment, poverty, oppression, and ignorance really *are* worth condemning. A sacred lexicon remains sacred only as long as it is revered in practice, and so the critic must help determine the fairest use of Ultimate Terms. One way to do so is by answering the following critical probes:

- What explicit or implicit God terms is the rhetor urging the audience to accept?
- What explicit or implicit Devil terms is the rhetor urging the audience to disavow?
- What evidence does the artifact offer for specific denotations and connotations of the terms?
- What are the social or political policy implications of these invitations?

A second approach to lexicon is to analyze **Code Words,** specialized terms that designate uncommon phenomena (or that designate common phenomena in uncommon ways) and which are unique to a subgroup. Typically, the more precise a word is, the more remote it becomes (e.g., "ribonucleic acid"). This remoteness makes for efficiency. The surgeon who asks a nurse for a trephine, for example, gets what is needed and gets it quickly. To have asked for "that saw-type thing over there" might have produced the same result but more likely would have produced an array of potential cutting instruments. Such inefficiency can be costly in surgery: A word lost can mean time lost and time lost can mean a patient lost.

For similar reasons, Code Words are used by scientists (they speak of an "angle of trajectory" instead of its tilt), by bureaucrats ("vehicular traffic" for cars and trucks), by lawyers ("indemnify" for protect), by athletes ("triple lutz"), and by other specialists ("blog," "fortissimo," "abstract impressionism"). As tastes become more refined, as people become more segregated, as ideas become more technical, Code Words become more common.

Code Words have an unsavory reputation because they are inherently discriminatory: They set their users apart from the larger society—even if the word's meaning is no secret. "One of the privileges men enjoy in a sexist society is the greater latitude in the use of emotionally charged words," writes Sol Saporta [1988–1989:163]. Women, Soporta argues, are in a double bind: If they reject "ladylike" behavior, for example, by using the word *bitch,* they may be disrupting men's privilege, but they are also participating in their own degradation. As a result, many people react to Code Words defensively, as if such terms constituted a rhetorical conspiracy against them. Sometimes, Code Words are just that. But sometimes, they result from practicality. We use linguistic shortcuts because grunting "torque!" is easier than orating: "Seeing as how I am lying on my back fixing the transmission linkage and hence cannot extricate myself to reach that curious, wrench-like implement at your feet, would you be so kind as to. . . ."

Others' Code Words keep us out of the picture and hence we resent them. *Their* Code Words are arcane, obtuse, an affront to civility. *Our* Code Words are "the language of our fathers" or our "distinctive linguistic heritage." Our Code Words are our semantic birthright while theirs become legalese, scientism, or bureaucratese. The agony of indecision that was the 2000 presidential election was punctuated with hilarity as the Code Words "dimpled, pregnant, and hanging chads" came into popular use as the subject of jokes. Often, Code Words function as rhetorical currency, enabling members of a particular group to demonstrate their legitimacy, their right to belong. When one is not fully integrated into a particular community, the results can range from disastrous to comical. In the film *Catch Me If You Can*, set in the late 1960s, con artist Frank Abagnale (played by Leonardo DiCaprio) impersonates a doctor in an emergency room. He repeats a line from the popular TV show *Dr. Kildare* ("And do you concur, Doctor?") which doesn't quite fit the situation, and his colleagues are suitably bewildered.

Code Words are standard rhetorical tools that perform a number of functions, among which are the following:

1. *Code Words insulate.* Code Words are a way of hiding in public, of sending messages to select persons without risk of interruption or interference from the unselected. Hayes [1976] documents this in a study of "gayspeak" where he describes two distinct cultures within the gay community, one that uses Code Words openly (including such terms as "nelly number," "S/M," and "Chippendale queen") and another that uses ordinary language in jargonized ways (e.g., "liberal-minded," "artistic," "tendencies"). This latter group, says Hayes, is seeking to maximize its rhetorical range while simultaneously guarding against the social isolation the former group reluctantly accepts.

2. *Code Words unify.* Turner [1973] makes the point that slang (a set of informal Code Words) is a token that can be shared with new members of a group to make them feel included. By using slang, the neophyte participates in the group rhetorically but not financially, organizationally, behaviorally, etc. As Turner says [p. 189], "Slang may even have its usefulness among children as a protection, so that they can begin to learn social behavior without staking too much of themselves at once." He also notes that the very act of learning Code Words is an important ritual for new members: "The student of geometry is never to *draw* anything; he may *describe* circles, *construct* a triangle, *produce* its sides and *drop* a perpendicular, so that geometry is in part the learning of new collocations of words special to the subject" [p. 172]. Speechwriter Peggy Noonan [1998:41] confirms that in her days as a reporter, "So entranced were my young colleagues and I by what we heard in the newsroom

each day that we took to barking our own pidgin dialect to the boys on the desk: 'A.P. with an Urgent at twelve o'clock high, light-weave polyester.' "

3. *Code Words neutralize.* Code Words often drain emotion from social or political events. In the language of Chapter 7, Code Words are frequently found in the Periodic (or noun-filled) style that hides the essential action that verb styles reveal. Thus, Code Words help us deal with unpleasantness, a point made some years ago by George Orwell [1946:363]:

> Things like the continuance of British rule in India, the Russian purges and de-portations, the dropping of the atomic bombs in Japan, can indeed be defended but only by arguments which are too brutal for most people to face and which do not square with the professed aims of political parties. Thus . . . [d]efenseless vil-lages are bombarded from the air, the inhabitants driven out into the countryside, the cattle machine-gunned, the huts set on fire with incendiary bullets; this is called *pacification*. Millions of peasants are robbed of their farms and sent trudg-ing along the roads with no more than they can carry; this is called *transfer of pop-ulation* or *rectification of frontiers*. People are imprisoned for years without trial, or shot in the back of the neck or sent to die of scurvy in Arctic lumber camps; this is called *elimination of undesirable elements.*

4. *Code Words sanctify.* Code Words make bad things neutral (e.g., "neu-tralizing the enemy" sounds less brutal than "killing"), neutral things good (e.g., explaining one's religion becomes "witnessing"), and good things mag-nificent (e.g., cutting off-tackle becomes a "Heisman move"). Himelstein [1983] observes that Code Words can desensitize voters by making political issues seem technical issues. In analyzing racism, for example, Himelstein asked [p. 156] "How does one avoid blatant offense to black voters and at the same time communicate [to white voters] faithfulness to the racist canons of the recent past?" The answer? Code Words. Words like "ward politics," "sec-tionalism," and "neighborhood representation" filled the campaign rhetoric Himelstein studied, giving white voters directions without appearing to have done so: "The politicians had winked, and the [white] voters had understood" [p. 165].

5. *Code Words stabilize.* Edelman [1971] observes that Code Words keep people in positions of power. So, for example, those who have not learned the language of the bureaucracy or who cannot use it with authority are denied its riches. That is why there is so little semantic creativity in politics, an arena whose numbing technicalities make ideas technical and audiences numb. It is this numbing, this state of nonfeeling, that makes the voter ripe for political exploitation. For a politician to avoid Code Words, warns Edelman [p. 73], and "to speak and write in fresh or unconventional terms while jargon swirls all about one in an organization [would be] to state definitively that one is not buying the accepted values and not docilely conforming to authority." The political satire *Bulworth* [1998] depicted Warren Beatty as a candidate who

did just that. And the establishment was not pleased. Few politicians, says Edelman, run such risks.

When examining Code Words, the critic does what critics always do—asks questions. So we offer the following critical probes:

- Why are Code Words used here and not there?
- Why this lexicon and not another?
- What attitudes and values are the Code Words walling in? Which are they walling out?
- Whom do they protect? Whom do they disenfranchise?

There are many such questions for the critic to ask because there are so many Code Words. So the critic studies them, sorting out in each instance what is being said and what is not. All too often, Code Words make ideas do the bidding of language. It is the critic's job to reverse that process.

EXAMINING INDIVIDUAL LEXICONS

Thus far, we have focused on groups' sacred or specialized words. But individuals' language choices are also worthy of study. We tune into Oprah Winfrey each afternoon, not knowing exactly what she will say but confident that it will be familiar because her style is so distinctive. Style, the rhetor's characteristic or distinctive manner of communication (as compared to other rhetors), is therefore a basic force in everyday interaction. But how much of this manner of communication must a critic assess? Which of its patterns are really important? In this section, we will suggest some guidelines.

> Dear Roxanne,
> I met somebody else and she is real cute too.
> I hope I haven't hurt you but I probably did.
> It was really great knowing you and now I am going to Tahoe to be a dealer.
> Yours truley (T-R-U-L-E-Y),
> Chris

Roxanne [RCA/Columbia, 1987], a filmic retelling of the classic French romance *Cyrano de Bergerac* [Rostand, 1898], features Steve Martin and Daryl Hannah as the lovers separated by a nose. C. D. ("Charlie") Bales (Martin) is in love with Roxanne (Hannah), who becomes infatuated with a classically handsome (yet linguistically uninspiring) firefighter named Chris. Discouraged, Charlie agrees to help Chris woo Roxanne by feeding him dialogue and penning love letters on his behalf. Eventually, Roxanne is forced to confront the dramatic differences between the good-bye note quoted above and the previous letters she has received. In other words, when comparing the Individual Lexicons of the two rhetors, she realizes that she has succumbed to the charms of a shallow imposter. When she confronts Charlie, she is furious at the deception, and she challenges him to read both letters aloud. He does so, attempting to sound as if the language he authored were unfamiliar to him.

C: Uh, "All day long, I, I think, uh, 'Where is she? um . . . What is she doing now?' Occasionally, I see you on the street and I feel uh the nerves in my stomach, a wave crashing over me." Heh heh—it's so "him"!

R: Go on!

C: Uh . . . "I remember everything about you. Every move, no matter how insignificant it might seem. . . .—July 11th, 2:30 in the afternoon. I, uh, I—you changed your hair: not that much, but I noticed, and uh, it was as though I had looked at the sun too long. I could close my eyes and see it again and again: the way your hair moved, your walk, your dress, everywhere I looked."

R: It's nice, isn't it? . . . I went through all of the other letters, Charlie. They're all in the same hand. It was your voice that night under the balcony. Chris didn't write those letters; you did.

C: (with chagrin) Yeah. Yeah,

R: All this time, right there in front of me. And I couldn't even see you. You BASTARD! (she lands a right to his nose)

The audience is invited to see Charlie's last-ditch effort to escape detection as comical. When he chuckles lamely and says, "It's so 'him'!" he is making a pathetic final attempt to claim that Chris's style matches his own. Of course, it wouldn't take a rocket scientist (which Roxanne happens to be) to spot the differences in these rhetorical styles. But it would take a rhetorical critic to describe them. The Individual Lexicons differ, as well as the syntax and imagery, so we will bring all our stylistic resources from Chapters 7 and 8 to bear here.

In terms of syntax and imagery (Chapter 7), the repetitive sentence structure of Chris's good-bye note features the most basic compound sentences: this and this, period; that and that, period. Each sentence is about the same length. The audience can "hear" no variety in rhythm or complexity or pacing. This is "See Spot run" discourse, using and even misusing the most common one- and two-syllable words (misspelling "truly," using "real cute" instead of "really cute"). There is no preamble, no getting the reader ready for the breakup. Simply: "I met somebody else and she is real cute too." Apparently all it takes to disrupt the course of this rhetor's affection is another partner of sufficient "cuteness" to appear, and no other explanations are necessary. Each sentence juxtaposes two thoughts without any transitional aid, relying on the reader to supply the logical link with only the simplest conjunction (and, but). Appropriately, the abrupt sound of each sentence echoes the abrupt leaving of one lover for another. But the rhetor displays no imagination, no originality, no complexity, no depth.

In contrast, Charlie's letter includes a variety of sentence lengths and structures, providing the sophisticated reader (i.e., Roxanne) with a more diversified and hence pleasurable experience. Although still employing familiar words, this rhetor puts them into startling combinations of images (nerves in stomach, waves crashing), which disorient the reader, piquing her interest. The writer displays grammatical competence, using the subjunctive form appropriately ("it was as though" rather than "it was like"). The respectful admiration and devotion ("All day long . . . I remember everything about you") verge on obsession, but remain flattering, nonthreatening. The reader's effect on the rhetor is described as momentous ("as though I had looked at the sun too long"). In short, this writer appears highly unlikely to toss the reader aside for somebody else, no matter how cute. There is no jockish masculine reserve here. This love is extravagantly vulnerable, this lover willing to risk social embarrassment by expressing the overwhelming nature of his feelings.

In analyzing Individual Lexicons, the critic might ground her or his analysis by tallying actual word choices, as Gibson [1966] did with his "tough, sweet, and stuffy" styles (see Chapter 7). For illustration, we present a simplified version here, one that attends to variety, complexity, certainty, and references to self and reader. At 42 words, Chris's note is less than half of Charlie's (98)—but of course, size doesn't really matter. It's what the rhetor does with it that counts. While our analysis of syntax and imagery might lead us to assume that Charlie's letter uses longer, less familiar words, counting actual words leads to a more complex answer: yes, and no.

Perhaps surprisingly, Table 8.1 shows that on a percentage basis, Charlie actually uses *less variety* than Chris does. Numerical findings create questions, as well as answer them. As with the application of any critical system, the critic must account for and interpret the patterns in imaginative ways, in order to produce criticism that teaches us something. So what can the critic offer to explain what might seem a surprising finding (Charlie's greater repetition)? Rereading the letters, the critic might notice that Chris is covering a great deal of geographic, professional and relational distance—from here to Tahoe, from firefighter to card dealer, from one love to the next. So it makes sense that he would need different words. Charlie, in sharp contrast, is composing an Ode to Roxanne. He has a single subject around which he circles continuously. A large part of the repetition, then, makes sense: *your* hair, *your* walk, *your* dress. So Chris's variety serves to distance himself from Roxanne, while Charlie's repetition describes an orbit around her.

TABLE 8.1 Stylistic Features of Chris and Charlie's Letters

Verbal Category	Chris	Charlie
Variety (words used only once)	83%	73%
Multisyllable words	5%	7%
One-syllable words	79%	82%
Certainty	67%	64%
Self-Reference	12%	7%
Reference to Roxanne	7%	9%
Reference to New Love	7%	0%

Both writers are also about equal in certainty ("I am going" as opposed to "I hope"). How to explain this? Both genres of letters, both speech-acts, assume self-certainty: good-bye, I adore you. Accordingly, each writer is confident of his own feelings and actions, less sure about hers. Chris is unsure of whether he hurt Roxanne, whereas Charlie is only unsure about where she is and what she is doing at a given moment. He writes with confidence that he notices every detail about her, and provides several details as proof. The high percentage of one-syllable words gives rhetorical momentum to each letter, providing a sense of motion (in Charlie's case, toward Roxanne, and in Chris's case, away from her). Likewise, both writers use words of three or more syllables with similar frequency, perhaps reflecting that although these are supposedly written letters, they are really meant to be heard aloud, as movie dialogue, and hence they bear the stamp of conversational style. (Of course, Chris's "somebody" and "probably" are lower-grade-level vocabulary than Charlie's "occasionally" and "insignificant.")

The biggest difference between the two letters rests in the references to self and reader. Chris refers most often to himself and dedicates only three words to Roxanne (four, if one counts "yours truley")—about the same number he uses for his new love interest. Charlie, in contrast, refers to Roxanne slightly more often than he does to himself. (Since this is a missive about his devotion to her, he also must appear frequently as a subject.) It is revealing that the good-bye note symbolically spends as much time on the replacement lover as it does on the recipient, with almost double the focus on the rhetor. Each letter thus enacts the message it is sending, either breaking up or gaining intimacy, at the microlinguistic level.

The original French novel on which this film is based was a tragic romance because the heroine (an insufficiently sensitive stylistic analyst) never realized the deception. Contemporary adaptations such as *Roxanne* and *The Truth About Cats and Dogs* turn the tale into romantic comedy, optimistically allowing the deceived parties to benefit from their crash course in rhetorical criticism and recognize that the rhetorical style they love comes in an unconventional package. While stylistic differences more subtle than these (exaggerated in this film for comic effect) may be discernible to a casual reader, counting can help ground the critical claims in the data, rather than in the critic's presuppositions.

When doing lexical analysis of a small number of artifacts, then, critical probes can help. Of course, the critic can develop other probes, depending on the artifact. Here are some starters for general use:

- What words recur with frequency? (Usually, findings about content-words such as nouns, verbs, and adverbs will be of greater interest than articles such as "the" or conjunctions such as "and.")
- What are these recurring words? What words tend to modify them?
- How complex and lengthy are the sentences?
- How much is the rhetor relying on common, everyday words? How simple or complex is the vocabulary?

- To what extent does the rhetor rely on specialized words (Code Words)?
- How often does the rhetor refer to him- or herself?
- How often does the rhetor refer to other persons, events, times, places?
- How frequently does the rhetor invoke abstract symbols (God Terms)?

And most importantly, for all of the above questions, the critic can then ask:

- What conclusions can be drawn from these findings? Do these patterns seem appropriate and normal for this genre, role, audience, etc.? Why or why not? How can they best be explained and understood?

An interesting real-life example of the importance of individual style occurred in the case of Ted Kaczynski, otherwise known as the Unabomber. After years of unsuccessful pursuit by the FBI, this domestic terrorist, who had killed and maimed several people with letter bombs, was eventually caught because of his distinctive rhetorical style. In 1995, the Unabomber issued an ultimatum to the *Washington Post* and the *New York Times:* Publish his Manifesto and the bombings would stop. The papers complied and so did he. As Foster [2000] tells it, Kaczynski's sister-in-law, living abroad, read the rambling manifesto and noticed familiar linguistic patterns, including specific phrases that echoed the rants and diatribes she'd seen in letters from her brother-in-law. She brought her concerns to the attention of her partner, who eventually alerted the authorities to his brother's identity and whereabouts.

Naturally, lexical-analysis-as-detective-work is a conjectural business, and is especially pressurized when lives are at stake. But cases like this raise fascinating and important questions: How unique is an individual's lexicon? And how can it be reliably determined? To begin to answer broad questions such as these, at least two things are required: (1) a sizeable sample of a rhetor's style, representing diverse rhetorical conditions and (2) a sample of others' word choices to be used for comparison. As Enkvist [1971] says, the study of style can be the study of deviance from known linguistic patterns.

This sort of comparative logic has guided a number of studies. Knapp et al. [1974] compared the spontaneous (truthful) remarks of people to lies they told at the behest of experimenters. Individuals' styles changed dramatically from condition to condition: fewer words spoken when lying, fewer self-disclosures, more caution in their remarks, more repetition of words, and fewer factual citations. It was as if the "liars" were trying to step away from themselves, as if their natural lexicons would not cooperate with the lies being told. In another provocative study, Satterfield [1998] analyzed the rhetoric of Winston Churchill, Adolf Hitler, Franklin Roosevelt, and Joseph Stalin during World War II and documented a trend in their speaking: The most aggressive and risky actions of these world leaders were immediately preceded by relatively optimistic and simplistic discourse. Although Satterfield's analysis was retrospective, he argued that its real utility would come in predicting behavior. Thus, critics could predict invasions before they occur.

In each of these studies, scholars examined what Sedelow and Sedelow [1966:1] call the distributional properties of language use, meaning the systematic ways word patterns vary from rhetor to rhetor or from condition to condition. Research of this sort has a quantitative bent to it. It assumes that any claim about stylistic distinctiveness is ultimately a mathematical claim: Feature A does or does not appear in this text; Feature B appears more often or less often than Feature C; Feature D appears less frequently than the norm. Turner [1973:25] makes these same points when he says:

> If there are choices in language, there are probabilities . . . Even such basic concepts as a 'rare word' or a 'common word' are statistical concepts . . . To take a simple illustration, if I am about to spell an English word, the probability that I will use a particular letter to begin it, say *n* or *g*, can be roughly measured with a ruler and a good dictionary; if I choose *n* to begin with, the probability that the next letter will be g becomes zero; if I reach the stage *notwithstandin-*, the probability that the next letter will be *g* becomes certainty.

The stylistic critic need not trade in good sense for a ruler (or a computer). Counting things only takes one so far. But counting the right things at the right times under the right circumstances can guard against a researcher's natural biases [see Gastil, 1992]. Most usefully, systematic analysis of this sort can produce startling (or confirming) findings that become questions for the critic. The critic then interprets these patterns with the resources of creative intelligence, producing critical insight that might otherwise be unavailable. The rest of this chapter will show why.

Figure 8.1 presents a speech John Kennedy [1961b] gave to the Democratic National Committee the day after his inauguration. The speech is not remarkable: It is a back-slapping piece of political celebration. It is brief, convivial, and spontaneous. It includes teasing and bantering. But it is not John Kennedy. Not really. Although the speech conforms to popular stereotypes of the Kennedy Style, this speech was not a normal one for him. Most of his speaking was drier, less personal, more restrained. Table 8.2 shows how we know this to be true.

The information in Table 8.2 comes from analyzing Kennedy's text with a computer. Especially when examining a great number of texts, computer analysis can be a great timesaver. Hart [1985] developed a computer program called DICTION to guide the computer and tell it which words to look for in a passage. The computer breaks a message into its individual words and then searches for word patterns, thereby determining the rhetor's basic lexicon. The program does so by employing **dictionaries,** lists of words the critic specifies ahead of time. So, for example, if the computer were prompted with a dictionary called *Animals,* it might look for dog, cat, sheep, etc. After finding all such usages, the computer would report how many times these words were employed versus those found in other texts previously searched with the Animal dictionary.

FIGURE 8.1 Kennedy's Speech as Analyzed by the DICTION Program

I WANT to express my (appreciation) to all of you for your (kind)(welcome), and also to take this occasion to express my (great) appreciation—and I think the (appreciation) of us all—to Senator Jackson who assumed the chairmanship of the Democratic Party at the Convention, who was greatly responsible for our (success) in November and has been an invaluable (aid) during the transition. Whatever has been done that is useful in the party in the last 5 or 6 months he has played a great part in it. And I feel that the party has served a most useful national purpose—and while Senator Jackson is obligated to serve the people of Washington in the Senate, I know that we can continue to count on him in the days to come for counsel and advice and support. So I hope we will all stand and give a good cheer to Scoop Jackson.

[Scoop] automatically loses his share of the [$4-million] [debt]—we are not going to let him in on it. [John Bailey] has become the [proprietor,] along with [Mac,] of this [enterprise.] I think we are particularly fortunate to have [John Bailey.] I heard [Governor Lawrence] in his seconding [speech] say the trouble with everything is that they don't know enough of what is going on here in [Washington;] they ought to get out in the [field.] I agree with him completely. We have got a man from the field who knows what's wrong here in Washington, and I am delighted that John Bailey is going to take over this job. He is more popular today than he will be any time again in his life. I will feel that he is doing a good job when you all say, "Well, Kennedy is all right, but Bailey is the one who is really making the mistakes." That's the way it was in Connecticut. Ribicoff was never wrong, it was always Bailey's fault. So that is what he is going to do down here.

Upbeat introduction results from Kennedy's Optimism score of 238, which was one of the highest in the sample.

Heavy use of prepositional phrases and passive voice constructions decreases Kennedy's Activity score.

JFK's Realism score of 241 is exceptionally high and derives from a combination of personal, temporal, concrete, and spatial references.

Semantically, humor is often the product of overly assured language devoid of qualification, all of which results in a high Certainty score.

But/I/am/delighted/that/he/is/going/to/do/it./It/is/a/sacrifice/for/him./
But/I/think/we/are/getting/the/services/of/someone/who/works/in/the/party/
year/in/and/year/out,/understands/what/the/party/can/do,/understands/what/
the/role/of/the/Chairman/is—and/I/must/say/that/I/am/delighted/to/see/
him/assuming/the/position/vacated/by/Senator/Jackson./

Lastly, I want to thank all of you for being with us at the inaugural. The party is not an end in itself—it is a means to an end. And you are the people who, in victory and defeat, have maintained the Democratic Party, maintained its traditions and will continue to do so in the future. I hope the relationship between all of us can continue to be as cordial as possible. I believe in strong political organizations in our country. The Republican Party is strong and vigorous today after the election of 1960. I think we are, also. And when we do that, I think we serve great national purposes.

The party is the means by which programs can be put into action—the means by which people of talent can come to the service of the country. And in this great free society of ours, both of our parties—the Republican and Democratic Parties—serve the interests of the people. And I am hopeful that the Democratic party will continue to do so in the days to come. It will be in the interest of us all, and I can assure you that I will cooperate in every way possible to make sure that we do serve the public interest.

You have done so well in the past. We couldn't possibly have won without your help. I look forward to working with you in the future, and I want you to know that here in Washington, we may not know always what is going on as well as you do, but at least we are trying.

Thank you.

Colloquial phrases produce a very high Familiarity score; monosyllabic words result in a low Complexity score; and a paragraph devoid of adjectival constructions accounts for the low Embellishment score.

Parallel constructions linked in sequence produce a Kennedyesque flourish as well as a very low Variety score.

Kennedy uses hallowed, albeit stock, phrases to generate an uncharacteristically high Symbolism score.

This is traditional political peroration consisting of high Self-Reference and Human Interest scores which, together, build speaker–audience bonds.

TABLE 8.2 Stylistic Features of the Kennedy Speech

Verbal Category	1/21/61 Speech	Kennedy Average	Other Presidents' Averages
Activity (aggressive, planned)	192.0	204.0	200.5
Realism (concrete, specific)	241.0	198.0	91.0
Certainty (assured, totalistic)	196.0	190.0	185.3
Optimism (inspired, praising)	238.0	213.0	220.0
Complexity (large words)	4.70	4.58	5.20
Variety (different words)	.410	.493	.488
Self-reference (I, me, etc.)	18.00	4.68	8.57
Familiarity (everyday words)	135.0	102.0	102.1
Human interest (references to people)	32.0	26.0	27.8
Embellishment (colorizing words)	.042	.070	.066
Symbolism (God Terms)	6.00	2.21	5.45

From Hart [1984c:19].

DICTION does not have a category called Animals, but it does employ such word lists as **Activity** ("achieve," "change," "plunge," etc.), Realism ("city," "buildings," "farmer"), **Certainty** ("everyone," "shall," "entire"), **Optimism** ("pleased," "generous," "exciting"), **Self-Reference** ("I," "me," "myself"), and **Human Interest** ("boy," "friend," "you"). The program searches for God Terms (here called **Symbolism:** "America," "democracy," "peace") and also calculates how **Embellished** a passage is by comparing its proportion of adjectives and adverbs to its number of nouns and verbs.

Finally, the program studies the richness of the rhetor's vocabulary (a high **Variety** score means the text is not repetitious), its use of everyday words (i.e., **Familiarity**), and how complicated it is (a high **Complexity** score means the rhetor used large words frequently). Guided by such search tools, the computer proceeds through a message word by word, remembering which terms of which type were used when. Table 8.2 simulates how the computer did its "looking" when examining the Kennedy speech.

Although computers are dull-witted when compared to a sensitive critic, they can make up in efficiency what they lack in imagination. DICTION has these advantages: (1) It examines every text in exactly the same way; (2) it ignores all words except those it has been instructed to "look" for; (3) it performs its tasks with lightning speed; (4) it never gets tired; (5) it never forgets what it has "learned" about any message; (6) it can track many kinds of words simultaneously (i.e., it can tell which portion of a text is highly Certain and which is *both* Optimistic and Certain).

Another advantage is that a computer cannot be seduced by the rhetoric it examines. Because it rather stupidly looks only for what it has been asked to look for, it is never sidetracked by interesting imagery or a humorous aside or a tear-stained narrative. It looks only for words, words, and more words. But afterward, it can report on verbal *patterns* that the imagery-noting critic was too busy to spot when inspecting the same message.

DICTION therefore operates like the Secret Service personnel who watch the crowd while the crowd (and the president) watch the tennis match. At the end of the day, when the president relaxes with them recounting the excitement of the contest, the Secret Service folks cannot comment on the overhead smash that won the fifth set. But they can tell the president how the crowd's mood changed when Serena Williams threw her racket. Reporting on crowd behavior can also be a type of tennis criticism.

A computer will never supplant the critic's wisdom, but its comparative information calls attention to features the critic may have missed. Table 8.2 shows this. At first, these findings seem odd since the popular press continually ran newsclips of the John Kennedy displayed in the D.N.C. speech. The Kennedy in that speech was witty, almost frisky, the same Kennedy who regaled reporters during press conferences. But DICTION shows that this was a *rare* John Kennedy. While this speech did display his characteristically simple style (see Complexity and Familiarity), in other ways it was singular. He was more concrete here than normal (see Realism) and more disclosive (see Self-Reference); he used many more Ultimate Terms (see Symbolism) and was substantially more upbeat (see Optimism). No matter what this speech implies, then, Mr. Kennedy's *general* style was quite dry and institutional. While a conventional critic might have discovered this same thing eventually, DICTION did so more quickly.

An important limitation of a program like DICTION is that it examines words out of context. By not distinguishing between "The boy hit the ball" and "The ball boy was hit" but only noting that the word "ball" appears in both statements, DICTION violates one type of context, the internal context of the message. But this type of context is not all there is to rhetoric. For example, the fact that the word "ball" appears in both passages signals a common concern with game-related matters (as opposed to religion-related or landscaping-related matters). The traditional critic might well miss these themes. (As Hart [2001:58] says, "At its best, [DICTION] points up the true-but-not-noticed.") And such easily overlooked themes may have *additive* effects on audiences who hear game-centered reference after game-centered reference, thereby contributing to their perceptions of rhetorical tone. So, even when sweeping across a text quickly and "destroying" its linguistic unity, DICTION likely simulates what listeners themselves do when processing messages.

The DICTION analysis of the Kennedy speech largely squares with our intuitions. Even a casual reading of the text reveals its personal, pragmatic tones. Then why use a computer? Because computers capture these tones quickly, reliably, and, most important, comparatively. Consider, for example, Table 8.3, which compares the Kennedy text to others examined previously. Few persons would confuse the Kennedy message with Martin Luther King's

TABLE 8.3 Comparative Use of Rhetorical Style*

Verbal Category	Martin Luther King	Rabbi Prinz	John F. Kennedy	Franklin D. Roosevelt
Activity (aggressive, planned)	Low	Low	Medium	High
Realism (concrete, specific)	High	Medium	Very high	Low
Certainty (assured, totalistic)	High	Medium	Medium	Low
Optimism (inspired, praising)	Very low	Medium	High	Medium
Complexity (large words)	Medium	Low	Medium	Very low
Variety (different words)	Low	Low	Low	Low
Self-reference (I, me, my, etc.)	Medium	Medium	High	Low
Familiarity (everyday words)	Medium	Low	Very high	Very low
Human interest (references to people)	Medium	Low	Medium	Medium
Embellishment (colorizing words)	Medium	High	Medium	Medium

*In comparison to a total sample of 861 public messages.

"I Have a Dream" speech. DICTION is also not confused. It finds an assuredness in the King speech missing in Kennedy's (see Certainty), perhaps showing that social movements permit more exhortation than do political celebrations. This difference is striking since, *for Kennedy,* this was one of his most assured speeches. But as a practical politician, he could not paint with King's broad brush nor could he be as precise. On the other hand, Mr. Kennedy could be more upbeat than King (see Optimism) and do what politicians do best: flatter ("give a good cheer to Scoop Jackson") and promise ("I can assure you that I will cooperate in every way . . .").

All of this is in sharp contrast to Rabbi Prinz's speech, which DICTION profiles as lecturish: heavy use of unfamiliar words, little Human Interest, and heavy Embellishment (adjectives usually slow down a message). The Activity found in Rabbi Prinz's speech is also the lowest of the five, documenting the philosophical tone of his remarks. It is little wonder, then, that DICTION finds almost no similarity between the Prinz and Kennedy texts.

The main advantage of DICTION is that it remembers the features of thousands of other messages when analyzing a text. By doing so, DICTION does what listeners do (without knowing it): It uses old texts to interpret new ones. Although DICTION ignores context at the level of the sentence, it enables the critic to account for another type of context—the larger rhetorical environment—quite handily. As Hart and Jarvis [1997:1100] argue, computerized analysis operates on the assumption that texts exist in a "community of discourse," and that "no text is understandable apart from the rhetorical world from which it was drawn." When they listened to President Roosevelt on December 8, 1941, for example, most Americans knew they were hearing something extraordinary, in part because the president had just asked Congress to declare war but also because of the new tone in his remarks.

DICTION also senses this when featuring the Activity in Roosevelt's remarks ("Last night Japanese forces attacked Hong Kong. Last night Japanese forces attacked . . ."). While FDR's language is not hard to understand (low scores on Complexity and Variety), he does draw on the special vocabulary of war ("hostilities," "air squadrons," "torpedoed") and of international geography ("Honolulu," "Guam," "Midway Island"), thereby scoring low on Familiarity. No doubt, the *divergence* between his familiar and unfamiliar words told listeners that something unprecedented was afoot and that listening to Roosevelt at that moment would be like nothing they had experienced before.

Another interesting aspect of the Roosevelt message is its midrange score on Optimism. At first, this seems an anomaly since Roosevelt was delivering a war message. But DICTION prompts us to think anew about the President's rhetorical task. He of course had to discuss the war, and words like "infamy," "deceive," "invasion," and "danger" show that he did. But for each negative statement he made, he also included a positive one, thereby creating dialectical tension. Early on, for example, he contrasts the "treachery" of the Japanese ambassadors with the peace-seeking United States. Later, after detailing the evil done the night before, Roosevelt talks of "inevitable triumph," "unbounding determination," and "absolute victory." Naturally, Roosevelt wanted the American people to deal realistically with the new challenges he described, but he also knew that they could not hope to do so unless they had Hope to do so. DICTION shows that he provided it.

DICTION also records low Certainty and Realism scores for Roosevelt, which seems strange since the President needed to inspire the nation and help it deal concretely with the Japanese threat. But his Certainty score is curiously low, resulting from heavy use of the Passive Voice: "Japan has . . . undertaken," "The attack yesterday . . . has caused," "American ships have been reported. . . ." Roosevelt watched his words carefully perhaps because he did not know precisely what was then happening in other parts of the world, what military response the United States could make (or how soon), or what domestic problems he would face in the immediate future.

His low Realism score also signaled tentativeness. Roosevelt spoke of "implications to the very life and safety of our nation" without spelling out these implications. He promised that "always will our whole nation remember the character of the onslaught against us" but did not detail specifics. In short, he seems to have used the speech to buy time, to provide emotional reinforcement but also to preserve his military options. Hence, he opted for strategic ambiguity.

Primarily, computerized language programs are valuable not because they provide numerical answers but because they suggest new critical questions. This is the approach Hart [1984d] took when analyzing the speaking of Presidents Truman through Reagan via DICTION. In a follow-up to that work, Hart [2000] examined not only campaign speeches, but also debates, political ads, news coverage, corporate messages, social protest and religious discourse, and letters-to-the-editor during presidential campaigns from 1948 to 1996. Although these books reveal much about rhetorical styles, they more usefully reveal the factors having major impact on any rhetor's lexicon. We present these factors below as a series of critical probes:

1. **Does the rhetor's social upbringing affect style?** Of all the presidents, Harry Truman used the greatest amount of Certainty. His plainspoken, midwestern assuredness charmed his friends and irritated his enemies. But neither reaction changed him. Today, in contrast, politicians fear accountability. In such an era, Harry Truman's voice is sorely missed: "Business was never so productive, vital and energetic as it is today. All this talk about weakening private enterprise is sheer political bunk" [Truman, 1950:497].

2. **Does the rhetor's employment history affect style?** Politicians speak a dialect that blends social protest, institutional maintenance, and moral discourse, according to Hart [2000:151–2]. Although they borrow from all three realms, their discourse is distinct from each. For example, an excerpt from a corporate mission statement reads more like a greeting card than a campaign address: "Quality, innovation, and caring: the hallmarks of the Amdahl philosophy. These characterize our dealings with our employees, customers, stockholders, and the communities where we work and live" [Amdahl, 1994]. The high Commonality score here gives the corporation a positively socialist image, and the Optimism outdoes even the most upbeat politician. By comparison, DICTION found presidential campaigners to be cautious realists (lower on Certainty and higher on Realism).

3. **Does the rhetor's political vision affect style?** Of all ten presidents whose words are included in the DICTION database (Truman to Clinton), John Kennedy scored the lowest on Optimism. At first this seems surprising since Kennedy motivated a generation of young people to enter politics to do good. Apparently, however, politics for Kennedy was a matter of *righting wrongs*. For example, on civil rights, Kennedy asked: "Are we to say to the world—and much more importantly to each other—that this is the land of the free, except for the Negroes; that we have no second class citizens, except for Negroes; that we have no class or caste system, no ghettos, no master race, except with respect to Negroes?" [Kennedy, 1963b:547].

4. **Does the setting affect the rhetor's style?** Rhetoric that appears on the local paper's editorial page, for example, bears a certain stamp due to the constraints of its setting. Those who write letters to the editor, although strongly motivated to complain (or praise), are subject to strict word limits: they must make their points in a hurry. And so they sound particularly insistent. As Hart [2000:208] found, letter-writers use Embellishment more than either the press or the politicians, apparently attempting to convey their sentiments as strongly as possible in the smallest amount of space: "The recent slander of Dan Quayle, and vicariously, the National Guard by his opponents and members of the press, is offensive to the great majority of the American people. Service in the Guard is *honorable, decent, and patriotic*" ["Quayle Attacks Unfounded," 1988].

5. Does the rhetor's strategic mindset affect style? The stereotype of the cynical news reporter is well-founded. As Hart [2000:172] shows, the news media paint a much more negative picture of events than politicians do, in large part because they see their role as a sort of political superintendent. Even small stories—those that go nowhere politically—are reliably negative, as in the following: "The Bush campaign dismissed one of three campaign supporters accused of anti-Semitic or fascist involvements. A campaign spokes[person] said he was dismissed after it was learned he had been active in efforts to defend a man condemned to death over atrocities at the Treblinka death camp" ["Supporter Ousted," 1988].

6. Does the rhetor's social power affect style? In *Campaign Talk* [2000:220], Hart roughly summarizes the trend of the past half century as follows: "Candidates address political initiatives, the press concentrates on political actors, and the electorate emphasizes political communities. . . . letter writers make more Voter References (folks, voters, society, rank-in-file) than politicians, far more than the press." This self-interest on the part of voters makes sense, Hart says, "given how often their concerns are disregarded by elites" [p. 220].

7. Does the rhetor's cognitive habits affect style? Jimmy Carter saw himself as a problem-solver, not as a politician. Thus, even though he worked hard at his rhetoric, it never worked well for him, largely because of his high Complexity scores (they were twice as high as any other president). This professorial lexicon impressed "businesspersons who heard Carter refer knowingly to . . . 'energy pricing policy,' [and] 'synthetic alternatives'" but no doubt bored educators who once heard him describe a "'greatly magnified opportunity for the enhancement of better relationships'" [Hart, 1984d:162–3].

8. Does the rhetor's communicative history affect style? Journalists don't make the news, they just report it. . . . Or do they? Hart [2000:182–4] argues that the news is interpretive. In other words, while politicians ask one central question, What should we do?, reporters ask many questions. This allows them to offer audiences their interpretations of what facts and events mean, based on what their research has taught them about the history, ideology, logic, emotion (etc.) behind a particular story. Thus, the attacks of September 11, 2001, continue to be discussed years later, because their meanings have not yet been exhausted.

Computer programs like DICTION are hardly omniscient. They cannot think; they can only count. They cannot deal with the majesty of style, just its plumbing. They cannot give final answers, just pose initial questions. Ultimately, it takes an intelligent critic to decide what the printouts say about lexicon. But as we have seen in both this chapter and the preceding one, style is so subtle that even an army of critics could not solve its mysteries entirely. If the computer can thereby free the critic from the more mundane work of sorting and counting words, it seems a useful adjunct to criticism. Given the complexity of style, the critic can always find better things to do than to sort and count.

CONCLUSION

Knowing about Ultimate Terms, Code Words, and individual lexicons is important in studying style but the critic's best tool is developing a sensitivity to word choice. It is this sort of sensitivity that Wallman [1981] demonstrated in her study of blue-collar British politics. She traced the ways in which the word "race" was used by a counter-establishment figure named Enoch Powell. Wallman noted that Powell's discussions of "race" entered into the everyday conversations of British voters, even though the term was *not* used by them to designate skin color. Rather, they used Powell's rhetoric to explain virtually every problem then besetting them: unemployment, economic scarcity, urban violence, and more were all laid at the door of "the race issue." Powell's rhetoric was influential, Wallman observes, because it gave ordinary people a language to talk about their difficulties, even though many of its users had never heard of Enoch Powell.

Wallman's study demonstrates the essential message of this chapter: Words are important. This is true even though speakers often choose their words without thinking about them. Lexical study is therefore interesting because words never exist alone. They are always nestled in the company of other words, each of which produces its own special effect and each of which contributes to the overall impact of the message. These streams of words come tumbling rapidly, forcefully, sometimes chaotically, at listeners. At their most powerful, these words become a torrent, sweeping the audience into a sea of persuasion.

The critic stops all of this. By examining word choice carefully, often minutely, the critic becomes a spoilsport, refusing to be carried off by an unexamined rhetoric. This is upsetting to persuaders, who prefer that listeners appreciate, rather than study, their words. That is why critics study them.

TIPS FOR THE PRACTICING CRITIC

1. When analyzing word choice, carefully examine every word in the message and refer to the critical probes in Chapter 8. (What is this word doing there? Why this word and not another? etc.) Of course, the critic cannot present every possible answer he or she finds in the resulting essay. Instead, highlight the most important rhetorical features of the message by choosing the most interesting and important hypotheses to present. For example, focusing on the rhetor's choice of the phrase "military buildup" rather than "defense spending," and how that affected his or her argument, is more likely to reward attention than speculating on the use of "the" rather than "a" (although such words may be important in some situations, they are unlikely to warrant critical focus *most of the time*).
2. Rhetors and audiences usually do not pay as much conscious attention to individual word choice as the stylistic critic will. This fact makes stylistic

criticism a rewarding enterprise because critics notice things that others do not. However, it can make the process frustrating, as well. With practice, critics develop a sense of "how close is close enough" when doing stylistic analysis. Sometimes critics may be told that they are "reading too much into" the message. It is far better to be told *that* (because it is easy to tone down a microscopic approach) than to be told that one is missing the subtleties of the language. Whatever the feedback, however, strive for a balance between the microscopic level and the macroscopic level by keeping a few key questions central to your investigation:

- What rhetorical purpose does this (word, phrase, message, collection of artifacts) serve, and how does it work?
- Does the internal structure of sentences mirror or contradict the argumentative structure of the text? If so, how?
- What can we tell about the rhetor, the audience, the situation, etc. from the individual words used?

Keeping "the big picture" in mind even when while engrossed in the details of analysis will allow the critic, with practice, to strike an optimum critical balance.

3. Those interested in doing automated textual analysis with DICTION can e-mail Professor Hart: diction@mail.utexas.edu.

Chapter 9

ANALYZING MEDIA

September 11, 2001, presented American newsweeklies with a daunting challenge: How could they cover the news and convey the horror of attacks on the Pentagon and the World Trade Center, without further traumatizing citizens who had lost both loved ones and their sense of security in a few short hours? Their rhetorical task was complicated by the fact that footage of planes hitting buildings, and towers burning and collapsing, had been looped endlessly on television for days. *Newsweek* chose a fairly conventional cover, featuring small photos of the devastation bordering a larger image of firefighters raising the flag. *The New Republic*, in contrast, displayed a peaceful, lavender-hued photo (Figure 9.1), apparently taken at sunset sometime prior to the attack. The Statue of Liberty is foregrounded, the towers in the background. The caption? "IT HAPPENED HERE."

These different rhetorical choices comprise another chapter in the nation's visual history. Images from September 11 are now seared in our collective memory along with pictures of bombs falling on Baghdad, Rodney King being beaten senseless in Los Angeles, and Mark McGwire rounding the bases for his record-breaking 70th home run of the season. With entire generations being raised on such powerful mediated images, it is entirely possible that the American people can no longer think past their eyes.

The complexity of our visual age is significant. Audiences have become used to images from one medium (video) being routinely borrowed by another (a magazine), as in the case of *Newsweek*. In the case of *The New Republic*, the image itself is another mediation, a computer-edited composite of pictures taken from different angles. (The towers and the statue would not

FIGURE 9.1 *The New Republic* Cover of September 24, 2001.

have been visible together as depicted here.) In another layer of complexity, the Statue of Liberty symbolizes both New York City and the United States, while the twin towers symbolize both New York City and the destruction wrought upon the Pentagon and downtown Manhattan. Using a pre-attack image, however, runs counter to readers' expectations. Although a relief to nerves deadened by carnage, the lilac-hued Lady Liberty seems inappropriately serene, almost an abdication of the magazine's duty to report the news. Depicting the twin towers still standing creates tension in the viewer. The likely response is both nostalgia and grief, because the viewer knows that the towers will fall, have already fallen. The viewer knows that many of the workers whose office lights brightened this skyline have since died. So even the apparently idyllic photo is fraught with contrast. The contrast sharpens with the addition of the deceptively simple three-word phrase, in bold capital letters, announcing, "IT HAPPENED HERE." By offering audiences this shocking combination of simplicity and complexity, beauty and grief, safety and danger, *TNR* captures both the United States's previous rhetoric of invincibility and the counter-rhetoric that "it" can indeed happen anywhere . . . and the devastation that occurs when the two rhetorics collide.

During the last fifty years, the mass media have changed how we live. Because of television, we not only entertain ourselves differently, we eat differently (TV dinners) and go to school differently (distance learning). Our songs are now visual (MTV), our athletes beautiful (Tiger Woods), and our preachers political (Pat Robertson). All of this happens with lightning speed, as satellites feed thousands of images across the globe and computers sort them, discarding some and forwarding others to an editor's desk. Because these changes are so new, they present new challenges to critics. Even a cursory examination of *The New Republic* cover shows that there are important—thoroughly rhetorical—questions to be answered:

- *Historical backdrop.* Did Americans look at this cover photo with eyes trained by other, more explosive, recent images of DC and NYC? By other locales (bombed-out Beirut, picture-postcards of Paris)? In other words, did the American people see this picture before they actually saw it?

- *Immediate context.* What rhetorical possibilities do the juxtaposition of these images create? Does the Statue of Liberty symbolize a pre-9/11 nation? the survival of freedom, undiminished by terrorism? Do the towers represent a memorial to the victims? Is the sunset emblematic of the death of the invulnerability Americans had been conditioned to feel? Is Lady Liberty turned away in anguish? Does her lamp burning brightly symbolize U.S. determination to stand united, despite the attacks?

- *Linguistic set.* If *The New Republic* had titled its photo "Remnants of a Dream," would readers have "seen" the picture differently, perhaps regarding it as a testimony to endurance? Nostalgia? Editorial insensitivity? Does the picture have an "inherent" meaning regardless of how it is captioned?

- *Medium's ethos* (credibility, reputation). If the picture had been found on the cover of *The American Traveler* magazine, would it have been less startling than it seemed in *TNR*? Would it have seemed more or less fitting, had it appeared in the *U.S. State Department Bulletin*? In *Mad* magazine?

- *Audience's perspective.* Although immediately after the attacks, French headlines read, "Aujourd'hui, nous sommes tous Américains" ("Today, we are all Americans"), al-Qaeda members presumably rejoiced upon seeing the destruction. What might a North Korean or a Kurd have seen?

In this chapter we examine the media through a rhetorical lens, studying how "policy options" are made available or denied by the words and pictures media create. That lens is especially necessary when it comes to the "War on Terrorism." As historian Robert Dallek [1991:3] observes, "what makes war interesting for Americans is that we don't fight wars on our soil, we don't have direct experience of it, so there's an openness about the meanings we give to it. War for us is a tabula rasa, a blank slate, which we can turn into a moral crusade." Via television, radio, Internet, and print news outlets, journalists, politicians, and ordinary citizens now artfully etch upon that slate. In the aftermath of the attacks, rhetorical creativity abounded with the naming of the Patriot Act, the Axis of Evil, the Department of Homeland Security, even color-coded alert status, including detailed instructions on the deployment of duct tape for national defense. When 9/11 brought destruction to the United States, the president was quick to turn the attacks into a justification for an ongoing moral crusade. And the media publicized and enabled that crusade.

All of this is to say that war now requires a new delivery system— the mass media. As this chapter will show, almost everyone now requires the mass media. Advertisers and teamsters, preachers and senators, lawyers and fund-raisers, soldiers and comics—all now dance the mass media's dance or they do not dance at all.

RHETORIC AND MEDIA

Because the study of visual persuasion is new, we do not yet have a standard way of discussing it. Some scholars (we might call them **synthesizers**) argue that we can simply modify existing models of rhetoric when examining media products. So, for example, they might urge us to catalogue the pictures contained in a political advertisement alongside its words and then gauge how these different forces complement one another. Other researchers (they might be called **iconologists**) demand that we abandon all logocentric notions when studying mediated texts. They argue that the visual/electronic world is a radically new one and that scholars ought not examine it with language-based assumptions. Iconologists have invented terms—basic visual elements are called "memes" and missing photographic elements "elisions"—to deal with the "visual grammars" that affect how people perceive film or television.

We will not decide this controversy here. Instead, we will survey some practical ways of dealing with mass media products. Our approach will be a rhetorical one for we will focus on *how the verbal frames the visual in policy-relevant ways.* While rhetorical studies of the media are still new, some general principles are becoming clear:

1. *The mass media are changing people's mental habits.* The evidence abounds: Political campaigns are skyrocketing in costs, largely because candidates think they cannot "crack through" to voters unless they have a large media budget. In addition, via the kind of publicity only television provides, criminals are caught (*America's Most Wanted*), third parties are formed (the Green Party), and national celebrities are created overnight (*American Idol*'s Kelly Clarkson), largely because the media prize contemporary information over all else.

In other words, people are beginning to learn differently as a result of the media, a notion that Georges Dukomel [Benjamin, 1969:238] predicted when he said that, with film, "I can no longer think what I want to think. My thoughts have been replaced by moving images." Overstatement, perhaps, but the hyperrealism and dramatic movement of the mediated image surely has a special kind of authority over us.

Robert Pittman [1990:19], creator of MTV, agrees, arguing that teens differ from their parents in the most fundamental way possible—in how they process information: "TV babies . . . seem to be processing information from different sources simultaneously. They can do homework, watch TV, talk on the phone and listen to the radio all at the same time. It's as if information from each source finds its way into a different cluster of thoughts. And at the end of the evening, it all makes sense."

Perhaps. But as Abraham and his colleagues [1995] found, MTV makes a *particular* kind of sense. They tested young people's reactions to public service announcements done in MTV style and found that while teenagers found the PSAs more relevant than traditional announcements, they actually learned less from them. So message comprehension suffered as its catchiness quotient rose, which Abraham and company argue may have serious implications for public health and political awareness campaigns.

2. *The mass media have a distinctive mode of authority.* Todd Gitlin [1980] has made the case that television was central both in fueling the antiwar movement in the 1960s and in its undoing, as well. Why? Gitlin says the media are moored not by political principle, but by omniscience, the need to become viewers' earliest and best source of information. So television has become a reliable delivery agent of the grand event but also an agent for the bizarre and colorful. Viewers learn to depend on these things, endlessly searching for the novel scene or voice. And so the media did to the antiwar movement what any fickle lover does: They treated the movement as a means (for ratings) rather than an end (for a particular political reality).

The media's authority shows up in fascinating ways. A study by Donsbach and his colleagues [1992] asked people to attend a political rally in person and then compared their reactions to those who had watched the same rally on television. Fewer than 20 percent of those who saw the event in person were negatively disposed to the rhetor compared to almost 60 percent of those in the TV news audience. Another study compared the economic outlooks of watchers and nonwatchers. The results, says Hetherington [1996], were stark: Television viewers were much more pessimistic about the economy in 1992 than were the nonwatchers *even though there was no appreciable difference between their real-life economic circumstances.* In other words, when asked about the economy viewers gave back the media's messages rather than reporting the contents of their wallets.

3. *The mass media appear to be unmediated.* According to Hart [1994:60], television creates an "arrogance of the eye," a feeling that anything seen is, in fact, fact. Television constantly genuflects in front of us, making it seem stupid not to believe "what we have seen with our own eyes." And certain political techniques have evolved to enhance our sense of trust as viewers. Parry-Giles

and Parry-Giles [1999] examine *The War Room,* a documentary about Bill Clinton's successful 1992 presidential campaign. To a public fascinated with "access," the sense that we are seeing the "real" candidate "behind the image" is intoxicating. But in fact, we are still seeing a carefully crafted image, or rather, what Parry-Giles and Parry-Giles call a "meta-image," which "comes to be the 'reality' of political campaigning via the forms of documentary and news and their illusions of objectivity" [p. 40].

This happens because film, like television, is a **medium,** a coming-between. We were not with Governor Clinton on the bus. We did not have a chance to ask James Carville or George Stephanopoulos about strategy. And we do not have access to that-which-was-not-chosen, the miles of videotape on the cutting room floor. Perhaps this is what Henry Fairlie [1980:E1] means when he says "if you see it on television, it did not happen."

How can Fairlie say such a thing? When we watch a football game on television, after all, do we not watch real people playing a real game in real space and time? Yes and no. Television does not give us *all* of the game, after all. It shows us more of the players than the spectators, more of the quarterback than the linesmen, more of the sideline announcers than the popcorn vendor, more of the good teams than the sorry teams. When watching a TV game we see only what we have been allowed to see.

Television's power comes from two things: (1) it edits what it receives and (2) it hides the effects of that editing. So, for example, research by Adams [1986] shows that television is always carefully adapted to its local audience. Adams found that coverage of natural disasters was determined not by the severity of the disaster but by the political importance of the affected country to the United States. In other words, viewers may believe they get a complete view of the world when, in fact, they only get the news that is deemed fit to see.

4. *The mass media produce multidimensional texts.* The power of pictures is undeniably important but as Gumpert and Cathcart [1985:28] point out, pictures are "influenced by other factors such as genre, context, and the other sensory modalities" (like sound and texture). That is, a picture rarely means one thing since it is composed of sometimes rival sub-elements and because language gives it a context (that is, a con-text). Nowhere was this truer than in the famed Rodney King case where, despite a videotaped record of the beating, a jury acquitted the Los Angeles police of all wrongdoing (the verdict was later overturned). Political cartoonist Paul Conrad captured the irony of this result in Figure 9.2.

During the first King trial, the videotape was played again and again—in slow-motion, in stop-action, at full speed, in reverse, frame-by-frame—until overuse drained it of meaning. In addition, the defense constantly told the jury how to view the video. Eventually, a sufficient number of jurors "saw" things the defense's way. As Roland Barthes [1985:29] explains, in such cases language is used to direct the viewer "among the various signifieds of the image, causing him to avoid some and to accept others; through an often sub-

FIGURE 9.2 Paul Conrad on the Rodney King Incident

ONE PICTURE IS WORTH ZERO

tle dispatching, it teleguides him toward a meaning selected in advance."
Rather amazingly in the King case, the defense's interpretations were offered
after the videos had been seen by the jurors and still the defense was able to
dislodge their powerful first impressions.

Language can also *pre-exist* a visual as "latent registers of phantasy, memory, and knowledge" [Burgin, 1983:235] tell a viewer how to view a stimulus.
These registers instruct a news photographer, for example, which pictures to
take for the morning newspaper (a traffic accident, for example, rather than a
bowling match), thereby revealing the lurid agenda favored by today's media.
In a similar vein, Sloop [1996] was intrigued by the words our culture uses to
discuss prisons and prisoners. For example, in an article for *People* magazine,
one prisoner described her electronic home confinement as being like the

parent she never had. Such descriptions, Sloop argues, encourage readers to view punishment as deserved and even loving, and discourage healthy debate on what constitutes acceptable moral behavior.

5. *The mass media carry their own, compelling logic.* In a media-saturated age, people think and act differently. A famous example of this occurred in 1984 when CBS commentator Lesley Stahl sharply denounced the Reagan administration's manipulation of the American people. Stahl showed a series of lush photo opportunities in which President Reagan pressed the flesh and mouthed sweet nothings to the assembled crowds, all of whom were trapped in a sea of red, white and blue balloons. Stahl decried the emptiness of the scene, upbraiding the President for pandering to the American people and avoiding the important issues of the day.

While Stahl fully expected to incur the wrath of the White House for her documentary, she was shocked to receive a pleasant thank-you instead for depicting the President in warm, patriotic scenes, wrapped in the embrace of appreciative crowds. Stahl learned that, despite her negative commentary, pictures count a great deal in television, with viewers often discounting what they hear while remembering what they see.

It is for this reason, says Hart [1987], that presidents now spend so much time speaking in ceremonial settings (see Figure 9.3). Because political ceremonies televise so well, presidents are using them instead of more contentious formats like press conferences and briefings. "If you want us on the nightly news," presidents are telling reporters, "do it on our terms, not yours." To insure such coverage, White House handlers are now attuned to media deadlines,

FIGURE 9.3 Presidential Use of Speech Settings

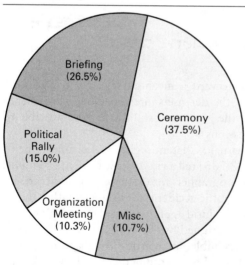

carefully arranging the president's schedule so that he is seen in crowd-receptive formats just in time for the nightly news.

Without question, then, the mass media place new demands on the rhetorical critic. They require a new language of description as well as a new language of critique. Visual images do not sit placidly waiting for the critic to discover them. Instead, they are folded into a dynamic and complex matrix of stimuli, parts of which—or all of which—may affect an audience. As a result, new questions arise each day: How are children affected by the hundreds of thousands of commercials they watch before becoming adults? Do situation comedies like *Friends* make us more convivial? Does a show like *South Park* make us more cynical? Is international reporting bringing the world closer together or is it merely providing new data for old prejudices? These are new questions and they require new moves from the rhetorical critic.

PERCEIVING TELEVISION

In *Seducing America: How Television Charms the American Voter*, Hart [1994b] argues that to fully understand the power of television, a critic must look at it **phenomenologically.** Phenomenology is the study of how people perceive the world around them. As the postimpressionist painter Paul Cézanne showed us, "nature is on the inside" [Spurling, 1977:46]; in other words, the most important stuff in life is easy to feel but difficult to explain because it is buried so deeply within us.

Phenomenology might ask, for example, how I become aware of the video arcade in the local mall. The no-brainer reply would be that flashing neon lights attract my attention. But how? the phenomenologist would persist. What in my prior experience has prepared me for these lights? What is being evoked by them? I may have learned that flashing lights signify excitement. Or I may associate neon with Las Vegas and lost fortunes. In either case, when I look, I yield to the attraction; I invest my attention. And the process of becoming aware of how I become aware is also of interest to the phenomenologist. How I feel about becoming aware helps determine my personal actions and reactions. A phenomenologist investigates such questions by giving language to our bodily experiences, by digging "up what is buried in our everyday, unthinking and prereflective experience" [Spurling, 1977:50]. The phenomenologist describes what is hard-to-describe.

Few things are harder to describe than the experience of watching television. That may sound odd. Perhaps watching television seems eminently understandable—body slumped, shoes off, beer in hand, brain on hold. This is complex? But what seems simple and sedentary is often neither. If nature is indeed on the inside, our sedentary watcher may not be so sedentary after all.

In *Seducing America*, Hart tries to explain some of the deeper pleasures of television, the deepest of which is the **intimacy** it delivers. Television puts viewers in touch with rock stars, athletes, and comedians and then lets viewers plumb their depths. Television lets us know that J.K. Rowling cries after writing the death of a *Harry Potter* character and gives us up-to-the-minute information on the status of Britney Spears's virginity and marital status.

There is nothing that television will not tell us. This builds what Horton and Wohl [1986] call "para-social" relationships between TV characters and their viewers. So, for example, Johnny Carson often complained that people would begin sidewalk conversations with him without ever introducing themselves. Because the *Tonight* show had illuminated their darkened boudoirs so regularly over the years, Carson's viewers felt they knew him personally. Johnny Carson seemed to be their neighbor, but who among them had ever borrowed his lawnmower?

Brummett and Duncan [1992:229] argue that television is powerful because (1) it is voyeuristic (I see others without being seen in return), (2) it is fetishistic (being knowledgeable about television shows gives me social power), and (3) it is narcissistic (TV's messages are directed at "my" personal life). Because of these features, television now affects how politicians and voters make decisions. The 1992 presidential debate in Richmond provides an example. During the debate, a citizen asked the candidates the following question: "How has the national debt personally affected each of your lives? And if it hasn't, how can you honestly find a cure for the economic problems of the common people if you have no experience in what's ailing them?"

In response, Ross Perot launched into a discussion of his grandchildren, Bill Clinton talked about his experience in rural America, and George Bush fell flat on his face:

MODERATOR: Thank you, Mr. Perot. Mr. President.
BUSH: Well, I think the national debt affects everybody.
MODERATOR: You personally.
BUSH: Obviously it has a lot to do with interest rates—
MODERATOR: She's saying, "you personally." You, on a personal basis. How has it affected you? Has it affected you personally? [Bush, 1992: 35–6]

Poor George Bush. He made three or four more false starts but ultimately flummoxed the assignment entirely.

Why? Because he was brought up in a pretelevision era and hence knew not the language of intimacy. His uptight, cerebral rhetoric was off the mark, as was his awkward body posture (he tried to half-sit on a tall stool during the debate) and his inability to make personal contact with his questioners. In general, he forgot, or had never learned, the iron law of television: Be intimate or begone.

This law is a law, says Schmull [1990:99], because people are increasingly "cocooning" themselves at home, alone except for a gaggle of electronic devices. As a result, they begin to think in private ways about public officials. Instead of asking themselves "What is the candidate's platform on the environment?" they talk to themselves this way: "The candidate is almost in tears when she talks about the environment. She must really care. Or maybe she can't handle the pressure of the debate. I wonder if all this talk about her pending divorce is true. And why is she wearing her hair that way? She needs a much softer look. But I'm glad she's still working out regularly. . . ."

In other words, television is a mass medium that presents itself as a coffee klatch. According to Gumpert and Drucker [1992:195], electronic home shopping is a case in point. When the host interacts with a call-in viewer, the researchers argue, "fragments of personal discourse punctuate the air: 'Hi, how are you today, good to hear from you . . . who are you buying this for? . . . your 14-year-old niece will love this." Only occasionally does the host suggest "Why don't you tell everybody why you ordered more of these so they will know what they would be missing." Being this bold would call attention to the public nature of the interaction, thereby piercing the veil of intimacy disguising the show's mercantile purposes.

Rawlence [1979:63] argues that the television audience "never has a sense of itself as an audience—only as individuals." Why is this important? Because it gives the viewer a sense of empowerment, a feeling of control over the interaction. The remote control symbolizes that empowerment, saying, in effect, "I and I alone will decide which message is granted access to my cranium."

Television also achieves intimacy by fitting in neatly with our everyday worlds. A morning newscast blends into a soap opera into a half-hour infomercial into a British documentary into late night comedy into Brazilian soccer at 3:00 a.m. As a result, says Langer [1981:356], "television's 'flow' is contemporaneous with the flow of life. So, not only is television 'always already' available, there will be something to watch immediately, as soon as the set warms up." In other words, television never announces itself. It becomes our unassuming friend from morning to night.

Genuine intimacy implies informality. An intimate relationship is one in which the rules of engagement are relaxed, in which people can speak to one another spontaneously and without fear of censure. Television adheres to these rules, too, giving viewers a sense of control even as it seeks to wrest control away from them. Carpignano and his colleagues [1990:117] argue that this explains the popularity of talk shows that inevitably trivialize discourse and pander to viewers' baser instincts (for example, when Morton Downey, Jr., "physically threatens his guests, the women sexually, the men with 'wiping the floor up' with them"). Such crude displays, say Carpignano et al., rule out all elite notions like expertise. Television puts everyone—performers and viewers alike—on the same level. In so doing it tells viewers that they are in charge of their lives and that nobody—nobody—stands above them.

What is the effect of television's intimacy? To addict us. Television's power comes from both its constant willingness to keep us company and its refusal to treat itself as powerful. Its informality gives us freedom and its remote controls give us creativity. A free, creative viewer, however, can also become cocky. The critic tries to warn people about that. The following critical probes for analyzing mass media artifacts can be of use in that endeavor.

- How does the artifact address the viewer verbally? What invitations does the artifact extend to the viewer? Invitations to let down one's guard and "merely" be entertained, informed, or consoled? Invitations to be carried away by the strong emotional display of the person depicted? (etc.)
- How does the artifact create its own credibility, or invite the viewer's trust and respect?
- Does the artifact deflect attention away from its own persuasive strategies? How?

EXPLORING VISUAL SYMBOLS

Because we live in a visual age, pictures count as never before. Documenting that claim is Lester [1994] who surveyed fifty years of magazine coverage, recording the number of times African Americans had been depicted in such outlets as *Time, Newsweek,* and *Life.* He discovered small but significant increases in the representation of African Americans, from an invisible 1.1 percent of the pictures in the 1930s to almost 9 percent fifty years later. Moreover, African Americans were increasingly depicted in advertisements as well as sports photos, in public forums and also in everyday scenes.

Lester found that the *quality* of minority coverage changed too, with the early, more stereotypical pictures giving way in the 1950s and 1960s to civil rights scenes and, later, to images of African Americans working within The System. Transformations like these are important since the media's pictures are often precursors to larger societal changes. So unless an activist group can deliver stirring visuals (for example, oil-soaked beaches) in time for the nightly news or unless a rally can be held in eminently photographable locations (for example, the Lincoln Memorial), persuasion suffers.

Out-of-sight, in other words, has become out-of-mind. But how do pictures persuade? And why are some more powerful than others? Do visuals follow the same rules guiding verbal rhetoric? Does language inevitably "frame" visuals, making them meaningless until captioned by an enterprising persuader?

The great modernist painter Pablo Picasso had a clear answer to the latter question: NO! "I don't want there to be three or four thousand possibilities of interpreting my canvas," said Picasso [Worth, 1981: 172], "I want there to be only one." Picasso went on:

> Otherwise a painting is just an old grab bag for everyone to reach into and *pull out what he himself has put in.* I want my paintings to be able to defend themselves, to resist the invader, just as though there were razor blades on all the surfaces so no one could touch them without cutting his hands. A painting isn't a market basket

or a woman's handbag, full of combs, hairpins, lipstick, old love letters and keys to the garage.

Picasso's notion of "visual inherency" is obviously debatable. At times, no doubt, pictures impose a single meaning upon us. A snapshot of a department store Santa Claus with a youngster astride his knee will probably not be interpreted as a Satanic ritual or as some sort of bizarre athletic event. That picture means good cheer, fanciful expectations, and little more.

But pictures like this are also rare. Most visuals are replete with several meanings, unprotected by Picasso's razor blades. The picture of a Liberian child refugee, for example, could represent (1) the luck of the geographical draw, (2) the divine will of an inscrutable God, (3) the evils of civil war, or (4) the moral bankruptcy of an uncaring West. That same picture could also be found (5) in a medical textbook on malnutrition, (6) in an anthropological study of tribal kinship, (7) in a UNESCO brochure on political realignment, or (8) clutched in the hand of a dying Liberian father.

Because pictures are "rivalrous" in this way, critics must ask complicated questions of visual texts. It is not enough to ask *what* a picture means. One must also ask *how* it means. There are countless such trajectories but here we will focus on four basic critical probes:

1. Does the visual image carry ideological force? That is, does it grow out of a systematically articulated belief system? Ideological images surround us. Pictures of the pope in his priestly garments, for example, signal a person set-apart from the world of business suits, a person who deals with matters more mysterious than those addressed at Citibank. A photo of men walking down Wall Street in their business suits, on the other hand, suggests a uniformity to the world of commerce, a place where people dress alike because they honor the same bottom line. Pictures of the pope in swim trunks could be unnerving, as could pictures of women wearing ties or tuxedos. The first image implies ideological slippage: Can a pope remain infallible on the beach at St. Tropez? The second image can spark ideological antagonism: Isn't it enough that they are taking "our" jobs? Must they also appropriate "our" uniform?

Cultures achieve distinction through their icons. Pictures of l'Arc de Triomphe tell Parisians they are cultured and subtle; Australia's kangaroo paraphernalia characterize it as an outdoors, muscular society. The United States, too, is known by its icons, which explains why the 9/11 terrorists chose to attack symbols of U.S. monetary and military might. (And of course the suspected third target, the White House, is an icon of political dominance.)

According to Olson [1987], however, the early United States was much less sure of itself. Its icons reflected that. His study focuses on two images that vied for popularity in the early colonies, each of which carried significant ideological freight.

In Figure 9.4 we see one of the earliest political icons in the U.S. Benjamin Franklin's *Join, or Die*, an image first published in the *Pennsylvania*

FIGURE 9.4 Benjamin Franklin's *Join, or Die*

(*Pennsylvania Gazette.* May 9, 1754, p. 2, col. 2, designer: Benjamin Franklin, publisher: Benjamin Franklin and David Hall, media: newspaper, size: 2″ × 2⅞″, photograph courtesy of the Library of Congress.)

Gazette on May 9, 1754, clearly sought to whip the colonies into a new kind of confederation. This is a bold and unrelenting image, its animalistic aspect suggesting a nation of rugged pioneers but its disjointed aspect suggesting the need for unprecedented political unity. But according to Olson, Franklin created *Join, or Die* to bring the colonies together for economic reasons, not to defy Mother England. As is so often true with visual rhetoric, however, *Join or Die* quickly took on a life of its own and came to symbolize the need for true separation from Great Britain.

Knowing that, Franklin produced a second icon, *Magna Britannia,* in 1765 (see Figure 9.5). Like its forerunner, this image exhorts the colonies to pull together. But note that England herself is the focal point here, with the colonies serving as her appendages. Franklin is warning his fellow colonists (and the lords back in London) that if certain economic and political problems remain unresolved, all will be lost. Franklin is peddling both subordination and interdependence here, trying to blunt the radicalism of *Join, or Die* which, by this time, had taken on strident ideological overtones as it circulated among the early colonists.

Like many nations, the United States began in political turmoil, as well as in political iconography. As Franklin's experience shows, a persuader can easily lose control over an image as secondary persuaders respond to, and then appro-

FIGURE 9.5 Benjamin Franklin's *Magna Britannia*

("MAGNA Britannia: her colonies REDUC'D." circa January 1766, designer: Benjamin Franklin, media: single sheet, size: $4\frac{1}{8}$" × $5\frac{7}{8}$", photograph courtesy of the Library Company of Philadelphia.)

priate, its elements. Even ostensibly innocent images can become embroiled in such ideological give-and-take. In the early 1990s, for example, underground murmurings had it that Proctor and Gamble's rather enigmatic logo—a bearded man-in-the-moon amidst a cluster of stars—proved that the company was sponsoring devil worship. The rumors persisted and became so feverish that the company eventually spent several million dollars to have its logo shorn of the offending associations. In a rhetorical world, it seems, there is no such thing as visual innocence.

    2. What condensations can be found in the visual image? Does the image act as a synecdoche for a particular set of ideas? In her book *Eloquence in an Electronic Age,* Jamieson [1988a] argues that television's pictures are now the central carriers of political information. Media events like pouring blood on draft cards during the Vietnam War became synecdoches for a rebellious generation. Traditionalists use visuals too. Former President Ronald Reagan was skilled at this, using horseback riding to signal youthful energy and the beaches of Normandy to signal his political vision. Reagan had an eye for what others liked to see and so he used the world around him to tell his stories.

A captivating visual is captivating in two senses: (1) it "contains" an idea or ideology, eliminating its extraneous or complicating aspects to make it more compelling; (2) it reduces the interpretations an audience can make, filling their eyes with a single, dominant meaning. Political cartoonists are particularly adept in this regard. According to Bostdorff [1987:52], synecdoche is naturally attractive to cartoonists because they operate in "the limited space and complexity of a one panel drawing." In *Doonesbury,* for example, Garry Trudeau represented President Bill Clinton as a waffle because he continually shifted political positions. Trudeau then reduced Clinton's successor to an empty cowboy hat, implying that George W. Bush was "all hat and no cattle," as they say in Texas. (When Bush took the country to war, Trudeau exchanged the cowboy hat for an empty Roman gladiator's helmet, symbolizing both war and imperialism.) Like all gifted reductionists, Trudeau zeroed in on exactly the right vulnerability. The deftness of his touch is proven by the anguished outcries of those he skewered (and their supporters).

A fine study along these same lines was undertaken by Goldman and colleagues [1991] who showed how corporate America has tapped into what they call "commodity feminism," or the selling of products using the ideals of feminism. For example, a recent Lucy.com ad for a "powermesh sports bra" features a playful blend of classical and contemporary. The ad depicts company founder "Lucy of Portland" in a pose reminiscent of female religious icons, hands clasped prayerfully as her eyes gaze heavenward. The text describes Lucy as a "righteous sister" who vows not to rest "until all the women of the world can run, spin and box in comfortable bras." Under Lucy's image is a photo of a row of women clad in workout wear. Confronting such an ad, Goldman and colleagues would note that certain signs (athletic-looking women, the invocation of sisterhood) stand for *feminist* goals of independence and solidarity while other signs (Lucy's long hair, clingy Lycra, and prayerful innocence) connote a more traditional *femininity*. "The mass media signify femininity," argue the authors, "by visually emphasizing the line and curve of the female body along with a code of poses, gestures, body cants, and gazes. This visual lexicon has become so familiar that we now accept the signifier, e.g., the close up curve of a calf or the hip or an ear lobe, to stand for the feminine" [p. 337]. The authors also note that, in ads, "the male world of commerce and status forms a silent, but present, party" to the dialogue between the feminine and the feminist [p. 343]. Rather than being a slave to the male world, the ads imply, the feminine feminist balances her work life with "privileged access to her own sensual body" [p. 343].

Such studies reveal advertising as a synthetic force, reducing people to their elemental needs even though some of these needs turn out to be oppositional when examined carefully.

 3. What significant tensions can be found in the visual image? Are these tensions easily resolved or are they deep and abiding? Jamieson [1984:449–50] argues that some images are "promiscuous" in that they contain many, often contrary, submeanings. Even the American flag can be read in this way, with the bars representing the original colonies and the fifty stars representing the modern states. This flag-image is so familiar by now that we rarely attend to the problems it hides—thirteen of the states (Massachusetts, Pennsylvania, Virginia, etc.) receive "double-billing" with both stars and bars. The remaining thirty-seven are short-changed. In addition, six of the colonies receive *long*

bars while the other seven get *short* ones. Worse yet, some of the colonies are assigned a white bar (purity, innocence) while the rest are blood red. And what about Puerto Rico, or the U.S. Virgin Islands, which get no recognition at all? In other words, even though the flag was designed to soothe intercolonial tensions, it still retains those tensions.

Are we over-reading the flag here? After all, no modern American notices such tensions. Precisely. The flag works its magic by "containing" its tensions. Over time we have come to see the flag holistically, as a testament to the *United States*. But are interstate tensions a thing of the past? In an era of welfare cost-shifting, medicare fund-matching, and differential immigration pressures, does not each state still have forty-nine (or more) rivals? So the U.S. may have one flag but that flag still contains its diversity, even though its rhetoric hides that fact from us.

An interesting study by Gallagher [1995] extends this line of thinking. Her study reminds us that, unlike the American flag, some icons cannot hide their tensions successfully. Her exemplar is the Martin Luther King, Jr., Memorial in Atlanta. Architecturally, says Gallagher, the Memorial is part mausoleum, part church, part library, part office building, and part school. The Memorial's complexity derives from the tensions in African American life itself: It cannot "afford" to be just a burial place or a church since it sits in a neighborhood hit hard by economic calamity. It must be an office building as well as a school since commerce and education are the keys to success in the United States. These conflicting needs cost the icon rhetorical integration, says Gallagher, but also represent the complexity of the task King faced. Rhetorical integration can wait, King might have said, until racial integration becomes a reality.

Likewise, the Vietnam Veterans Memorial in Washington, D.C., provided rich material for Foss [1986], who examined the "statements" it makes. The key thing, says Foss, is that this Memorial violates "conventional form" [p. 332]. As we see in Figure 9.6, the controversial wall is low, not high; black granite, not white marble; personal, not abstract. People approach it intimately—touching its engraved names, leaving personal notes and poems, walking its length to contemplate the scope of lost lives. "No heroic action is depicted to suggest bravery and nobility and to generate a sense of patriotism," says Foss [p. 332], "and no inscription quotes a general or a president on the goals or benefits of war to remind us of American values." Instead, the wall is pure wall—opaque, inscrutable.

The wall's inscrutability is fitting since, decades after withdrawal from the Vietnam War, Americans are still trying to determine its meaning. The Wall is a testament to the people who fought and died but not to the uncertain cause for which they fought. Given the turmoil of that war, it is not surprising that the Vietnam Memorial has grown over the years. The trio of soldiers in Figure 9.7 was added to appease American traditionalists. Later, the nurses in Figure 9.8 joined them to represent the sacrifices of the nation's women.

FIGURE 9.6 The Original Vietnam War Memorial

FIGURE 9.7 First Supplement to the Vietnam War Memorial

FIGURE 9.8 Second Supplement to the Vietnam
War Memorial

And so in a curious way the Vietnam Memorial represents its era. Its three components now "argue" with one another each day, just as the nation argued passionately during the war. This fractiousness may make it a postmodern memorial, as Blair and her colleagues [1991] have declared. But that makes sense too since the war had so many different meanings for so many people that it ultimately lost its meaning altogether.

As Savage [1994:135] has said, "public monuments do not arise as if by natural law to celebrate the deserving; they are built by people with sufficient power to marshal (or impose) public consent for their erection." We create monuments because time is fleeting, memory short, and life confusing. We resort to public displays to settle things down, to make one last argument about that which has gone before. Because the past is often conflict-ridden it produces symbolic tensions. The critic seeks out those tensions as guides to a complex world the visual has tried to simplify.

ANALYZING MEDIA CONTENT

Judging by the proliferation of scholarship in the area, mass media content has never been more heavily scrutinized. Many of these studies have taken a rhetorical approach, examining the policy-endorsing or policy-undermining aspect of the media. Often, they have focused on politicians and social movement leaders (i.e., traditional rhetors) but here we will concentrate on less obvious kinds of influence—advertising, news, popular entertainment, and the Internet—and see how these powerful forces insinuate themselves into our lives.

THE RHETORIC OF ADVERTISING

Halliday and his colleagues [1990] have made an important observation about modern advertising: It subsumes almost all other discourse within it. On any given night in any American home a viewer can see—in fewer than thirty seconds—turmoil and pathos, talking cats and dancing toilet bowls. Each societal discourse, each human emotion, is fodder for the modern advertiser. And as Hitchon and Jura [1997] argue, ads are increasingly relying for meaning on references to other texts, thus becoming more and more allegorical. (Aristotle called this type of argument, requiring that the audience provide some unspecified bit of cultural knowledge, an *enthymeme*.) Some years ago, Diet Pepsi produced an advertisement that was almost an exact duplicate of a Robert Palmer music video—except that the leggy dancers sipped Diet Pepsi as they grooved. The ad both recalled and delivered the sensual pleasures of the video and implicitly congratulated savvy viewers for knowing the original referent, for getting the joke. Advertisers "graze" the cultural landscape, grabbing emotions and cultural experiences and retrofitting them for a product pitch. Advertising begins and ends within us. It knows what we know and feels what we feel. It absorbs our most sacred historical moments and connects them to a magical future time when all is perfect (cheaper, slimmer, newer, and less toxic).

Figure 9.9 is an ordinary advertisement for an ordinary product—a device for making business graphics. But it is also an *extraordinary* advertisement. It places its product on a literal pedestal, a pan-cultural sign of power and authority, and surrounds it with an ancient piece of alabaster. It gives us a human Athena and a cyber-ATHENA, even though Athena herself was neither. (And when the Greeks visualized Athena, they probably pictured olive skin and raven hair, rather than the light-skinned blonde posed here.)

But these are quibbles, and advertising brooks no quibbles. Advertising carves its territory boldly, making ancient legend pragmatic: "Simple, yet brilliant. Like the lady herself." Advertising creates its own rhetorical space, disorienting us in order to reorient us. It blends the human (female) with the nonhuman (computer), the aesthetic (her form, her flower) with the prosaic (statistics and prices). It promises an unlikely thing—a relationship with a goddess—and does so in a typically American way—efficiently ("just use the reader service card").

FIGURE 9.9 The Goddess and the Machine

As Chapman and Eggar [1983] suggest, critics need to examine an advertisement's **referent systems,** those desirable values and moods enjoyed by Group A that become the envy of Group B. Our ad collects a host of these jealousies: Ideal people are practical (ATHENA is priced from $450) but also whimsical ("something for framing"). They are resolute and competent ("forecasts, trends") but swayed by group opinion ("critically acclaimed in all leading journals"). And ideal people are at home in the heavenly hierarchy even as they embrace the democratic mandate ("anyone in the office can understand and work with ATHENA"). Advertising is a pluralistic discourse, enticing all, refusing none.

According to Leiss and his colleagues [1990], Figure 9.9 is a fairly typical contemporary advertisement. Surveying the research, they note the following trends: (1) "status ads" (e.g., a heavenly goddess) have increased over time, as have (2) lifestyle ads (ATHENA's white-on-white elegance suggests a bourgeois culture). In addition, (3) compared to earlier times, products themselves are rarely the focus of today's advertisements, having been replaced by "poetic distractions" suggesting escape or luxury (ATHENA provides both product and distraction). Also, like the ATHENA example, (4) contemporary ads emphasize themes of self-transformation—they do not reflect what people are *doing* but what they are *dreaming*. And, curiously enough, (5) actual product users are depicted less and less often these days (our ad features no computer geeks, for example).

Advertising guru Tony Schwartz [Leiss, 1990: 301] has observed that, in a highly litigious and accident-prone world, advertisers get into trouble when making claims about their products. So they don't. They make claims about other things. The Maytag Corporation, for example, refuses to guarantee a fault-free washing machine but does produce heart-rending vignettes about its lonely repairman. As we see in Figure 9.10, "utility appeals" have dropped off in advertising over time while "sensual appeals" have steadily risen. Why is this important? Because it means advertising has become a **cultural discourse,** not just a mercantile one. And why is that important? Because cultural discourses affect policy preferences in the most basic of all ways.

In other words, there is a politics of advertising. According to Christopher Lasch [Leiss, 1990:26], advertising does not sell specific products as much as it *promotes consuming as a way of life.* Advertising works to keep us in a constant state of dissatisfaction so the nation's economic engine can run at top speed. After World War II, say Leiss and his colleagues [1990:52], advertising took on an "anxiety format" in which the fear of social mortification (epitomized by concern with "keeping up with the Joneses") became a dom-

FIGURE 9.10 Changing Emphases in Advertising over Time

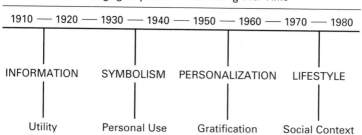

inant theme. As a result, despite *real changes* in economic growth during the postwar years, the number of people who rate themselves as "very happy" has not changed.

The ultimate effect of advertising, according to Gitlin [1987], is to make us politically docile. After all, a society that sees consumption as its raison d'être has precious little time to throw itself into political causes, thus leaving affairs of state in traditional hands. Advertising does so via its escapist, anti-establishment appeals. The jeans ad featuring the "loner" with a "blank and cynical" look, says Gitlin, sends out a series of clear political messages: Power has already corrupted society; do not get involved; consume instead; that will teach them.

There is another sense in which advertising is escapist. Politics deals with the concrete and the tangible—What is the best location for the new prison?—while the world of advertising is decidedly abstract. It deals in essences, not forms; feelings, not practices. According to Geis [1982], it accomplishes much of this work through language. For example, advertising uses **abstract nouns** rather than concrete nouns (e.g., "more tomato for your money" vs. "more tomatoes for your money") and also **weak verbs** rather than strong ones (e.g., "Ethanol *helps* your engine run cleaner"). In addition, we find in advertising an abundance of **elliptical comparatives** in which the product being advertised is compared to an unmentioned norm (e.g., "Carlton—the lighter 100"). Finally, **mysterious modals** imply a large world (e.g., "many people say it relieves their pain") but specify a much smaller one.

Advertising has become part of our consciousness. We hum jingles absentmindedly; our politicians quote ad copy more often than the Constitution; we stay seated during halftime waiting for the Super Bowl ads. But what is advertising saying about us as a nation? After all, advertisers are often the first to spot—and exploit—emerging trends in society. Thus, critics are wise to look over advertisers' shoulders to see how they go about making us believers of a certain sort.

In addition to the previous critical probes presented in this chapter, critics examining advertisements can benefit by asking the following questions:

- To what extent is the advertisement engaging in implied, but not actual, promises, through the use of abstract nouns, weak verbs, elliptical comparatives, and mysterious modals?
- How do these implied promises invite audiences to respond?

THE RHETORIC OF NEWS

It took a fairly long time for critics to look at the news rhetorically. Traditional reporters, after all, had surrounded themselves with the trappings of objectivity, declaring to the world "Nothing but the facts here; look elsewhere for persuasion." A news documentary for example, does not have the "scars of mediation and transformation" [Silverstone, 1986:81] to signal it has been manufactured from odds and ends. And so we have tended to trust documentarists and to discount the often arbitrary decisions they make.

Scholars have been rethinking this approach to the news. Patterson [1993], for example, found the news producing an **alternative authority structure** in recent years, with the voices of political leaders increasingly being de-emphasized in favor of news personnel. Hart and his colleagues [1984] report a similar finding. Focusing on televised news coverage, they discovered that U.S. presidents were directly quoted in only 8 of the 45 broadcasts sampled *even though the newscasts dealt exclusively with the president's most recent speech!* And tellingly, Kenski [1996] suggests that TV news influences not only which issues we focus on, but what standards we use to judge governments, officials, and policies. In other words, the news establishment is increasingly positioning itself as an independent source of political authority.

Griffin [1992] investigated how this is done. Focusing on television's visual conventions, he observes that the mass media use "symbols of access" (e.g., stand-up footage in front of the Capitol) to suggest that they and they alone can enter the corridors of power. Similarly, they use "signs of information"— on-location photos in far-flung places, for example—to give viewers the sense that television is omniscient. So, for example, one plane crash story carried less than 30 seconds of on-site video in its three-minute lead story. But the footage was sufficiently spread out during the report so that it seemed both authentic and comprehensive. Griffin says these few shots were used to

> metonymically represent the drama of rescue. Most of the report is taken up with interviews filmed away from the crash. The use of a few selected images to represent a much larger story and more complex series of events is especially evident in the way this story centers on the shot of the little girl crying from the top of the plane's tail section. This shot is longer than the rest, includes a camera zoom for emphasis, and is paired with interview footage of a rescue worker identifying this as his most-vivid memory. The editing and placement of this shot have made it a central dramatic symbol for the rescue story. [pp. 135–6]

The rhetoric of the news, then, is a rhetoric of authority, with news institutions constantly making bids for preeminence. One such bid can be seen in how the press covers politics. Hart and colleagues [1990] inspected four hundred news stories in *Time* magazine between 1945 and 1985. They learned that the presidency has been described as increasingly besieged over the years: by international crises, material want, lapses of character, and so on, as well as disagreement between the president and Congress, the electorate, the press, etc.

But have presidential traumas *fundamentally* increased over the years or have only *descriptions* of that institution changed? That is a complex (perhaps unanswerable) question. But clearly the press has found it convenient to feature political turmoil. Institutionally, this is a useful choice because it allows the press to portray itself as a politically neutral, and therefore slightly superior, profession. Rhetorically, it has allowed the media to tell a suspenseful story. As all dramatists know, conflict sells. As political dramatists know, conflict at the highest echelons sells especially well. Notions like these now seem to guide political reporting in the United States.

But these approaches come at a cost: Milburn and McGrail [1992] found that overly vivid reporting actually *decreases* an audience's ability to learn from the news or to think in complex ways about public affairs. Worse, Kerbel [1994] discovered that conflict-ridden coverage makes the electorate cynical, causing them to lose faith in democratic governance. Most ominous of all are the findings of Jamieson and Cappella [1996] who found that such coverage can actually decrease voter turnout.

Our discussion thus far suggests a jealous relationship between journalism and the political mainstream. But this is not to say the American media offer a fundamental critique of the western, capitalistic mandate. In fact, numerous scholars have shown how the rhetoric of news is a **source of system maintenance.** For example, Miller [1987] notes that while newscasters often smirk at the *individuals* holding office, they rarely question basic aspects of the American creed. Instead, they criticize politicians' techniques or qualities (e.g., shortsightedness), leaving the democratic/technocratic commitment untouched.

A variety of studies demonstrates this. Entman [1991] compared U.S. news coverage of two airplane disasters, one involving the downing of an Iranian airliner by a U.S. Navy ship and one in which the Soviet Union shot down a Korean jet. Although the events seemed similar, the rhetoric surrounding them was quite different. The Soviets were described as acting with "deliberate cruelty" in committing a "barbaric atrocity." Instead of referring to "passengers" the press described "victims" and "loved ones," using the Korean jet incident to offer global commentaries (almost always negative) about the Soviet Union. In contrast, the Iranian airline situation was described as a "tragic accident." Later research showed that that same description applied equally well to both affairs.

Other studies found similar biases. Steuter [1990] notes that coverage of political "terrorism" in newsmagazines has reflected the victim's viewpoint rather than complex economic and political forces. "The analysis revealed a picture of terrorism that was volatile and sensational," says Steuter, "the product of [. . .] conspirators whose aim is the destabilization of Western democratic society." No doubt that is part of the story. But the critic must scrutinize any narrative told this consistently. "Terrorism," after all, is a value-laden word. It implies evil motivations (i.e., political anarchy) and cowardly behaviors (i.e., the terrorist's anonymity). By this definition, those who dumped tea into the Boston Harbor in 1773 were terrorists as were those who protested the World Trade Organization in Seattle in 1999. But it is uncomfortable for Americans to think of such persons as terrorists. That is why they like the rhetoric their newspapers make.

The news, then, is a rich source of persuasion. The critical probes presented for the study of television (earlier in this chapter) will be useful to the critic studying the rhetoric of news, with an especial focus on the process by which the news creates its own credibility and hides its status as persuasion.

Critics are beginning to learn more about it and its odd, often conflicting, features. Here are several:

1. *The news is present-focused.* When we watch the news we watch the moment. Rarely does the news give us a sense of history. That can cause us to lose a sense of perspective as well as to lurch about from solution to solution. Reflecting on such presentism, some scholars worry that it will cause us to act precipitously and to abandon historic compacts in favor of untried, potentially dangerous, solutions.

2. *The news is undertheorized.* That is, the news appears to have no encompassing worldview; it seems innocent of over-arching prejudice. It reports only "the facts" and thus seems more trustworthy than does partisan rhetoric with its hortatory style. But no rhetoric is devoid of a worldview. The critic's job is to find the story behind the media's stories. In 1991, the Senate confirmation hearings of Supreme Court Justice Clarence Thomas riveted the nation when former employee Anita Hill testified that Thomas had sexually harassed her. Vavrus [2002] argues that sensational coverage of the hearings depicted American society in crisis, providing a rationale for unprecedented numbers of women to run for office the following year.

3. *The news is calibrated.* Newswriters are not fools. They adjust their texts to their market. So, for example, Hart and his colleagues [1980] found that *Time* magazine's religion sections were carefully pegged to its Eastern, Episcopalian (vs. Southern, Baptist) subscription base, even though the nation's Baptists outnumber its Episcopalians and even though *Time* is, ostensibly, a national newsmagazine.

4. *The news is fantastic.* Much of what we read in the news does not exist. There is no such thing as "public opinion," for example, until a writer *labels* a particular set of attitudes as popular. Similarly, as Meyers and her colleagues [1978] discovered, newswriters often argue that a political candidate has a great deal of "political momentum" even though no human being has ever seen or touched such a quality.

The essence of rhetoric is selectivity. To make a rhetorical decision is to choose this image rather than that one, to frame an argument for this audience rather than another. Because so much happens in the world each day, and because reporters operate under such tight constraints (e.g., what they know about a topic, what their budget will let them find out), they tell only part of the world's story. That makes them selectors of the first order and hence makes what they write a vital source of insight for the rhetorical critic.

THE RHETORIC OF ENTERTAINMENT

Some argue it is silly to criticize unserious texts. After all, is deconstructing *Everybody Loves Raymond* really worth it? Should we waste time teasing out grand insights from pop music? Can a baseball broadcast really tell us something important about the world? It is clearly possible to wax philosophical about such matters, but should we?

Many critics say yes for these reasons: (1) rhetoric is most powerful when it is not noticed and nobody notices popular culture; (2) people are easiest to persuade when they are in a good mood and entertainment creates such moods; (3) some of our most basic values come to us when we are young and the young consume entertainment voraciously; and (4) the mass media disseminate entertainment far and wide, affecting millions. Perhaps the only thing sillier than studying popular culture, then, is not studying it at all.

Critical studies of mass entertainment have exploded during the past thirty years. We cannot survey that vast literature here but we can feature three of its most suggestive findings. Several critics have noted, for instance, the **radical individuality** found in entertainment texts. Consider Jonathan Crane's [1988] research. He studied the "slasher movie," finding amidst the gore one consistent argument: Collective action is doomed. The real power of the horror movie, says Crane, is its ability to reduce the individual to the primordial endangered body.

For example, in films like *Night of the Living Dead* and *Halloween* we are thrust into Everytown, an amorphous but recognizable place that has "no architectural identity or historical specificity" but whose very ordinariness "generates reality effects among the audience members" [Crane, 1988:379]. The real horror, says Crane, is that evil has become situated in our most private and unprotected locations. One by one the townspeople are killed, with the hero remaining to battle the Feared Invader. Evil is eventually dispatched but the greatest horror is this: Each of us is alone; community is a myth.

Perhaps this seems absurd. After all, we do not live in horror films. But these themes of radical individuality are now repeated so often that they aggregate within us. Rasmussen and Downey [1991] discovered these themes in Vietnam War films where the politics of war were sidestepped in favor of cameo stories about the boy-in-the-rice-paddy and the girl-back-home. "Therapeutic" films like this, say Rasmussen and Downey, never really let the American people learn anything from the war because they focused so heavily on the individualistic and hence provided no *policy* guidance for the future.

Popular entertainment is also distinguished by its **radical presentism,** an ahistorical understanding of human problems and an antihistorical rejection of old truths. For example, Schlenker and colleagues [1998] examined issues of *Seventeen* from 1945 through 1995. Perhaps unsurprisingly, they found that although the focus of the magazine's articles shifted slightly toward personal growth in years when the women's movement was especially strong, women's progress toward parity in the public realm was not reflected on a long-term basis. When women's lib was not in the headlines, *Seventeen* reverted to its emphasis on eyeshadow and how to talk to your big crush.

When presentism and individualization combine, popular culture becomes somewhat rootless. What makes presentism attractive? It allows grand experimentation, setting the individual loose to explore the lived moment.

And abandoning the past (and bracketing the future) lowers our sense of responsibility. As Daughton [1996:146] notes, much of the humor in the 1993 Bill Murray film *Groundhog Day* results from the hedonistic extremes to which Murray's character descends, upon learning that no matter what he does, there will be no consequences, "no tomorrow." He will wake up the "next" day and it will still be February 2. Here, however, this presentism takes a paradoxical, Zen-like twist. In contrast to the responsibility-free presentism encouraged by many media artifacts, in *Groundhog Day* it is the almost meditative practice of accepting and learning from each moment, Daughton says, that allows Murray's character to evolve and ultimately escape his dilemma.

Responsibility can exact a heavy toll, after all, and so hearing the smack of a home run or feeling the energy at a Dave Matthews Band concert both rewards and distracts. But as Tucker and Shah [1992] have shown, presentism can also blind us. They compared Alex Haley's epic slave narrative, *Roots,* to the television miniseries by the same name and found it had been turned into a "classical immigrant story" suitable for modern Americans. In doing so, say Tucker and Shah, the adapters tore the story from its historical moment, diluting "the horror, complexities, and seriousness of slavery as a societal institution" [p. 325]. No doubt, it would have been uncomfortable to watch the horrors of slavery for five nights in a row. Deft rhetorical restructuring allowed for other possibilities.

Armstrong and his colleagues [1992] add a chapter to this story. They noted the increased presence of African Americans in TV dramas and wondered how these portrayals affected viewers. The more that people of European descent were exposed to such shows, the researchers found, the more they overestimated the socioeconomic status of African Americans in general. That is, by focusing on the unrepresentative lives of Cliff and Claire Huxtable each week, television implies they are the norm. Predictably, white viewers respond: "Haven't we gotten past this race thing by now? Surely we've done our penance; things have changed. Just look at Bryant Gumbel." Such is the power of the image that elevating a few very visible members of an oppressed group can make political remedies (e.g., affirmative action) seem unnecessary. Armed only with their statistics, sociologists have a hard time countering such claims.

Another study details the power of presentism. Lowry and Towles [1989] examined portrayals of sexuality in soap operas and found (1) a substantial increase over the years in sexual promiscuity and, more important, (2) *no attendant consequences* (e.g., STDs, pregnancies) to such actions. Does this imply, as conservatives have argued, that television publicizes licentiousness? Perhaps. But even worse it robs us of consequence. On television, behavior occurs suddenly, often devoid of context. It comes from nowhere and (often) leads to nothing. This makes television escapist. But what does it make of us?

A third aspect of popular culture is its **radical ambivalence.** That is, while popular entertainment often delivers exciting and clear-cut *characters,* it delivers a clear-cut *message* less often. For example, when Jasinski [1993] wrote about the film *The Big Chill,* he noted that critics on both the right and the left found its 1960s nostalgia mildly objectionable, for different reasons. Producers of these artifacts justify this open-endedness commercially: It keeps audiences reading or watching, pleasing many, truly alienating few. Films, magazines, and TV shows often use this strategy rhetorically to deal with complex and divisive issues without losing their audience.

The daytime controversy-magnet known as *The Jerry Springer Show*, on the other hand, would seem to court disaster, potentially offending large segments of its audience. However, in her analysis of 100 episodes of the show, Grabe [2002] argued that the outrageous behaviors of the show's guests are actually balanced by the harsh public punishment they receive from the host and the studio audience, with results that actually reinforce traditional family values. So even though they are rewarded with notoriety, because they are also punished for their transgressions, Grabe reasons, the show's "villains" serve as morality lessons for the rest of us.

Especially on social change questions (such as race, class, gender) the media's tendency toward radical ambivalence comes to the fore. For example, Douglas [1994:14] explored a range of media texts from the 1950s to the 1990s targeted toward female baby boomers, "the first generation of preteen and teenage girls to be so relentlessly isolated as a distinct market segment." She found that

> American women today are a bundle of contradictions because much of the mass media we grew up with was itself filled with mixed messages about what women should and should not do, what women could and could not be. This was true in the 1960s, and it is true today. The media, of course, urged us to be pliant, cute, [hetero]sexually available, thin, blond, poreless, wrinkle-free, and deferential to men. But it is easy to forget that the media also suggested we could be rebellious, tough, enterprising and shrewd. And much of what we watched was porous, allowing us to accept and rebel against what we saw and how it was presented. [p. 9]

Likewise, in concluding her own study of TV series featuring women, Dow [1996:214] proclaims, "No feminist viewer should attempt to deny her pleasure in these prime-time feminist visions: they offer sophisticated, entertaining, often quite satisfying images of the personal struggles and triumphs of women. The danger is not in enjoying them but in mistaking them for something more than the selective, partial images that they are." Almost any pop culture artifact could provide glimpses into our conflicted, collective psyches, whether it be the music of Beyoncé Knowles or Garth Brooks, the films of Spike Lee or Jackie Chan, *Maxim* magazine or *Curves* magazine. It is the job of the rhetorical critic to tease out the tensions and see where they lead, keeping in mind that any one artifact only tells part of the larger story.

Critics wishing to study artifacts from entertainment media can focus their attention on critical probes such as:

- What tensions exist in the artifact? How are they represented?
- Are audiences encouraged to see these tensions and appreciate them? struggle with them? accept them uncritically?
- How do the tensions in these artifacts relate to a larger social, cultural, or political story?

Critical work in the area of entertainment is becoming increasingly important since global viewers now consume individuality, presentism, and ambivalence on a nightly basis. *The Simpsons* embodies these strains as does *60 Minutes*. The rhetorical critic is left to ponder this: How do such motifs affect what we think and how we feel about what we think? Are consumers destined to become what they consume? Will they grow happy with their individualization and comfortable with their uncertainties? Or are the effects of entertainment being overemphasized? Perhaps we all need to relax and watch more TV. Or perhaps not.

THE RHETORIC OF THE INTERNET

Because the Internet has evolved from and helps constitute this media culture, it demonstrates a combination of the rhetoric of news, narrative, advertising, visual imagery, and entertainment. This boundary-blurring is justifiably fascinating for students of rhetoric: Is online communication entertainment? Consciousness raising? Private discourse? Sales? Information gathering (public or private)? News? Information sharing? In a word, yes.

Certain features of the Internet seem especially relevant for rhetorical critics.

1. In the language of Chapter 6, *online communication borrows from and adapts other media genres.* For example, at times, the Internet appropriates the form and hence the credibility of news or personal narrative, breathing new life into urban legends, chain letters, and hoaxes. To some extent, the Internet's norms resemble those of the offline world. At times this is commonsensical, at other times, comical. In an ironic twist, Warnick [1999] found that early appeals aimed to bring women online actually excluded some women, by focusing on stereotypically masculine traits and values (aggression, opportunism, technological proficiency). Traditional gender expectations flourish online, but that is not all. Fürsich and Robins [2002] investigated the official government websites of 29 sub-Saharan countries, noting that Westernized cultural values and corporate appeals predominated. African nations were advertising themselves, trying to attract business and tourism by attempting to create brand-name recognition with slogans such as "The Warm Heart of Africa" (Malawi), "The Switzerland of Africa" (Swaziland), and "The Gem of Africa" (claimed by both Botswana and Namibia) [p. 197]. The proliferation of discourse online makes such niche marketing especially attractive to producers of rhetoric, and the language of advertising is easily adapted to this new setting.

2. *The Internet highlights the fluid possibilities of personal identity.* Some theorists, such as Judith Butler [1999:181], argue that all identity (such as gender) is fluid and constructed moment by moment: "My argument is that there need not be a 'doer behind the deed,' but that the 'doer' is variably constructed in and through the deed." But even those who see identity as relatively fixed have argued that gender, sex, sexual orientation, age, size, race, class, disability—all excuses for prejudice—drop away at the keyboard. Users

can carefully construct their online identities, determining which features of themselves to reveal, which to conceal, and which to simply "change" for their self-presentation during these interactions. Although he may not have foreseen the Internet, Aristotle accounted for such self-construction when he wrote about the importance of *ethos*, the rhetor's image or credibility created through the performance of the rhetorical act itself. Samp and her colleagues [2003] attempted to investigate this fluid identity by surveying users on their habits of gender-swapping on the Internet; however, the nature of the self-report survey meant that the authors could not swear to the "accuracy" of their results! Similarly, Ferris and Roper [2002] observed the interactions that occurred in a specialized setting, an interactive online community based on the "Pern" novels of Anne McCaffery. Such communities, or MOOs (multi-user dimension, object oriented), transcend time and space in that participants are both sitting at their computers and experiencing the settings and events of the novel, play, or TV program on which their MOO is based. Ferris and Roper focused on how the participants ("players") displayed intimacy online, comparing these patterns to offline observations about males and females. But because of the possibility that some players were gender-swapping, the authors limited their claims to descriptions of the characters, not the players themselves. Intriguingly, the very factors that make Internet research challenging also make it attractive. The almost limitless possibilities of self-creation on the Internet will provide fascinating sites for study by rhetorical scholars.

3. *The Internet offers instantaneous access—to those with access.* Without question, the Internet offers unparalleled opportunities for fast global research and contact among persons and institutions. All you need is the use of a networked computer, right? Wrong, say folks concerned about the "digital divide." This divide shows up in differential access to the actual hardware, as well as in basic literacy, language (most Internet discourse is in English), and attitudes toward the technology. The digital divide is global as well as national. As of 2000, in over half the countries in Africa, 99 percent of the population had no access to the Internet [Hafkin, 2001:326].

But even in economically privileged nations where public libraries and cybercafés offer online access, these benefits are neither universally free nor available. In January 1995, then-Speaker of the House Newt Gingrich suggested that perhaps poor people should receive tax credits for buying laptop computers, in order that their children not be left behind during the "information revolution." Although his proposal may have been well-intentioned, critics were quick to ridicule the idea on practical grounds, likening it to Marie Antoinette's famous (but apocryphal) statement when told that the poor had no bread: "Let them eat laptops."

Rhetorically, the speed and reach of Internet access will probably contribute to a growing sense of global connectedness, informality, and familiarity. Some would say this is illusory; others would say it is as real as any other perception. In either case, the effects are likely to show up in discourse. As

Benson [1996] notes, political debate on Usenet/Newsnet bulletin boards is often marked by angry certainty, ideological abstraction, even insulting diatribes against opponents. While we might not expect this in a televised presidential debate, for example, such changes may not be too far in the future. The Internet now leads even television in informality, and it does so by creating a sense of addressability, of being able to say anything to anyone at any time. The possibilities and tensions inherent in this cultural and interpersonal access/intrusion will no doubt shape online verbal and visual artifacts in intriguing ways.

4. *The Internet decenters traditional power centers.* Since there is no central command or clearinghouse, the Internet allows the mundane to coexist alongside the staid alongside the bizarre. One result pertinent to rhetorical criticism is that the Internet enables grassroots activism (e.g., MoveOn.org) and the easy broadcasting of alternative news (e.g., Indymedia.org) and personal perspectives on world events. Sometimes this requires critics to rethink what counts as political action, as Koerber [2001] argues we must do in order to consider the liberatory possibilities of, for example, websites for progressive young mothers. DeLuca and Peeples [2002:125] agree, proposing that rather than simply investigating the discourse of the public sphere, rhetorical critics must now think in terms of events playing out on the "public screen," including new "forms of activism adapted to a wired society" as crucial elements in a participatory democracy. Seeing events such as the World Trade Organization protests streamed live and narrated online from different perspectives lessens audiences' reliance on news frames provided by Tom Brokaw or Dan Rather. The mass circulation of online petitions and preconstructed emails to congressional representatives have returned to many citizens the sense that they have a daily voice in their democracy, rather than only being consulted on election day.

In addition to using the critical probes developed in earlier and later chapters, critics may find several other questions useful for the study of the Internet.

- To what extent does the online artifact resemble offline communication? Are there clear generic parallels? Does this artifact borrow from more than one offline genre? Are there unique qualities that distinguish this artifact from those offline genres? From other online discourse? How do these borrowings and differences shape the way audiences are likely to receive this message?

- What attempts, if any, have been made to address a particular audience (through links, mass emailing, etc.)? What is this artifact asking of the viewer? What strategies does the rhetor use to make this request clear? How clear is the request? How are these qualities of rhetorical address likely to influence the way the artifact is received?

- How mutable is the artifact? Does the artifact invite interactivity, immediate feedback? If so, how? Is there an implicit or explicit expectation that audience participation will influence the artifact's construction in the near or distant future? How might this level of interactivity (or empowerment) invite or discourage audiences' future involvement?

CONCLUSION

At first glance, the ancient study of rhetoric may seem alien to an electronic world. The discipline of rhetoric was invented to deal with the great declarations of individual orators patiently explaining the affairs of the day to a learned citizenry. Things have gotten stranger. In an era of 300+ cable channels the individual rhetor now swims in a sea of competing hucksters. With network airtime costing hundreds of thousands of dollars a minute, "patience" has gone by the boards as persuaders try to hit'em hard and hit'em fast. The "affairs of the day" also struggle against a tide of distractions: reruns of *The X-Files,* Australian rules football, the plaintive sounds (and sights) of the Country Music Channel. In such an era the "learned citizenry" seems to have taken a permanent vacation as well.

But just because public discourse has changed does not exempt the critic from showing up for work. Why? Because too many important questions are still unresolved: Do situation comedies increase or decrease racial tolerance in the United States? Are network executives operating as patriots or serfs when re-presenting the Pentagon's press releases? Does the Internet recreate or obliterate the individual political empowerment of the ancient city-state?

The world of persuasion has changed, yes, but that only means the critic must stay on top of things. Late night impresario Larry King [1994:136] explains why when discussing the challenges America's Founders would face today:

> [Just think about] Jefferson, who was shy, kind of introverted: "Who is this woman, Tom? Black woman, mistress," they'd want to know. "Who is this woman?"
>
> Imagine Ben Franklin, with "Hard Copy" following him over to Paris. All over. Film of Ben Franklin in Paris? "Exclusive, tonight, at 5:00, Mrs. Franklin speaks out on 'Inside Edition' . . .". I mean, they were just as raucous—it's just that they didn't have television.
>
> Today, if we had a July 4th Declaration of Independence, it still would have been signed, let's say, in Philadelphia. But all the signers would have been on all the shows the next three nights, putting a spin on it: "Hancock, how come your name's so big? Are you plugging the insurance company? What do you mean by 'When in the course of human events. . . .'?"
>
> And try to picture the wacko right-wing talk show host on the Declaration of Independence—he'd have gone berserk: "Who *are* these people? Revolutionaries, mercenaries, violating the king?"

Some may be inclined to shed a tear for Jefferson and crew when reading King's imaginings. But the critic cannot be among them for, today, there is too much work to do. There will be time enough for tears tomorrow.

TIPS FOR THE PRACTICING CRITIC

1. Because we see thousands of media messages everyday, most manage to sneak by beneath our conscious awareness. The ubiquity of media messages often leads us to take them for granted. But all rhetoric asks something of its audience, and the most powerful rhetoric is often that which we do not, at first, detect.

2. Approaching the media from a rhetorical perspective requires that we achieve some critical distance from the texts we analyze. However, familiarity (or liking) makes it harder for us to be as critical of *Sesame Street,* for example, as we could be of a president's State of the Union Address. In order to develop this critical distance, try to develop a sense of dis-ease by making strange that which is familiar. The easiest way to feel dis-eased is by asking questions. For example, if a particular media message depicts "American Life," ask how representative the message is. Which groups are included in this portrait? Which groups are overlooked? Whose America is this? Is it a good America? For whom would this rhetoric work? For whom would it fall flat? Questions such as these allow critics to step back and view mediated messages more critically.

Chapter 10

ROLE CRITICISM

WOW! JESUS REALLY LOVES YOU
—Church sign, early July, 2003

ETERNITY—SMOKING OR NON
—Same sign, one week later

No doubt these messages in front of the Heartland Christian Center (and others of their ilk all over the country) are designed to quickly grab the attention of passing drivers, to invite them to consider their salvation, and to entice them to attend Sunday worship services. So what in Heaven's name makes them rhetorically noteworthy? The critic may suspect that bubbly reassurance one week, and dire warning the next, might create a sort of rhetorical whiplash. But what aspect of these messages would be responsible for such reactions?

This chapter focuses on the nature of **rhetorical role,** *a regularized set of verbal strategies resulting in a distinctive personal image.* That is, we will try to understand how a rhetor's words interact with an audience's perceptions to create social change. The first message does not just inform the reader of Jesus' love, it trumpets it. There is nothing the reader can do to change Jesus' unconditional love. Regardless of whatever horrible things the reader might have done, Jesus (and this church) still offer a loving welcome. This is Son-of-God, New Testament love and forgiveness with a contempo-twist. The "WOW!" and "REALLY" distinguish the message from the more clichéd "Jesus loves you." "WOW!" and "REALLY" emphasize the nature of this love, the strength of which is apparently startling even to the knowledgeable rhetor. Although announcing this as "news" to the reader, the rhetor sounds more impressed than even the bubbliest news anchor delivering her report. The rhetor combines the roles of Approving Teacher and Enthusiastic Cheerleader, singling out the reader for distinction ("You mean, Jesus really loves *me,* in particular?!").

The following week's message would seem to come from a different source, with a different view of God. God-the-Father of the Old Testament, who wrought vengeance with plagues and damnation, seems to be the rhetor. Or if not God, then one who can speak confidently for God, in the roles of Judge and Reformer. The reader of the first message could do nothing to lessen Jesus' love. However, the second voice knows with certainty that particular Life Choices result in particular Afterlife Outcomes, and the reader is provided with a humorous-but-sharp reminder of the dichotomous options available. The role adopted in the second message is reminiscent of fire-and-brimstone colonial preacher Jonathan Edwards, who here appears to be moonlighting as Restaurant Host, offering the reader the final choice of Eternal Seating.

In framing these messages, Angel Marjanovich, the worship leader of the Heartland Christian Center, knew that she would be facing **role constraints,** *the communicative rules imposed on a rhetor by the rhetorical situation.* A church's signs must sound authoritative and be congruent with the philosophy of the church. Religious leaders have the daunting job of being God's Voice on Earth, Shepherd to the Flock. They need to display credibility to current and potential congregants. To do so, those who post inspirational messages must demonstrate, week after week, familiarity with the Christian Bible and at least a modicum of cleverness, as well as heaps of rhetorical ingenuity, here signified by role flexibility: Teacher-Cheerleader-Reformer-Judge-Restaurant Host.

And so these messages create a distinctive **rhetorical persona,** *that complex of verbal features that makes one person sound different from another.* Each rhetor has a distinctive sound resulting from the combination of role and person. Perhaps religious leaders need to be able to be stand-up comics these days, able to do different voices: an admiring enthusiast one week, and within a few days, Jonathan Edwards helping you to your seat in the Hereafter. The combination of these roles makes the resulting persona richly layered—if not schizophrenic. Whatever the role, this persona has the ability to know and judge actions, for good or ill. The quick role changes and slight irony of "SMOKING OR NON" indicate a lack of pretension, which charms audiences. And in an MTV world, as we saw in Chapter 9, the rapid splicing together of different images makes sense. Most importantly, it attracts our attention. That is half the challenge in persuasion, and this is why these rhetorical contortions are both productive for rhetors and rewarding for critics.

It is one thing to be amused, annoyed or intrigued by messages such as those from the Heartland Christian Center and another to understand how they do what they do. This chapter is devoted to the latter pursuit. We will investigate the impact of social obligations on discourse, how roles create rhetorical limitations and possibilities, and how rhetors work to take on such roles. Our premise will be that selfhood and text collude to produce rhetoric. Here, we will monitor those collusions.

THE EMERGENCE OF ROLE

If role does not come at birth, it arrives soon after. "Infant" becomes "son" or "daughter" and learns to gurgle or smile on cue. "Infant" may also become "sibling" and, despairingly, learns to share. Learning to become a "niece" or a "nephew" is trickier if aunts and uncles are around infrequently. But these roles, too, are learned and after them "student," "goalie," "burger-flipper," "best friend," "lover," "lawyer," "homeowner." Each stage of life brings its jobs, each job a clientele, each clientele a rhetoric.

Rhetorical personae come from many sources. Often, one's **personal rhetorical history** produces a distinctive way of saying things. Being brought up in a particular locale (say, the Midwest), learning a particular style of speech (directness), identifying with a particular group of people (the middle class), having distinctive learning experiences (being the daughter of a businessman), and attending a particular kind of college (Wellesley) can produce a modest, conservative young woman like Hillary Rodham.

But **ideological influences** can also shape the social self. Attending a progressive law school (Yale) during a particular era (the 1960s), marrying a distinctive fellow (a handsome young politician) with a particular philosophy (high-tech populism) can produce a sharply transitional Hillary Rodham Clinton.

And rhetorical role can also be the product of **institutional affiliations.** When making the transition from Little Rock to Washington, D.C., Rodham Clinton increasingly found herself in role difficulty. She was part wife, part mother, part lawyer, part politician, and all First Lady. Each job had its own, long-standing rhetorical roles associated with it. It is small wonder then that as her time in Washington proceeded, Rodham Clinton learned to speak very, very carefully.

At times, institutional affiliations may conflict, which can lead rhetors to seek more creative role solutions. By 2000, Rodham Clinton had had eight years to practice her role-balancing, which prepared her for the next challenge: running for Senate. As Anderson [2002] found, Rodham Clinton managed to serve as First Lady while simultaneously running for and winning a seat in Congress. How? By performing the roles of Madonna (the mother of Jesus) and Madonna (the Material Girl). First, Anderson argues, Rodham Clinton emphasized her domesticity with the traditionally feminine role of "holy mother." But Anderson notes that Rodham Clinton's persona resisted easy categorization. In this regard, her public image bore similarities to the persona of pop icon Madonna, another woman famous for her ambition, her boundary-crossings, and her ability to divide public opinion.

Hillary Rodham Clinton's story shows that the critic has to be careful when doing any sort of rhetor-centered analysis since public people are so tightly role-constrained. This explains the importance of the final vowel in the term *persona.* Person and persona are not the same. The former is hidden within layers of self-hood while the latter is presented for public inspection. The American people know the persona of Hillary Rodham Clinton (e.g., "It takes a village . . .") but only her intimates know her person. (Even tell-all memoirs never do tell all.) Since every public message is made for a unique audience in a unique situation, it will necessarily bear their imprints. Thus, *the good critic never presumes that a text faithfully reflects the unique mind and personality of its author.*

The importance of this notion cannot be overestimated. Too often, critics become amateur psychoanalysts, searching for a rhetor's psyche within the metaphors the rhetor uses. This is a hazardous and unproductive game. Psychologizing about rhetors by looking at their public statements is normally both inaccurate and inconclusive. Instead, the critic must describe a rhetor's persona, the person-type the audience is being *invited* to see.

Thus, a research question like "What good or evil lurks inside the Hillary Rodham Clinton who uttered these remarks?" equates person with persona and hence is unanswerable. But a question such as "What sort of person were audiences invited to notice when hearing Hillary Rodham Clinton speak?" is answerable because the critic has Rodham Clinton's explicit and implicit self-descriptions as guideposts. Keeping this biographical fallacy in mind, we can consider several critical probes useful for describing a rhetor's persona:

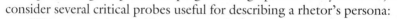

What reasons-for-speaking are offered by the rhetor? To study claimed motivations is to study the rhetor's self-portrait and, hence, the rhetor's understanding of audience values. Earlier in this book, for example, we heard Harold Hill proclaim his solemn duty to stave off corruption in River City, Iowa. Why a duty and not a whim? What is it about "duty" that sells in Iowa? In his speech, Rabbi Prinz said that he spoke not as a Jew, not as an American, but as an American Jew. Why the double motivation? In his speech, George Patton made no mention of his reasons for speaking. What did his audience make of that?

As Kenneth Burke [1962] said, motive is never not at issue in rhetoric, in that all such situations prompt the question: What is this person trying to do to me? As Arnold [1968] says, motive is especially crucial in oral persuasion. There, the rhetor's physical presence and nonverbal behavior (e.g., shifty eyes, perspiration) provide personalized information unavailable to the reader. This complicated package of cues brings the humanity of the rhetor into the picture more directly, both for good and ill. Naturally, the clever rhetor will try to de-emphasize this question of motive, often by providing flattering self-characterizations early in a message. In so doing, he or she also provides an understanding of what it takes to do business with this sort of audience in this sort of culture.

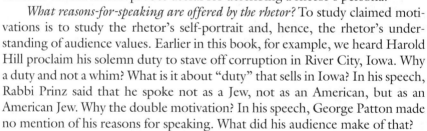

How sharply delineated is the persona of the message? According to Harrell et al. [1975], persona gives authority to a text that it would otherwise lack. For this reason, says Carlson [1991], lawyers in court sometimes try to "borrow" a persona from the literary realm (e.g., The Tempting Seductress or The Evil Leech) when defending their nonfictional clients in court. As Pauley [1998] notes, adopting the persona of Prophet allowed controversial Nation of Islam Minister Louis Farrakhan to generate widespread support for the Million Man March in 1995. On other occasions, argue Erickson and Fleuriet [1991], presidents issue "unattributed" messages shorn of persona so that public reaction can be gauged without the proposer risking personal censure. A middle ground between the distinct and indistinct personae was described by Darsey [1995] who found Senator Joseph McCarthy's persuasive power to derive from his ability to create a "fantastic" world so captivating to its audience that they never bothered to inspect McCarthy's own motives.

Hillbruner [1974] suggests that a critic distinguish between the **signature** of a message (verbal tics unique to the rhetor) and its use of **archetypes** (cultural stories and traditional language used by all rhetors). In these terms, the Heartland Christian Center's signs were all archetype and no signature. The opposite condition is found in the following variation on a personal ad:

> Intelligent guy (38–55) wanted by beautiful woman to love, honor, and obey. Want to leave the hustle and bustle of a superficially glamorous career to raise a family. I'm 35, but can pass for 28. I'm attractive (many say gorgeous, some say cute), sincere, passionate. I like power and settle for nothing less than excellence. I'm also caring, loyal, faithful, monogamous, artistic, spiritual, physically fit, health oriented but indulgent, traditional (I've never written to a personal column before!). Sweet, caring, sexy, bright, demonstrative. Enjoy opera, elegant restaurants, hayrides on starlit nights, goofy affection, Chinese food, satin sheets, bubble baths, Bach, shopping malls, and playing Monopoly by the fire on winter nights. Write on company letterhead to Box 223, *The Times*.

This passage is a benchmark for clarity of persona! Upon reading it, the reader can quickly decide whether or not to pursue the possibility. The Self described here is a unity of diversity, all of it well buoyed by a very healthy ego. Strine and Pacanowsky [1985] describe texts of this sort as having **prominent authorial status** whereby the author becomes central to the rhetorical action. In sharp contrast is the rhetoric of science which derives its authority from a distanced, pedantic style containing no self-references or personal reflections. In rhetoric with such **diminished authorial status,** the rhetor's faithful adherence to role-constraints, rather than personal flair, provides its suasive force.

 Does role, not situation, dominate the rhetor's message? This question encourages the critic to track rhetors across situations to find regularities. And it takes a *critic* to do so since most people pay little attention to their social habits. Simply raising one's hand in class, for example, marks a learner's deference to the instructor and a willingness to abide by the norms of politeness. If hand raising is a product of role constraints, then so too are the infinitely more complex patterns of daily discourse.

Sigelman [2001:15] looked at the "onstage" and "backstage" personas of Presidents Johnson and Nixon and found that "the onstage Johnson had more in common with the onstage Nixon than with the backstage Johnson, and the onstage Nixon was a fraternal twin of the onstage Johnson but only a distant cousin of the backstage Nixon." Hart [1984b] studied such role-related demands by searching for the "natively presidential" features of political language. He tracked the use of ten verbal factors (described in Chapter 8), comparing Presidents Truman through Reagan to a group of nonpresidents that included preachers, corporation executives, social activists, and candidates for political office. Table 10.1 presents samples from the texts studied.

Generally speaking, three features seemed linked to presidential role: (1) **humanity** (presidents used the most self-references, were most optimistic, and compared to business executives, were more people-centered); (2) **practicality** (presidents used concrete language and chose a simpler style than their counterparts); and (3) **caution** (presidents used less assured language than those running for office, and dramatically less than the preachers studied). Not only did these factors distinguish presidents from others but Lyndon Johnson and Richard Nixon also changed their speaking in these ways when moving from the vice presidency to the presidency.

These findings suggest that the president's *job itself* has built-in rhetorical requirements, dictating that presidents both humanize technical problems and present them as solvable. The president's job demands language laypersons can understand, rather than geopolitical abstractions. Finally, the president must choose words carefully: A Dwight Eisenhower must avoid the formulas

TABLE 10.1 Presidential and Nonpresidential Speech Contrasted

Presidential	Nonpresidential
"I have tried to base my decisions and my thinking and my actions on what I think is really best for this country. I believe that is what my country expects me to do." {Johnson, 1966:659]	"The Democratic Party does not believe that we can hold back and go forward at the same time. We do not believe that we can get ahead by standing still. We do not believe that we can be strong abroad and weak at home." [Johnson, 1960:4]
"We have the chance today to do more than ever before in our history to make life better in America, to ensure better education, better health, better housing, better transportation, a cleaner environment, to restore respect for law, to make our communities more livable, and to ensure the God-given right of every American to full and equal opportunity." [Nixon, 1973:14]	"There are some threats to our existence which are fundamentally environmental. . . . The urbanization problem is so severe over the world today. . . . Here is a single example from outside the United States of how we can make very silly mistakes. . . . These are the people who are looting and polluting the world." [Erlich, 1972:118-9]
"Now as we strive to bring about that [peaceful] wisdom, there is, in this moment of sober satisfaction, one thought that must discipline our emotions and steady our resolution. It is this: we have battleground, not peace in the world." [Eisenhower, 1953:642]	"Mark these words well. This is what the Communists really mean by 'peaceful coexistence.' They do not mean 'peace.' 'Peaceful coexistence' is simply the Communist strategy for world conquest." [Goldwater, 1964:37]

of radical politics used by a Barry Goldwater [see Table 10.1], a Richard Nixon cannot be as pessimistic as environmentalist Paul Erlich, and a President Johnson must personalize issues that a Senator Johnson might have made more general. For several reasons, then, presidents follow a rule book when they speak, clearly showing how role can dominate person on occasion.

THE MANAGEMENT OF ROLE

Among the most primitive resources in persuasion are the qualities of mind, behavioral habits, and factors of personal appearance that attract people to one another. But like a talented but raw young boxer, one's person must be "managed" if it is to have social effect. Generosity of spirit and a twinkle in the eye cannot advance a rhetor's goals if they are not noticed by others. And so rhetoric requires the rhetor to make choices in self-presentation; criticism demands that the critic track these choices. These critical probes are useful for doing so.

 What is the rhetor's theory of discourse? How are audiences' and rhetors' roles defined in this model? Everyone has a theory of discourse, whether they know it or not. Mary Poppins's classic refrain, "A spoonful of sugar makes the medicine go down," affirmed that common premises can win over hostile audiences. Similarly, when Harold Hill's rival in *The Music Man* proclaimed "You've gotta know the territory," he isolated audience analysis as the key to persuasion. And when Toula Portokalos's father in *My Big Fat Greek Wedding* promised "Give me a word, *any word*, and I show you how the root of that word is Greek," he demonstrated his affinity for communication-as-competition. As Johnson [1975] notes, these **implicit communication theories** are just that: implicit. Mary Poppins and Gus Portokalos could not discuss their rhetorical theories with precision, for life had taught them such lessons in its taken-for-granted way. More important, however, Poppins and Portokalos *used* these unspoken assumptions when talking, thereby providing the critic with an important, and accessible, object of scrutiny.

Seven such theories seem particularly useful to the critic. Perhaps unsurprisingly, conspiracy theorists often favor **Magical** theories of communication, in which great power is attributed to unseen forces. Theatrical producer Henslowe in *Shakespeare in Love* [1998] provides a lighter version. As he explains to a skeptic,

HENSLOWE: The natural condition [in the theatre business] is one of insurmountable obstacles on the road to imminent disaster.
FENNYMAN: So what do we do?
HENSLOWE: Nothing. Strangely enough it all turns out well.
FENNYMAN: How?
HENSLOWE: I don't know. It's a mystery.

A related model is more **Mechanical** in nature. It warns that society is being worn down by "implements of propaganda" that "overwhelm" the stalwart but "inept" citizen. Within such rhetoric, Benson [1968] found metaphors of poison used to explain why people succumbed to error (i.e., they were "helpless" to resist). With the Magical theory, then, the rhetor becomes a master wizard who uncovers vile deceptions or celebrates mystical order. With the Mechanical theory, the rhetor becomes a concerned mechanic, working to repair the audience's attitudinal systems with the right ideological tool.

Lake [1983] discusses a third, **Experiential,** theory of persuasion. Here, language is seen as an obstacle to truth. For example, the rhetoric of the American Indian Movement argued that the world of words is the white person's world and therefore corrupt. These rhetors argue that Whites' treaties have subverted Native Americans and, as a result, only natural and supernatural forces can be trusted. The persona here is defiant and emotional, a rhetoric suited to insiders.

In contrast is the **Rationalistic** theory of economic progress displayed, for example, in the famous opening of Jane Austen's *Pride and Prejudice* [1993:1]: "It is a truth universally acknowledged, that a single man in possession of a good fortune, must be in want of a wife." The "logic" of this theory when applied to love is, Austen implies, less than appropriate. Predictably, the rhetoric this theory produces is bland, spare, and remote.

Another popular theory of communication is **Parental.** Here, the persona of the rhetor is a clear, dominating presence. The image is that of a kindly shepherd leading a flock, helping even the weakest traverse the difficult course. Rhetors operating on this model become all-knowing and yet patient, sage but nonpartisan helpmates to the audience. The leaders of both religious and social movements often opt for this image, especially after their movements have reached maturity. Coles [2001] depicted Bill Clinton as assuming this mantle in the late 1990s, after scandals threatened to destroy his presidential legacy.

Rhetors operating on the **Antagonistic** model of persuasion see the audience as an enemy to be assaulted; submission, not cooperation, is their goal. The rapid-fire salesperson and the fact-spewing trial attorney often project this persona when "attacking the fortress of public opinion." Hart's [1978] study of modern atheists shows this theory in action, with the atheists producing pamphlet after pamphlet, most of which were badly written, poorly documented, and terribly edited but which still had tremendous rhetorical energy ("We *can* turn the tide!"). The idea here is to produce *enough* persuasion so that religion is washed away in a sea of rhetoric. The logic of this approach also holds that atheistic ideas, even when unadorned, are so powerful that the merest contact with them will produce conversion.

A final, **Formulaic,** theory is especially popular. This model holds that audiences will succeed if they use certain recipes for personal profit. The shelves of bookstores bend under the weight of these recipes: *Fit for Life; Men Are from Mars, Women Are from Venus; Mayan Wisdom Made Easy.* The persona here is supremely confident: The formula works for all customers under all circumstances. According to Payne [1989], this rhetoric sharply increased during the 1960s when scores of capitalistic gurus appeared on the American scene. As with the other implicit theories, these persuaders endorse a policy ("Reach paradise. Follow the Way") but also peddle a philosophy of listening ("Record this list of tips; don't question them") and a philosophy of life ("Even difficult things can be made easy").

Most people are unaware of their assumptions about discourse and might well deny these assumptions if brought to their attention. Still, the good critic realizes that to speak is to reveal attitudes—about oneself and one's ideas, but also about one's audience and what is best for them. The good critic is always on the lookout for such attitudes.

How consistently does the rhetor opt for a particular role? What does this show about the rhetorical situation? Consider the following exchange, from the film *Miss Congeniality* [2000]. The evil and scheming beauty pageant host, Kathy Morningside, addresses the crucial interview question to klutzy FBI agent Gracie Hart. With the grudging cooperation of Morningside and makeover guru Victor Melling, Gracie has gone undercover as Miss New Jersey to foil the plot to kill the pageant's winner.

KATHY: (poisonously) New Jersey: As you know, there are many who consider the Miss United States Pageant outdated and antifeminist. What would you say to them?

VICTOR: (watching from the wings, smells doom) Oh, my God.

GRACIE: Well, I would have to say, I used to be one of them.
(Uncertain laughter and murmurs from the audience)
And then I came here and realized that these women are smart, terrific people who're just trying to make a difference in the world. And we've become really good friends.
(Applause begins, which she interrupts)
I mean, I—I know we all secretly hope the other one'll trip and, and fall on her face. . . . Oh, wait a minute! I've already done that! (Shared laughter)
And for me this experience has been one of the most rewarding and. . . . *liberating* experiences of my life.

VICTOR: (appreciatively) Oh my God. That did it!

GRACIE: (not finished) . . . And if anyone, anyone, tries to hurt one of my new friends, I would take them out. I would make them suffer so much that they'd wish they were never born. And if they ran . . . [she turns to look at Kathy] . . . I would hunt them down. (Shocked silence)

GRACIE: (smiling graciously) Thank you, Kathy.
(Scattered applause begins)

VICTOR: A brief, shining moment, and then that *mouth!*

Kathy's question is clearly meant to trap Gracie, whom Kathy knows primarily in her persona of Jeering Pageant Critic, a graceless federal agent impatient with the rituals of femininity. In contrast to the knee-jerk "feminist" reaction Kathy hoped to provoke, Gracie's answer reflects more complexity. The initial portion of her reply presents a collection of personae we might title the Wise and Integrated Self. Rather than being defensive, she is the Perceptive Philosopher, self-reflective and honest ("I used to be one of them"), open to admitting and learning from her mistakes ("And then I came here and realized"). She is the Self-Mocking Comedian, aware of petty competition but rising above it ("Oh, wait a minute! I've already done that!") and the Generous Spirit ("smart, terrific people . . . just trying to make a difference"). The real triumph of her response, however, the one that gladdens Victor's heart, is her **role appropriation.** She presents herself as a Recovering Stereotypical Feminist, which the audience can tell because (a) she knows karate and (b) prior to her makeover, she eschews conditioner in favor of career. Hence, she can adopt a rhetorical posture otherwise unavailable to her. As a Converted Feminine Feminist, she can legitimate the pageant in ways no "typical" contestant could do, by claiming that it has achieved the goals of feminism . . . without all that unsightly hair: "And for me this . . . has been one of the most rewarding and . . . *liberating* experiences of my life." Because feminism values self-determination for women and men, critiquing another's chosen means of liberation can be tricky.

In the final portion of her answer, Gracie reverts to Ruthless Crimefighter: "And if anyone . . . tries to hurt one of my new friends, I would take them out." She is still on the job, and must protect the vulnerable. But in *Miss Congeniality*, protection is ironically achieved through femininity, which Susan Brownmiller [1984:19] identified as the appearance of weakness—thus "proving" the paradox that, in order to be strong, feminists sometimes have to meet idealized beauty standards. As with all such "makeover" movies, the heroine's heretofore unsuspected **role flexibility** is her rhetorical hat trick, here resulting in the double payoff of both career and romantic advancement. Produced during a conflicted time of gender questioning and political realignment (are progressive young women and men third wave feminists? postfeminists? something else entirely?), *Miss Congeniality* is trying to have it as many ways as possible. This passage therefore establishes an important proposition: *role signals circumstance.*

Critics have investigated a variety of roles to learn about circumstances. For example, Ware and Linkugel [1973] found that one of the roles adopted above, that of **Apologist,** featured four ways of rebuffing attack: outright denial ("I'm not guilty"), bolstering ("We've got better things to be concerned about"), differentiation ("Here's a new way of thinking about it"), and transcendence ("There's a larger principle at stake here"). Along similar lines, Scott [1987] observed that when Senator Edward Kennedy tried to explain the tragic Chappaquiddick affair (in which one of his aides died by drowning), he directed his remarks to the people of Massachusetts (even though the address was televised nationally), thereby claiming the role privileges of a native son.

Another rhetorical character is the **Agent** who speaks in behalf of some institution. At first, this role seems attractive since it gives the rhetor legitimate authority. But what power gives, power can also deny. Jablonski [1980] found that when Catholics resisted certain liturgical reforms in the 1970s, American bishops tried to strong-arm them by using doctrinal materials, thereby cloaking themselves in the mantle of the Church. More recently, Murphy [1997] examined Bill Clinton's 1993 speech on race, crime, and welfare. Clinton spoke to five thousand African American ministers in the church where Dr. Martin Luther King, Jr., preached on the eve of his assassination. Clinton took on the diction and vocal patterns of Dr. King, invoking him as if he were there, rendering his judgment of the world in the twenty-five years since his death. In effect, Murphy argues, by adopting King's vision and rhetorical style, Clinton became an Agent for the African American church: "By [subordinating himself to King], he paradoxically gains communal authority" [pp. 80–81]. The downside, of course, is that Agents can at times misinterpret the party line, thereby creating more trouble than they are worth.

While Agents filter their words through revealed truth, the **Partisan** strikes out in new directions, speaking the truth with power and passion. For these reasons, Partisans prosper during times of turmoil, using their charisma to galvanize public opinion by goading entrenched powers. Gregg [1971] notes that such rhetoric is often auto-suggestive: Its strong, negative tone better serves to reinforce in-group feelings than to make new converts. In Murphy's [1997] reading of Clinton's Memphis speech, he also presents Clinton as a Partisan for American liberalism. Both Agent and Partisan were necessary because "Liberalism [alone] leaves Americans, black and white, with a vision of freedom minus community responsibility. . . . While he retains the liberal emphasis on work, it is now animated with the ethical light of King's vision" [Murphy 1997: 82–83]. Together, the argument goes, liberalism and ethics, Partisan and Agent, offer hope for helping African American individuals and communities break the destructive cycle.

The role of **Hero** is not easy to play although many try to play it. Ronald Reagan played it better than most. According to Fisher [1982], Reagan's rhetoric combined two key heroic features: a *romantic* quality and a commitment to *action*. Years later, George W. Bush, Mr. Reagan's would-be legatee, used this same role to build and maintain political power (e.g., by offering a $25 million reward for Saddam Hussein "dead or alive" and fostering a continual state of medium-to-high antiterrorist alert).

Whether one attempts to become Apologist, Agent, Partisan, or Hero, however, one must bring to that role **emotional integrity,** so that its pieces and parts fit together, and **dramatic consistency,** so that one does not try to become an Apologist one day and a Hero the next. Role-enactment can therefore fail for many reasons: (1) The role may be played poorly, (2) it may be unsuitable for the times, or (3) different roles may become ineffectively intertwined. As McGee [1998] shows, Louisiana gubernatorial hopeful David Duke faced all of these problems during his 1991 campaign, as he tried to: (1) outlive his image as a neo-Nazi and former Grand Wizard of the Ku Klux Klan; (2) cast himself as a newly born-again Christian somehow immune from criticism by other Evangelicals, and (3) convince voters of his (Partisan) "conversion" to mainstream politics despite remaining true to his (Apologist) beliefs in segregation and white majority rule. Tracking the maneuverings of people like Duke can tell the critic much about the theater of everyday life and about the players who walk its stage.

THE ASSESSMENT OF ROLE IN RHETOR-CENTERED DISCOURSE

This final section presents two practical ways of analyzing speaker-based rhetorical patterns. Although not exclusively for use in investigating oral discourse, they are ideally suited for it. Neither approach is especially sophisticated, but together they can round out the critic's analysis of persuasive role. Once again, we will begin our discussion with critical probes:

 Does the rhetor make *overt* use of credibility devices? Do these uses vary across time and circumstance? In September of 1960, John F. Kennedy had a credibility problem: Although his campaign for the presidency was moving apace, he could not shake the charge that his Roman Catholicism would curtail his political independence as a chief executive. Because he was heir to several generations of antipapist sentiment in the United States, Kennedy tried to defuse the issue by speaking to the Greater Houston Ministerial Association and thereby make the Catholic issue a nonissue.

Kennedy's speech was a remarkable success. Some say it won him the presidency. The speech not only charmed the Texas ministers but also moved the religious issue to the back burner throughout the United States (either by convincing or by cowing his critics).

The speech itself was perhaps less remarkable than the speech-act. Kennedy's willingness to face his detractors in a volatile situation impressed people, even though his message had few rhetorical flourishes. Kennedy began by thanking the ministers for the invitation to speak, commented on several international and domestic problems, and then framed the central issue succinctly: "It is apparently necessary for me to state once again—not what kind of church I believe in, for that should be important only to me, but what kind of America I believe in" [Kennedy, 1961a:427]. Kennedy then spoke with unusual directness about the issues: Would he become a political captive of the pope? Would he encourage mindless bloc voting? Would other religious groups suffer at his hands? No, no, no, he replied.

The second half of the speech was more positive, with Kennedy discussing freedom of speech, religious tolerance, and the sacrifices that had been made for both: "Side by side with Bowie and Crockett [at the Alamo] died Fuentes and McCafferty and Bailey and Bedillio and Carey—but no one knows whether they were Catholics or not. For there was no religious test there" [p. 428]. In the final portion of his statement, Kennedy made a series of highly specific predictions for his intended administration: No aid to parochial schools; no religious litmus tests on abortion, censorship, or gambling; no untoward alliances with Catholic countries. He concluded his speech with a warning: "If this election is decided on the basis that 40,000,000 Americans lost their chance of being President on the day they were baptized, then it is the whole nation that will be the loser . . . in the eyes of history, and in the eyes of our own people" [pp. 429–430].

When speaking, Kennedy used a number of credibility strategies, six of which are presented in Table 10.2 (a seventh dimension, Dynamism, is largely a nonverbal factor signaled by bodily action and vocal activity). While all rhetorical situations involve these dimensions, the rhetor's *words* perform only some of the work of image-making. That is, credibility is also determined by such factors as human prejudices, the rhetor's sponsor, media effects, the time of day, audience confusion, etc.

Moreover, credibility bestowed one day is sometimes withdrawn the next, often for reasons having little to do with what the rhetor says. (For example, the highly publicized Arthur Anderson, Enron, and WorldCom frauds led to a loss of trust in CEOs in general [Gibbs, 2002]). In short, the devices listed in Table 10.2 are available for control by the rhetor but this is not to say that they alone "produce" credibility.

Table 10.3 presents the credibility strategies used by John Kennedy and some of the other rhetors discussed earlier. The chart has been produced by using the "Methods of Demonstration" listed in Table 10.2 and searching for sample instances of them in the four messages studied. We claim nothing like scientific precision here, but the results are interesting. Kennedy, for example, tried a bit of everything. He used Competence ("the hungry people I saw in West Virginia"), Good Will ("Today, I may be the victim [of religious prejudice]—but tomorrow it may be you"), Idealism ("this is the kind of America I fought for in the South Pacific"), Similarity ("I am wholly opposed to the state being used by any religious group"), and even Power ("judge me on the basis of my fourteen years in the congress") and Trustworthiness (when he cites his previously "declared stands against an ambassador to the Vatican"). Kennedy's speech is therefore quite experimental since there were no guidelines for handling such an unprecedented situation.

George Patton's situation was obviously more comfortable than Kennedy's so he used Trustworthiness heavily. In a sense, Patton's address was a counterstatement to the anxieties his men were experiencing on the eve of battle. He therefore used his long-standing relationship with the military to become part of his men's internal dialogue and to become identified with the emotional life of the footsoldier. Patton also used his speech to empower the troops, explaining that they were braver and stronger than any who preceded them. While Patton used Good Will and Similarity to also show concern for the GI's daily lives, he spent virtually no time on Competence, no doubt because he already had a legendary reputation.

TABLE 10.2 Verbal Dimensions of Credibility

Credibility Dimension	Perceived Capacity	Methods of Demonstration	Example (United Fund Campaign)
Power	Rhetor can provide significant rewards and punishments (either material or psychological) for audience.	(1) Indications of previous victories the rhetor has won in behalf of the topic.	"I've had the honor of directing the last three successful campaigns and. . . ."
		(2) Suggestions of how audience can share influence already possessed by the rhetor.	"I'd now like to pass out the gold pins to the ten-year volunteers."
		(3) Subtle reminders of status differences between rhetor and audience.	"Just last week the mayor said to me, 'John, . . .'"
Competence	Rhetor has knowledge and experience the audience does not have.	(1) Association with recognized experts.	"Studies of malnutrition by the federal governments show conclusively that. . . ."
		(2) Unique, personal familiarity with the topic is demonstrated.	"Having worked with the Meals on Wheels Program, I. . . ."
		(3) Mastery of relevant technical vocabulary.	"The hospital's new Epidemiology Lab is now complete, thanks to the last campaign."
Trustworthiness	Rhetor can be relied on beyond this one moment in time	(1) Present and past behaviors are consistent.	"The United Fund stands on its record: low overhead, maximum help to the community."
		(2) Verbal and nonverbal behaviors are consistent.	"A full two percent of annual salary. That's what I give. Here's my canceled check."
		(3) Explicitly address alternative viewpoints.	"Yes, the Harris scandal did set us back. But there are no more skeletons in the closet."
Good will	Rhetor had the best interests of the audience in mind.	(1) Benefits of rhetor's proposal are dramatized.	"People get sick. Those of you who aren't people needn't bother giving to the Fund."
		(2) Reasons for rhetor's concern for audience are specified.	"My family's been in town for three generations. *That's* why I kill myself for the Fund."

(continued)

TABLE 10.2 (continued)

Credibility Dimension	Perceived Capacity	Methods of Demonstration	Example (United Fund Campaign)
Idealism	Rhetor possesses qualities to which the audience aspires.	(1) Socially acceptable eccentricities are revealed.	"Yes, a 'Uni Fnd' license plate is strange. So call me strange. Publicity is publicity."
		(2) Rhetor's risks in behalf of the proposal are specified.	"I put in thirty hours a week for the Fund in addition to my regular job. How about you making ten phone calls for us?"
Similarity	Rhetor is seen as resembling the audience in important ways.	(1) Association with valued beliefs.	"We've got to remember that folks should care for folks. And that's doubly true for folks who have no folks to care for them."
		(2) Disassociation from unattractive beliefs.	"Communism and the United Fund are both collective actions. That's where the similarity ends."

After Hart et al. [1983].

TABLE 10.3 Comparative Uses of Credibility Strategies*

Credibility Strategies	Rabbi Prinz	Harold Hill	George Patton	John Kennedy
Power	0	9	19	5
Competence	44	61	4	22
Trustworthiness	0	0	32	8
Good will	18	5	26	26
Idealism	2	2	9	27
Similarity	36	23	18	12

*Percent usage in text.

Rabbi Prinz and Harold Hill operated in a remarkably similar manner, a finding that would no doubt be disconcerting to the good Rabbi. But their behavior makes sense: Given the time constraints, neither could count on extended interaction with their hearers and, given their status as unknowns, neither could base their case on personal biography. Power, Idealism, and Trustworthiness were thus eliminated as rhetorical options.

So Harold Hill went with what he had—his imagination—and used Competence to demonstrate his authority about the wages of sin. He alluded to corruptions found in the pool hall ("your son playin' for money"), at the racetrack ("some stuck-up jockey-boy settin' on Dan Patch"), and in the dance hall ("libertine men and scarlet women"). Rabbi Prinz also used Competence but did so far differently: He simply told his own story of persecution. This "I've been there" approach is universally compelling and was especially appropriate for a person trying to build bridges in the early civil rights movement.

Similarity also builds bridges. Prinz offers an almost perfect equation between his life in Nazi Germany and his audience's experiences with racial discrimination in the United States. Hill responds in kind, disassociating himself from middle-American evil (e.g., not getting the screen door patched) and associating himself with cherished values and traditions: "Remember the Maine, Plymouth Rock, and the Golden Rule!" As we have seen earlier, Hill's speech is largely a sermon. The correspondence between its credibility structure and that of a legitimate member of the clergy like Prinz further attests to Hill's talents at generic transference.

One value of canvassing such strategies is that it shows which aspects of image were *overtly* dealt with by the rhetor and which aspects the audience may have supplied on its own. For example, General Patton could have spoken about Competence directly, but to have dwelt on his previous exploits at this time could actually have rebounded, by calling them into question ("Why is he suddenly feeling the need to prove himself? What's wrong?"). So he concentrated his efforts elsewhere, counting on the aspects of credibility he did cover to reinforce the taken-for-granted nature of his ability to plan and lead an attack. That is presumably the response most of his soldiers had to his remarks.

How often does one find self-references in the text? Why are they there? I-statements are important because they are not particularly common and because they index a person's feelings and ambitions in especially prominent ways. Some rhetors refer to themselves constantly while others never do. What accounts for such patterns? Personality? Social norms? Situation? Do certain rhetorical tasks (e.g., being a morning-show host on television) encourage self-references while others (e.g., being a diplomat) discourage them? Why do speeches typically contain twenty times the number of self-references found in writing? Why do presidential campaigners significantly increase their I-statements once elected and why have recent chief executives increased this rate dramatically? [See Hart, 1984b]. We have plenty of such questions. Answers are less available.

A critic should look with special care at I-statements since they make special claims on the audience's attention. Even in casual chatter this is true. When a speaker suddenly starts to tell a personal anecdote, listeners' ears perk up as they sense a shift in the discussion. Naturally, their expectations can be quickly dashed if the story turns into a boring monologue. But, temporarily at least, they are open to influence because identifying with one another is such a basic human instinct.

A useful critical procedure is to extract from a text any phrase or clause containing an "I" and then to lay out these statements one after another (paraphrased, if necessary). Even this simple procedure gives the critic a fresh perspective on the message, as context is torn away and the Self made more prominent. Table 10.4 shows the results of this procedure for an address given

TABLE 10.4 I-Statements in Ronald Reagan's Speech of 3/4/87*

(01) I have spoken before (from the Oval Office).
(02) I want to talk (to you).
(03) I have been silent (about Iran-Contra revelations).
(04) I guess you're thinking (I'm hiding).
(05) I haven't spoken before (because of sketchy details).
(06) I felt it was improper (to react precipitously).
(07) I have paid a price (for silence).
(08) I have had to wait (for the whole story).
(09) I appointed (Abshire).
(10) I appointed (the review board).
(11) I am often accused (of optimism).
(12) I have had to hunt (for good news).
(13) I will discuss criticisms.
(14) I was relieved (by the Tower Commission report).
(15) I want to thank (the panel).
(16) I have studied the report.
(17) I accept the Board's findings.
(18) I want to share my thoughts (about the findings).
(19) I am taking action (to implement the findings).
(20) I take responsibility (for my actions).
(21) I am angry (about aides).
(22) I am accountable (for their actions).
(23) I am disappointed.
(24) I must answer (to the people).
(25) I find secrets distasteful.
(26) I told the American people (there'd be no arms trade).
(27) I didn't trade arms for hostages.
(28) I undertook (Iran initiatives).
(29) I let my concern for hostages (spill over).
(30) I asked questions (about the hostages).
(31) I didn't ask about the plan (to swap arms for hostages).
(32) I promise we'll try to free the hostages.
(33) I must caution (Americans in Iran).
(34) I am confident (the truth will come out).
(35) I told the Tower board (I didn't know about diversions).
(36) I didn't know (about diversions of funds).
(37) I cannot escape (responsibility).
(38) I identify (problems before acting).
(39) I have found (delegating to be effective).
(40) I have begun (to correct problems).
(41) I met (with professional staff).
(42) I defined values (that should guide them).
(43) I want values to guide policy.
(44) I told them (integrity was essential).
(45) I want a justifiable policy.
(46) I wanted (an "obedient") policy.
(47) I told them (freelancing was over).
(48) I can tell you (the NSC staff is good).
(49) I approved (an arms shipment).
(50) I did approve (an arms shipment).
(51) I can't say when (approval was given).
(52) I have been studying (the report).

(continued)

TABLE 10.4 (*continued*)

(53) I want people to know (the ordeal has not been in vain).
(54) I endorse (the Board's recommendations).
(55) I am going beyond recommendations.
(56) I am taking action in three areas.
(57) I brought in (a new team).
(58) I am hopeful (that experience will prove valuable).
(59) I am honored (by Baker's acceptance).
(60) I nominated Webster.
(61) I will appoint Tower.
(62) I am considering other changes (in personnel).
(63) I will move "furniture" as necessary.
(64) I see fit (to make staff changes).
(65) I have ordered NSC (to review operations).
(66) I have directed NSC (to comply with correct values).
(67) I expect to have an honorable covert policy.
(68) I have issued directives (about covert operations).
(69) I have asked Bush (to reconvene task force).
(70) I am adopting (Tower report's model).
(71) I am directing Carlucci (to improve staff operations).
(72) I have created a post (of legal advisor).
(73) I am determined (to make new policy work).
(74) I will report to Congress (about new policies).
(75) I have taken steps (to implement Board's recommendations).
(76) I have gotten (the message).
(77) I have heard (the message).
(78) I have a great deal to accomplish (in the future).
(79) I want to accomplish much (in the future).
(80) I intend to accomplish much (in the future).

*Paraphrased.

by Ronald Reagan on March 4, 1987. This speech was Mr. Reagan's first response to the Tower Commission's report on the Iran-Contra affair, a scandal in which certain agents of the Reagan administration sold arms to the South American "contras" so they then could trade for American hostages in Iran.

While not charging Mr. Reagan with high crimes or misdemeanors, the Commission did find that the President had been lax in managing those responsible for the arms-for-hostages deal. Because the Commission was a distinguished one (chaired by a Republican) and because its report received ample media attention, Mr. Reagan had little choice but to face the music.

This much-awaited speech cast Reagan in an unaccustomed role—that of Apologist—and began a long period of frustration for him as well. To his credit in the speech, Reagan accepted a good deal of blame for what went wrong, although he chalked up some of the problem to incomplete reports, faulty memory, irresponsible aides, and general miscommunication. All in all, it was a speech Ronald Reagan did not enjoy giving.

One way of capturing the tenor of his remarks is to categorize his I-statements by means of a crude, but straightforward system consisting of four elements: (1) **Emotional/Moral Action:** the rhetor's reports of feelings experienced, moral lessons learned, and hopes and desires for the future. Reagan's statements 6, 14, 21, 37, and 58 are examples of this type; (2) **Narrative Action:** references to allegedly factual events, sometimes occurring in the distant past, that led up to the speech, (e.g., statements 1, 5, 16, 27, 35, and 39); (3) **Behavioral Action:** specific *policy* behaviors the rhetor has engaged in immediately prior to the speech event itself (e.g., statements 10, 44, 56, 65, 71); (4) **Performative Action:** a more complex category consisting of references to the rhetor's intentions for the speech (e.g., statements 13, 18, 24,) or to commitments and certifications being made by the fact of the speech itself (e.g., statements 54, 63, 70, 77).

This system highlights the **locus of action** in a text. That is, it describes whether the rhetor is being acted upon by events (i.e., when the message is high on Narratives) or whether the rhetor is taking charge (i.e., when it is high on Behavioral Action). This critical system can also track internal versus external action (i.e., Is the rhetor a "feeler" or a "doer"?) by scrutinizing the number and types of Emotional/Moral statements. Finally, the system identifies whether or not the rhetor is personally willing to become part of the bottom line for policy initiatives (i.e., the number and force of Performative statements).

Although Ronald Reagan used all four types of I-statements in discussing the Iran-Contra affair, the first half of his message was dominated by Emotional/Moral and Narrative Action and the latter half by Performative and Behavioral Action. That is, Mr. Reagan commenced his remarks by backpedaling, recounting how the tide of events swept him up: "As angry as I may be about activities undertaken without my knowledge, I am still accountable for those activities" [Reagan, 1987:12].

The locus of *observable* action in the early part of the speech is therefore external to Mr. Reagan while the *emotional* action lies inside, establishing the President as a sensitive, compassionate person ("I let my personal concern . . . spill over"). He felt deeply about the events of the day but was not responsible for them.

Reagan corrects this latter error in the second part of his address. There, he takes charge of events by "adopting," "endorsing," "telling," "nominating," "issuing," "creating," and "ordering." Like a phoenix rising from the ashes, Reagan ends his remarks by promising that there will be action, he is once again in charge, and his audience need no longer worry. But while the emphasis changes dramatically during the speech, Mr. Reagan never completely abandons the Emotional/Moral note on which he began.

For Ronald Reagan, this was unquestionably the most difficult speech of his life and so he concluded by redocumenting his personal seriousness: "You know, by the time you reach my age, you've made plenty of mistakes if you've lived your life properly. So you learn. You put things in perspective. You pull your energies together. You change. You go forward" [p. 12].

I-statements are only a part of rhetoric and comparatively little is known about them at present. But when examined in the manner suggested here, they can shed light on the motivational dynamics of discourse. Rhetors who use a great many self-references hint strongly that a special personae is being created in the texts they produce. They may also hint something of importance about the persons behind the personae, although that is far less certain.

On the other hand, rhetors who never refer to themselves also make an important personal statement by not making one, a condition that should be particularly inviting to the imaginative critic. It would be interesting to know, for example, *why* a particular rhetor adopted a particular ideology, what personal grievances the rhetor may have suffered in the past, and how they may have affected her or his view of the world. Naturally, tracking such humble uses of language as I-statements is a speculative business, but if it moves the critical enterprise forward even slightly by shedding light on the personae rhetors adopt and what they might gain from those personae, it is a worthwhile business indeed.

CONCLUSION

Within one seven-year period, two very different events occurred in the state of Texas. In 1976, President Gerald Ford gave a speech at the Waco Suspension Bridge. His speech was not magnificent, but suspension bridges rarely evoke eloquence. Mr. Ford did his best with the situation, declaring the bridge "a tribute to your forefathers, their vision, their foresight to have something like this over this great river, the Brazos river" [1976b:1335]. Having made this observation, Mr. Ford could apparently think of nothing else to say and so he thanked the people in attendance and sat down.

Seven years later, rock star Ozzy Osbourne urinated on the Alamo. Clearly, an ungracious act. Mr. Osbourne's poverty of spirit was explained to him by virtually everyone over the age of nineteen in San Antonio and explained in especially great detail by one irate city judge. What Gerald Ford had given to the Lone Star State, Ozzy Osbourne had taken away.

In this chapter, we have examined the roles rhetors play—how those roles come to be, how they are managed, how they can be studied. Although we may not like it, we all play roles. Roles, after all, facilitate social traffic. They help us think of things to say. It is probably true, for example, that even a kindly person like Gerald Ford would have willingly passed up the chance to orate at a bridge. But being a trooper he carried on, appropriating a ceremonial role that he might have used previously at the opening of a new restaurant in Idaho or the fishing fleet in Massachusetts.

His persona was friendly, engaging, and respectful, and he carried it off without a hitch. His audience in Waco probably knew that he was playing a role but they hardly minded. After all, it was their bridge built by their ancestors that their president had come to commemorate. Mr. Ford's role, in effect, was owned by his audience as well.

As mentioned earlier, it is *motive* that audiences are keen to discover in almost any rhetorical situation. Rhetors use roles to help audiences assign them proper motives. This was, among other things, Ozzy Osbourne's problem at the Alamo. Had he been some unfortunate derelict who in a state of inebriation had relieved himself, Osbourne might well have escaped San Antonians' wrath. But Osbourne had motive working against him. The irreverent persona he had nurtured over the years via his bizarre stage antics, his antisocial lyrics, and his satanic costuming made it rhetorically impossible for him to claim uncontrollable bladder problems.

Osbourne had long since established a *purposive* image and no amount of explaining could make it seem otherwise. That which he had worked so hard to create—persona—and that which he paid his staff thousands of dollars a year to manage for him—role—was the same thing that made him a cause célèbre on that fated evening in Texas. Like Frank Sinatra before him, Ozzy Osbourne did it his way.

TIPS FOR THE PRACTICING CRITIC

1. Thou shalt not confuse person with persona nor role. While critics cannot "psychoanalyze" a rhetor based on public messages, they can investigate stated and unstated motives in presenting a certain persona for public inspection. (Remember that person plus role equals persona.)

2. Base assessments of the rhetor's role securely in the artifact. Review the chapters on style, especially Gibson's "Tough, Sweet, and Stuffy" criteria. What "tone" or "voice" is the rhetor adopting? (Don't limit yourself to Gibson's characterizations; refine them or invent others.) Getting a sense of "tone" usually furthers the task of role assessment.

3. Use the critical probes in Chapter 10 to begin the process of analyzing rhetors' role choices. You can borrow or create categories for describing role and characterize different parts of the same message differently—simple survival dictates that contemporary rhetors learn a variety of roles; clever rhetors can switch gracefully.

4. As with any category system, keep your application of the types of role, credibility devices, etc. *adaptive*. Categories can tyrannize and the good rhetorical critic must be flexible. Use the category systems presented here and elsewhere as intellectual stretching exercises to prepare for the balanced workout of approaching a message from multiple perspectives. Mental agility, as well as strength and endurance, are essential for the healthy critic.

Chapter 11

CULTURAL CRITICISM

The United States dollar took another pounding on German, French and British exchanges this morning hitting the lowest point ever known in West Germany. It has declined there by 41% since 1971 and this Canadian thinks it's time to speak up for the Americans as the most generous and possibly the least appreciated people in all the earth.

As long as 60 years ago when I first started to read newspapers, I read of floods on the Yellow River and the Yangtze. Who rushed in with men and money to help? The Americans did. They have helped control floods on the Nile, the Amazon, the Ganges and the Niger. Today the rich bottom land of the Mississippi is under water and no foreign land has sent a dollar to help. Germany, Japan and to a lesser extent Britain and Italy were lifted out of the debris of war by the Americans who poured in billions of dollars and forgave other billions in debts. None of those countries is today paying even the interest on its remaining debts to the United States. *When the franc was in danger of collapsing in 1956, it was the Americans who propped it up,* and their reward was to be swindled on the streets of Paris. I was there. I saw it.

When distant cities are hit by earthquakes, it is the United States who hurries in to help. Managua, Nicaragua is one of the most recent examples. So far this spring, 59 American communities have been flattened by tornadoes. Nobody has helped.

The Marshall Plan, the Truman Policy all pumped billions upon billions of dollars into discouraged countries. Now newspapers in those countries are writing about the decadent, warmongering Americans. I'd like to see just one of those countries that is gloating over the erosion of the United States dollar build its own airplane. Come on, let's hear it. Does any other country in the world have a plane to equal the Boeing Jumbo Jet, the Lockheed Tri-Star or the Douglas 10? If so, why don't they fly them? Why do all international lines except Russia fly American planes? *Why does no other land on earth even consider putting a man or woman on the moon?*

You talk about Japanese technocracy and you get radios. You talk about German technocracy and you get automobiles. You talk about American technocracy and you will find men on the moon—not once, but several times and safely home again.

You talk about scandals and the Americans put theirs right in the store window for everybody to look at. Even the draft dodgers are not pursued and hounded. They are here on our streets. Most of them, unless they are breaking Canadian laws, are getting American dollars from Ma and Pa at home to spend here. When Americans get out of this bind, as they will, who could blame them if they said the hell with the rest of the world.

Let someone else buy the Israel bonds. Let someone else build or repair foreign dams or design foreign buildings that won't shake apart in earthquakes. *When the railways of France, Germany and India were breaking down through age, it was the Americans who rebuilt them. When the Pennsylvania Railroad and the New York Central went broke, nobody loaned them an old caboose.* Both are still broke.

I can name you 5,000 times when the Americans raced to the help of other people in trouble. Can you name me even one time when someone else raced to the Americans in trouble? I don't think there was outside help even during the San Francisco earthquake. Our neighbors have faced it alone and I'm one Canadian who's damned tired of hearing them kicked around. They will come out of this thing with their flag high and when they do they are entitled to thumb their nose at the lands that are gloating over their present troubles. I hope Canada is not one of these, but there are many smug, self-righteous Canadians.

And finally, the American Red Cross was told at its 48th annual meeting in New Orleans that it was broke. This year's disasters have taken it all—and nobody has helped. [Sinclair, 1973]

These remarks were made over thirty years ago by Gordon Sinclair, a radio personality for station CRFB in Toronto, Canada. At the time, the United States faced inflation at home and an unfavorable dollar abroad. Unemployment was high and America's superiority in manufactured goods, high technology, and natural resources was being questioned on many fronts. The Vietnam war had cost the United States considerable prestige in the eyes of many Europeans and the Watergate affair was beginning to unravel the administration of Richard Nixon. All in all, this was not a happy time for the American people, which is why Sinclair spoke as he did during one of his daily radio commentaries.

The effect of Sinclair's remarks was immediate and dramatic. The text was reprinted in full in many American newspapers and commented upon in virtually all. Similarly, at the request of their listeners, U.S. radio stations ran his commentary for days on end. Numerous television interviews were conducted with Sinclair, he received some 50,000 appreciative letters from U.S. citizens, and Westbound Records of Detroit, Michigan eventually distributed a recording of the Sinclair apologia.

What could account for such an unprecedented popular reaction? What was it about Sinclair's rather pedestrian philosophizing that caused so many listeners to respond so viscerally?

The Sinclair statement probably reveals more about his audience than it does about him. (And the appeal of this message—appreciation for those feeling beleaguered—is timeless, for it has been recirculated on the Internet in recent years, usually presented as "new.") U.S. citizens appreciated the speech because it had cultural resonance for them. In the language of Chapter 3, Americans liked Sinclair's speech-act itself. It was fearless, assaultive, and totally unexpected. In the language of Chapter 7, Americans liked Sinclair's style. It was simple, hard-hitting, unembellished, concrete, and concise—five adjectives often used to describe the American people themselves. In the language of Chapter 10, Americans liked the Sinclair persona, an independent, blue-collar tough guy—part Sean Penn, part Jesse Ventura.

But perhaps the most important feature of Gordon Sinclair's statement lies in the evidence he used. Sinclair lionizes the United States not on the basis of the goodness of its people, its educational system, its artistic and cultural achievements, or its form of government. Rather, he burrows into the fundaments of U.S. culture for his arguments when claiming that its entrepreneurship has made it a great nation. Gordon Sinclair speaks like a classic empiricist, one who believes that tangible knowledge is the best sort of knowledge. He spoke this way because his ultimate audience, the American people, are themselves classic empiricists.

It is *American money,* not American missionaries, that he mentions in connection with Africa. It is *American technology,* not American diplomacy, that he mentions in connection with the former Soviet Union. It is *American engineering,* not American science, that he mentions in connection with the space program. Sinclair's praise is praise not based in ethics or social theory. It is homage based on war reparations, airline safety, moon walks, dam building, and earthquake relief.

In short, Sinclair complimented the American people as they compliment themselves—for what they have *done* and for what they have done *alone.* When he spoke, Sinclair implicitly invoked Americans' most cherished self-portraits: of seventeenth-century Puritans carving out communities on the windswept Atlantic coast; of eighteenth-century farmers venturing south and west to plow with tools fashioned by hand; of nineteenth-century miners and ranchers settling the great American west. The American people have been raised on these ethnocentric stories, and they derive fierce pleasure from "facing it alone."

Like Sinclair, they too get "damn tired" of being "kicked around." But their national history, or that portion they choose to remember, sustains them in moments of trouble. American confidence knows no bounds. Americans hold "their flag high" and take special delight in "thumbing their noses" at their detractors. And this delight is doubled if the "smug, self-righteous" detractors have the Old World mentality especially repugnant to a nation founded by dispossessed persons with chips on their shoulders. And the fact that Gordon Sinclair was himself a Canadian, a citizen in a faintly Eurocentric culture, made his statement especially welcome.

In this chapter, we will study rhetoric's cultural features. That culture seeps into all messages is beyond question. Nobody escapes such influences completely.

While Henry Higgins may have changed Eliza Doolittle's speech patterns in *My Fair Lady,* he surely did not change the engine that drives language—Doolittle's thoughts, feelings, values, and cultural experiences. Eliza Doolittle may have become less a cockney rhetor but she always remained, in part, a cockney thinker. Such cultural influences did not make her less an individual but they did make her an individual *somewhere.* It is this somewhere that the cultural critic studies. Three features of culture are especially important to study:

1. Values—deep-seated, persistent beliefs about essential rights and wrongs that express a person's basic orientation to life;
2. Myths—Master Stories describing exceptional people doing exceptional things and serving as moral guides to proper action;
3. Fantasy Themes—abbreviated myths providing concrete manifestations of current values and hinting at some idealized vision of the future.

While we will separate these key cultural elements for ease of discussion in this chapter, everyday rhetoric finds them working in concert. Gordon Sinclair, for example, uses them all. The values he champions—charity is laudatory, technology is sacred, free speech must prevail—are drawn from the very sinews of the American value system. Similarly, Sinclair draws upon exploration myths (the moon landing), the good Samaritan myth (floods on the Yellow River), and the savior myth (the Marshall Plan) in his address as well. But full mythic development takes time, something that persuaders rarely have enough of, so fantasy themes, a kind of mythic shorthand, become its workhorses. Gordon Sinclair's fantasy themes become evident when he imagines Europe without American aircraft and Israel without U.S. materiel. These projective "snippets" are among the tales Americans tell each other constantly and, in repeating them, Gordon Sinclair became an American for a day.

When a critic peels back culture from a given message, there is often no message left. Our cultural assumptions, treasured stories, ways of valuing, and linguistic preferences are so deeply ingrained within us that we become mute without them. One cannot, for example, fully appreciate the masculine, hyperactive tone of Saturday morning cartoon shows without understanding that such shows have been produced in a nation historically led, for good and ill, by hyperactive males. Fortunately, even the most sophisticated persuaders carry their culture absent-mindedly. That is a real boon to the rhetorical critic who can look through message to culture and hence to the roots of persuasion itself.

VALUES: THE BEGINNINGS OF CULTURE

How can you tell whether a person is a good citizen? The *Webelos Scout Book* tells us that there are "a few signs":

- He obeys the law. If he thinks a law is wrong, he tries to have it changed. He does this by telling the people who are elected to make laws.

- He respects the rights of others. He does not try to get special privileges for himself.
- He tries to be fair and honest with everyone.
- He tries to make his country or town a better place.
- If in school, he "does his best" to learn all he can about his country.
- If grown up, he learns all that he can about his government. Then he votes on election day. [Webelos, 1979:71]

Children growing up in any culture confront such litanies. Texts like this tell people who they are and, equally, who they are not. In some senses, the values framed here are obvious and unremarkable—honesty, justice, participatory government. These are the values lying at the surface of the message. A more careful inspection of the text's "deep structure" finds still other values worth noting.

For example, Americans have always believed that values can be taught, just like mathematics. Americans, like other Westerners, tend to be quite linear in their thinking: "Learn these propositions and proper behavior will automatically follow." Americans believe that all instruction, even value-based instruction, can be systematized, personalized, and efficiently delivered. Their (originally) radical notion of universal public education was based on this read-a-book-learn-a-construct model. It is therefore only slightly more ambitious to try to teach national values in the same way.

Americans are an impatient people. They do not, by and large, value the indirection that polite behavior requires in some cultures. As philosophers, they favor pragmatism, not metaphysics. They not only believe that a question like "What is a good citizen?" is answerable but they believe that it is answerable (1) universally and (2) behaviorally. They believe that "signs" of a citizen's goodness are empirically observable and that, no matter what form of madness may lie in a voter's head, the act of voting on election day is what really counts.

Americans are also passionate believers in free will and self-determination. They feel that any country or town can be made "a better place" by human effort. Their skyscrapers and hydroelectric dams stand as evidence of such beliefs. In contrast to cultures ruled by clergy, American culture teaches that governance is an essentially cognitive matter. U.S. citizens believe that learning "all one can about one's country" will somehow translate into an effective political system and, for that reason, they believe that sublimating intense political passions is highly desirable. Unlike more traditional peoples, Americans were brought up on change, challenged and stimulated by it as well. They believe that if a person "thinks a law is wrong," that said law can be altered just as easily as one's name, one's spouse, or one's brand of deodorant. No matter what the evangelical Christians among them might argue, Americans are "evolutionists" of the first order.

So the *Webelos Scout Book* tells both a simple and a complex story, as does most rhetoric. The critic's job thus becomes one of examining the *presuppositions* imbedded in discourse, its *non-argued* premises, its *taken-for-granted* assumptions. Consider, for example, the research of Lionel Lewis [1972] who did a careful content analysis of 300 letters of recommendation written for applicants to graduate school in sociology and for faculty positions in chemistry at such institutions as Cal Tech, Berkeley, and Harvard. Here are some of the statements he found in the recommendations:

1. He is a very serious and determined student of sociology. In most assignments he goes beyond the call of duty [by producing] more than is expected. [p. 22]
2. Although she is rather short, she compensates by drive and perseverance and usually attains her goal. [p. 22]
3. He is the oldest son in a family wherein the mother is widowed and has contributed substantially to his own education through outside work. [p. 22]
4. There is no question about the fact that he was one of the best liked of our students. He is mature and reserved, yet very friendly and cooperative. [p. 25]

Lewis titled his study "On the Genesis of Gray-Flanneled Puritans" but he might as well have called it "The *Webelos Scout Book* Revisited." We see in these endorsements of modern scientists very little that is modern and even less that is scientific. What we do find is American axiology writ large—effort, stability, overcoming great odds, likability. The ghosts of Horace Greeley and Horatio Alger beckon here and there is something of television's Beaver Cleaver and *The Simpsons'* Lisa as well. Lewis was understandably distressed by much of what he found and he warns that such letters of recommendation threaten to give scientific excellence a permanent backseat to public relations. By replacing scholarly qualities with "the social ethic" and by judging professionals on the basis of their "whole beings" rather than their work, Lewis warns that universities could well become populated by personable but incompetent faculty members.

Lewis may be right, but the letter writers wrote, inevitably, in the only language available to them—the language of their culture. White [1949] discovered, for example, that Adolph Hitler denied not a single major democratic value when he spoke to the German people, even though his political actions embraced none of those values. It was as if a cultural frame had preshaped the contours of Hitler's remarks, thereby preventing many in his audience from sensing his totalitarian ambitions.

Similarly, in *The Captain America Complex*, Jewett [1973] observed that the long-standing Puritan image of the United States as a Redeemer Nation contributed substantially to the "millennial" fervor of American pro-(Vietnam) war rhetoric. Following Jewett's analysis, one could argue that the American people have since fought two Gulf Wars to uphold their self-image as Preservers of World Freedom. To deny such a rich rhetorical heritage would threaten what Jewett sees as the nation's "mythic base of moral superiority" [p. 222].

Although it is risky to present a list of values for 280 million Americans, Table 11.1 attempts just that. Based on work done decades ago by Minnick

TABLE 11.1 A Catalog of American Values

I. Theoretical Values of Contemporary Americans

1. Americans respect the scientific method and things labeled scientific.
2. They express a desire to be reasonable, to get the facts and make rational choices.
3. They prefer, in meeting problems, to use traditional approaches to problems, or means that have been tried previously. Americans don't like innovations, but, perversely, they think change generally means progress.
4. They prefer quantitative rather than qualitative means of evaluation. Size (bigness) and numbers are the most frequent measuring sticks.
5. They respect common sense.
6. They think learning should be "practical," and that higher education tends to make a man visionary.
7. They think everyone should have a college education.

II. Economic Values of Contemporary Americans

1. Americans measure success chiefly by economic means. Wealth is prized and Americans think everyone should aspire and have the opportunity to get rich.
2. They think success is the product of hard work and perseverance.
3. They respect efficiency.
4. They think one should be thrifty and save money in order to get ahead.
5. Competition is to them the most important aspect of American economic life.
6. Business can run its own affairs best, they believe, but some government regulation is required.
7. They distrust economic royalists and big business in general.

III. Aesthetic Values of Contemporary Americans

1. Americans prefer the useful arts—landscaping, auto designing, interior decorating, dress designing, etc.
2. They feel that pure aesthetics (theatre, concerts, painting, sculpture) is more feminine than masculine and tend to relegate the encouragement of them to women.
3. They prefer physical activities—sports, hunting, fishing, and the like—to art, music, literature.
4. They respect neatness and cleanliness.
5. They admire grace and coordination, especially in sports and physical contests.
6. They admire beauty in women, good grooming and neat appearance in both sexes.
7. They think many artists and writers are queer or immoral.
8. They tend to emphasize the material rather then the aesthetic value of art objects.

IV. Social Values of Contemporary Americans

1. Americans think that people should be honest, sincere, kind, generous, friendly, and straightforward.
2. They think a man should be a good mixer, able to get along well with other people.
3. They respect a good sport; they think a man should know how to play the game, to meet success or failure.
4. They admire fairness and justice.
5. They believe a man should be aggressive and ambitious, should want to get ahead, and be willing to work hard at it.
6. They admire "a regular guy" (one who does not try to stand off from his group because of intellectual, financial, or other superiority).
7. They like people who are dependable and steady, not mercurial.
8. They like a good family man. They think a man should marry, love his wife, have children, love them, educate them, and sacrifice for his family. He should not spoil his children, but he should be indulgent with his wife. He should love his parents. He should own his own home if possible.
9. They think people should conform to the social expectations for the roles they occupy.

(continued)

TABLE I I.I (continued)

V. Political Values of Contemporary Americans

1. Americans prize loyalty to community, state, and nation. They think the American way of doing things is better than foreign ways.
2. They think American democracy is the best of all possible governments.
3. They prize the individual above the state. They think government exists for the benefit of the individual.
4. The Constitution to the American is a sacred document, the guardian of his liberties.
5. Communism is believed to be the greatest existing menace to America.
6. Americans believe the two-party system is best and should be preserved.
7. They think government ownership in general is undesirable.
8. They believe government is naturally inefficient.
9. They think a certain amount of corruption is inevitable in government.
10. They think equality of opportunity should be extended to minority groups (with notable minority dissent).

VI. Religious Values of Contemporary Americans

1. Americans believe Christianity is the best of all possible religions, but that one should be tolerant of other religions.
2. They think good works are more important than one's religious beliefs.
3. They believe one should belong to and support a church.
4. God, to most Americans, is real and is acknowledged to be the creator of the universe.
5. They think religion and politics should not be mixed; ministers should stay out of politics, politicians out of religious matters.
6. Americans are charitable. They feel sympathy for the poor and the unfortunate and are ready to offer material help.
7. They tend to judge people and events moralistically.

Wayne C. Minnick, *The Art of Persuasion*, Second Edition. Copyright © 1968 by Houghton Mifflin Company. Used with permission.

[1957], the list confirms the 1831 observations of French writer Alexis de Tocqueville. The test of such a list is its "face validity": Do the values seem familiar to a discerning member of the culture?

Admittedly, these are the values of white, heterosexual, Christian, middle-class males, a powerful minority, which Minnick (and his 1950s contemporaries) took as "the norm." The cultural critic can therefore ask: To what extent do these values remain relevant? While values wax and wane over the years, they only change radically after massive social upheaval because, as we stated earlier, values represent *basic life orientations*.

When Minnick formulated his list, he could not have predicted that half a century later Americans would be purchasing hybrid automobiles, debating whether Laci Peterson was in fact killed by her husband Scott, or struggling with the issue of multicultural education. But knowing that Americans value efficiency, are fascinated by male aggression and, for the most part, believe in equality of opportunity, such contemporary events would perhaps not surprise him.

The cultural critic can use Minnick's schema to reveal the value emphases in a particular message, uncovering why and how often a given persuader dipped into this satchel of sacred beliefs. When cataloguing the values in an artifact, analysts can rely on the following critical probes for help:

- How sharply and clearly are these values appealed to?
- Where and how frequently does this occur in the artifact?
- What sort of response does this invite from the audience?

For example, Gordon Sinclair's message was in many ways just a prose version of Minnick's telegraphic list. Although Sinclair does not invoke aesthetic values, he mentions all of the other value-types. The result is a rhetorical shotgun approach: Presumably, almost everyone can find something appealing here. Similarly, Lewis's [1972] letters of recommendation almost appear to use Minnick's list as a kind of artificial intelligence system: II.6 + IV.4 + VI.3 = a letter of recommendation. That impression is heightened when one examines some of the unfavorable letters Lewis studied:

1. He is an individual capable of working long hours at his chemistry, with the aid and encouragement of his splendid wife . . . But I believe he has dissipated a good deal of his energy in nonscientific endeavors—including two unsuccessful marriages and a substantial business venture. [p. 28]
2. The only objectionable feature that I have noted is that this last semester he has raised a beard. I thought his appearance without the beard was very nice. I do not know how permanent the beard is. Otherwise I am sure you would be well pleased with him in this position. [p. 26]

Perhaps the most interesting feature of such value-based rhetoric is how *automatically* and *confidently* these value-centered observations are made, as if the warrants for such data-claim movements were beyond question.

According to a number of scholars, one of the most distinctive things about American rhetoric is its curious combination of **Transcendental** and **Pragmatic** themes. Kristol [1972] has identified the blending of these themes as quintessentially American. The Transcendental themes stem from the "prophetic-utopian" strains of colonial religion, the Pragmatic themes from the rugged mercantilism that motivated the nation's earliest European settlers. Arnold [1977] observes that almost every major debate in American history has borne witness to this struggle between "doing the will of God" and "doing business."

The statement Brinton [1938:34] makes about all revolutions—"grievances, however close they are to the pocketbook, must be made respectable, must touch the soul"—has been especially true in the United States, a nation that seems to need a Holy Purpose for doing almost anything. The Transcendent strain in discourse gives it an "elevating" tone, the sort of tone one hears on Inauguration Day in the United States. On such days, Americans have been told, for example, that they are explorers of a "new frontier" or the guarantors of a "new covenant." Such rich abstractions were often attended by the levying of new taxes, a bitter dose of Pragmatism made easier to swallow because of the Transcendent chaser. Ostensibly, new policy cannot be effected in the United States without this mixture.

Kristol [1972:148] explains why: "Just imagine what our TV commentators and 'news analysts' would do with a man who sought elected office with the promise that, during his tenure, he hoped to effect some small improvements in our conditions. They would ridicule him into oblivion." Some commentators have argued that pushing Pragmatic policies with Transcendent tones results in an offensive self-righteousness, making all Americans Ugly Americans.

In most American discourse, the astute critic can find both transcendental and pragmatic themes. Smith [1980] did so when investigating the lyrics to 2,300 country music ballads. He found there a struggle between Transcendent Southern values (close family ties, natural beauty, strong religious values) and the Pragmatism of the North (often depicted as cold but efficient, a source of jobs as well as sin).

No doubt, non-U.S. cultures also blend Pragmatic and Transcendent themes. But Americans appear to have a special penchant for *institutionalizing* rhetoric of this sort and for maintaining the *balance* between Pragmatism and Transcendence. Because they have no universally shared ethnic roots, cultural folkways, or religion, the American people have been especially susceptible to discussions of national purpose. But it is also because they *lack* these common ties that they are attracted to Pragmatic discussions. After all, a diverse citizenry can more often reach agreement about oil import fees or sewer systems than they can about political abstractions. In any event, the presence of this twin value cluster is a special boon to the critic interested in monitoring cultural continuity and change in the United States.

MYTHS: THE SUBSTANCE OF CULTURE

Earlier, we defined myths as Master Stories describing exceptional people doing exceptional things. These stories serve as moral guides to proper action. Among the most common types are **Cosmological** stories—why we are here, where we came from, what our ancestors were like. We hear myths like these at an early age from our parents (why Great Uncle Ezra moved off the farm), textbooks (how the Declaration of Independence came to be), churches (what Moses heard in the burning bush), and even popular films (how Pocahontas helped the English colonists). (As Giroux [2001:585] notes, "films both entertain and educate." We can say the same about any use of myth.)

Societal myths teach one the proper way to live. Tales of George Washington's childhood honesty and Rosa Parks's refusal to move to the back of the bus become richer in detail and more heavily drenched in meaning each time they are told. They also often become more erroneous, but the literal truth of a myth is rarely its most important measure. Rather, a myth's serviceability is judged by its *evocative potential*, its capacity to impress upon an audience the "Truth" of an event, not by its facticity.

Identity myths are also common. They explain what makes one cultural grouping different from another. Stories of the United States as a "non-aggressor" nation, as "peacekeeper to the world," are used to distinguish it from political rivals such as Russia (once thought to be committed to "world conquest") or economic rivals such as Japan (a "fiercely dedicated" but somewhat "fanatical" nation).

Finally, **Eschatological** myths help a people know where they are going, what lies in store for them in the short run ("full employment," "an end to the nuclear fear") as well as in the long run (a "heavenly reward," the "transmigration of souls," etc.).

Virtually all rhetoric depends on myth for its effect. A political announcement of rising employment rates is especially heartening to citizens who have heard of the Great Depression. Ethnic jokes are funny only if one knows (and believes) the supposedly peculiar story of the group being teased. Sermons of hellfire and damnation are frightening only if a worshipper is familiar with a certain brand of Christian mythology. Even if a rhetor does not retell a mythic tale in full, he or she will use some device (a quick allusion, a metaphor) to invite the audience's remembrance of that tale.

But why use myth? There are at least six reasons:

1. *Myths provide a heightened sense of authority.* When using myths, rhetors expect audiences to treat the myths seriously. Such stories are not presented for the sake of mere diversion but to justify a data-claim movement ("If you don't buy Clearasil you'll be a wallflower") by inviting audiences to search through their mental files and to contemplate anew the life of a wallflower. McDonald [1969:144] claims that "without myths there is no authority and without authority there is no politics," thereby suggesting that no government can succeed unless it can link its preferred policies to its historical truths.

2. *Myths provide a heightened sense of continuity.* As one event merges into another, its "meaning" becomes hard to discern. Myth helps out by grabbing up huge chunks of time and thousands of individual events to make some sort of patterned sense. As Einhorn [2000:83] notes, many Native American storytellers speak about "death and rebirth as inherent and natural parts of life," reminding listeners of connections to ancestors and descendents. As a result, *myth gives meaning to the present and future by making them seem continuous with the past.* So, for example, the Kennedy assassination meant very different things to different people depending on the stories they were exposed to prior to the assassination itself [Zelizer, 1992].

3. *Myths provide a heightened sense of coherence.* Just as myth can reach across time, it can also reach across intellectual space by fashioning "whole" stories out of bits and pieces of ideas. So, for example, Adolph Hitler wove British nationalism, Marxist imagery, Roman Catholic pageantry, and Freemason eschatology into Nazi wholecloth [Bosmajian, 1974]. Pocock [1971] describes such rhetoric as using "ancestral ghosts" to fashion something ostensibly new

and complete. Through such combinations, myth serves a kind of tidying up function, bringing together diverse parts of an audience's emotional life.

4. *Myths provide a heightened sense of community.* Community is born when people admire the same heroes and revere the same moments in history. Studies of colonial America (with its diverse and unsettled citizenry) show how myths create community. Merritt [1966] studied the newspapers of the day and found that revolutionary fever increased as references to "the American colonies" (vs. "the British colonies") increased. According to McGee [1975], almost all references to "the people" are based more in myth than in history. As McGee [p. 242] says, the people "are conjured into objective reality, remain so long as the rhetoric which defined them has force, and in the end wilt away, becoming once again merely a collection of individuals."

5. *Myths provide a heightened sense of choice.* People rarely change their behavior unless a choice is forced upon them. Myths dramatize such choices by depicting **dialectical struggles** between Good and Evil. Such grappling heightens the importance of the issues at stake ("the path of Light or the path of Darkness") and clarifies the alternatives ("a life in chains or a chance to breathe free"). The struggle may be between Progressivism and Orthodoxy, as Lee and Lee [1998] discovered in their analysis of how the Little Red Schoolhouse myth continues to influence debate over multicultural public education. At other times, the struggle is between Rationality and Irrationality, as Ivie [1980] found when studying myths of savagery in prowar rhetoric.

6. *Myths provide a heightened sense of agreement.* Although myths often describe concrete events, they do so in a marvelously abstract way. Myths of the Abortion Clinic Bomber and the Welfare Queen are useful to Leftists and Rightists even though such stereotypes are vague. But vagueness is valuable, says Hart [1977], since an abstraction like "One Nation Under God" has kept church-state tensions to a minimum in the United States for over two hundred years. In sanctioning invocations at political banquets and nondescript prayers before sessions of Congress, the American people have forged a civil-religious "contract" between church and state, using myth, not law, to handle these potentially dangerous matters.

How can critics best study myth? The work of respected anthropologist Claude Lévi-Strauss provides a rich approach. Lévi-Strauss, the father of **structuralism,** was particularly fascinated by the folk stories of the cultures he studied. A broad and imaginative thinker, Lévi-Strauss [1955:431–440] has provided six guidelines (here paraphrased) for the critic of myth. We have added critical probes in parentheses:

 1. The critic tries to track the **source** of the myth (where it came from, what forms of the myth existed before) in order to understand its emotional power for people. (Is this a Cosmological, Societal, Identity, or Eschatological myth?)

2. The key to a myth's effectiveness lies not in its individual narrative elements but in how such elements are **combined.** (How does this particular combination work? For example, does it offer a sense of Authority, Continuity, Coherence, Community, and/or Choice?)
3. The critic's task is to discover the unique sort of **harmony** (of emotions, images, ideas, etc.) this combination provides. (How smoothly do these elements work together?)
4. The critic calculates how the myth treats standard chronology (historical time) versus **synchronic time**—the narrative progression as imaginatively constructed by the storyteller. (What happens to time in the narrative? Is it elongated? shortened? Is it presented as linear, circular, or illusory? Are there flashbacks and foreshadowings?)
5. Narrative elements that are temporal neighbors, sharing the same **context,** often lead the critic to the myth's basic "argument." (What does the specific contextual logic tell us about what matters most to the rhetor and what the rhetor would have audiences remember?)
6. Similarly, the critic pays special attention to the myth's **oppositional** (or dialectical) forces in order to discover its motivational base. (How are dramatic conflicts or contradictions presented?)
7. How do each of these mythic choices invite audiences to respond?

Lévi-Strauss's suggestions are a good starting point for the critic even though critics have discussed its shortcomings [see Warnick, 1979; Harari, 1979; and McGuire, 1977]. A good case in point is a speech given by Major, an aging pig in George Orwell's *Animal Farm.* In his book, Orwell tells of a society populated largely by animals who, like people, struggle daily with life's ups and downs. In the beginning of Orwell's book, Major gives a classic revolutionary address. When reading it, one can easily imagine the same rhetorical ploys being used to inspire any oppressed class in any era. This is Major's speech:

> (1) Comrades, you have heard already about the strange dream that I had last night. But I will come to the dream later. I have something else to say first. I do not think, comrades, that I shall be with you for many months longer, and before I die, I feel it my duty to pass on to you such wisdom as I have acquired. I have had a long life, I have had much time for thought as I lay alone in my stall, and I think I may say that I understand the nature of life on this earth as well as any animal now living. It is about this that I wish to speak to you.
>
> (2) Now, comrades, what is the nature of this life of ours? Let us face it: our lives are miserable, laborious, and short. We are born, we are given just so much food as will keep the breath in our bodies, and those of us who are capable of it are forced to work to the last atom of our strength; and the very instant that our usefulness has come to an end we are slaughtered with hideous cruelty. No animal in England knows the meaning of happiness or leisure after he is a year old. No animal in England is free. The life of an animal is misery and slavery: that is the plain truth.
>
> (3) But is this simply part of the order of nature? Is it because this land of ours is so poor that it cannot afford a decent life to those who dwell upon it? No, comrades, a thousand times no! The soil of England is fertile, its climate is good, it is

capable of affording food in abundance to an enormously greater number of animals than now inhabit it. This single farm of ours would support a dozen horses, twenty cows, hundreds of sheep—and all of them living in a comfort and dignity that are now almost beyond our imagining. Why then do we continue in this miserable condition? Because nearly the whole of the produce of our labour is stolen from us by human beings. There, comrade, is the answer to all our problems. It is summed up in a single word—Man. Man is the only real enemy we have. Remove Man from the scene, and the root cause of hunger and overwork is abolished forever.

(4) Man is the only creature that consumes without producing. He does not give milk, he does not lay eggs, he is too weak to pull the plough, he cannot run fast enough to catch rabbits. Yet he is lord of all animals. He sets them to work, he gives back to them the bare minimum that will prevent them from starving, and the rest he keeps for himself. Our labour tills the soil, our dung fertilises it, and yet there is not one of us that owns more than his bare skin. You cows that I see before me, how many thousand of gallons of milk have you given during this last year? And what has happened to that milk which should have been breeding up sturdy calves? Every drop of it has gone down the throat of our enemies. And you hens, how many eggs have you laid in this last year, and how many of those eggs ever hatched into chickens? The rest of you have all gone to market to bring in money for Jones and his men. And you, Clover, where are those four foals you bore, who should have been the support and pleasure of your old age? Each was sold at a year old—you will never see one of them again. In return for your four confinements and all your labour in the fields, what have you ever had except your bare rations and a stall?

(5) And even the miserable lives we lead are not allowed to reach their natural span. For myself I do not grumble, for I am one of the lucky ones. I am twelve years old and have had over four hundred children. Such is the natural life of a pig. But no animal escapes the cruel knife in the end. You young porkers who are sitting in front of me, every one of you will scream your lives out at the block within a year. To that horror we all must come—cows, pigs, hens, sheep, everyone. Even the horses and the dogs have no better fate. You, Boxer, the very day that those great muscles of yours lose their power, Jones will sell you to the knacker, who will cut your throat and boil you down for the foxhounds. As for the dogs, when they grow old and toothless, Jones ties a brick round their necks and drowns them in the nearest pond.

(6) Is it not crystal clear, then, comrades, that all the evils of this life of ours spring from the tyranny of human beings? Only get rid of Man, and the produce of our labour would be our own. Almost overnight we could become rich and free. What then must we do? Why, work night and day, body and soul, for the overthrow of the human race! That is my message to you, comrades: Rebellion! I do not know when that Rebellion will come, it might be in a week or in a hundred years, but I know, as surely as I see this straw beneath my feet, that sooner or later justice will be done. Fix your eyes on that, comrades, throughout the short remainder of your lives! And above all, pass on this message of mine to those who come after you, so that future generations shall carry on the struggle until it is victorious.

(7) And remember, comrades, your resolution must never falter. No argument must lead you astray. Never listen when they tell you that Man and the animals have a common interest, that the prosperity of the one is the prosperity of the

others. It is all lies. Man serves the interests of no creature except himself. And among us animals let there be perfect unity, perfect comradeship in the struggle. All men are enemies. All animals are comrades . . .

(8) I have little more to say. I merely repeat, remember always your duty of enmity towards Man and all his ways. Whatever goes upon two legs is an enemy. Whatever goes upon four legs, or has wings, is a friend. And remember also that in fighting against Man, we must not come to resemble him. Even when you have conquered him do not adopt his vices. No animals must ever live in a house, or sleep in a bed, or wear clothes, or drink alcohol, or smoke tobacco, or touch money, or engage in trade. All the habits of Man are evil. And, above all, no animal must ever tyrannise over his own kind. Weak or strong, clever or simple, we are all brothers. No animal must ever kill any other animal. All animals are equal.

(9) And now, comrades, I will tell you about my dream of last night. I cannot describe that dream to you. It was a dream of the earth as it will be when Man has vanished. But it reminded me of something that I have long forgotten. Many years ago, when I was a little pig, my mother and the other sow used to sing an old song of which they knew only the tune and the first three words. I had known that tune in my infancy, but it had long since passed out of my mind. Last night, however, it came back to me in my dream. And what is more, the words of the song also came back—words, I am certain, which were sung by the animals of long ago and have been lost to memory for generations. I will sing you that song now, comrades. I am old and my voice is hoarse, but when I have taught you the tune, you can sing it better for yourselves. It is called "Beasts of England":

(10) Beasts of England, beasts of Ireland,
    Beasts of every land and clime,
    Hearken to my joyful tidings
    Of the golden future time.
Soon or late the day is coming,
Tyrant Man shall be o'erthrown,
    And the fruitful fields of England
    Shall be trod by beasts alone.
Rings shall vanish from our noses,
    And the harness from our back,
Bit and spur shall rust forever,
    Cruel whips no more shall crack.
Riches more than mind can picture,
    Wheat and barley, oats and hay,
    Clover, beans, and mangel-wurzels
    Shall be ours upon that day.
Bright will shine the fields of England,
    Purer shall its waters be,
    Sweeter yet shall blow its breezes
    On that day that sets us free.
For that day we all must labour,
    Though we die before it break;
    Cows and horses, geese and turkeys,
    All must toil for freedom's sake.
Beasts of England, beasts of Ireland,

> Beasts of every land and clime,
> Hearken well and spread my tidings
> Of the golden future time. [Orwell, 1946:17–23]

Taken at its broadest level, Major's speech is a myth of rebirth. In paragraph #1, Major mentions his own advancing years but at the end of the speech he returns to a story from his infancy, thereby giving the speech a mythic frame of death and rebirth. The propositional content of the speech progresses in precisely the same way: Animals have been horribly exploited in the past but a new day is dawning. Paragraphs #2 through #5 amplify the death motif as Major details the horrors his comrades must abide daily. Paragraphs #6 through #8 proceed differently as Major describes the mythic labor pains attendant to any birth, even the birth of a movement. Not unlike an instructor in a natural childbirth class, Major comforts, coaxes, and inspires his charges during this painful, yet glorious, parturition. The final two paragraphs detail how glorious this birth will be and it is not incidental that Major mentions his own mother's love in paragraph #9.

Within this overall frame, three major substructures can be detected. Table 11.2 sketches one such mythic substructure—how Major generates dialectical tension in the speech. Paragraph #1 is comparatively peaceful, with Major reflecting on his dream of the night before. Here, he also foreshadows mythic transcendence when mentioning his desire to donate what he has learned to posterity. But this tranquility is sharply arrested in paragraph #2 as Major introduces the first of seven major clashes. He begins on the most general note (freedom) and quickly introduces the theme of exploitation that he will subsequently develop. In this second paragraph, however, the precise source of the exploitation is left unstated, as Major tries to engage his listeners' imaginations.

But paragraph #3 begins with gusto as the rhetor warms to his subject—the depravity of humankind. Thenceforth, Major maintains mythic continuity, successively contrasting human exploitation with the things his audience most

TABLE 11.2 Myth and Dialectic in Major's Speech

Paragraph	Negative Mythic Elements	Positive Mythic Elements
1	None	Wisdom, nostalgia
2	Unspecific exploitation	Personal freedom
3	Human exploitation	Fruitfulness
4	Human exploitation	Productivity
5	Human exploitation	Longevity
6	Human exploitation	Deliverance
7	Human exploitation	Equality
8	Human exploitation	Personal integrity
9	None	Wisdom, nostalgia
10	Human exploitation	Freedom, productivity, fruitfulness, solidarity

treasures. Paragraph #3 focuses on basic survival needs. Paragraph #4 makes an incipiently Marxist argument about the distribution of capital. Paragraph #5 ups the stakes by considering death itself.

Beginning with paragraph #6, however, the mood shifts substantially as higher needs are introduced—self-achievement, companionship, a sense of honor. In each case, humankind is again made the foil as Major contrasts each animal virtue with a human vice. Finally, in paragraph #9, dialectic fades into synthesis as Good subsumes Evil. The speech ends in paragraph #10 on the dream motif with which it began but, this time, the dream is amplified majestically.

Structuralists emphasize the importance of time to myth. That is clearly the case here as well, as we see in Figure 11.1. Unlike historical time, mythic time does not have to move moment by moment. Persuaders sometimes violently rearrange chronology in order to place the audience in the proper "emotional time." Major, for example, begins his speech in the distant past, no doubt because it gave him special credibility (he was the patriarch of the community). He quickly moves forward in time but, interestingly, returns once again to the distant past at the end of his speech, thereby sandwiching all that has transpired with his omniscience.

Temporally, paragraph #2 is a complex unit of discourse because it foreshadows the entire speech. Here, Major establishes himself as a person of perspective, one who can move easily across time. In addition, this paragraph establishes that his topic is grounded in the reality of the past, linked to the saliency of the present, but also relevant to the uncertainty of the future. Major

FIGURE 11.1 Myth and Time in Major's Speech

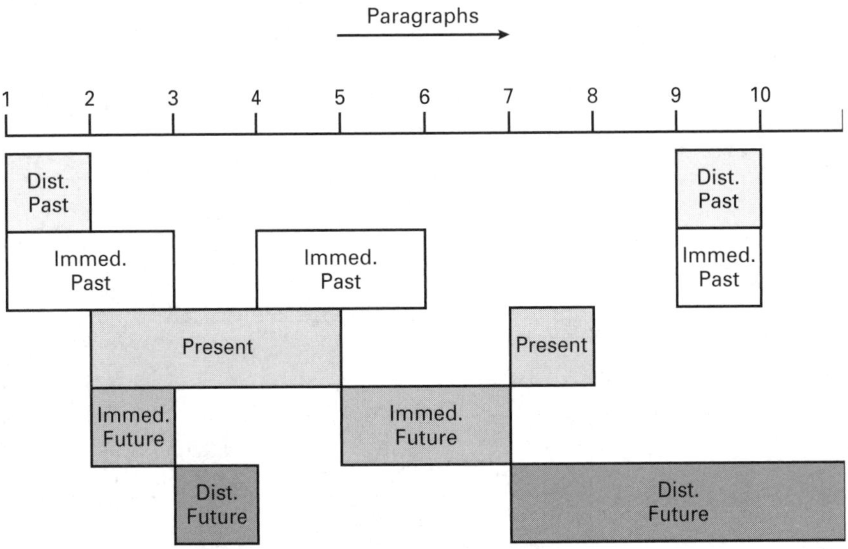

juxtaposes the immediate past and the present in paragraphs #2 through #6. These paragraphs give emotional force to the speech because the data he cites spring directly from the dreadful lives of his listeners (he even mentions some in his audience by name, as if to heighten their sense of personal crisis).

The use of the *immediate* future is perhaps most unsettling of all in these paragraphs as Major argues that his audience's current desperation cannot compare to tomorrow's hardships. It is the *structural* relationship between these temporal elements—the fact that they occur together at this point in the message—that makes for such powerful mythic effects.

When Major says in paragraph #3, "Remove Man from the scene, and the root cause of hunger and overwork is abolished forever," he briefly shows the light at the end of a tunnel he is about to make considerably darker. He returns to this theme briefly in paragraph #6 ("Only get rid of Man, and . . . almost overnight we could become rich and free"), drops it in paragraph #7, develops it in the two penultimate paragraphs, and finally lets it blend into the transcendent future in his concluding paragraph.

Moving in and out of the distant future in this way clearly encourages mythic tension within his audience until it becomes almost unbearable. This is a primitive rhetorical device that serves to heighten appreciation for the full-bodied, self-contained myth with which he concludes his remarks.

A final structural pass over Major's speech reveals the use of three different mythic themes, as we see in Figure 11.2. **Naturalistic** myths introduce his topic, properly so since his audience members are animals. In these passages, images of bodily processes (sleeping, eating) interact with images of nature (growing, fertilizing) so as to establish the real-life import of Major's remarks.

These themes are extended in paragraphs #4 and #5. There, images of fertility (bearing foals) are linked to organic images (excreting) and aging images (toothlessness). But these paragraphs create dialectical tension as Major contrasts the naturalness of the animal world with the artificiality of the human

FIGURE 11.2 Myth and Topic in Major's Speech

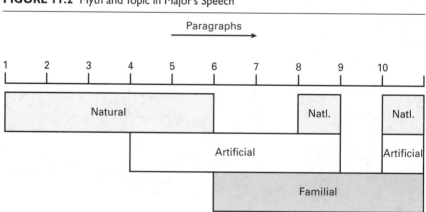

world. The rhetor lists humanity's sins serially: overconsumption, materialism, the arbitrary foreshortening of animal life. He also contrasts natural objects (eggs) with the contrivances of human society (knives).

Humanity continues as the mythic foil in paragraphs #6 through #8 as the poverty of the human spirit (tyranny, selfishness) is linked to humankind's depraved, unnatural habits: sleeping in beds, drinking alcohol. But a third mythic grouping arises at this same time—images of solidarity—and these images begin to change the tone of the speech from outrage to inspiration.

The **family** myth is developed *across species* ("whoever goes upon four legs . . . is a friend") as well as *across time* ("pass on this message . . . to those who come after"). The terminology changes too as "comrades" appears more frequently, and kinship terms (mother, brothers) are used explicitly. Specifications for this new family of animals are also provided. They include political admonishments (reference to the "common interest"), sociological enjoinders (avoid human habits), and moral advice (no killing of other animals).

In paragraph #9, this newly fabricated family is linked, magically, to an ostensibly pre-existing family by means of a song that was "sung by the animals of long ago." Finally, in paragraph #10, "beasts of every land" are united in a grand eschatological myth that describes a "golden future time."

Although we have made three *separate* critical passes over Major's speech, we must remember that, like any message, this is a *coalescence* of all three different mythic structures. Unlike critics, audiences do not have the luxury of unraveling that which they hear when they hear it. Major implicitly asked his audience to deal with the dialectical, temporal, and topical structure of his myths *simultaneously*. It is this simultaneity that gives rhetoric its richness. It is the delicate interweaving of these themes that makes for rhetorical genius. As Claude Lévi-Strauss demonstrated, the study of myth is necessarily a complex undertaking. But myth's powerful appeal makes it a study the critic dare not abandon.

FANTASY THEMES: THE GRASS ROOTS OF CULTURE

Considerable research has been done in recent years using an approach called fantasy theme analysis. Originally identified by social psychologist Robert Bales, fantasy themes have also been studied extensively by communication scholar Ernest Bormann. In this section, however, we adapt the notion of fantasy themes in order to make it immediately useful to the critic.

For our purposes, fantasy themes can be thought of as *mythic shorthand*, the stories told by subgroups in society. If myths are the prized tales of humankind in general, fantasy themes are the *local variations* wrought on these themes. If myths are vague, fantasy themes are specific. Whereas myths are enduring, fantasy themes are short-lived. While myths are universally suited to public discussion, fantasy themes change from topic to topic. Myths are cross-cultural; fantasy themes are culture-specific.

An example: One of the most popular master myths in the United States has been that of America-as-New-Israel, a conviction that God specially created and guided the nation for a special purpose—that of delivering the world's peoples from a state of Darkness. The belief was that God gave U.S. citizens an incredibly bountiful land because He especially favored them. In recompense, however, He expected the American Message (read, His message) to be spread far and wide.

It may seem preposterous that any group could feel so self-important as to believe the literal truth of this tale, especially when the myth is laid out so bluntly. That is how fantasy themes help. They round out the bluntness with attractive vignettes that disguise the myth's presumptions. In a sense, fantasy themes become the everyday language of myth.

The early Puritans embellished the New Israel myth, and it soon sank deep roots into the American psyche. One cluster of fantasy themes it spawned argues that the United States is the peacekeeper of the world, and must keep itself strong in order to protect all of God's children. Another set of fantasy themes preached that Americans must be the first to colonize space because of God's charge to go forth into the wilderness with His word. Westward expansion in the early 1800s was launched in a similar way, as were Woodrow Wilson's League of Nations, Harry Truman's Marshall Plan, John Kennedy's Peace Corps, and both Bushes' Wars in the Gulf.

New Israel fantasy themes were used to launch the public education movement in the United States, broaden participation in the Olympic Games, and support a host of charities such as the Red Cross. Social movements of both the Right and the Left have used such themes as well, with Teddy Kennedy marching off in the mid-1980s to explain civil rights to South Africans and televangelist Pat Robertson urging greater U.S. involvement in Central America. Fantasy themes have also been used to endorse the Voice of America. It is noteworthy that there is no Voice of Canada nor, for that matter, no Voice of Israel either.

According to Bormann and his colleagues [1994], the purpose of fantasy themes is to dramatize ideas for audiences who sometimes lack the imagination to see what the world will be like if they accept new beliefs. A study by Kidd [1975] demonstrates how rhetoric performs this task. Kidd was interested in how popular magazines represented the social world to their female readers. She found two major "visions" of the world being projected. One vision stressed that women (1) were fundamentally different from men and should behave accordingly, (2) should avoid conflict under all circumstances, and (3) should follow clearly established guidelines when interacting with others. Kidd cites magazine passages that exemplify this traditional vision:

- In New York City the 'career woman' can be seen in fullest bloom and it is not irrelevant that New York City also has the greatest concentration of psychiatrists. [p. 33]
- A man can feel kinship with the gods if his wife can make him believe he can cause a flowering within her. If she doesn't feel it she must bend every effort to pretend. [p. 34–5]

The more modern vision Kidd found embraced a more fluid conception of life, far fewer social strictures, and more numerous societal roles for women. She offers the following passages to represent that vision:

- Specialists who study family life now agree that it is pointless to compare real marriages with some imagined ideal. The model marriage is a myth . . . We must begin with a basic fact. Not all marriages are alike and they cannot be measured by the same standards. [p. 35]
- Unpleasant feelings, petty resentments and frustrations do not go away simply because one refuses to let them show. Rather, they can build up a deadly store of bitterness. [p. 36]

Kidd found that after these premises were laid out for readers, the fantasy themes were developed in considerable detail, with countless "case studies" of happy and unhappy women used to add dramatic intensity to the ideas being stressed.

By finding so many instances of these two visions in so many different magazines, Kidd demonstrated another feature of fantasy themes: They "chain out" in society because of their rhetorical power. People become caught up in these visions and then repeat them for others. Thus, because of the rhetoric of the 1940s "everybody knew" that cigarettes were a healthy way to relax. By the 1970s, "everybody knew" that cigarettes caused cancer. In the early 1980s "everybody knew" that only homosexuals and Haitians could contract AIDS. More recently, "everybody (in the Bush administration, at least) knew" that Saddam Hussein was linked to the 9/11 attacks. Fantasy theme analysts are thus especially interested in calculating the *breadth* of such appeals, discovering those that "echo" through society and those that are unique to a subgroup.

Fantasy themes can be highly sustaining. A fascinating example of this was reported by Weisman [1980] who studied the activities of prisoners held in Nazi concentration camps during the second world war. Weisman argues that the capacity to generate and share fantasy themes helped the prisoners maintain their sanity. By repeating for one another sacred religious tracts, by engaging in "public dreaming" (e.g., by describing the elaborate meals they would prepare upon their release), and by recording their visions for the future in their diaries (a punishable activity itself), some of the prisoners were able to distract themselves usefully from the horrors surrounding them.

Given the importance of fantasy themes, how might they best be studied? Bormann and others have developed a number of elaborate social scientific methods for testing their popularity. Here, however, we will take an approach better suited to the beginning critic. Table 11.3 presents eight major questions that can be asked of discourse. In a sense, these critical probes operate at the philosophical level because they question the *presuppositions* underlying a group's rhetoric. These probes ask the critic to **isolate the stories** told most often in a given body of rhetoric and then to **ask what "lessons" they appear to be teaching:** about people in general, about the capacity of individuals, about right and wrong. However, Bormann cautions, *it is not sufficient to*

TABLE 11.3 Critical Probes for Fantasy Theme Analysis

1. Given the rhetor's story lines, what are people like?
   Are they dependable? Fundamentally deceived? Are people essentially alone? Evil or duplicitous at root? Do they care for one another?
2. Given the rhetor's story lines, what are the possibilities of group action?
   Is group effort morally superior to individual effort? Practically superior? Are groups doomed to disharmony? Does group action bring out the best in us? The worst?
3. Given the rhetor's story lines, on what can people most depend?
   Their mental agility? Physical skills? Spiritual resources? Hard work? Other people? Nothing at all?
4. Given the rhetor's story lines, what is humankind's fundamental purpose on earth?
   To help others? To self-actualize? To change the world? To fulfill historical mandates? To right wrongs?
5. Given the rhetor's story lines, what are the fundamental measures of right and wrong?
   Personal ethics? Some religious code? Social obligations and agreements? Political utility? Legal duty?
6. Given the rhetor's story lines, how can success best be measured?
   By assessing quantitative gain? By enhancing self-knowledge? By fulfilling group destiny? By being faithful to certain abstract principles? By defeating an enemy?
7. Given the rhetor's story lines, what sort of information is most dependable?
   Book learning? Empirical observation? Personal experience? Folk wisdom? Secret revelation?
8. Given the rhetor's story lines, why do things happen as they do?
   Because of some hidden design? Because of individual or group effort? Because of random chance? Because of some extrahuman force?
9. What responses do these story lines invite from the audience?

answer these questions for a single text. Rather, the cultural critic must track answers to them across rhetors. Only then can genuine thematizing be established and the critic's claims sufficiently grounded.

Using a single artifact (for demonstration purposes only), we present a cursory example of how such questions can prove useful in rhetorical analysis. The following passage is an excerpt from an oft-circulated flyer entitled *Ideals of a Klansman* by Robert Shelton [n.d.], one-time leader of the Ku Klux Klan. Although brief, it gives us a feeling for the Klan's mythic orientation and the fantasy themes it utilizes most frequently:

> We believe in the upholding of the Constitution of these United States.
>
> By upholding the Constitution, is meant the whole Constitution, anyone who violates one clause of the Constitution, would as quickly break every other one if it serves his purpose to do so. . . .
>
> We believe in a free press, uncontrolled by political or religious sects.
>
> The press should be free to spread news without coloring it to suit any person or sect: But such is not the case, scarcely a newspaper anywhere dares to publish the truth: the whole truth and nothing but the truth. The press is largely controlled by the Roman Catholic priesthood and Judaism, and as a result the great masses of people are fed on propaganda instead of true facts. When an article is read in either a newspaper or magazine, one does not know but what there is a sinister motive back of it. And a paper that publishes nothing but the truth can hardly exist.
>
> We believe in law and order: In other words, the Klan believes in keeping the laws and in enforcing the laws. Many accusations have been brought against the

Klan as lawbreakers. These accusations against the order are purely newspaper propaganda. So far we have not heard of a single instance where the Klan, by an official act, has violated any law.

We believe in white supremacy.

The Klan believes that America is a white man's country, and should be governed by white men. Yet the Klan is not anti-Negro, it is the Negro's friend. The Klan is eternally opposed to the mixing of the white and the colored races. Our creed: Let the white man remain white, the black man black, the yellow man yellow, the brown man brown, and the red man red. God drew the color line, and man should so let it remain, read Acts 17:26 if you please.

We believe in the protection of our pure womanhood, the home, the church, our public school system, our Constitution, and our American way of life.

This is a stand for the purity of the home, for morality, for the protection of our mothers, our sisters, our wives, our daughters, against the whiteslaver, the homewrecker, the libertine. And to live up to this principle a Klansman must keep himself pure and above reproach. He must treat other women as he would have those of his own household treated.

Here, we begin to see the fantasies that chain out among Klan members and motivate their labors. Throughout the passage, one gets the clear sense that the world is divided into two groups: one (small) group sees things clearly, and another (much larger) group includes people too lazy to see the truth or who have been captured by the forces of evil (e.g., the press). Life as described by the Klan is a dog-eat-dog existence. Laws are broken with impunity, immigration threatens to pollute the gene pool, churches deceive their flocks. Only the Klan stands for righteousness; even the courts cannot be trusted. Men are strong, but sheep; women are innocent, but weak.

These conditions give the Klan a reason-for-being. In a lethargic, disordered world, even a small band of fearless patriots can turn back the slovenly forces massing against them. Because the enemy is in *moral* disarray, group action is indeed possible—but only if the entire group adheres to the essential truth of the Klan philosophy. It is perhaps for this reason that we find so much repetition in even this short passage. The repetition gives energy to the prose ("the truth, the whole truth and nothing but the truth") and it also serves to document the inevitable coherence to be found in Klan philosophy. A small but powerful truth sustains a crusade best.

Philosophical allegiance, then, will best advance Klan goals. Like much doctrinaire rhetoric, this passage places little faith in "great persons" leading the group to moral victory. Given the tremendous number of people who have already accepted what they see as the insanity of civil rights, Klan members have little confidence in human discernment. Nor does the Klan have much hope for change via natural evolution. The Klan's world is fixed: The NAACP is in league with the Communists; foreign ideas are inherently bankrupt; Klansmen are "pure and above reproach." "England for Englishmen, France for Frenchmen, Italy for Italians, and America for Americans," says Shelton elsewhere in the pamphlet.

Because so much in the world is thereby "set" in the eyes of the Klan, the only possibility for change is *complete* eradication of evil, *total* removal of Blacks and Jews, and *unqualified* acceptance of the Constitution ("anyone who violates one clause of the Constitution would . . ."). Given the genetic deficiency of the offending groups, no cosmetic change is possible. Similarly, given the inherent bias of the media, the courts, and the established churches, their pronouncements can be completely disregarded as well.

Generally speaking, the Klan does not discover its purpose in self-actualizing, in helping others or, for the most part, in changing public policy in a piecemeal fashion. While it does seem motivated by an "historical mandate" of sorts, the precise source of that mandate is unclear (the advancement of Christianity? returning to the chivalric code?). Despite this vagueness, the Klan points to the past as it looks to the future. The Klan finds right and wrong in religion ("an infidel is a person who rejects Jesus Christ"), in law ("we have not heard of a single instance where the Klan . . . has violated the law"), and in morality ("this is a stand for the purity of the home").

Given the magnitude of the Klan's goals, only long-term success is possible. Given the galaxy of challenges the Klan identifies, its rhetoric will not appeal to those looking for a quick fix. Rewriting an entire nation's laws, disbanding the media, eliminating three-fourths of the world's religions, removing all "foreigners" from the United States, and protecting womanhood in all its varieties (mothers, sisters, wives, and daughters) is clearly a tall order. Only the tireless need apply.

The Klansman is an empiricist. He believes in what his eyes tell him: the length of a nose, the pigmentation of skin, the existence of "true facts" (as opposed to "propaganda"). His sensory organs are all that he needs. "God drew the color line," says Shelton, "and man should so let it remain." The world he projects is therefore a tidy world with people and ideas housed in the categories to which they are natively suited. Books (and, we suspect, education in general) merely serve to confuse because they build higher and higher abstractions and mangle categorical distinctions (e.g., by entertaining the notions of a Black patriot or a White libertine). By keeping one's eyes on what one "knows for sure," the Klansman is not likely to underestimate the enemies who threaten to further sully the nation. "Let him who has eyes see," argues the Klansman, for it is through vision that one finds Vision.

One cannot help but notice in Klan rhetoric a certain tired quality. The fantasy themes are old and shopworn: rapacious Blacks, crooked lawyers, liberated women, power-mongering Catholics, usurious Jews. The pamphlets issued from its national headquarters do not differ from year to year, or from decade to decade for that matter. It is as if all that is known has already been learned. Klan persuaders have long since found their major claims and now seem interested only in collecting copycat data. As a result, the rhetorical visions they generate are not particularly clear or compelling. The repetitiveness of their fantasy themes makes for a lazy rhetoric, one that can be heard in every age but which seems peculiar to no age. This may be why the Klan has been consistently relegated to marginal status in the United States, a rhetorical fate for which we may all be grateful.

CONCLUSION

In this chapter, we have observed the rhetoric of Klansmen, magazine authors, Boy Scouts, aging pigs, and a U.S.-loving Canadian. All embraced values. Each depended on myth. All traded in fantasy themes. Each went about their rhetorical business in a different way because each had a special message to share. Each had a vision of what a perfect world would be like and each tried to share that vision with others. Some, like the Boy Scouts, succeeded because their goals were so traditional while others, like Gordon Sinclair, succeeded because they had the right message for the right moment.

There is much that is unique about each of these persuaders but there is something they share as well—a culture. For all of them it was Western culture; for most of them, U.S. culture. But having said that, what have we said? After all, each had a different rhetorical goal and a distinct rhetorical style. But each possessed something else—cultural confidence—a sense that they had the right message for the right place. Also, like the authors of the *Webelos Scout Book,* they believed they could talk people into behaving better than they had been behaving. This is a thoroughly Western kind of confidence and it is very much in the tradition of American political evangelism as well.

At the moment, we do not know what will happen when some of these old values are fashioned for some new purpose, or who will win and who will lose when certain other fantasy themes become tired and die. We do not know what will happen but we can guess about such matters. Cultural criticism helps with the guessing.

TIPS FOR THE PRACTICING CRITIC

1. When doing cultural analysis, keep asking, "Why is the rhetor using *this* (strategy, image, myth, value, etc.) *here*? How would it work or not work? What kinds of associations does/should it call up? What does this tell us about the culture in which this message was produced, the rhetor who produced it, and the rhetor's assessment of the audience's morals, values, etc.?" Try to take nothing for granted: If a rhetor begins by referring to the occasion, do not just conclude that it was "the appropriate thing to do." Consider *why* such a tradition has become accepted in that rhetor's culture. What would happen if such customary formulations were not observed?
2. Refer often to the tables in Chapter 11. Table 11.1 should serve as a useful checklist of values (and brainstorming prompt for alternatives) upon

first examining a message, and Table 11.3 suggests critical probes for doing fantasy theme analysis. Defamiliarize yourself with the assumptions behind familiar messages by continually questioning what you know and how you know it. Cultural analysis is necessarily slippery; if the members of a culture were conscious of every cultural influence upon their actions, they would not have time to think of anything else. As a result, most cultural assumptions are accepted without question. So asking critics to go back and question the unquestionable is a somewhat unnatural act! But, ultimately, the urge to "question authority" is necessary for the survival of any intellectual enterprise.

Chapter 12

DRAMATISTIC CRITICISM[1]

Remember when you knew most of your neighbors and their children? Wasn't it a comfort to know if your child was playing a couple of blocks away and had a bump, bruise, or skinned elbow that one of your friends would take care of the immediate problem and let you know, because you'd show the same concern? This is how small neighborhoods used to be. This is how Wimbledon Country is! [Wimbledon Country, 1988:3]

***

Legend Oaks is a carefully planned neighborhood of nearly 300 thickly-wooded acres in the very heart of Southwest Austin. Here, Mother Nature, preserved and even enhanced by new plantings, lives in harmony with a new standard of neighborhood amenities. Right now, children laugh and swing on our playscape, tennis balls bounce across our lighted court, and the surface of our pool is broken by a swimmer's rhythmic strokes. [Legend Oaks, 1988:F12]

***

When you purchase a home site in Weston Lakes you can enjoy the prestigious Weston Lakes Country Club and build your dream home when you're ready. The country club features one of the finest 18-hole championship golf courses in Texas, adult and family swimming pools, tennis courts, croquet lawn and fine dining.

---

[1] With thanks to David Payne for his contributions to this chapter in the first edition.

Situated among huge century old pecan and oak trees and shimmering natural lakes, Weston Lakes offers a distinctive and private life style. The lakes act as a clearwater moat surrounding the property and enhance the privacy and security of the development. They are also stocked with catfish and trophy-size bass. [Weston Lakes, 1988:5]

***

The homes in Ember Oaks Estates are built on lush, wooded homesites and are surrounded by gently rolling hills, giving the entire area a peaceful country atmosphere . . . Ember Oaks offers a secluded atmosphere, yet it is close to Southlake, the new IBM complex, Las Colinas, the Mid Cities and Dallas/Fort Worth International Airport. [Fox and Jacobs, 1988:J5]

***

Our company sells houses. Nothing more. If you need to live near the third busiest airport in the United States so that you can travel four days out of five for Transcontinental Computers, you're going to hear a lot of planes. Now, we'll be happy to plant a few begonias next to your house so you can be reminded of Mayberry R.F.D., but you'll still be living within twenty miles of three million people. We've been in business for twenty-five years, so see us if you want a house built. As for illusions, you'll have to shop elsewhere. For a hundred and fifty thousand bucks we can't give you prestige—you'll have to earn that by becoming president of your company, playing ball for the Dallas Mavericks, running for Congress, or writing a best seller. Our company can't relieve your guilt feelings about your latchkey kids and we sure as hell can't stop the air pollution you and your neighbors will generate on I-30 each morning. When we build houses, we supply the two-by-fours, the duct tape, the corner molding, the electrical circuits, and the paneling. You supply the baloney.

In the last of these ads, something has gone awry. Or perhaps something has gone wry. The first four ads, drawn from the Homes sections of various Texas newspapers, represent their genre nicely. Filled with overly rich images, these ads turn brick-and-wallboard boxes into much grander places by focusing on what their products symbolize rather than what they are. The last ad, however, misses the game plan entirely. Its depressing frankness fails to do an essential job of rhetoric: blending an audience's lived life with its psychic life.

Critic Kenneth Burke said that it takes mystery, adventure, community, and magic to make a human creature. He said that to thwart people's imaginations (as in the fifth ad) is to deny people the resources they need to cope with rootlessness and anomie. He said that our need for drama is universal, and as basic as the needs for food, sex, and shelter. Burke would probably say that the need for drama is so profound that the fifth advertisement could only have been written by a textbook author to make a point. And he would be right.

This chapter details the critical approach of Burke, a critic who explored the complex relationships among aesthetics, politics, language, and social organization. Burke's ideas have influenced countless students of rhetoric and literature as well as sociologists, political scientists, historians, linguists, and philosophers. Burke urged the doing of criticism not because rhetoric is powerful, although it is, and not because criticism is interesting, which goes without saying. Rather, said Burke, tracking the "rhetorical motive" is central to understanding what human beings are at root (symbol-users), what they strive to do (rise above themselves), and what they have the potential to do (rise up together).

Especially in his younger days, Burke viewed criticism as social activism. One of his most famous essays, "The Rhetoric of Hitler's Battle," is a trenchant analysis of the persuasion in Adolph Hitler's *Mein Kampf* [1973: 191–232]. Today, of course, academic discussion of Hitler's techniques have become something of a cliché, but it was Burke who traced the trajectory of Hitler's rhetoric in the early 1930s. Unlike his contemporaries, who viewed Hitler as just another politician, Burke treated the Führer as a medicine man who had concocted an elixir for the ailing German spirit.

In 1939, few commentators anticipated the scapegoating of the Jew but Burke saw that potential in the scenarios Hitler sketched in *Mein Kampf*. Burke reasoned that any person who saw himself striding—alone—across a grand political stage could dispatch unthinkingly the lesser characters in his self-made play, much as Shakespeare's kings dismissed their fools with nary a thought. Accordingly, Burke feared Hitler's rhetoric more than he feared Hitler's politics. Burke knew that political systems come and go as a nation's economy, sociology, and demography evolve. But a galvanizing drama can be repeated endlessly, Burke warned, because people's deepest fears and anxieties never change. As a result, Burke became a kind of political psychoanalyst and Hitler became his first, and most disturbed, patient.

Burke wrote his initial book, *Counter-statement,* in 1931 to "counter" the view that art and literature were merely ornamental. Rather, he said, all of the verbal arts, including literature, drama, speech, pedagogy, and reportage, affect both social knowledge and political decision making. While exploring this thesis, Burke put over six million words in print in fourteen books and hundreds of essays, lectures, poems, stories, and even a modest novel. Throughout his work, Burke refused to treat life *as* drama. Rather, he believed, life *is* drama: People's actions are themselves symbolic statements. In this view, rhetoric employs primitive dramatic forms that enable people to see more than their eyes alone would allow.

Such forms abound in the passages above. In the first ad, the reader is asked to **identify** with a simpler, safer time and place. For many people (e.g., urban dwellers, newly arrived immigrants, single-parent families, etc.), such a place never in fact existed. But these idealized neighborhoods exist throughout American literature (and on *Sesame Street*), so they are familiar nostalgia trip destinations. Burke would also call attention to how the second passage uses **language clusters** to build its images of innocence. Thick woods, Mother Nature, children, water, harmony—these are primal terms, the stuff of dreams. Judging by its advertising, "Legend" Oaks is aptly named.

Burke believed that the principle of **hierarchy** is especially helpful in explaining rhetorical force. The third passage provides evidence of hierarchy with its talk of "prestigious" country clubs, "fine" dining, and "distinctive" life styles. "Moving up" when buying a home would be more than just a metaphor for Burke since one's house has psychic as well as material properties and is intimately tied to one's sense of relative worth. When bass are described as "trophy-sized," Burke might have noted, somebody, somewhere, is feeling inadequate. Also, while this passage celebrates old hierarchies with its talk of "century old" pecans, secure "moats," and "croquet lawns," it implies that even the Newly Arrived can scale the summits if they have the price.

While issues of hierarchy pose the central questions of drama, **transcendence** provides the answers. When considering the fourth passage, for example, Burke might note how "secluded closeness" splits the difference between the inconveniences of rural living and the hectic pace of city life. "Secluded closeness" does not actually make living in the Metroplex easy as much as it transcends such problems by offering a construct around which all persons—country bumpkin as well as city slicker—can rally. Even if it takes an hour on the interstate to get home, a "lush homesite" in a "country atmosphere," not a tract house in a subdivision, awaits. This image adds dramatic action to the suburbanite's commute and calls attention to what people are: actors living out their lives speaking scripts to one another.

The dramatistic critic reads these scripts, although there can be danger in doing so. Too often, critics use Burke's ideas to merely label textual elements rather than explain their symbolic power, a point nicely made by Chesebro [1994]. To avoid this trap, we will discuss Burke's system selectively here so that the principles of dramatism, not its terminology, become our focus. But discussing Burke selectively also has its disadvantages since Burke's mind has ranged so far over so many subjects. Burke's writings show him to be a topical critic, a narrative critic, a structural critic, and a rather scientific student of syntax and lexicon. He commented on role, imagery, and speech-acts and his treatment of myth was consummate. He was also an early devotee of Marxist thought and linguistic skepticism and he was Freudian to his core (topics to be treated in Chapter 14). Burke, in short, followed his own advice when doing criticism: He used all there was to use.

THE PRINCIPLES OF DRAMATISM

Almost as soon as drama existed in Western culture, criticism existed as well. Among the first critics were the *theoria*, a troupe commissioned to travel about in ancient Greece gathering local information about society. Often, they would comment upon local rituals and festivals, activities designed to call attention to what is noble and base in people and their motives. By adopting the dramatistic model for criticism, Burke therefore seized on features of drama that had long been recognized but inadequately developed as a critical paradigm.

Burke presented his theory of dramatism before the advent of television. With fewer people going to live theater these days, does a dramatistic model still make sense? Indubitably. Current estimates are that the average American child will watch 30,000 television stories by the time of maturity. High drama this is not, but television is often good low drama. Each day, TV reintroduces the child to the very heart of dramatic action: why people do what they do, a phenomenon Burke calls **motive.** Cartoons teach that exasperation leads to irrationality (as with Sylvester and Tweetie); situation comedies teach that callousness can be profitable, if censurable (as in *Will and Grace*); adventure stories teach that evil must be punished at all costs (as in *NYPD Blue*). All such dramas throw light on human motives, inviting viewers to examine—and judge—how people behave.

Equally important, television employs age-old dramatic conventions. Because of television, political conventions turn into prime-time extravaganzas and electronic preaching adopts the form of modern morality plays. Through television, even the most pedestrian American has been made drama-literate. But when Burke introduced his notion of dramatism in 1939, people were less sophisticated about the mass media. (Recall that 1939 was the year in which Orson Welles's radio spoof, *The War of the Worlds,* capitalized on its audience's ignorance of dramatic forms). Today, in contrast, most of us have a second sense about drama. Burke's critical system depends upon this second sense by making six key assumptions:

1. *The range of rhetoric is wide.* Wherever he looked, Burke found rhetoric. In the language of Chapter 1, Burke rarely analyzed obviously rhetorical messages (commercial sales, political solicitation, religious pamphleteering, etc.). Instead, he teased out the unspecified policies hidden in implicit rhetoric: poems, plays, polite conversation, signs, maxims, histories, scientific treatises, folklore. One of Burke's most famous studies was an analysis of Antony's address to the mob in Shakespeare's *Julius Caesar.* Instead of detailing how Antony cleverly bested Brutus and company in the speech ("So are they all, all honorable men"), Burke focused on how Shakespeare adapted the play to his Elizabethan audience. Why, for example, did Shakespeare's audience wind up respecting Caesar and not Brutus or Cassius? After all, Caesar was deaf in one ear, suffered from falling sickness, "cried out like a sick girl" on occasion, and was timid and superstitious. Who would wish to identify with him? Burke asked. And yet is it not crucial that we do so? He solved his puzzle thusly:

> For such reasons as these you are willing to put a knife through the ribs of Caesar. Still, you are sorry for Caesar. We cannot profitably build a play around the horror of a murder if you do not care whether the murdered man lives or dies. So we had to do something for Caesar—and you would be ashamed if you stopped to consider what we did. I believe we made Caesar appealing by proxy. That is: I, Antony, am a loyal follower of Caesar; you love me for a good fellow, since I am expansive, hearty, much as you would be after not too heavy a meal; and as one given to pleasure, I am not likely to lie awake at night plotting you injury. If such a man loves Caesar, his love lifts up Caesar in your eyes. . . .

[Although I, Antony, was a reveler before Caesar's death], in expanding to my expanded role, I must break the former mold somewhat. Let *savants* explain the change by saying that carefree Antony was made a soberer man, and a bitter one, by the death of Caesar. But it is an obvious fact that if an important cog in the plot vanishes in the very middle of our drama, something has to take its place. In deputizing for Caesar, I found it impossible to remain completely Antony. Let *savants* explain my altered psychology as they will—*I* know it was a playwright's necessity. [Burke, 1964:66,67]

Like all good rhetorical critics, Burke focused here on the rhetor-audience relationship, looking through the text to readers' needs and expectations. Because he thereby focused on the "strategic business" of literature, Burke is persona non grata for orthodox critics interested in a text's inherent merit. But such inherency did not exist for Burke. He believed that truth is human and therefore negotiated, so any attempt to share unaltered reality with an audience is doomed to failure: "Even if any given terminology is a *reflection* of reality, by its very nature as a terminology it must be a *selection* of reality; and to this extent it must function also as a *deflection* of reality" [Burke, 1966:45].

Sharing ideas with others, Burke believed, is always an act of misdirection, a condition required by the complexity of language. Even the simple image of the shepherd, he observed, remains innocent only if an audience half-thinks about the shepherd's duties. Upon fuller consideration, the job becomes ominous: "If the shepherd is guarding the sheep so that they may be raised for market, though his role (considered in itself as guardian of the sheep) concerns only their good, he is implicitly identified with their slaughter. A total stress upon the autonomy of his pastoral specialization here functions *rhetorically* as a mode of expression whereby we are encouraged to overlook the full implications of his office" [Burke, 1966:301–2].

In his writing, Burke insisted that we study *formal discourse* carefully since it often escapes public scrutiny. He saw the "drama of human relations" on display in the wording of political constitutions, bureaucratic injunctions, academic treatises . . . and especially scientific discourse. Burke was concerned that the technological establishment (which grew up around him in the 1940s and 1950s) was escaping critical examination because of its rhetoric of nonrhetoric. The Scientific Word, Burke argued, is often exploitative and combative; it typically dissociates thought and feeling and too often rejects its communal responsibilities [Frank, 1969:84]. "Scientism," Burke argued, "needs to be counter-balanced by a stress on 'intuition,' 'imagination,' 'vision,' and 'revelation'" [Rueckert, 1963:38].

Were he alive today, Burke might therefore appreciate Al Sharpton, not because of his politics, but because his rhetoric stresses social and moral possibilities rather than systemic constraints, personal responsibility rather than determinism. Burke might worry that the technocratic realism of a Bill Clinton would reduce politics to "mere motion" rather than to "dramatic action," thus hiding the *choice-making* that politics involves. Burke appreciated persuasion that owned up to its nature as persuasion. But whenever rhetoric denied itself, Burke perked up his ears.

2. *All life is drama.* Burke believed that drama is present whenever people congregate but that the essential drama of a situation is not revealed until rhetoric exploits it. The New Journalists, writers who describe real events but who do so as novelist/journalists, exemplify Burke's point. For example, Truman Capote's *In Cold Blood* told of an innocent farm family slaughtered by strangers. Before Capote got to this story, it was just another random rural crime. Capote's writing skills, however, added back the dramatic action hidden by the cold statistics of the local police blotter. Capote's rhetoric returned life to the victims and revealed the tortured motivations of the perpetrators.

The beat journalists in western Kansas had also covered this crime but their reports did not help readers hear the dull thud of the death instruments or feel the murderers' adrenalin rush. But Capote's redramatization allowed his readers to feel these things and more. Thus, in a Burkean reading we might dub the New Journalists 'Dramatic Recreationists' since they *reestablish* the dramatic action of prior events, rather than allowing it to seep away.

Rhetoric is therefore a compass for dramatic action: It points out what is at stake, for whom, by affixing labels to activities. Without such labels, Burke says, people cannot describe what they feel, even to themselves. Burke was especially interested in definitional labels [Heath, 1986:96]. When Truman Capote titled his book *In Cold Blood,* for example, he revealed his view of the crime's motivational dynamics (i.e., he did not entitle it *Accidental Mayhem*). Similarly, says Weldon [2001:10], news coverage depicting rare Ebola-type viruses as "predators" create drama by displacing responsibility (which Burke called **agency**) for any outbreaks onto the virus, rather than onto the human **agents** who failed to follow appropriate safety precautions. Thus, such reporting breeds public hysteria, steals rhetorical energy from epidemic prevention efforts, and distracts attention from the "real killers" such as tuberculosis and typhoid fever.

To appreciate rhetoric, then, one must understand a culture's dramatic library. As Rueckert [1963:20] observes, the "quest" drama alone has inspired countless works of literature, from *The Odyssey* to *The Adventures of Huckleberry Finn. The Lord of the Rings* is a classic quest trilogy, but people also invoke quest narratives when speaking about advancements in virtual reality and ridding the world of cancer and AIDS. Becoming aware of these formulae, especially when they are used in nonnarrative discourse (e.g., in expert testimony before Congress), can help the critic disestablish dangerous forms of dramatic action.

So, for example, Burkean critics like Payne [1992] have told us that the acclaimed film *The Dead Poets Society* at first appears to be a celebration of adolescent rebellion and creativity but, because a creative rebel is killed at the end of the movie, the film ultimately pays homage to their dramatistic opposites: order and stability.

3. *Dramas feature human motives.* This is a key Burkean assumption. It says that the central purpose of drama is to spotlight why people do what they do. It also says that our natural curiosity about human motives can seduce us. As an illustration, let us consider the headlines from a randomly chosen front page of the *Christian Science Monitor* (Wednesday, December 17, 2003):

> "Dean vs. Bush: Would It Be Close?"
> "Doubt Over 'Disability Abortions'"
> "The Next Century of Flight: Inventing the Jetsons' Car"
> "Iraqi Women Raise Voices—For Quotas"

Dramatism is not difficult to find here: the media's impatience with the pre-primary process, legal challenges with moral implications in Britain, a quest to realize science fantasy, and gender politics in post-Saddam Iraq. But these are not just random happenings; they are motivated. In each case, the *Monitor's* headline writers have taken us behind the scenes to show that someone is acting for/with/against someone else for some set of reasons. If Iraq's new government reserves seats for Shiites, Sunnis, Kurds, and Assyrians, shouldn't some seats be saved for women? Do parental desires for healthy infants constitute the first step toward eugenics? Months before the first primary, should Howard Dean be running against George Bush rather than against other Democratic presidential hopefuls?

Even a staid journal like the *Christian Science Monitor*, that is, cannot resist the motive mandate. In the Dean versus Bush story, for example, it was "a matter of speculation" whether the president's "rare morning press conference, scheduled at the last minute, was timed to trump Dean's [major foreign policy] speech" that same afternoon [Feldmann and Marlantes, 2003:10]. The *Monitor* invites readers to become caught up in this drama, contrasting Bush's apparent recognition of Dean as his opponent with the intra-Democratic Party skirmishes. By focusing on motive questions—Was Bush's timing a political stratagem? Is opposition by the incumbent sufficient to anoint Dean as the Democratic nominee?—the paper makes a front-page story out of no story at all. With dramatism, there is no such thing as a slow news day.

With regard to motive, the critic's job is (1) to inspect discourse for its model of motivation and (2) to explain the rhetor's dramatic actions parsimoniously. That is a tall order. Motives, after all, are complex, overlapping, and sometimes contradictory. So Burke began simply by examining a rhetoric's **vocabulary of motives**—the language it uses to explain human behavior—in order to outline that rhetoric's theory of volition. It is this motivational apparatus, said Burke, that makes one piece of rhetoric different from another.

For example, in 1989, the American Football Coaches Wives Association began meeting in conjunction with the annual coaches' conference. Their motive, says Tucker [2001], was not fame or fortune, but legitimation. If masculinity is glorified in American culture generally, then football is its Cathedral, where these forces are concentrated and sanctified in weekly rituals. The incessant, behind-the-scenes, unpaid work of coaches' wives in recruiting, tutoring, entertaining, and caretaking is largely invisible. Tucker found that AFCWA's efforts to publish its cookbook and newsletter served to recognize and validate the crucial *feminine* presence that undergirds the football system and allows it to function.

And different viewers will ascribe different motives to the "same" act, depending on their perspective. A scientist may describe drinking-while-driving as "conditioned behavior," a phrase that downplays motive, while the libertarian and the religious cleric may highlight motives but do so oppositely (i.e., "drinking as personal freedom" vs. "drinking as sin"). For the scientist, decisions are made by the brain; for the libertarian they are made by the mind; for the preacher they are made by the conscience. Each sketches a different theory of life: random reinforcement, political conversion, a divine plan. Each differs as to human possibility (there is much, some, none) and each proposes a unique solution to problems (scientific analysis, political propaganda, moral submission).

Different still is the rhetoric of Mothers Against Drunk Driving. For them, drinking is a social act, often a public act, and only the *public's motives*—not the driver's motives—are relevant to the discussion. MADD's vocabulary of motives is therefore neither long nor textured: "Killing while drinking and driving is murder, plain and simple."

4. *Hierarchy is fundamental to human symbolism.* Every page of the daily newspaper shows the centrality of hierarchy. *Page 1:* "Martinez Edges Bradley in Mayoral Runoff." *Editorial Page:* "Sanitation Workers Should Strike." *Obituary Page:* "Local Surgeon, Grandmother Dies." *Sports Page:* "Serena Tops Venus in Straight Sets." *Society Page:* "Howard Grad Marries Social Worker." *Entertainment Page:* "*Star Wars: Episode Nine* Opens Friday."

In these ways and more, the newspaper tells who has gotten how far in life, which is why young brides and old mayors alike prepare their press releases carefully. Even after death, hierarchy remains, and so the good doctor's survivors labor over her obituary notice. Yet it is also true that people read newspapers not just to find out about the rich and powerful but to regain hope that the trash collectors among them will receive justice as well.

Hierarchy is, by definition, incremental, so dramatic tension is highest when the increments are small (e.g., when an election is too close to call). Hierarchy is also bidirectional: It recounts failure as well as triumph. *Star Wars: Episode Nine* will likely depict the progeny of Luke Skywalker, a child born into a time of relative peace and privilege, which is shattered by a re-emergence of the Dark Side of the Force. Alone and friendless, young Skywalker must then retrace father Luke's footsteps, training with a Jedi Master to develop the skills and sensitivity until, like Dad, the young hero finally conquers the forces of evil (at five times the original ticket price, of course).

Burke says that people are "goaded by hierarchy" to do more, to be more, and to have more. But Burke's hierarchies are not just monetary. Values, knowledge, and even beauty standards are hierarchical, which is why preachers preach, teachers teach, and cosmetics are a multibillion-dollar industry. Even though none of us has yet found an ideal person, idea, or object, the *principle* of hierarchy goads us on. Despite suffering, many believe that "Jesus is the answer." Despite the sorry track record of consumer products, others "Buy Panasonic, the last TV you'll ever own." In their heart of hearts, many people harbor religious doubts and even more distrust home appliances. And yet the principle of hierarchy will not let them rest. They become gluttons for the rhetoric of perfection.

Rhetoric is filled with overstatements because it often focuses on the endpoints of the hierarchy, inspiring us with the Highest Highs, frightening us with the Lowest Lows. As Nichols [1969:279] observes, the rhetoric of Karl Marx had special power for many because his political cosmos was structured so hierarchically: The worker worked for the State, the State worked for the worker, all worked for the Motherland. As a result, the peasant could perform menial chores happily, knowing that he or she was contributing *directly* to the great historical drama of Communism. Griffin [1969:460] argues that many successful movements have used similar motivational tactics when positing utopian visions.

Burke [1966:18] says that rhetoric can also tilt in the opposite direction when it describes perfect evil: the Christian's devil, the Nazi's Jew, etc. According to Appel [1987], this sort of "rhetorical perfection" is especially attractive to the alienated in society, persons who cannot be persuaded via incremental appeals.

5. *Rhetoric promises transcendence.* If hierarchy gives rhetoric a quantitative dimension (how much, how often, how high), transcendence gives it a qualitative dimension (how good, grand, or noble). Hierarchy argues that people can get more; transcendence argues that they can become better. Hierarchy suggests how people can improve; transcendence tells them why they should. Rhetoric has transcendent themes because people want to rise above the ordinary and do something important with their lives.

According to Burke, meeting these needs turns rhetoric into a kind of **secular prayer.** Perhaps this is why Black preachers have been such an important emotional resource in their communities throughout American history. They secularized Christian motifs for the Black slaves (and, later, for the Black underemployed), assuring them that their hard, physical labors would earn them rewards in Tomorrow's Tomorrow. Transcendence can also be found at the other end of life's hierarchy: An aging millionaire suddenly decides to become an aging philanthropist. Fund-raisers know full well that some people will trade millions for meaning.

Transcendence is also an incorporative device. When a U.S. president speaks of "all Americans," momentarily at least Texans may become less Texan, American doctors less medical, and American politicians less partisan. Similarly, each time we wear the sorority's colors, we transcend to another level of symbolic identity, acquiring new "motives" for what we do. Moving upward in this way gives people a sense of drama and also offers them new explanations for their actions: "I am protesting in the rain not because I am a masochist but because I am a concerned citizen."

Naturally, Burke was wary of transcendent rhetorics, since so much evil has been done at their behest. And yet his reading of history resigned him to their drumbeat. From the time of the Pharaohs' pyramids to that of the modern organizational chart, people have been attracted to hierarchies and the promise of transcending them.

6. *Rhetoric is fueled by the negative.* Burke was fascinated by the negative. He accounted for the omnipresence of rhetoric by looking to the inevitable divisions among people and between people and their personal goals. This makes people "relentlessly rhetorical" [Rueckert, 1982:22] as they try to bridge the gap between themselves and their dreams. He argued that social problems lead to feelings of guilt [Burke, 1969]. When sharing rhetoric with one another, people then use "collectivist effort" [Rueckert, 1963:47] to slay the "guilty part" of themselves and become "purified." In doing so, rhetoric serves important purposes, symbolically defending us against ignorance, estrangement, and impurity. In these ways, rhetoric becomes, like literature, what Burke would call **equipment for living.**

"C-SPAN junkies" who fear World War III and who, as a result, gorge themselves on Congressional rhetoric seem to use rhetoric as equipment for living. They do so because such speechmaking is highly controlled and predictably boring ("Why should I be afraid when the Representatives in the chamber are falling asleep?"). Similarly, people watch soap operas to steel themselves against disease and loss. Each day, series characters confront these evils and persevere (the show *will* resume tomorrow), thereby providing viewers with steady doses of emotional medicine. In other words, "passive" television viewing may not be passive at all but a safe, active way of coping with loss.

Burke says that nature itself is completely "positive," that it is people who invented the negative, which is why, wherever he looked, Burke found formulae of guilt and redemption. As Rueckert [1963:130] says, "a 'No Trespassing' sign on a piece of property is the infusion of a linguistic negative into nature" (the fenced-in pasture has no "preference" as to who walks where) and "the proposition that adultery and fornication are sinful is the infusion of a linguistic negative into pure sensory experience" (the sex drive, after all, does not mandate a spouse).

Rhetoric, in short, puts people in charge of people by saying "thou shalt not." Why celebrate the Fourth of July? To stave off tyranny. Why buy aluminum siding? Because weather can be brutal. Why watch *The West Wing*? Because real-life politicians cannot live up to President Jed Bartlett. In each case, a rhetor steps forward to shout "no!" to nature.

In nature, time passes. In nature, memory fades. As Bostdorff [1987:45] observes, political cartoonist Tony Auth could not personally fire James Watt (a probusiness Secretary of the Interior in the Reagan administration) but he could symbolically rearrange nature by creating a Ronald Reagan National

Forest and populating its hillsides with oil derricks. In this case, the rhetor has reduced evil to a **scapegoat:** a person, group, or idea treated as the incarnation of evil. Hitler, of course, used this technique, but Burke identified scapegoating whenever people build unity by identifying a common enemy. Sometimes, the scapegoat is made obvious (like James Watt) and sometimes it is not. At still other times, the scapegoat is not a person at all but an object (crack cocaine), an idea (homosexual marriage), or even a bodily process (Alcoholics Anonymous's notion that alcoholism is a disease). Burke noted that while rhetoric often scapegoats others (which he called **victimage**), it can also scapegoat the self (which he called **mortification**). In either case, rhetoric cleanses the soul of sin and provides new "attitudes" for use in daily decision making.

Burke was ambivalent about his discovery of the negative. He understood that, to construct social order, groups must develop shared conceptions of evil. He realized that morals must be taught somewhere, either through formal institutions (church, school) or everyday experience (popular entertainment, family interaction). If advertisements, for example, teach people how to deal with romantic or work problems, they serve an educational function. But Burke would also note that these same ads purge something or someone to get their messages across.

For example, the recent "epidemic" of vaguely-defined "codependency" is made possible through the universal appeal of such rhetorical practices, says Messner [1996], because it urges people to recognize their codependent pollution and then engage in purification through mortification and surrender to God. Only then can they be redeemed through rebirth as "recovering codependents" [Messner, 1996: 101]. Similarly, Brummett [1986] was distressed to learn that young, sexually active women were overwhelmingly chosen for victimage in contemporary horror films. What lessons are being taught here, when young women are punished for their sexuality? Rhetoric may indeed be equipment for living, but critics must ask, what sort of life is that equipment endorsing?

THE METHODS OF DRAMATISM

Burke's interpreters often describe his critical approach as a system of conceptual principles, but it sometimes appears as a loose confederation of ideas that Burke used—brilliantly, but erratically. Not being Kenneth Burkes, we must proceed more carefully. The key to Burkean criticism is asking how and why a text is dramatized. The principles from the first section of this chapter can become our vantage point. Phrased as critical probes, they are:

1. Can principles of hierarchy be found in the discourse? Who or what has great or little value? Is movement up or down the hierarchy possible or are things "set"? Are there many gradations or only a few? Are the hierarchical stages clear or hazy?

2. What is the rhetor's vocabulary of motives? Why do things turn out as they do? Why do people think and act as they do? Are their motives described clearly or mysteriously? Does the rhetor give personal reasons for communicating? Why or why not?
3. Who or what is being scapegoated? Is the scapegoating obvious or subtle? If the scapegoat is within ourselves, what sort of mortification is needed to purge it? If the scapegoat is another person or group, why have they been selected for victimage?
4. Are strategies of transcendence in evidence? What will help the audience overcome its problems? Are the transcendent forces human (a group, a nation) or extrahuman (God, fate)? Are they concrete (new legislation) or abstract (renewed spirit)?

Since Burke believed that we cannot speak without dramatizing, these questions are not alien intrusions into a text. The average college party proves this. Informal chatter about which majors are the most challenging (hierarchy), who is sleeping with whom (mortification and victimage), why good parking is hard to find (motive), and who will be graduating soon (transcendence) constitute the daily drama. As the refreshments and dramatizing are ingested, the increasingly loud buzz of conversation proves the increasing influence of both.

Burke, of course, was interested in weightier matters. He was interested in texts like this:

When I speak to you today and thus to millions of other Americans, I have more right to do this than anyone else. I have grown out of you yourselves. Once I myself stood among you, I was among you in the war for four and one-half years and now I speak to you to whom I feel myself to be bound still today, and for whom in the final analysis I carry on the struggle. As far as I was concerned the struggle was not necessary. Nor would I wage it for a class or any certain stratum of society. I lead the struggle for the masses of millions of our honest, industriously working, and creative people. . . .

In my youth I was a worker like you, and then I worked my way up by industry, by study, and I can say, by starving. In my innermost being, however, I have always remained what I was before. When, after the war, I entered political life, I did so with the conviction that our people was poorly advised by its political leadership, that a horrible future awaited the American people as a result of this bad leadership. I acted then with the most sincere self-justification because I did not belong to those who were in any way responsible for the war. I was just as little responsible for the war as anyone among you, for at that time I was, just like you, an unknown person, whom fate passed over in the order of the day. In any case I have not counted myself among those who set themselves against their own nation at the time.

I was convinced that one had to enter the struggle for the destiny of the nation, if sooner or later the entire people was not to suffer a terrible ordeal. That is what separated me from the others who turned against America. When the war was over I, as a front soldier, assumed the right to represent that which I had recognized to be right. Before this I had not made any speeches, nor had I engaged in any activity. I was simply a man who earned his daily bread. Not until I saw after the conclusion of the war that the political leadership did not live up to what it had promised the nation, but that the contrary was true, did I go among the people and work with six other quite insignificant workers and found a movement.

I began with six or seven men. Today it is the greatest American Movement; this is so not by chance and not because the way was made easy for me, but because the ideas upon which I built are right. It was only for this reason that they could be carried through. For you can imagine, my friends, that when a man in my station in life begins a movement, success does not just fly to him. That is self-understood. One needs great tenacity and a tremendous will to begin such an enterprise at all. And I should like to say this to you: If I had this faith, I had it only because I knew the people and because I had no doubts as to the quality of the American people. The intellectual groups did not give me the courage to begin this gigantic work; I took courage because I knew the American worker and the American farmer. I knew that these two classes would one day become the bearers of the new spirit and that the group of college professors would also join them of itself. A gigantic program! When I was called on January 30th, after a bitter struggle of fourteen years, I had only one wish and that was to fulfill this great task. What does a title mean to me? I do not need a title. My name, which I achieved with my own strength, is my title. I only wish that posterity would sometime confirm the fact that I have striven to achieve my program decently and honestly. . . .

In America I am the guarantor that this community will not work out to the advantage of any element of the American people. You can look upon me as the man who belongs to no class, who belongs to no group, who is above all such considerations. I have nothing but my connections with the American people. To me everyone is entirely equal. What interest do the intellectuals have for me, the middle class, or the working class? I am interested only in the American people. I belong exclusively to the American people and I struggle for the American people. . . .

These immortal words were spoken by Samuel Adams just after the Revolutionary War. Or are they the remarks of Ulysses S. Grant during reconstruction, or John Kerry post-Vietnam? Any of these ex-soldiers could claim these remarks for they dramatize fundamentally American themes: working hard, staying close to the common folks, defending the country, succeeding because of effort, not privilege. We have heard these themes since childhood and they resonate with us.

But Burke knew that dramatism respected neither national nor temporal boundaries. So he would have been unsurprised to learn that this speech reflects not the American dream, but the American nightmare, for these are the words of Adolph Hitler to the German people in November, 1933. But when we restore the words "German" or "Germany" (for "America" and "American") in the passage above, what changes? Would thirteen little substitutions fundamentally alter the message's emotional impact? Clearly not. Hitler had his finger on *human* drama here. He, better than virtually anyone, knew the prerequisites of political theater.

Even when altered, Hitler's speech retains its **dramatic form** and thus its ability to persuade. It is therefore really only an accident of history that these words were spoken by Adolph Hitler and not Abraham Lincoln. Altering the passage in this way simply makes it easier for contemporary Americans to identify with Hitler's drama. Naturally, one may be put off by the egotism of the speech, but Hitler's nationalism compensates for it. So do his word-pictures, which make life larger than life. Hitler tells how he starved and struggled to start his movement, how his people had seen hard times, how their destiny was at hand, how the values of equality and classlessness could soon be achieved. Hitler told his audience they were standing at an unprecedented moment in human history. Who could refuse to become part of such a moment?

A dramatistic critic. An overriding concern of Burke's was that such moments of great drama tend to unhinge people, making them co-actors rather than critics of dramatic action. Our needs for drama no doubt rise and fall. Early 1930s Germany, for example, was a gray and lifeless place. Precious little food, few jobs, the national disgrace of having lost the first world war, an uninspiring, old-line leader in office. These were brutal times. In response, Hitler turned Germany's black-and-white into technicolor. In many ways, Hitler's rhetoric was a rhetoric waiting to happen.

How might a critic use Burke's insights to better understand Hitler's persuasion? Two starting places are Hitler's use of **hierarchy** and **transcendence.** One of Hitler's most ingenious ploys is to identify each subgroup in German society (workers, farmers, intellectuals) and relate them directly to the supreme values of prosperity and nationhood, moving his audience up the hierarchy until they are surrounded by "millions of our honest, industriously working, and creative people." Hitler also establishes the possibilities of hierarchical movement by using himself as a case study. Having been a lowly worker, he recounts how "industry" and "study" enabled his ascent. Even more dramatically, he shows how "starving," the lowest point to which one could sink, also contributed to his upward mobility so that he could now become the "guarantor" of civil equality.

But an audience will not strive upward without guidance. They must be teased into doing so, so Hitler dramatizes the slowness of his rise. He recounts his beginnings ("I was, just like you, an unknown person, whom fate passed over"), his growing consciousness ("[I labored] with six other quite insignificant workers"), his current success ("Today it is the greatest German movement"), finally reaching his rhetorical mountaintop ("I knew that these two classes would one day become the bearers of the new spirit"). Hitler removes himself from the meanness of practical politics, transcendently declaring that he "belongs to no class" and does "not need a title." He offers himself "exclusively to the German people," all of whom, in his eyes, were "entirely equal" to one another. History might question his sincerity about this latter point.

Hitler also cleverly managed **motive** in his speech. He did so immediately by asserting "I have more right to [speak] than anyone else," presumably because his emotional investment in the movement had long since extinguished his natural human reticence ("Before . . . I was simply a man who earned his daily bread)." Hitler paints the picture of one who has been "overcome" by the need to speak. He is not a clever manipulator who has carefully planned his address nor is he motivated by ego. Instead, his "ideas" have pushed him forward and he has become a kind of political mannequin: "I have grown out of you yourselves."

Today, we think of such strategies as stock forms of identification. But perhaps we do so because Hitler defined the acceptable vocabulary of motives for a mass movement. There had, of course, been other people's movements before Hitler, but they were less rhetorically based, depending more on sudden uprisings (e.g., the American revolution) or upon bitter, long-term struggles (e.g., the Russian revolution). Hitler, in contrast, largely talked his way into power and so the matter of symbolic motives was always on his mind.

Hitler uses historical revisionism to find an acceptable **scapegoat** in this speech. He catalogues the motives of the political establishment, always finding them wanting. The "quality," "courage," and "spirit" of all the German classes, he alleges, could be trusted implicitly. Then why have the German people suffered? Because they have been "poorly advised" by the previous leadership that "did not live up to what it had promised." This leadership, which was "responsible for the war," offered only a "horrible future." Hitler's motivational universe here is not one of Innocence versus Malevolence. Rather, he derides Incompetence since, in 1933 at least, he could not afford to completely alienate the supporters of the Prussian government that his Third Reich would eventually replace. Nevertheless, by indirection, Hitler found wellsprings of the negative sufficient for his rhetorical purposes.

In addition to the general critical tools of hierarchy, motive, scapegoating, and transcendence, Burke introduced other methods for dissecting rhetorical texts, which we can use as critical probes. Three of them are particularly important:

What invitations for *identification* does the message extend? Identification is now a fairly common term (e.g., "I can identify with that") but Burke had something more subtle in mind. He saw that people identified with one another when their common interests were dramatized for them, just as if they were biological organisms exchanging chemical properties in order to survive. Even "naturally unaligned" groups—rich and poor, black and white—said Burke, will become motivated to share new identities when their unmet needs are made salient to them. Rhetoric provides this salience.

For Burke, drama could not succeed unless it invited an audience to (1) reexamine and (2) activate its identity. Identifications are the "aligning symbols" that serve such functions. These symbols can be as simple as a politician saying "I was a farmboy myself" when stumping through Iowa. Or they can be as complex as the intricate web of symbols that links one Virginian to another, unless one of them happens to be a transplanted North Carolinian, which is alright as long as she is not a liberal, which could, of course, be forgiven if their kids happen to be in the second grade together. Burke believed that these complex intertwinings were indeed weblike, "trapping" complex psychological materials so that communication becomes functionally possible. He wrote a poem that illustrates:

> He was a sincere but friendly Presbyterian—and so
> If he was talking to a Presbyterian,
> He was for Presbyterianism.
> If he was talking to a Lutheran,
> He was for Protestantism.
> If he was talking to a Catholic,
> He was for Christianity.
> If he was talking to a Jew,
> He was for God.
> If he was talking to a theosophist,
> He was for religion.
> If he was talking to an agnostic,
> He was for scientific caution.
> If he was talking to an atheist,
> He was for mankind.
> And if he was talking to a socialist, communist, labor leader, missiles
>   expert, or businessman,
> He was for PROGRESS. [In Simons, 1986:131]

In the Hitler passage, identifications abound. Everyone has been hungry; Hitler has been hungry. Everyone has been upset; Hitler has been upset. Everyone has had a moment of bravery; Hitler has had many such moments. And even though contemporary Americans cannot appreciate exactly what it was like to be a poor peasant in Hitler's Germany, such feelings and experiences can be approximated.

Common *rhetorical* experience makes it possible. For example, documentaries about the Depression in the 1930s and news stories about terrible droughts in Africa help explain hunger and social disintegration to well-fed Americans. In similar ways, movies like *Boyz N the Hood* and *American History X* tell rural residents and suburbanites about the struggles of urban youth to find a sense of self-respect, how violence becomes attractive, and the challenges of breaking that cycle. All of these sentiments can be shared via identification, perhaps suggesting that there is a universal language of the emotions.

Identification can also partially bridge hierarchical separations. This bridging is only partial because **dramatic force** comes from difference while **dramatic comfort** comes from similarity. For example, Huxman [1997] noted that American Mennonites, a pacifist religious sect, dealt paradoxically with the challenges of being called up for military service in World War I. They petitioned Congress and emphasized the ways in which they were willing to conform to society's expectations, offering their services to the country in noncombat roles, thus inviting dramatic comfort. But they also created dramatic force within their own communities, reminding one another of the rightness of being different from society by invoking their ancestral heritage as martyrs for their faith. For Burke, then, "rhetoric occurs when individuals examine their identities to determine who they are and how they fit into groups with others who share those identities" [Heath, 1986:202]. It is this interest in identification that makes Burke such a manifestly "psychological" critic.

 What *associational/dissociational clusters* can be found in the message? Burke frequently took what he called a "statistical" approach to style, examining language elements for patterned relationships. Such patterns, he believed, work additively on an audience without their knowing it. By tracking which images went with which images, which opposed which, or which followed which, Burke often had novel things to say about rhetorical tone.

When doing this sort of analysis, Burke looked for increasingly abstract relationships among stylistic elements. Unless the critic tracks word patterns up the ladder of abstraction, they become mere tidbits of data that have been tidily assembled by the critic but whose conceptual importance is impossible to discern.

Berthold [1976] did just such patient tracking. She examined John Kennedy's rhetoric and discovered that his references to "peace" were typically found adjacent to references to "freedom," ostensibly because Kennedy's liberal instincts were vying with the conservative realities of the early 1960s. A second finding corroborated this inference: Berthold found the terms "freedom" and "Communism" consistently *opposed* to one another in Kennedy's speeches, again suggesting that there was more of the Cold Warrior in John Kennedy than many had noticed.

Burke is particularly interested in these opposed or **agonistic** patterns since conflict lies at the heart of drama [Brock, 1985:88]. When he battled his fate, for example, Oedipus "agonized" with the gods over his personal destiny. Oedipus' situation is no different from those played out by the prot-agon-ists and ant-agon-ists of everyday life, which is why Burke took special interest in how significant symbols line up in a text to produce conflict.

These alignments often tell the text's basic plot: who is good, who is evil, what the future portends, and why. For instance, when American Private Jessica Lynch was captured in Iraq in 2003, people in the United States were anxious to get the basic "story" as quickly as possible. During wartime, however, reliable information is scarce at first. And so the initial reports deployed stock agons, with the "evil Saddam" and his "disregard for human life" counterpoised to the "injured hero" who accidentally wandered into the line of fire (therefore becoming a helpless "damsel in distress"). However, later British press coverage cast doubt on the fairy-tale rescue scenario, reporting that Iraqi hospital administrators had actually *attempted to return the injured prisoner of war*—but American forces had opened fire on the ambulance carrying her. Their overtures had been rejected in favor of the carefully staged, televised rescue—conducted with blanks and the sound of explosions, even though witnesses said that the American special forces were aware that the Iraqi military had fled the day before [Kampfner, 2003]. The U.S. press largely spurned this revised version of events in favor of the more clear-cut good versus evil drama already scripted, a story so powerful it impelled both a made-for-TV movie and a book contract.

The job of the dramatistic critic, then, is to discover the "calculus of meanings" in a text. For instance, in the now-classic movie *Poltergeist*, a family does battle with an evil force hoping to drive them from their home. The force steals the smallest child (through the television set, no less!) and generally traumatizes the rest of the family. As we watch, there is an almost direct "statistical" alignment between good and evil: The family is good, the television ghosts evil (a comment that TV destroys the American family?). The spiritualist who comes to the house is also on the side of right and becomes a kind of hero for the family. The movie's dramatic tension comes from questions about who or what has selected the family for harassment and why.

In Hollywood fashion, the denouement reveals all: Real estate developers have built the family's home over a graveyard without first removing the bodies. This conclusion "solves for *x*" in the dramatic equation: Big is evil, new is evil, capitalism is evil. Although *Poltergeist* displays little subtlety in selling its rape-of-the-countryside moral, it does exemplify what Burke found being done (well or poorly) in virtually all rhetorical exchanges.

 What is the *foreground/background ratio* in the discourse? One of the most frequently used Burkean tools is also one of the most frequently misused: his "pentad" of dramatic elements—Agent (who acted), Act (what was done), Agency (how it was done), Purpose (why), and Scene (in which context). This all seems straightforward, but application of this format has proven tricky. Accordingly, we shall abbreviate Burke's system here, focusing just on Act, Purpose, and Scene, and use these tools to examine TEXTUAL materials only. Thus, we shall be concerned with the Scene *the rhetor* depicts, the Purpose *the rhetor* claims, and the Act *the rhetor* recounts.

Our key critical probes will be these: (1) Which factor dominates the discourse generally? and (2) When two factors are discussed simultaneously, which predominates and why? By roughly calculating the ratio among these usages, the critic begins to appreciate how dramatic tension and excitement are produced. Definitionally, we can proceed simply: **Act**—*when the rhetor describes the freely chosen activities of some protagonist;* **Purpose**—*when the rhetor details the protagonist's feelings, intentions, and value systems;* **Scene**—*the kind of stage the rhetor sets when describing community conditions, social influences, historical causes, or natural events (e.g., a severe storm).*

The value of Burke's approach here is that it looks at the same rhetorical situation from multiple perspectives and thereby explains the otherwise unexplainable. For example, a fascinating study by Tonn and her colleagues [1995] examined the case of one Donald Rogerson who, while deer hunting in rural Maine, shot and killed Karen Wood, a wife and mother who had just moved to

Maine from Iowa and who at the time of the shooting was standing in her back yard. Hapless manslaughter? Not according to Mr. Rogerson, who argued in court that his Act (hunting) had a long and honorable tradition and that his Purpose (being prudent) was beyond question since he thought he had spotted a deer. But Rogerson was acquitted because of Scenic arguments—all folks in rural Maine know that you don't poke your head out the back door during hunting season. Case closed.

Within the same text or set of texts, rhetors will sometimes shift ratios from moment to moment. By examining these different "featuring" strategies, a critic can gain a rich perspective on a dramatic encounter, as we see in Table 12.1. The case study is that of Brummett [1984] who examined news coverage of John DeLorean, a one-time automobile executive at General Motors who left a promising career at GM to found his own automobile company (and to live the life of a jet-setting bon vivant). When his company began to founder, DeLorean allegedly sought venture capital in the cocaine industry but was eventually tried and found innocent of the drug charges. Because of DeLorean's flamboyant approach to business and personal affairs, his story became front-page material for months on end in the 1980s.

Brummett's deft analysis recounts the "ironic frame" the press used to tell this tale and explains why they were able to keep the story alive for so long. As we see in Table 12.1, the press could do so because so many *different* ratios were available to them for creating dramatic clash. Table 12.1 also shows that these rhetorical ratios produced both favorable and unfavorable stories, depending on the reporters' intentions, further adding to the overall, ironic storyline. As Brummett's study shows, dramatistic ratios can prove endlessly fascinating.

In many ways, Kenneth Burke is the most daring of the well-published critics. One of his favorite techniques was to extract from just a bit of text some intricate conceptual design. He looked at a piece of discourse for its **representative anecdote** (a Scene/Act imbalance, a narrative habit, a pattern of imagery, a telling example, etc.), that summed up its rhetorical tone. According to Burke, such an anecdote will be representative if it contains the basic agon or master metaphor of the discourse system in general. So, for example, the Hitler speech reviewed earlier is probably a representative anecdote since it captures the senses of struggle and revenge that fanned the flames of the Third Reich.

Most rhetorical critics, however, are not as adventurous as Kenneth Burke nor should they be. Burke's penchant for establishing sweeping psychological and cultural *answers* on the basis of isolated bits of rhetoric is probably not the Kenneth Burke the beginning critic should emulate. But the Kenneth Burke who asked wonderfully imaginative *questions,* who was bold enough to search for rhetoric where others would not, who inquired constantly about how such discourse affected the human condition, who asked about the sundry victimizations of persuasion as well as its glorious transcendences, who was concerned, constantly, with those on the bottom of life's hierarchies as well as those at the

TABLE 12.1 Dramatistic News Strategies in the DeLorean Case*

Act Dominates Scene

What is featured? Freely chosen activities of some protagonist

What is muted? Community conditions, social influences, historical causes, or natural events

Eulogistic use: Describes a protagonist's actions as being of such heroic proportions that the actions of others pale in comparison

> *Example:* "[At General Motors, DeLorean stood out] like a Corvette Stingray in a showroom full of GMC trucks."

Dyslogistic use: Characterizes a person or group's behaviors as being so reckless or self-centered that they dwarf normal, social obligations

> *Example:* "I don't know how you square the description of a community-minded man with that of a man who engineered the delivery of China White."

Scene Dominates Act

What is featured? Community conditions, social influences, historical causes, or natural events

What is muted? Freely chosen activities of some protagonist

Eulogistic use: Draws attention to the personal sacrifices a protagonist faced as a result of some larger social trend or societal condition

> *Example:* "Sales of domestically built cars have been sagging for more than three years, while imports are thriving under precisely the same market conditions . . . [all of which resulted in] 'the failure of the enterprise.' "

Dyslogistic use: Emphasizes that the larger community can ultimately constrain the actions of even the most powerful

> *Example:* "DeLorean, a man accustomed to gold bracelets, was led away in steel bracelets . . . [his jail was] not the Ritz [and was filled with] male prostitutes, muggers, and murderers."

Scene Dominates Purpose

What is featured? Community conditions, social influences, historical causes, or natural events

What is muted? Protagonists's feelings, intentions, value systems

Eulogistic use: Emphasizes the social attractiveness of one who is so responsive to societal needs that no questions of character can be raised

> *Example:* "If DeLorean was driven to drug dealing in an effort to raise capital, underlying the resentment there is some compassion for him . . . [since he was trying to protect] the DeLorean family [his employees]."

Dyslogistic use: Describes a protagonist-as-puppet who has become so enmeshed in the social world that his or her values and priorities have been forsaken

> *Example:* "DeLorean was vulnerable to the magic aura of the cocaine trade and its promise of euphoric profits. After eight years of superhuman struggle . . . DeLorean appeared to crack."

Purpose Dominates Scene

What is featured? Protagonist's feelings, intentions, value systems

What is muted? Community conditions, social influences, historical causes, or natural events

Eulogistic use: Argues that one's feelings and thoughts are of such importance that they override social and other consequences

> *Example:* "There is a very high price to pay for such a dream [as DeLorean had]."

(continued)

TABLE 12.1 *(continued)*

Purpose Dominates Scene *(cont.)*

Dyslogistic use: Shows the tragic results of allowing personal pride or idealogical zeal to override social obligations

>*Example:* "How could a shrewd businessman like DeLorean fall so stupidly and easily into the hands of drug suppliers and federal agents?"

Purpose Dominates Act

What is featured? Protagonist's feelings, intentions, value systems

What is muted? Freely chosen activities of some protagonist

Eulogistic use: Features the significant personal costs borne by some person or group because of their beliefs and values

>*Example:* "[DeLorean] improbably as it seems, detected parallels between his life and that of Jesus Christ."

Dyslogistic use: Indicates that a protagonist has become so preoccupied with personal goals that he or she is now behaving erratically and irresponsibly

>*Example:* "He [DeLorean] was drawing $475,000 a year and $1,000 a week in expenses, even when the company was dying. . . . All the things he despised at G.M. he became himself."

Act Dominates Purpose

What is featured? Freely chosen activities of some protagonist

What is muted? Protagonist's feelings, intentions, value systems

Eulogistic use: A person or group's actions are described as so grand in scale that to raise questions of motive would seem pedestrian

>*Example:* Adjectives for DeLorean: "feisty," "swashbuckling," "awesome," "charismatic," "phenomenal," "savvy," "remarkable," filled with "creativity," "éclat," and "flair" and never losing his "cool"

Dsylogistic use: A person or group's actions are described as noteworthy and yet ill-advised, thus opening the door to questions of intelligence and decency

>*Example:* Headlines in DeLorean case: "Coke, Cars, and Capitol" *(New Republic),* "DeLorean Drove the Fast Lane" *(Washington Post),* "DeLorean's Scramble Ends with Arrest" *(Business Week),* "When You Wish Upon a Car" *(New York),* "Superstar and Maverick, DeLorean Never Fit the Mold" *(New York Times).*

*Adapted from Brummett [1984].

top—this is the Kenneth Burke who teaches capably, often brilliantly, and who has lessons for all.

CONCLUSION

In 1935, before he developed his theory of dramatism, Kenneth Burke published *Permanence and Change.* In it, he argued that all persons, not just those interested in literary and rhetorical matters, must become critics. He said that even a trout whose mouth has been ripped apart by biting into an angler's hook becomes a critic as a result of the experience, sharply revising its understanding of food, bait, time, and tide. But all living things are not necessarily *good* critics, Burke argued further, which is why the critical faculty must be nurtured so carefully and so insistently.

People are not fish. Human judgment is complicated because people must respond to both a physical and a symbolic world. To fail to become a critic of symbology, warned Burke, would be to ignore human motives—and that is often disastrous. Some people write their poems on paper, he [1984:76] observed, while others "carve them out of jugular veins." Accordingly, the social responsibility of the critic extends even to a consideration of human warfare since wars are "statements" two countries are trying to make to one another ("stay off our land," "give us back the money your grandparents stole," "let us practice our religion in peace," etc.). Burke thought that critics could help "purify war" by discovering what rival nations were attempting to say to one another and by suggesting symbolic ways of saying such things.

Criticism was therefore not a trivial activity for Burke since he saw that people make their grandest and most heinous statements with symbols. He believed that by becoming better critics people would come to understand how complicated human motives are and how inadequate ordinary communication can be for sharing that complexity. Burke reminds us that criticism is a profession exclusively devoted to asking questions . . . and never stopping. Therefore, Burke believed, critics should never abide facile, incomplete, or doctrinaire answers. He believed, too, that criticism is an "art of living," humanity's best chance to nurture our unique capacity for reflection. Burke concluded that understanding what people are saying—or trying to say—is therefore a badly needed enterprise.

TIPS FOR THE PRACTICING CRITIC

1. In doing dramatistic analysis, it is easy to feel overwhelmed by Burke's example. But rather than trying to do everything at once, make several passes through a message, looking each time for one specific feature and how it is operating in the text (hierarchy, motive, scapegoating, etc.) Then fit the different parts together to see how they interact and influence one another.
2. Refer to Table 12.1 for guidance in analyzing the dramatization of the message. Remember that simply labeling the parts (scene, act, purpose) does not constitute rhetorical criticism.
3. Burke's playfulness and imagination make his criticism engaging. Take advantage of the prescription implicit in the praise of Burke's work: Allow yourself to play with language, ideas, choice of critical artifact, etc. Sometimes apparently "insignificant" or "unpersuasive" discourse can reveal important insights to the astute critic: insights about the nature of rhetoric, those who use it, and the context and ways in which they do so.

Chapter 13

FEMINIST CRITICISM[1]

A woman's mouth should look soft and feminine, and sensuous and sophisticated.
All at the same time. That's why new Love's Reflections Lip Cremes were created.

Lip Creme colors are soft-spoken. From the rich, clear shades to the mellow,
muted ones. And when they're pearled, it's done delicately. With just a touch
of shimmer.

Lip Creme textures feel sensuous. Because Love used 3 special moisturizers to
make Lip Cremes moist, creamy, richer on your mouth.

Love's Reflections Lip Cremes will give your mouth a look that's soft-spoken
and sensuous. And that's the way a woman's mouth should look. ["Love's Reflections," 1971:14]

***

This cosmetics advertisement, from a women's magazine during the hey-
day of the women's liberation movement, is clearly ripe for feminist critical
analysis. Like most ads, it invites insecurity on the part of its audience by setting up a daunting goal: in this case, looking soft and feminine, sensuous and
sophisticated, all at the same time. The un-self-consciously bossy assertion—
"A woman's mouth should look"—may appear dated to our contemporary
sensibilities, much more blatant than the appeals in today's ads. (As Neuborne
[2001:183] writes, "What my mother taught me to look for—pats on the butt,
honey, sweetie, cupcake, make me some coffee—are not the methods of choice
for today's sexists. Those were just the fringes of what they were really up to.

---

[1] With thanks to Joanne Gilbert for her contributions to this chapter in the second
edition.

Sadly, enough of them have figured out how to mouth the words of equality while still behaving like pigs. They're harder to spot.")

In this chapter, we will be considering **feminist rhetorical criticism,** which can be practiced on its own or in conjunction with any of the other approaches we have described thus far. Because it is a form of **ideological criticism,** or criticism that analyzes and challenges the ways in which the status quo of unequal power relations is maintained, feminist criticism can be seen as threatening. It challenges oppression and privilege (and often, not just sexist oppression, but racism, heterosexism, classism, etc.) with a set of attitudes and activist presumptions about how the world could be improved through changing discourse. Feminist criticism assumes, like Chapter 11's Cultural Criticism, that artifacts both shape and reflect the cultures that produced them, including the expectations those cultures have about what it means to be male and female, masculine and feminine. Feminist critics ask how messages explicitly describe (and thus implicitly prescribe) "appropriate" gendered behavior.

Some readers may come to this chapter with trepidation because of previous exposure to (mis)conceptions of feminists as humorless, angry, hairy, manhating lesbians. First things first: True, feminists do not often laugh at sexist jokes. Similarly, people of color do not often laugh at racist jokes—*but no one implies that they should.* Connection and trust with other, likeminded women and men bring both joy and playfulness to the feminist's life and critical efforts. Moving on to the next charge: Anger (along with grief) can be a logical response to the recognition of mistreatment, and often an important wake-up call for change. Naomi Wolf's [1993] attempt to make feminism more palatable by promoting the term "power feminism" (vs. "victim feminism") seems a well-intentioned but misguided tactic. While of course people wish to see themselves as powerful rather than as victims (this holds true with all kinds of oppression), the ability to recognize past and present injustice is a crucial part of "consciousness-raising," which allows us to better ensure justice in the future.

Indeed, there is nothing wrong with being sometimes angry, or hairy. (In fact, implying otherwise is a transparent attempt to limit women's choices.) But hatred is not a value most feminists espouse. And Findlen [2001:xv] answers the last part of this stereotype thoughtfully:

> The idea that all feminists are lesbians is scary enough to keep some women, even those who are equality-minded, away. When a young woman decides to identify as a feminist—a person who believes in the full equality of women and men—she soon discovers at least two things: that women of all sexual identities are feminists, and that, even so, she will now be subject to the same stereotypes and dyke-baiting that may once have scared her away. But simply denying that all feminists are lesbians is not the way to right this wrong. We need to take the harder road of challenging the homophobia that gives this image its power.

Indeed, the vast majority of feminists are also humanists, believing that no one should attempt to limit another's ability to develop based on characteristics such as sex, sexuality, race, age, class, disability, marital status, etc.

As practicing feminist critics, then, we might be tempted to conclude simply that the Lip Cremes ad above is "sexist," but that would be comparable to, in the language of Chapter 12, simply labeling the parts of Burke's pentad and going home. Unpacking the interpretive possibilities of a message is likely to be more productive of insight. Feminist critics find critical probes such as the following useful for beginning analysis:

- In what ways does this artifact suggest that women and men should look, think, feel, behave?
- Overall, how might this message challenge the mystiques of femininity and masculinity?
- And how might this artifact reinforce them? (Beware an either/or logic; most artifacts—and the best feminist critics— are more complex than that.)
- What are the implications of these messages?
- In what ways are women and men advantaged or disadvantaged by such portrayals?

The Lip Cremes ad, for example, tells women how to be appropriately feminine: be muted, subtle, soft-spoken, delicate and sensuous. In effect, women should be decorative, seen and not heard, and their lips should be moist, creamy, virtually edible—presumably, for the pleasure of male sexual partners. But "sophisticated" is also on the list, and "sophisticated" is not submissive; it implies knowledge, even expertise: How to do this, without threatening men in power? The ad thus briefly appears to undermine its own rules for femininity, acknowledging that this seems an impossible task "all at the same time." (If it were not an impossible task, there would be no need for cosmetic enhancement of women's "natural" femininity.) Fortunately, purchasing a new tube of lipstick should do it.

But the fact that this ad appeared in *Ladies' Home Journal* in the same issue with articles such as "Myths That Keep Women Down" complicates matters. Perhaps part of the complicated instructions for how women "should look" was due to (white, middle-class) North American women's increasing sense that they had a right to self-determination. Perhaps "sensuous and sophisticated" was a nod to feminism's second wave, which was cresting at about that time. Perhaps the "shoulds" that form the beginning and end of the text, attempting to symbolically contain women, are in fact a sign that the **patriarchy,** the rule of men in society, was starting to get a wee bit jumpy.

Would all feminist critics agree with this analysis? Probably not. So what is feminism, exactly? Given the many kinds of feminists today, there is more than one answer, and some would argue that we must use the term "feminisms," or "feminism and womanism." (Some African American women, such as Patricia Hill Collins [2000], embrace the term "black feminist thought." But many African American women have felt excluded from the feminism of white, middle-class women, due to both its goals and the unexamined racism of their white "sisters." Womanism is the term Alice Walker suggested for African American women, which takes into account African American women's commitment for "race up-lift," bettering the lives of African American men in U.S. culture, as well.)

Feminist exploration often involves the painful and humbling recognition of one's own part in perpetuating oppression, and the resolve to try to be more conscious of this, and change it when possible. (When this becomes clear, men usually relax, realizing that they are not, as individuals, being held responsible for all injustice.) For example, women's studies helped McIntosh [1998] begin to identify her own white privilege, previously invisible to her. She describes white privilege (and by extension, middle-class, heterosexual, etc., privilege) as a knapsack she has unknowingly carried, full of unearned benefits systematically denied to others (such as the trust that if she happened to be late for a meeting, it would not reflect negatively on her race).

Feminism can be attitudinal, as Barreca [1991:178] wryly points out: Feminists are those who recognize that "the earth doesn't revolve around any-body's son." But as Burke taught us, attitudes have consequences in how we live our lives. Prolific feminist cultural critic bell hooks [1984:26,17], for ex-ample, defines feminism as "the struggle to end sexist oppression" but also as-serts that "A central problem with feminist discourse has been our inability to either arrive at a consensus of opinion about what feminism is or accept defin-ition(s) that could serve as points of unification." Obviously, this applies not simply to feminisms within the United States. Until recently, most widely pub-lished feminist theory has originated from within North America and Europe, but the perspectives of women from Central and South America, Asia, Africa, and Australia are beginning to be published, as well. Unlike the situation in many Western societies, for example, African cultural traditions legitimate fe-male organizations and collective actions by women of all classes, and so the issues and starting points for their feminist actions differ from those of North American women [Mikell, 1995]. Because "feminism" has meant a series of *so-cial movements* as well as intellectual positions, and because feminists' specific goals have shifted over the years as the concerns of different groups of women have been voiced, we will have to approach feminism in a complicated way as well.

Of course, not all feminists are women. "Men's studies" have proliferated since the 1970s with the recognition that the social constructions of masculinity and femininity as "opposites" damage men as well as women. (This is especially true since, as Faludi [1991:61–2] notes, masculinity always needs to prove itself superior!). As Newton [1998:594] observes, masculinity studies and feminist theory can mutually benefit from sharing knowledge: "Building community, we should remember, was never the work of one sex or race alone."

And not all women are feminists. But in many cases, this is an issue of "spin" rather than substance. Douglas [1994] devotes a chapter in her excellent book *Where the Girls Are: Growing Up Female with the Mass Media* to unpacking the statement "I'm not a feminist, but. . . ." What follows the "but" is invariably a statement in support of some feminist goal involving women's right to self-determination (in education, livelihood, spirituality, partnership, parenting, etc.). The "I'm not a feminist" part of the statement receives the most public attention, usually, as do surveys that ask whether women call themselves feminists. But given the ways in which feminists are targeted for harassment by conservative opinion leaders, it takes courage to embrace the term. Many women are working hard merely to survive; why invite more abuse? And so intimidation tactics serve to keep feminism's real numbers underground. But they are there. As Findlen [2001:xiii] observes, "many . . . young women and men have integrated feminist values into their lives, whether or not they use the label, and this is also an important barometer of the impact of feminism." Wolf [1993:278] writes that ". . . any woman who believes in women's right to self-definition and self-respect is a feminist in my book." And Latina talk-show host and media tycoon Cristina Saralegui says, "I consider myself a feminist, and to me a feminist is nothing more than a full and complete human being with all the available rights and no limitations" [Muñoz, 2002–2003:60].

But even among women who embrace the label of feminist, philosophical disagreements remain. Fox-Genovese [1991:56] writes:

> Today, as in the past, feminists divide over whether women should be struggling for women's rights as individuals or women's rights as women—whether women need equality with men or protection for their difference from men. . . . This debate over equality versus difference lies at the core of contemporary feminist thought, not merely because of the way in which it divides feminist theorists, but, perhaps more important, because of its ability to link theory and practice.

Given these political and philosophical complications, this chapter can hardly embrace a single brand of feminism. Instead, our goal will be to discover how rhetorical texts become gendered and how such gendering blinds audiences to some realities while opening them up to others. Philosophically, we will embrace a basic sexual egalitarianism, the idea that humanistic and pluralistic values best guide human affairs and that the privileging of one sex over another harms social life. Critically, we will highlight these feminist assumptions:

1. *Traditional rhetorical acts are androcentric (consider male as the "norm").* Feminist critics do not introduce politics into a text, but rather expose the politics already there. As Carol Tavris [1992] notes, for example, the teaching of students in medical school may seem a rhetoric-free zone, but the "normal body" presented for study is always male. Thus, students learn about the effect of medications on men, but not women, and yet go on to prescribe such medications for women as well—with sometimes disastrous results. And most college students have heard of the gender-bias inherent in the English language, and know of inclusive, nonsexist alternatives (e.g., "firefighter, police officer, humankind," rather than language that specifies a male body). (Some people persist in believing that "man" means everybody, but even they are usually convinced by the jarring nature of the statement, "Man, being a mammal, breastfeeds his young.") In more obvious rhetoric, it may seem familiar and therefore "normal" for a male U.S. president to sing the praises of the "father of our country" on Washington's birthday and then relinquish the podium to

a male prelate intoning the benediction, "Our Father, who art in heaven." Feminist critics would point out that this "normal" androcentrism is "man-made," not natural: Ceremonies are conducted by those in power (presidents, ministers), who are steeped in a tradition of masculine motifs (the Washington myth, the King James bible). As a result, the very act of participating in these ceremonies reinforces the power of those who speak (often wealthy, white, heterosexual men) and the relative powerlessness of those who listen (women, poor people, people of color, etc.).

Because of the growing number of activist women today, it is easy to forget how recently feminism has developed in the United States. Prior to the nineteenth century women could not study Latin (the language of education, religion, and the law) and thus were denied the key to the established professions [Donovan, 1980]. It was not until 1920 that women in the United States won the right to vote. The 1970s brought U.S. women laws against marital rape and battery, as well as Title IX, which resulted in the creation of women's sports programs in colleges. Married women can now establish their own credit. Most people reading this will have grown up with the idea that women and men can do anything they aspire to do, given the talent and the will. But as Findlen [2001:xiv] points out, "feminism has unfinished business. . . . When we experience the sometimes brutal realities of gender inequity, we are enraged. Almost every woman knows what it feels like to be mistreated, trivialized, kept out, put down, ignored, assaulted, laughed at or discriminated against because of her sex." Rather than being ancient history, the Equal Rights Amendment guaranteeing protection from discrimination on the basis of sex, first proposed in 1923, *is not yet a part of the U.S. constitution.* In every domain, women have gone to great lengths to claim their rightful rhetorical practices. Feminist critics seek to expose, and offset, the patriarchal customs that threaten women's (and men's) human rights.

2. *Traditional rhetorical texts are androcentric.* Feminist criticism employs two different modes. In the **universalizing mode,** a critic examines a text for its general descriptions of the human condition and then asks how "general" those descriptions really are. This is crucial, says Showalter [1985:143], because texts have heretofore asked women to "identify against themselves" by presuming that *male* (and usually also white, heterosexual, wealthy) standards for beauty, truth, and justice are basic *human* standards. That these masculine premises have been accepted without reflection is especially dangerous, a prime example of rhetoric that has successfully denied its own status as rhetoric, rendering itself "invisible." As Ruthven [1984:64–65] points out, "men are able to conceive of their own subjectivity as being non-gendered, and therefore wonder why feminists make such a fuss about gender. But because women are not aligned with the universal, they are much more inclined to see themselves as women than men are to see themselves as men."

Accordingly, says Rich [1972:20], critics must practice what she calls re-vision, the act of "entering an old text from a new critical direction" so that these male-centered premises can be thought anew. U.S. legal statutes, for example, are rhetorical artifacts with tremendous power. Many laws rely on definitions of what the "reasonable man" would do, without taking into account that men and women are practically raised in two different cultures. Men are encouraged to fight an attacker; women are cautioned that fighting might "enrage" an attacker. Women are taught to fear and feel helpless before men's physical power, and are thus often so intimidated that they will not use the physical power they do possess. The staggering numbers of women who are raped, battered, and murdered by men is a direct outcome of the divergent rhetorical messages about what is "appropriate" for men and women. When abused women do attempt to leave, their partners often threaten to kill them. (And tragically, many succeed.) The woman who escapes by means of killing her abuser while he sleeps is often jailed for murder. And so, men who batter, then murder, their partners are less likely to serve time than women who kill their abusers. (The man's crime is presumably one of passion; the woman's, since it often occurs *after* rather than *during* abusive episodes, does not "count" as self-defense, but premeditation.) In short, feminist critics urge us to take nothing for granted, but to re-examine the implications of virtually all of the "great" historical texts—in speeches, law, literature, religion, science—every arena of life.

3. *Traditional criticism is androcentric.* The **particularizing mode** of feminist scholarship tries to find an authentic female voice by calling into question the established, universal norms for literary and rhetorical excellence. Seventy-five years ago, Virginia Woolf [1929:77] understood the inherent bias in these "universal" norms when she did an impersonation of the usual (male) standard of literary excellence: "This is an important book . . . because it deals with war. This is an insignificant book because it deals with the feelings of women in a drawing room." In reaction to such biases, feminist critics frequently use the phrase "women's writing" rather than "women's literature" to define their interests because the former, more generous phrase, includes the schoolbooks, diaries, and letters that were the only outlets available to generations of literarily inclined women.

Operating on these three major premises, feminist criticism has been especially productive during the last three decades. Feminist critics have found patriarchal **intellectual conventions** problematic since they typically endorse (1) abstractions such as "duty" and "honor" rather than people's lived experiences and (2) dichotomies such as male (good)/female (bad). Ruthven [1984: 72] notes, for instance, that whereas male characters have been given full definition in literature, female characters have more often been given binary options: "sensuous roses or virginal lilies, pedestaled goddesses or downtrodden slaves, Eves or Marys, Madonnas or Magdalenes, damned whores or God's police."

Feminist critics have pointed out that political discourse is especially laden with these dichotomies and abstractions, leading men in power to conflict rather than negotiation, to martyrdom rather than flexibility, to independence rather than interdependence. Women's historical reality—childbearing and caretaking—has encouraged the development of relational skills such as compassion and nurturing. Accordingly, many feminist critics prize concrete experience and contend that "the personal is political," meaning that women's "individual" experiences are often actually part of a larger pattern of oppression.

Feminist critics are also interested in the **mythic conventions** used in rhetoric, for many standard mythic patterns have marginalized women, if not victimized them. Ruthven [1984:80], for example, argues that the typical fairy tale describes a passive princess "who waits patiently on top of the Glass Hill for the first man to climb it" and who, as a result, is "symbolically dead" and can only be brought to life by a man. Radway's [1984:212–213] classic study of why women read romance novels stirs up parallel concerns. She finds similar kinds of passivity there and, although she notes that reading such fiction is a somewhat "rebellious" act, it is also mythically entrapping: "They do nothing to challenge [women's] separation from one another brought about by the patriarchal culture's insistence that they never work in the public world to maintain themselves but rather live symbiotically as the property and responsibility of men."

Feminist critics also focus on the **role conventions** of discourse. Perhaps the most cherished role, the role of authority, has been an especially male (and white, heterosexual, wealthy) preserve. Press coverage invariably focuses on "the first woman" to achieve high status in male-only occupations, often ignoring those who come after her. (A parallel phenomenon occurs with the first African American, Latino, Asian American, openly gay person, person with a disability, etc.) Although often well-intentioned, such publicity can (ironically) invite the audience to view these "firsts" as abnormal exceptions, rather than as representative of women's (or "minorities") potential for accomplishment. This robs "minorities" and women-in-general of respect and credibility and reinforces hierarchy, which is automatically oppressive, and against which many feminists fight. As Poirot [2004] points out, the (second wave) women's liberation movement attempted to use collective action rather than spokespersons, but the media insisted on anointing authorities (such as author Kate Millett) to stand for the group; these authorities could then be individually targeted and discredited. Paradoxically, this sets up a double bind: those who are not in positions of authority will not be taken seriously; people who cannot be taken seriously will not be heard.

The *projected* roles of women—how they are portrayed in rhetoric and literature—are also frequently demeaning. These roles, too, have consequences. Not only do they affect how men see women but also how women see themselves. For example, Charlesworth [2003] analyzed AIDS education brochures directed at women, and found that women were consistently depicted as transmitters (when, in fact, they are far less likely than men are to transmit the disease), as caretakers of those with the disease, and as "flowerpots" whose main responsibility was incubating a man's seed. Notably, none of these identities encourages women to take precautions in order to preserve their own health—but only to preserve the health of others, a strategy that has proven dramatically ineffective in preventing further infection. And Barbatsis et al. [1983] did a comprehensive analysis of television programming, finding that men talked most of the time (even in cartoons), that females received significantly more orders, and that women asked more questions than they gave answers. Even in romantic fiction, says Snitow [1986:138], women's roles are circumscribed. Despite the perhaps comforting familiarity of such characterizations, their *rhetorical* impact on women's attitudes can be devastating:

> When women try to picture excitement, the society offers them one vision, romance. When women try to imagine companionship, the society offers them one vision, male, sexual companionship. When women try to fantasize about success, mastery, the society offers them one vision, the power to attract a man. When women try to fantasize about sex, the society offers them taboos on most of its imaginable expressions except those that deal directly with arousing and satisfying men. When women try to project a unique self, the society offers them very few attractive images. True completion for women is nearly always presented as social, domestic, sexual.

These, then, are some of the major themes characterizing feminist perspectives. Phrased as additional critical probes, we can ask:

- What does the rhetor present as "the norm"?
- Are the specific experiences of people from diverse ethnicities, nationalities, sexes/sexual orientations, and classes included, or are people assumed to be "all the same"?
- How explicitly or implicitly is this handled?
- What intellectual, mythic, or role conventions does the artifact offer?
- What are the implications of these depictions for men and women (people of different classes, body sizes, sexualities, ethnicities, nationalities, etc.), both in terms of how they see themselves and in terms of how others see them?

Individual critics deploy these perspectives differently and the result is a multi-hued feminism. Here, we will focus on four of its hues. Our category system will be neither exhaustive nor definitive but it will expose some of the ways in which power becomes gendered and in which gender becomes powerful. (As we go along, we will suggest specialized critical probes from previous chapters to be used in conjunction with the feminist critical probes outlined above.)

POLICY CRITIQUE

Feminist critics have long sought to challenge how public policy has reflected a masculinist view of the world. Enshrining the male orator as the font of political wisdom, they have argued, has thereby privileged a narrow sort of discourse: public, agonistic, competitive. (Critics may choose to combine this perspective with **critical probes** on argument, genre, or style from Chapters 5, 6, or 7.)

In her landmark study of early feminist rhetoric, Campbell [1989:11] explains the social costs women suffered when trying to embrace the male tradition:

> . . . a woman who spoke [in public] displayed her "masculinity"; that is, she demonstrated that she possessed qualities traditionally ascribed only to males. When a woman spoke, she enacted her equality, that is, she herself was proof that

she was as able as her male counterparts to function in the public sphere. That a woman speaking is such proof explains the outraged reactions to women addressing "promiscuous" audiences of men and women, sharing a platform with male speakers, debating, and preaching, even on such clearly moral issues as slavery, prostitution, and alcohol abuse. The hostility women experienced in reform efforts led them to found female reform organizations and to initiate a movement for women's rights, at base a movement claiming woman's right to engage in public moral action.

Recovering women's rhetorical history is a worthy goal, and Campbell and others (e.g., Japp [1985], Jorgensen-Earp [1990], Carlson [1994], and Griffin [1994]) have provided important analyses of early feminist oratory. Other scholars, such as Mattingly [2002:99] have reminded us that, since women's rhetorical opportunities did not usually include public speaking, we must "rethink what counts in rhetoric" and, as Enos [2002] argues, include alternate modes of expression in our historical research. Along these same lines, Foss and Griffin [1995] call for greater use (in the public as well as the private spheres), of an "invitational rhetoric," a discourse grounded in the feminist principles of equality, immanent value, and self-determination. By seeking understanding rather than control, they argue, rhetors can avoid the zero-sum game that politics too often becomes.

Some policy critiques are quite specific, targeting particular laws. María Cristina Rangel [2001:191–192], reflecting on her treatment by caseworkers during her college years as a single mother on welfare, offers a cogent feminist criticism of the rhetoric of the system:

> I had to explain myself over and over again, always living with the fear that I would not be believed and my benefits would be cut as a result. After each humiliating, intimidating interrogation, I would make my way back through the waiting room and glance at the Welfare to Work posters hanging on the waiting room walls. "Mommy, will we always be on Welfare?" "Work Works!" "Think of your children. . . . Whose footsteps do you want to see them follow in?"
>
> I was struck by how patronizing, how blaming these statements were, and how they were designed to inflict guilt on women because of the circumstances of our lives. Poverty is a matter of personal failure, they seemed to say, and ending poverty a matter of personal will. You have failed, but with our help you can become better, and then maybe your children won't be ashamed of you. Even the name of the welfare reform law hints at this blaming attitude: The Personal Responsibility and Work Opportunity Reconciliation Act. Implicit in the title is the assumption that welfare recipients refuse to accept responsibility for their lives.

Rangel, like many feminist critics, is dealing with **power, discrimination, discourse,** and **relationship.** These important foci came together quite publicly in October, 1991, during the Senate confirmation hearings for Supreme Court Justice nominee Clarence Thomas. Professor Anita Hill, a former assistant to Thomas (ironically, at the Equal Employment Opportunity Commission) charged that Thomas had sexually harassed her. She made these charges to a nervous group of U.S. senators and to a fascinated nation as well. Because the Hill/Thomas hearings involved all three branches of government (as well as the fourth estate), they were widely viewed and discussed. More important, the Hill/Thomas hearings named and displayed in public what women had suffered in private for years.

Feminist critics have treated the hearings as a microcosm of competing rhetorics. Fraser [1992:599], for example, saw the distinction between the private and public spheres as crucial to the hearings' outcome. She argues that the (first) Bush administration's attempt to forbid interrogation into Judge Thomas's private life reinscribed the public/private distinction that has long favored men over women. Such a strategy, for example, excluded expert testimony on sexual harassment, a move that:

> cast Clarence Thomas and Anita Hill in very different relations to privacy and publicity. Thomas was enabled to declare key areas of his life "private" and therefore off-limits. Hill, in contrast, was cast as someone whose motives and character would be subjects of intense scrutiny and intrusive speculation, since her "credibility" was to be evaluated in a conceptual vacuum. When the Senate Judiciary Committee adopted these ground rules for the hearings, they sealed in place a structural differential in relation to publicity and privacy that worked overwhelmingly to Thomas's advantage and to Hill's disadvantage.

Fraser shows how the advantage quickly became Thomas's when she quotes directly from the hearing itself:

SENATOR LEAHY: Did you ever have a discussion of pornographic films with . . . any other women [than Professor Hill]?

JUDGE THOMAS: Senator, I will not get into any discussions that I might have about my personal life or my sex life with any person outside of the workplace. [p. 600]

In defending his privacy so vigorously, Fraser maintains, Thomas was defending his essential masculinity since to have one's "privacy publicly probed is to risk being feminized" [p. 601]. (In other words, Thomas was resisting symbolic violation.) In addition, says Fraser, when Judge Thomas played the race card by complaining the hearings were a "high-tech lynching," he rendered Hill "functionally white." Rather quickly, says Fraser, "the black woman was erased from view" [p. 605].

Other studies show how democratic governance itself was used as a scapegoat for the abuse that otherwise might have been directed at Thomas. By engaging in a "proceduralist rhetoric," Regan [1994] discovered, participants succeeded in condemning the political process rather than sexual harassment itself. Not surprisingly, Thomas [1991:283] himself most artfully used the proceduralist approach:

> In my 43 years on this earth I have been able with the help of God to defy poverty, avoid prison, overcome segregation, bigotry, racism and obtain one of the finest educations available in this country, but I have not been able to overcome this process. . . . When there was segregation I hoped there would be fairness . . . some

day. When there was bigotry and prejudice, I hoped that there would be tolerance and understanding some day. Mr. Chairman, I am proud of my life, proud of what I have done and what I have accomplished, proud of my family and this process . . . is trying to destroy it all.

This is a dangerous rhetoric, says Regan, because it focuses attention on "extraordinary" issues (issues that lie safely beyond adjudication), rather than on ordinary crimes committed by ordinary people.

Lipari [1994:300] examined press coverage of the hearings, arguing that the press treated them as melodrama, using eroticized news stories that "trivialized the issue of sexual harassment and, by extension, women's collective claim to social and political legitimacy." Headlines like "Next Act in Drama Fails to Disappoint" domesticated the hearings, Lipari claims, thereby undercutting the charges of *illegality* made by Anita Hill.

Such rhetorical flourishes are amply demonstrated in a snippet from one of the news reports: "What happened on TV yesterday was an electric thunderbolt, a riveting tragicomedy that combined the sugar of kinky sex with the salt of power, passion and propriety" [p. 303]. Such coverage turned the hearings into a case of "he said/she said," writes Lipari, making it hard for many Americans to see sexual harassment as a crime and insuring that "the systematic subordination of women [would] appear personal and hence not at all political" [p. 307].

Finally, Beasley [1994] explains the hearings by describing their competing logics of freedom and power. The logic of freedom, Beasley notes, assumes that people are free to choose their own courses of behavior. It is this glorious logic that funds the "American Dream." The grittier logic of power, in contrast, holds that people are sometimes compelled to do "irrational" things. Employing the logic of freedom, many people (especially those unaware of their own privilege) asked why Hill would continue to work for Thomas after being so mistreated. The logic of power explains: Those with little influence (subordinates, women, people of color, the poor) do what they must to survive. The testimony of Ellen Wells, a witness for Hill, is illustrative:

> . . . I get Christmas cards from people that I do not see from one end of the year to another, and quite frankly, do not wish to. And I also return their cards and will return their calls. And these are people who have insulted me and done things which have perhaps degraded me at times, but there are also things that you have to put up with. And being a black woman, you have to put up with a lot, so you grit your teeth and you do it. [p. 297]

Many Americans fortunate enough to live their lives according to the logic of freedom (without understanding that this logic was not universally available) never really understood Wells's statement here. They could not grasp the psychology of the downtrodden. But as Susan Brownmiller pointed out in her groundbreaking book *Against Our Will: Men, Women, and Rape* [1975:5], the barely submerged threat of force (rape) is what ultimately keeps women "in their place" in patriarchal culture. Although Thomas claimed to be the victim of a high-tech lynching, many feminist critics reverse the metaphor, seeing Anita Hill as the victim of a high-tech gang rape. While the hearings did publicize the problem of sexual harassment, Thomas's successful confirmation and Hills's public humiliation also served as an intimidating object lesson: "Do not accuse the men in power above you. You, too, could get dragged through the mud, revictimized like the rape survivor in a courtroom."

NARRATIVE CRITIQUE

The narrative critique focuses on women as readers and fiction writers, and how narrative in general interacts with the female consciousness. Ever since Kate Millett's landmark book, *Sexual Politics* [1970/1990], feminist critics have called into question the androcentric "canon" of "great books" long popular in the West. Millett argued that male writers typically distorted female characters, often associating them with deviance and, simultaneously, insuring that masculine perspectives would dominate literature. (Critical probes from any of the previous chapters—e.g., Chapters 5 [narrative], 8 [lexicon], 9 [media], 10 [role] and 11 [culture]—may be fruitfully combined with this critique.)

In *The Resisting Reader*, Fetterly [1991:492–493] casts feminist criticism as inherently an act of resistance. Surveying writers from D. H. Lawrence to Ernest Hemingway, Fetterly explodes the notion of a universal "human experience," insisting that the emotional lives of women have rarely been faithfully reproduced by even great male novelists. Writers like Lawrence and Hemingway lead their female readers to think like men, says Fetterly [1991:493], arguing that:

> "Rip Van Winkle" is paradigmatic of this phenomenon [identifying with men]. While the desire to avoid work, escape authority, and sleep through the major decisions in one's life is obviously applicable to both men and women, in Irving's story this "universal" desire is made specifically male. Work, authority, and decision making are symbolized by Dame Van Winkle, and the longing for flight is defined against her. She is what one must escape from, and the "one" is necessarily male.

Most literature is dangerous, Fetterly believes, because through it women are subtly encouraged to identify against themselves. Hence, she urges women readers to adopt a strategy of constant vigilance.

Similarly, Schweickart [1991:531] is concerned with "feminist readings of [both] male . . . [and] . . . female texts." Because the Western canon has such monolithic power, she notes, a feminist:

> cannot simply refuse to read patriarchal texts, for they are everywhere, and they condition her participation in the literary and critical enterprise. In fact, by the time she becomes a feminist critic, a woman has already read numerous male texts—in particular, the most authoritative texts of the literary and critical canons. . . . The feminist story stresses that patriarchal constructs have objective as well as subjective reality; they are inside and outside the text, inside and outside the reader. [p. 541]

Feminist criticism is therefore at times a humbling enterprise, involving as it does the painful recognition of one's one patriarchal "programming."

Some feminist scholars envision dramatic ways of purging this programming. Among the most theoretically challenging of this corps are French feminists such as Luce Irigaray and Hélène Cixous, who, according to Jones [1991:359] believe that women are instinctively repelled by masculine logics and language habits and "must recognize and assert their *jouissance* [physical pleasure, first experienced in infancy and later, through sexual expression] if they are to subvert phallocentric oppression at its deepest levels" [p. 360]. Cixous holds that "women's unconscious is totally different from men's" and that women need "to overthrow masculinist ideologies and to create new female discourses" [Jones, p. 360]. Cixous develops what she calls "écriture féminin," a way of literally "writing the [female] body." "To the extent that the female body is seen as a direct source of female writing, a powerful alternative discourse seems possible: to write from the body is to recreate the world" [Jones, 1991:361]. As Jones explains, both Irigaray and Cixous believe that for women to escape oppression they must start by experiencing their unique sexuality, a sexuality that ". . . begins with their bodies, with their genital and libidinal difference from men" [p. 361].

Feminists have struggled to find ways to write that are not co-opted by masculinist expression. As poet Audre Lorde [1981:99,100] so famously said, "the master's tools will never dismantle the master's house," and therefore feminists must be on guard not to replace male forms of hierarchy with white ones:

> If white [A]merican feminist theory need not deal with the differences between us, and the resulting difference in aspects of our oppressions, then what do you do with the fact that the women who clean your houses and tend your children while you attend conferences on feminist theory are, for the most part, poor and third world women?

In response to such concerns, contemporary "third wave" feminism has included a greater emphasis on diversity issues, while maintaining the commitment to valuing individual women's life experiences. Feminist critics recognize that the power to tell one's own story is a key political move. As Daughton [1991] notes, first-person narrative is a rhetorical first resource as well as a last resort, for no one can deny the validity of another's experience. Perhaps this is why, for centuries, women were not allowed to "publicize," to make their stories known, to become their own authors. But now, according to Olsen [1978], women are filling in the silences of their missing texts.

Autobiography is an important genre because it deals with the complex issues of self, identity, authority, and experience. hooks [1991:1038] notes that "The longing to tell one's story and the process of telling [are] symbolically . . . gesture[s] of longing to recover the past in such a way that one experiences both a sense of reunion and a sense of release." Some scholars are pushing these notions further by bringing autobiographical style to the scholarly essay. In "Disciplining the Feminine," for example, Blair, Brown and Baxter [1994] respond critically to both an earlier publication (which is normal in academic journals), *and to the earlier reviews of their critique* (previously unheard of in academic journals!). Their essay illustrates the twofold purpose of autobiographical critique—to validate the author's individual voice and to invite reconsideration of what discourse (and in this case, the "discipline" of communication) is itself all about.

Sharon Olds's poem, "Rite of Passage" [1984:66], is a provocative example of both feminist criticism and autobiographical rhetoric:

RITE OF PASSAGE
As the guests arrive at my son's party
they gather in the living room—
short men, men in first grade
with smooth jaws and chins.
Hands in pockets, they stand around
jostling, jockeying for place, small fights
breaking out and calming. One says to another
How old are you? Six. I'm seven. So?
They eye each other, seeing themselves
tiny in the other's pupils. They clear their
throats a lot, a room of small bankers,
they fold their arms and frown. *I could beat you up,*
a seven says to a six,
the dark cake, round and heavy as a
turret, behind them on the table. My son,
freckles like specks of nutmeg on his cheeks,
chest narrow as the balsa keel of a
model boat, long hands
cool and thin as the day they guided him
out of me, speaks up as a host
for the sake of the group.
We could easily kill a two-year-old,
he says in his clear voice. The other
men agree, they clear their throats
like Generals, they relax and get down to
playing war, celebrating my son's life.

Clearly, Olds's poem represents the personal (autobiography) and the political (critique). The story she tells involves several rites—her son's birth, his birthday celebration and, less directly, her own passage on the journey of parenting. The poem comically and ironically blends the juvenile with the mature ("men in first grade/with smooth jaws and chins"), thereby helping the poet (and reader) integrate the various phases of life and thus get at the essential human experience of change (and our reactions to it). Olds lovingly notices "freckles like specks of nutmeg on his cheeks, / chest narrow as the balsa keel of a / model boat, long hands / cool and thin as the day they guided him / out of me." Reflecting so intimately on her birth experience turns the public poem into a private interaction with an unknown reader. Masterful though he was with language, John Donne did not write this way.

But "Rite of Passage" is also critique, with Olds's depiction of the strutting youngsters offering an acerbic commentary on patriarchal values. Calling her party guests "a room of small bankers," she cleverly reveals the incipient machismo of her son and his friends: "Hands in pockets, they stand around / jostling, jockeying for place, small fights / breaking out." The poem condenses their rumblings of aggression and invites reflection about the eventual, perhaps inevitable, loss of innocence these rumblings will exact on her son. But Olds does not assert that "boys will be boys;" instead, she makes the larger, more poignant (even sinister?) claim: "boys will be men." Including bankers and generals in her metaphors makes the poem highly political, implying direct links among male authority, economic domination and physical violence.

But Olds's poem, because it is a poem and because it is a careful feminist analysis that avoids oversimplification, does not close us down entirely. She leaves us wondering about the precise "policy options" she might endorse. Her poem is richly ambiguous, leading us to see the boys' strength and vulnerability, inviting complicated reactions. Should we celebrate (or laugh indulgently at) their confidence? Enjoy their innocence? Mourn the normalization of violence, hierarchy, domination? All of the above, we suspect. The best feminist criticism, like the poem itself, is multidimensional, exploring the layered possibilities for a text's interpretation. Olds is a feminist, yes, but she is also a mother, making her poem both portrait and lens. Her autobiographical approach lets us see Olds-the-mother, but Olds-the-critic lets us see *through her* as well. Her move is deft. As we saw in Chapter 10, featuring the self can create quite an appeal. Olds capitalizes on that, making it harder for readers to dismiss her as an unthinking ideologue. Rhetoric and poetry conjoined are a potent blend indeed.

REPRESENTATIONAL CRITIQUE

The representational critique examines female portrayals in culture, especially in television and cinema, with an eye to determining how social policies are advanced or retarded by these portrayals. (Critical probes from Chapter 9, especially those about the visual image, may be especially helpful here.) Laura Mulvey's oft-anthologized 1975 essay, "Visual Pleasure and Narrative Cinema," has been a springboard for much criticism. Mulvey [1991:436] maintains that there are three "looks" in a Hollywood film: (1) the look of the camera, (2) the look of the audience, and (3) the look of the character. Of special interest is her notion of the "male gaze" of the camera, which means that women are "simultaneously looked at and displayed, with their appearance coded for strong visual and erotic impact" so that they come to have that most precious of Hollywood qualities, *"looked-at-ness."*

Mulvey argues that in Hollywood films men serve as the "bearer of the look" and this grants them special subjectivity, a preferred point-of-view. Women in films are denied these essential aspects of character and hence function as pure spectacle. In essence, the rhetoric of the film teaches an audience (even its female members) to see female characters from the male character's perspective—as erotic, perhaps pathetic, but hardly dimensional. Mulvey's point is thus like Fetterly's, in that women are being taught to identify against themselves. Although Mulvey's essay is thirty years old now, the male gaze (of camera, actor, and spectator) is still at work in selfconsciously postfeminist television programs such as *Ally McBeal* [Vavrus, 2000] and Hollywood blockbusters like *Charlie's Angels.* Even in the Academy Award–nominated *Catch Me If You Can,* each female character serves to refocus us on Frank Abagnale's *chutzpah,* charm, and unparalleled success.

Williams [1984:83] notes that the horror film is a particularly interesting genre for examining "when the woman looks." Almost always, says Williams, the horror film punishes the female character for her gaze (the gaze, after all, being a primordial act of human empowerment). So there are excellent reasons for the female spectator to cover her eyes during such films, "not the least of which is that she is often asked to bear witness to her own powerlessness in the face of rape, mutilation and murder." But there are more subtle reasons to do so as well since "women are given so little to identify with on the screen." Unlike her male counterpart, the female character in horror films looks directly at the "monster's freakishness," thus having her wits scared out of her (literally). And yet a bizarre kind of "sympathy and affinity" often develops between monster and female victim, Williams continues, an eventuality that is "less an expression of sexual desire . . . and more a flash of sympathetic identification" between two marginalized entities [p. 88].

Similarly, in *Tough Guise* [2000] Jackson Katz notes that horror films usually time the monster's attacks for a moment immediately following the partial disrobing of one or more nubile young women, thus ensuring that young heterosexual males are aroused—and learn to associate violence with sex. Katz posits that such imagery helps us make sense of the continued rise in rape statistics, even while numbers of other violent crimes have declined.

The male gaze has reached the news media, as well. Feminist critics might note (as did the BBC [2003:1]) a disturbing pattern in the obsessive U.S. press coverage of young, beautiful, slim, white, blonde females as "tragic victims": Nicole Brown Simpson; JonBenet Ramsey; Elizabeth Smart; Jessica Lynch. Of course these *are* tragedies—"The point is not to downplay these girls' suffering, it is to show how the media obsesses over the stories when attractive white people are involved, and shows little or no interest in the 'tragedies' that don't involve blonde little white girls. It is not more tragic when beautiful females are victims, but it is certainly tragic that the media treat it that way." Lynch, for example, was not the only POW, nor even the only American female taken prisoner that day. Shoshana Johnson—a member of

Lynch's unit, wounded in the same ambush (Johnson was actually shot, whereas Lynch sustained injuries from a vehicular accident), was also kept as a POW—*for 12 days after Lynch was rescued*. Upon her release, the military offered Johnson 30% disability pay, in comparison to the 80% Lynch was receiving. Where were the media angst, the book deal, the TV movie? Johnson was not blonde and blue-eyed, but African American. She did not fit the requirements of the male gaze and did not thus become a media darling, although her "tragedy" was quite similar to Lynch's.

Are males the only ones who look? Of course not. Mayne [1984:55] uses the metaphor of a woman looking through a keyhole to describe the *female* gaze in traditional cinema, claiming that "the history of women's relationship to the cinema . . . has been a series of tentative peeks." In the "woman's film" genre popular throughout the 1930s, 1940s and 1950s, Mayne explains, male filmmakers tried to create films for a female audience. The melodramatic nature of such films earned them the sobriquet "the weepies" (precursors to soap operas). Doane [1984:80] points out that these films typically desexualized the female body, removing the focus from female action to the most superficial of emotional experiences. This is ultimately problematic, says Doane, because "to desexualize the female body is ultimately to deny its very existence." In other words, Hollywood has typically given women two choices: Be objectified or be invisible.

Even films hailed by Hollywood as triumphs for women are not necessarily seen as such by feminist critics. For example, in the *Bridget Jones's Diary* films, women's common experiences are affirmed, yes, but the title character's strength gets frequently undermined (or backgrounded) by her obsessive concern about her sexual attractiveness to men. This is not to say that feminist critics must deny the pleasures of such films, but rather (in the language of Chapter 2), when they do their criticism, they seek to remain skeptical, discerning, and hard to distract. And just as with the Lip Cremes ad that began this chapter, feminist critics often find cause for celebration *and* concern, amusement *and* chagrin—in the same artifact. In short, we do well to remember two things: (1) placing women in leading roles often has little to do with feminism and (2) the male gaze still insures a box office draw.

A subset of the representational critique we might call the **corporeal critique,** which focuses on how the human body becomes implicated in the messages we share with one another. For example, Nelson [1994] writes about the ways in which female athletes have been sexualized to appeal to a male sports audience, so that the well-toned body becomes decorative instead of "merely" functional. Likewise, Feder [1994] dissects the "overdetermined femininity" in "ladies" figure skating, positing that its main purpose is to reassure men of women's frailty, even in the face of the Olympians' incontrovertible strength. And as Hayden [2001] found, even simple descriptions of biology can prove wildly amusing, demonstrating mad attempts to naturalize female passivity and male activity—*at the cellular level!* Hayden found that contemporary sexuality education texts reproduced strict gendered assumptions, in statements such as "in a dream-like, slow motion ballet, the tiny cilia caress the ripe ovum and gently move it along," and "Semen is very powerful stuff. You know how during a game football players drink Gatorade, which is packed full of sugar and vitamins, to give them an instant energy boost? Well, semen is like Gatorade for sperm. . . . Once the sperm get a shot of semen, they start whipping their tails around like wild and moving all over the place" [pp. 42–43]. The stylistic differences between the two texts could hardly be more pronounced, thus assuring teenage readers that girls really are naturally soft, gentle, and graceful, while boys really are, well, rather frenetic.

Corporeal critics often note how the male gaze has been transferred from cinema to advertising, for example, and how women have been taught to internalize this gaze, and turn it upon—and against—their own bodies. One such critic, Susan Bordo, has been particularly influential. In her book, *Unbearable Weight* [1993], Bordo critiques American culture (as well as educational, social, and economic institutions) for creating the kind of low self-esteem among women that results in eating disorders, plastic surgery, and rampant consumerism. Examining the causes of anorexia and bulimia and the relentless advertising campaigns that foster them, Bordo finds that "The general tyranny of fashion—perpetual, elusive, and instructing the female body in a pedagogy of personal inadequacy and lack—is a powerful discipline for the normalization of *all* women in this culture" [p. 254]. Bordo identifies two rhetorical moves that are especially debilitating: (1) normalization, whereby women are urged to conform to a particular standard of beauty and femininity and (2) homogenization, which tells all women to look alike. Along with teaching women to be insecure about their bodies, she says, society teaches women how to *see* their bodies. When the cultural ideal becomes progressively slimmer, therefore, women at or even below their optimum weight tend to feel fat.

As she writes in the preface to the tenth anniversary edition of the book [2003:B6],

> "How to Interpret Your Body 101." It's become a global requirement; eventually, everyone must enroll. Fiji is just one example. Until television was introduced in 1995, the islands had no reported cases of eating disorders. In 1998, three years after programs from the United States and Britain began broadcasting there, 62 percent of the girls surveyed reported dieting. The anthropologist Anne Becker was surprised by the change; she had thought that Fijian aesthetics, which favored voluptuous bodies, would "withstand" the influence of media images. Becker hadn't yet understood that we live in an empire of images and there are no protective borders.

Bordo illustrates this problem by comparing advertisements from both the 1960s and the 1990s, noting that "What was considered an ideal body in 1960 [Figure 13.1] is currently defined as 'full figure' [Figure 13.2] . . . , requiring special fashion accommodations!" Given the changing standards, Bordo argues,

FIGURE 13.1 Lady Marlene Ad

FIGURE 13.2 Figure Plus Ad

". . . the anorectic does not 'misperceive' her body; rather she has learned all too well the dominant cultural standards of *how* to perceive" it [1993:57].

In the decade since her book's first and second editions, Bordo notes that, once an oddity, plastic surgery has become normalized, almost required.

> Am I immune? Of course not. I want my lines, bags, and sags to disappear. . . . There's a limit, though, to what fruit acids can do. As surgeons develop ever more extensive and fine-tuned procedures to correct gravity and erase history from the faces of their patients, the difference between the cosmetically altered and the rest of us grows more and more dramatic.
>
> "The rest of us" includes not only those who resist or are afraid of surgery but the many people who cannot afford basic health care, let alone aesthetic tinkering. . . .
>
> Undergraduates . . . are the ones most likely to "get it." . . . They know. They understand that you can be as cynical as you want about the ads—and many of them are—and still feel powerless to resist their messages. They are aware that virtually every advertisement, every magazine cover, has been digitally modified and that very little of what they see is "real." That doesn't stop them from hating their own bodies for failing to live up to computer-generated standards. [2003:B7]

We can hope that the standards will change again soon. Perhaps they will. (Bordo [2003:B9] notes a glimmer of hope in the low-rider jeans and soft, exposed bellies of today's young women, unashamed of their rounded flesh.) But the bottom line is always power. Whose interests are served when women (and increasing numbers of body-conscious men) are kept busy by the never-ending task of consuming in order to "perfect" the body? It is important to realize that these self-obsessions have an invisible cost. They encourage women to devote a great deal of their time, energy, and money to working out, clothes shopping, glamorizing, dieting and surgically enhancing their bodies. If, instead, the average woman spent that minimum of 5–15 hours (and $10–20) a week working for hunger relief/political reform/support services for the disabled, etc., what might our world look like? It is a safe bet that power and material resources would be more evenly distributed, and of course, this would disgruntle those who currently have most of them. Feminist critics want to remind women that these choices are still available, although our culture often hides the choice-making involved by positing certain "requirements" for femininity.

PERFORMATIVE CRITIQUE

Sociologist Erving Goffman is well-known for his notion of the *Presentation of Self in Everyday Life* [1959], which, like Burke's dramatism (Chapter 12), sees our daily life as performance. Similarly, but more specifically, Judith Butler

[1990:278] asserts that gender "is real only to the extent that it is performed." Unlike biological determinists, performative critics argue that gender is not a static thing but a fluid process open to change. Imagine, for example, a long clothes rack. The outfits at one end represent hyper-femininity; at the other, hyper-masculinity. At the center is androgyny, the balancing of masculine and feminine. We can then think of gender as coming into existence only when a person tries on an outfit and *performs* a role. Performative rhetorical criticism studies the embodiment of gender (race, class, etc.), through written analysis, staged productions, and various levels of enactment between the two. (The critical probes on role analysis [Chapter 9] and dramatism [Chapter 12] are especially well-suited to this critique.)

When a male student is asked to perform a female heroine in class, for example, he may confront his maleness in a self-reflective way for the first time. More important, he is asked to experience gender in a way that the silent reading of *Little Women* could never teach him. While biological *sex* is ours at birth, we are taught *gender* by society. The challenge for the critic, then, is to examine the performed artifact (whether in everyday life or onstage) to see how it becomes gendered and what happens to performer and audience as a result.

Take stand-up comedy, for example. While men have dominated that arena, female performers increasingly populate U.S. comedy clubs and cable shows. But given the aggressive history of the genre, how can a woman know what to do, or be, in such a venue? Can she even perform femaleness in such a format? Comic performances are revealing because they often use exaggeration (of gender, race, etc.), and the *public* pressures of performance make obvious what ordinary social life typically leaves unclear.

Gilbert [2004] describes the most popular rhetorical postures of the female comic, tracing these postures back to the limited options available to women on the nineteenth-century stage. Gilbert argues that the five comedic roles she found are all ways of performing marginality. By ingratiation, intimidation, or supplication, the female comic exemplifies some of the stock options available to women in the less dramatized spheres of everyday life. "The Kid" urges us to pay no attention to the fact that she is a woman while "The Bawd" demands otherwise. "The Bitch" habitually uses "'putdown' humor as a form of social critique" and thus makes an active play for social dominance [p. 108]. Like The Kid, "The Reporter" performs gender androgynously, using observational remarks carefully adapted to middle-class tastes. "The Whiner" apologizes for her femaleness, hoping to curry favor on patriarchal terms. Admittedly, these personae are terribly conventionalized, and everyday life presents women with richer options. But studying humor is important for it points us to our vulnerabilities.

And we feel most vulnerable when most acutely aware of our inability to control events such as birth and death. A great deal of performative, rhetorical critique happens during staged performance. For example, in her solo show and follow-up essay, Pineau [2000] narrates and theorizes about her experiences with the medical establishments in Canada and the United States, respectively, as her mother was dying and her daughter was being born. In an attempt to avoid major surgery (Caesarean section) when her baby was "overdue," Pineau agreed to have her labor artificially induced by the drug Pitocin, which brings on contractions more painful and forceful than those experienced naturally. Her poetic prose evokes both her feminine cultural training as a "good little girl" and the sense of violation and loss that ensues when hospital personnel (strangers) become "intimate," doing things good little girls should not have done to them:

> It is the afternoon of the second day and we've been working hard, the machine and I, to count each drip of my chemical labor, to make each drip count. To breathe and relax and count the contractions and visualize them working the way that they should, the way I've been told that they would if I follow directions, if I do . . . what they want. . . . It's got to be working, just look at the monitor. And so I smile when they greet me this afternoon of the second day, like a child offering up to her teachers her homework on which she is sure to receive a gold star.
>
> Good afternoon. I am Robin, Mary, Ellen, Sue, Bob, Nancy, Francis, Tom, Dick, and Harry and I am here to examine you. To assess your cervix. To measure progression. Just lie back and relax. . . .
>
> I try to relax. I really do. I try my hardest. . . . And we all look away while they do it. . . . Look away to a place where it's OK to have strangers put their hands on your body, where it's OK to say yes and not mean it, to think no and not say it, where penetration is necessary, where sex is the site but never the issue; it's never at issue and you both understand that sex isn't at issue and so it's OK.
>
> But it isn't. It just isn't.
>
> Because even when it's gentle, and even when it's considerate, and even when it's necessary, they are still strangers: Robin, Mary, Ellen, Sue, Bob, Nancy, Francis, Tom, Dick, and Harry who have entered my body and made me stranger to myself.
>
> Because it's not about sex. It's about access. [p. 7]

Pineau's performed narrative both critiques and enacts the complex dance between the public and the private, between compliance and resistance, that is "woman birthing in a hospital" in this culture. Although she does not offer a dispassionate argument on the advantages and disadvantages of home birth versus hospital birth, the bitterness of her irony implicitly critiques the system that empowers any and every passing stranger (from "Robin" to "Tom, Dick, and Harry") to "peer" at a most private part of her body and judge her "success" in meeting standardized rules for "birthing progress." And she implicitly critiques her own participation in this system, as well. Performative critiques such as Pineau's "make the personal political" in exceptionally powerful ways, thereby inviting audiences to explore their own performed lives with greater awareness.

The critic operating from this perspective gives women (and men) an extraordinarily liberating option by assuming that **rhetorical performances**—not biology, sociology, history, or destiny—makes woman woman. Performance has always asked us to confront life itself. With regard to gender, it asks if we have yet discovered all our ways of being. We act out our self-definitions each day, says the performative rhetorical critic. By behaving, in other words, we become who and what we are.

CONCLUSION

Feminist criticism challenges business as usual, requiring that we examine power inequities in everyday life, particularly in the area of gendered assumptions. At times this can be uncomfortable, because it involves opening our eyes to sometimes harsh realities. But the rewards can be great and the stakes can be high. (And, to paraphrase the bumper sticker, if ignorance really were bliss, wouldn't more people be happy?)

A particular strength of feminist criticism is in helping us see traditional texts in new ways. As Ruthven [1984:13] says, it is not so important that we all "write criticism" as that we "incorporate the lessons of feminism into everything [we] write." And those lessons are twofold: (1) to question what we think we know about rhetoric in case it is only what men know and (2) to assess the consequences of rhetoric that historically has treated half the human race as inconsequential.

Although, as Green [2001:275] puts it, "no one owns the definition of feminism and . . . all feminists don't agree on every issue," most feminisms coalesce around a set of shared values. In the language of Richard Weaver, feminists' "God Terms" (Chapter 8) are the very human values of Respect, Dignity, Fairness, and Compassion. Like other ideological critics, feminist critics work to uncover and thereby weaken the structures of oppression. Ideological critics recognize that the greatest oppression of all occurs when our minds are "colonized" by popular discourses. It is one thing for rhetoric to change behavior. Far more profound is when it alters our very habits of mind. But resistance is empowering, and feminist criticism offers on-the-job-training in resistance.

TIPS FOR THE PRACTICING CRITIC

1. Feminist criticism is a set of questions rather than answers. These questions can be used with other critical probes about argument, style, narrative, genre, dramatism, and so on, as the critic sees fit, in order to get at

the ways in which artifacts are gendered, and how they invite us to perform our own genders.

2. Critics of feminism often assume that because feminist criticism leads with its ideology it is less valid. But in truth, there are no ideology-free approaches to criticism. Every text, and every reading of a text, is ideological in that the critic privileges some questions and fails to ask others. It is those approaches that claim "objectivity" of which we should be most suspicious.

Chapter 14

IDEOLOGICAL CRITICISM

Last month, a survey was conducted by the U.N. worldwide. The only question asked was, "Would you please give your most honest opinion about solutions to the food shortage in the rest of the world?" The survey was a HUGE failure. In Africa they did not know what "food" meant. In Western Europe they did not know what "shortage" meant. In Eastern Europe they did not know what "opinion" meant. In the Middle East they did not know what "solution" meant. In South America they did not know what "please" meant. In Asia they did not know what "honest" meant. And in the USA they did not know what "the rest of the world" meant. [received via email, 2002]

This bit of cultural reportage blends political and social critique to form a bitter joke of the sort circulated so often on the Internet. Relatively few places, it would seem (Canada, Greenland, Central America, Australia, New Zealand, and assorted small islands) are exempt from this equal-opportunity offender. The anonymous rhetor here operates as an **ideological critic,** one who specifies (or in this case, clearly implies) the political standard (Chapter 2) by which the critic believes rhetorical acts and artifacts should be judged. Like feminism (Chapter 13), other forms of ideological criticism serve as lenses through which critics focus not only on the rhetorical strategies of a particular artifact, but on its social and political goals. Thus, they focus on **the ends as well as the means** of rhetoric, and subject those ends to **judgment.** In this sense, ideological critics merely make explicit what other rhetorical critics do more implicitly, often without being aware they are doing it. In this chapter, we will briefly discuss three types of ideological critique: deconstructionist, Marxist, and postcolonial criticism.

Like a deconstructionist critic, the joke above playfully demonstrates the way the meanings of words refuse to stay put, even within a single sentence. Like a Marxist critic, the narrative reveals the shocking disparities of material wealth in the world, from not knowing what "food" meant, to not knowing what "shortage" meant. Like a postcolonial critic, the joke reserves its most pungent critique for those who do not reflect upon the exploitive relationships between "the West and the rest."

Although each of these types of criticism is unique, they share some features. Each grew out of disillusionment with the established order in Europe and in the former colonies of European nations. And since the latter part of the twentieth century, each has become a powerful source of influence upon scholars in the United States, despite the long-standing American preference for liberal or pluralistic philosophies and pragmatic, functional methodologies.

What do they have in common? Like feminist criticism, each type of criticism can be practiced in conjunction with other specific critical foci and can borrow **critical probes** from other chapters in this text. In general, they are more leftist than rightist, and they share a concern with exposing the power dimensions of rhetorical artifacts. How do they differ? Marxists believe in undermining exploitive economic systems, postcolonial critics believe in privileging the voices of the oppressed, those previously colonized, and deconstructionists believe in . . . not believing.

Not surprisingly, then, each type of critic would offer distinctive observations about the joke with which we began this chapter. Deconstructionists are interested in the **linguistic integrity** of a text: how well its arguments hang together, how internally consistent its images are, how well it resists vacuums (or **aporia**) of meaning. Such critics might note that, as the joke progresses, it invites the reader to laugh (or cry) at the painful dispensation of each region or continent, presuming that the reader understands each key term in the survey question. Therefore, as each country is listed, its citizens ("they") are shown not to be the designated readers of this text. Given which country has the most English-language Internet users and appears last on the list, we can guess that the joke is intended for an American audience. But, a deconstructionist might observe, even as the joke purports to stand outside of (and critique) multiple cultures, that supposedly "superior, objective" standpoint, vanishes beneath the rhetor's feet. (By the end of the joke, if the reader is a U.S. American, he or she should not be able to understand anything but the last clause of the joke.) Deconstructionists make no attempt to honor a rhetor's intentions since they observe that all meanings are the arbitrary products of rhetor-audience negotiations. Such readings create problems for a text—or rather, point up problems a text creates for itself. They try to reduce the rhetor's hold on the audience by showing the inevitable **self-contradictions** in human discourse.

A Marxist might applaud the apparent concern for a more equitable distribution of resources, but be skeptical that the top-down, merely linguistic approach (a survey from the United Nations) would be likely to effect local,

material change. Marxist critics would also investigate the context of the joke itself, to question how these food shortages have occurred in the first place: What **economic systems** have allowed starvation and malnourishment in the midst of record-breaking crop production? How and why has it been possible for such extremes to co-exist? What rhetorical discourses have been used (and how) to make these food shortages seem to be a "natural" (though surely regrettable) occurrence?

A postcolonial critic might point out that the joke clearly presumes that Western, Enlightenment standards for rational civil discourse (please, honest, solution) are universal standards. Also, the critic would say, the narrative totalizes, or overgeneralizes, about citizens by continent, rather than recognizing the complex of factors that go into the formation of identity, knowledge, and attitudes. Postcolonial critics recognize that the former colonial subjects (and their descendents, wherever they live) are unable to claim a single, coherent national or cultural identity. Thus, the joke claims to speak about and for the oppressed, but in fact, further silences them, by refusing to recognize their distinctive voices.

These schools of thought are not part of a single, monolithic consciousness but they embrace three general themes:

1. *All criticism is politically self-interested.* As Jameson [1981:58] argues, virtually any statement a critic makes has latent historical or theoretical assumptions. Whenever we look at something, we do so with all of our habitual ways of looking, including our biases, hunches, and deep-seated uncertainties. Thus, to enjoy a Dr. Pepper commercial featuring dancing teenagers and their dancing grandparents may expose our belief that physical energy is central to a meaningful life. This assumption may betray yet other assumptions we have about aging (i.e., that it is best when it looks like non-aging) as well as about politics (i.e., that state funding for the care of sedentary geriatric patients should not be increased). In other words, ideological critics believe that feigning objectivity when doing criticism denies who we are as people.

2. *Criticism should be expansionistic.* Ideological critics often study previously ignored texts. In contrast, says Wander [1983:3], U.S. critics have typically studied texts produced by "the monopoly of officialdom"—white, Anglo-Saxon, centrist males—thereby producing rhetorical theories of doubtful generalizability. To correct for such limitations, says Lentricchia [1983:15], the ideological critic tries "to re-read culture so as to amplify and strategically position the marginalized voices of the ruled, exploited, oppressed, and excluded." Immigrant family stories, experimental fiction, and punk rock culture offer the critic opportunities to "open a space within which . . . resistance may be heard" [Grossberg, 1984:416]. Such critics practice what Ricoeur calls a "hermeneutics of suspicion" [Ruthven, 1984:35], which helps prevent them from being tripped up by the forces of power and insure that they listen to the voices that had been muted or ignored.

3. *Criticism should be oppositional.* Ideological critics believe that their U.S. counterparts have been too willing to honor the text the author had in mind. The very title of E. D. Hirsch's classic, *Validity in Interpretation* [1967], suggests that, heretofore, the only way for a traditional critic to know a text was the author's way, resulting in a gospel of "intentionalism" that reproduced the author's worldview. Ideological critics show no such obeisance to the author. They often become "resistant readers" [Fetterly, 1987] who accept no utterance at face value and who instead examine a text for what they find interesting, whether or not it coincides with the author's intended interpretation.

In short, ideological critics ask questions not always asked, indeed, questions they cannot always answer. However, this especially recommends them, for such critics are now producing some of the most interesting work being done. Kenneth Burke, in many ways a kindred spirit, counseled that criticism should be more than just an intellectual exercise. For criticism to be insightful, as it must be, probing, as it can be, and pluralistic, as it should be, we must "take our work home" with us and become "responsible to the larger social project" [Lentricchia, 1983:151].

When beginning ideological analysis, critical probes such as the following may be useful:

- What kind of social or political attitudes or statements would fit in with this text? What would not? Why?
- How is this text contributing to oppression and/or helping to throw it off?
- What elements of the message contradict and/or reinforce the status quo?

DECONSTRUCTIONIST CRITIQUE

Born out of the social turmoil that swept through Europe in the 1960s, deconstruction is "intensely skeptical of all claims to truth" [Norris, 1982:57]. To deconstruct is to take apart a rhetorical message, to examine how well a text "holds" its author's ideas without revealing unintended meanings. Given such obstreperous goals, it is not surprising that deconstruction was spawned by frustration. Its founders were French thinkers—Jacques Derrida, Michel Foucault, and Roland Barthes—who disdained the Western Establishment that fostered the Vietnam War, student repression, and racial segregation.

Moreover, they decried Establishment academics for their embrace of positivism (a love of things scientific), formalism (a reverence for the aesthetic, rather than the social, aspects of texts), and structuralism (the scientific study of texts). Deconstructionists, then, are *post*-structuralists, meaning that they take as problematic the structuralist commitment to uncovering the rules that govern texts. They do not view language "as a complex but stable system whose constituents can be securely established" but as "an unreliable structure that violates its own rules" [Barney, 1987:179].

Deconstructionists have been accused (e.g., by Michael Walzer [1988]) of being anarchists who treat communication as an impossibility and who are, as a result, nothing more than radical debunkers. Their detractors charge that deconstructionists flee from the patient work of disciplined criticism. But such criticism, deconstructionists respond, too often becomes unenlightening, "mere paraphrasing" of a message rather than rich analysis.

The alternative, say the deconstructionists, is criticism that challenges rather than confirms critics' assumptions, explores rather than retraces textual features, and subverts rather than accepts rhetorical artistry. Deconstructionists resist the charge that they are political saboteurs costumed as critics, arguing that the nature of textuality demands their approach, because of three crucial premises:

1. *Meaning is problematic.* The mystery of language is the central issue here. Language is **polysemous:** the "same" word means different things to different people, and to the same person on different occasions. Accordingly, deconstruction turns into linguistic skepticism because of what Derrida has called the constant "deferral" of meaning in a text.

One factor demanding such deferral, says Moi [1985:106], is **language structure.** For example, the simple sentence "She sat on the camp fire stool" defers understanding until the final word, and in fact, changes its meaning with each ensuing word. If instability is true at such elementary levels, the deconstructionists argue, how can a critic expect to settle, once and for all, the complete meaning of a verbal text?

Cooper [1988] provided an interesting example of this principle. She noted, for example, that Richard Nixon's famed "Checkers" speech succeeded in exonerating him in 1952. At the same time, says Cooper, that speech put the *personal* lives of politicians on the press's agenda forevermore. Ironically, then, it may have been this Nixon-inspired concern over personal character that sustained the media's investigation of the Watergate burglaries twenty years later. According to this logic, the ultimate "meaning" of the "Checkers" speech was Nixon's resignation from the presidency.

Verbal context further complicates the picture, says Ryan [1982:12], who notes that the "God" in "God damn" and in "God of our Fathers" are very different Gods indeed. As a result, says Sumner [1979:149], every text will have a "surplus of meaning," which changes the critic's job considerably. Rather than looking for a message's "best" meaning, deconstructionists seek out its widest range of meanings by asking: In how many *different* ways might people come to understand this text?

Dow [2001] provides an example, writing on the 1997 "coming out" episodes of the sitcom *Ellen.* While many interpreted the title character/performer's coming out as liberation, Dow sees reason for caution in the mostly heterosexual audience the show's producers (and DeGeneres herself) were targeting for appeal. Following Foucault, Dow notes that confession to a potentially unsupportive audience, rather than being freeing, can be "to escape from one power relation only to enter another" [p. 127].

Social context, therefore, makes meaning difficult to establish. Take a statement like the following, says Belsey [1980:52]: "Democracy will ensure that we extend the boundaries of civilization." Would this statement sound different, Belsey asks, to residents of Western democracies (suggesting free speech, consumer choice, open elections) than to residents of the so-called Third World (invoking colonial exploitation, guerilla warfare, cultural decadence)? Belsey says that such a statement would sound different still if mouthed by a conservative member of Parliament in Great Britain, by a committed socialist, or by the International Vice President of Pepsi Cola. This sentence will not stand still, Belsey argues, and we cannot pretend in criticism that it will.

Given these roadblocks to easy meaning, someone must become equipped to deal with what Culler [1982:220] calls "the uncanny irrationality of texts." Someone must realize that chaos is not something the radical critic adds to a text but something that constitutes the text initially. Someone must ask the questions about "real meaning" that traditionalists have been afraid to ask. The deconstructionist does.

2. *All messages are intertwined.* Every text bears the markings of its persuasive field (Chapter 3), the messages to which it responds and which respond to it. The ideal critic, says Barthes [1981:39], views the text as an "intertext" woven from the threads of other texts. The critic looks for the traces of these other messages within the text so that its "pluralistic" effects can be gauged. As a result, deconstructionists "often show scant respect for the wholeness or integrity of individual works" [Culler, 1982:220] but are more interested in the general themes that echo through society. While deconstructionists sometimes visit with an individual text, they rarely stay for long.

To take a pedestrian example of intertextuality, we might ask why Internet chatrooms are so popular. A deconstructionist might observe that they contain (and are contained by) gossip, flirting, counseling, obscene phone-calling, stage drama, and even prostitution (available companionship 24/7). Each of these genres carries its own "charge" for participants, which can "detonate" from time to time, thereby increasing the medium's overall rhetorical "explosion." And because these subdiscourses are mutually implicative, their power is increased all the more. Hence the job of the deconstructionist: to reveal the seams in the fabric of Internet chatrooms by asking whether audiences really wish to become addicted to discourse emerging from the rather squalid worlds of gossip and obscene phone-calling.

As Goodall [1994] demonstrates, a political campaign is no different. After all, when the average citizen "inhales" a campaign, he or she absorbs snippets of campaign rock music, head shots of the candidates, newscasts, long-winded speeches, *Daily Show* parodies, and thousands upon thousands of additional images. "A" campaign, then, is a rich but unstable thing and hence its meanings must be plural.

Deconstructionists say that we cannot escape intertextuality, that subtexts affect not only how we listen and read, but how we are *prepared* to listen and read. So, for example, U.S. Americans view the Civil War (or, the War Between the States) differently depending upon their previous exposure to Northern or Southern myths. Because of this complexity, deconstructionist criticism challenges the univocal interpretation of any text. As Foucault [1981:70] points out, for example, madness and hypersexuality have been the object of scorn *and reverence* at different points in human history. Thus, unless a text's meanings are pluralized, an old rhetoric may gain new, unwarranted popularity because its "textual history" has been forgotten or not plainly established in the first place.

3. *Rhetoric is problematic.* Heretofore, most deconstructionists have spent their time unmasking authors by demonstrating the clever tricks they have used to fabricate rationality in a fictional world. While traditional critics have assumed that the author knew what he or she was doing when composing a text, deconstructionists have made no such assumption. They proclaim "the Death of the Author" [Belsey, 1980:139], approaching texts in ways that might well horrify their creators. As a result, deconstructionists often call authors to task for the "texts" they wittingly or unwittingly reproduce anew.

Partly because deconstruction has been used primarily in literary studies, but mostly because they are good skeptics, deconstructionists approach rhetoric as if it were literature. They emphasize rhetoric's fabricated status so that people will learn to question the Declaration of Independence just as sharply as they do the *Canterbury Tales.* Equally, the deconstructionist approaches literature as rhetoric, warning readers not to become so relaxed in its presence that they forget it can also affect their social attitudes and expectations. Tracking strategic devices in an artifact—rhetorical or literary—sheds light on how a rhetor privileges one meaning over its many alternatives. By "pluralizing" an artifact in this way, the critic disrupts its power.

Given these premises, we may envision deconstructionists as ordinary rhetorical critics on steroids, having had extra doses of the key critical qualities (Chapter 2) of **skepticism, discernment,** and **imagination**—along with large doses of **self-reflexivity** and **playful free association.** But how does one deconstruct a text? And what political values serve as the standard here? The deconstructionist's answers to questions of purpose and method can be frustrating. For one thing, they rarely worry about producing answers. Their business is producing (or reproducing) questions. Deconstruction is therefore never a completed process. Its goals are (1) to "exhaust" a text so that its multiple meanings become clearer and (2) to contrast what a rhetor intends for an artifact with the other intentions a critic might find in it.

As for critical method, there is none. Not really. Rather, the critic operates creatively, teasing out themes and inconsistencies in a text, starting down one path and then another, looking for semantic uncertainty until it is time to stop. (A deconstructionist never definitively *concludes.*) When doing criticism, a deconstructionist will frequently "seize on some apparently peripheral fragment in the work—a footnote, a recurrent minor term or image, a casual allusion—and work it tenaciously through to the point where it threatens to dismantle the oppositions which govern the text as a whole. The tactic of the deconstructive critic . . . is to show how texts come to embarrass their own ruling systems of logic" [Eagleton, 1983:133].

But while deconstructionists might dismiss purpose as illusory and critical method as pedantic, they do persistently focus on certain textual features. To avoid complete bewilderment, we will critically probe these features (**absolute, figurative, hierarchical,** and **inconsistent language**) during a sample deconstruction. (Critical probes from Chapters 7, 8, and 12 may also be of use, given the deconstructionist's close attention to style and hierarchy.) But what sort of text deserves the rather rough treatment deconstruction can hand out? Aune [1983:260] provides a clue when he recalls that Derrida and company were especially suspicious of the "transcendental significations" of formalized rhetoric. Derrida had in mind here such things as legal statutes, religious coda, scientific reports, and political oratory.

He might also have had Gerry Ford in mind. We will assume that he did, and here consider the simple remarks President Ford gave on July 1, 1976, just prior to the opening of a Centennial safe that had been sealed at the U.S. Capitol a century before.

(1) Thank you very much, Senator Mansfield, Mr. Speaker, Senator Scott, Senator Brooke, Congressman Boggs, distinguished Members of the House and Senate, ladies and gentlemen:

(2) Obviously, I am deeply honored to have the opportunity this afternoon to open this historic Centennial safe. It contains many items of interest to us today as we celebrate the completion of our second century. But it symbolizes much more than a valuable collection of mementos, it symbolizes something about the United States of America that is so mighty and so inspiring that it cannot be locked up in a safe—I mean the American spirit.

(3) When this safe was sealed, Americans looked forward to the future, to this year of 1976. There was no doubt in their minds that a President of a free government would participate in a ceremony here in the United States Capitol Building.

(4) Just as American men and women 200 years ago looked to the future, those who sealed this safe 100 years ago also looked to the future. So it is today with Americans. But there is no safe big enough to contain the hopes, the energies, the abilities of our people. Our real national treasure does not have to be kept under lock and key in a safe or in a vault. America's wealth is not in material objects, but in our great heritage, our freedom, and our belief in ourselves. . . .

(5) In 1876 our immense wealth, both natural and inventive, commanded world-wide attention. We grew from coast to coast in greater industrial and agricultural development than humanity had ever known. In 1876 America was still emerging from a terrible fraternal war. A lesser people might have been unequal to the challenge, but 1976 finds the confidence of 1876 confirmed.

(6) Today there is far greater equality of opportunity, liberty, and justice for all of our citizens in every corner of America. There is rising prosperity for our Nation and peace and progress for our people.

(7) We look back to the evening of July 4, 1776. It was then, after the adoption of the Declaration of Independence, that the Continental Congress resolved that Franklin, Adams, and Jefferson begin work on a seal as a national symbol. We are all familiar with the front part of that great seal. But the reverse side, which also appears on every dollar bill, is especially instructive. It depicts a pyramid which is not completed and a single eye gazing out radiantly. The unfinished pyramid represents the work that remains for Americans to do. The Latin motto below is freely translated: "God has favored our undertaking." Two hundred years later, we know God has.

(8) Though we may differ, as Americans have throughout the past, we share a common purpose: It is the achievement of a future in keeping with our glorious past. The American Republic provides for continued growth through a convergence of views and interests, but that growth must be spiritual as well as material.

(9) As we look inside this safe, let us look inside ourselves. Let us look into our hearts and into our hopes.

(10) On Sunday we start a new century, a century of the individual. We have given meaning to our life as a nation. Let us now welcome a century in which we give new meaning to our lives as individuals. Let us look inside ourselves to unleash the God-given treasures stored within. And let us look outside ourselves to the needs of our families, our friends, our communities, our Nation, and our moral and spiritual consciousness.

(12) Thank you very much. [Ford, 1976a:1941–3]

Most Americans would judge this a fine speech. It says nothing terribly new but it re-says old things in a pleasing way. Mr. Ford develops a trite metaphorical theme (spiritual values as riches), touches on the expected bits of Americana (the Revolutionary War, Adams and Jefferson), and ends his speech by looking toward a glorious future. There is nothing startling here but nothing distasteful either. Even many cynical observers would find it harmless. Not so, says the deconstructionist: This speech subverts the dignity of the average citizen and promotes a new American oligarchy. Where is the proof?

The deconstructionist might first examine any **absolute language** in the text that implies that the audience can rise above partiality. President Ford's brave phrases—"so mighty and so inspiring," "devotion to the principles"—merely float in rhetorical space, the deconstructionist would argue. Similarly, when Ford speaks of "us," or "Americans," he conceives of a dormant citizenry. Of the twenty-one such references in the speech, over half refer to *looking*, not acting. Americans look forward, backward, inside their hearts and their national safe. But what sort of citizen merely "looks"? Why does Ford use only three *behavioral* verbs to describe what Americans are like? How can such an inert speech comfort an audience? And if the American people are not "acting," who is?

The speech's **figurative language** answers this latter question. Deconstructionists warn that people depend heavily on metaphors for meaning but often forget how imagery can trap them. The critic would note, for example, that during Mr. Ford's speech-act he not only opens a safe but uses that safe figuratively. Why choose that metaphor, the deconstructionist would ask, when most Americans have no immediate connection with a convenience the upper class uses to hide its money? Is Mr. Ford really describing a *national* safe or is he just taunting blue-collar Americans by alluding to valuables they do not possess residing in a safe they do not own? Besides, how "safe" can a safe be for ordinary people when opened but once every hundred years and then only by the ruling-class individuals who have its keys?

Deconstructionists might even find a certain cruelty in Mr. Ford's teasing, since the safe we are locked out of *contains our hopes:* "As we look inside this safe, let us look inside ourselves. Let us look into our hearts and into our hopes." So, it appears, we are (1) inside a safe that (2) we do not own and (3) for which we do not have a key. We are thus a people trapped and isolated, separated from our fellow citizens by steel walls, unable even to hope for community since the President has urged us to "give new meaning to our lives *as individuals.*"

But why do the American people deserve this fate? Too many of them were born on the wrong side of the tracks, says Mr. Ford via his **abstract language.** "[T]hrough abstractions," says Ryan [1982:50,56], people can be manipulated by making things "seem outside the movement of time and the productive processes of society." Such is the case with Mr. Ford's concept of "wealth," which he says lies "not in material objects" but is "spiritual as well."

Is Ford arguing here that monetary and spiritual wealth are necessarily separate, with some people deserving one and some another? Apparently so, since he claims that *our* "real national treasure does not have to be kept in a vault." But why can't *we* have secured riches, Mr. Ford? Because there is "no safe big enough to contain the hopes . . . of our people," he replies. Thus, we must resign ourselves to the lot of all non-elites (only "*work* . . . remains for Americans to do") and to inequality as well ("We may differ, as Americans have throughout the past"). The American Dream, it appears, is ultimately just a dream.

Like Kenneth Burke (Chapter 12), deconstructionists also key on **hierarchical language** because of their theory of meaning: A thing can only be known by its opposite; if one thing is good, some things must be worse and others better. This sense of relativity is rarely explicated in a text, which is not to say that it is not there (by implication). Mr. Ford's unfinished pyramid on the back of the dollar bill is a case in point.

By the time he makes this allusion, Mr. Ford has already affirmed (in paragraph 6) that there are greater and "lesser" people in the world. Presumably, then, some people are on the pyramid's bottom and some at its top. When finishing the construction of such a pyramid, one would presumably work at (for?) its apex and not at (for?) its base. This implies that the real beneficiaries in the future will be those who are already at the top of the pyramid, powerful persons looking with "a single eye gazing out radiantly" on the day laborers in society.

Might Mr. Ford's hierarchy be leveled in the future? Apparently not, since we can only look toward "a future *in keeping with* our glorious past," a past that Mr. Ford admits included a civil war, insufficient opportunity for the nation's citizens, denial of liberty, and an inadequate judicial system. While there apparently will be some increases for "our citizens in every corner of America," one wonders whether cornered citizens will even notice such improvements, sitting as they do at the base of the Ford pyramid.

Deconstructionists can be particularly devilish when it comes to **inconsistent language.** For example, despite his lionizing of "spiritual treasures," Ford declares that the "valuable collection of mementos" in the national vault symbolizes "something" (some-*thing*) important, thereby endorsing materialist values. He repeats this theme when recollecting that "our immense wealth . . . commanded worldwide attention" in 1876, attention he clearly appreciates. If Mr. Ford were not a materialist, why did he choose the dollar bill as his central rhetorical image?

Moreover, why tell us to look "outside ourselves" to the "needs of our families, our friends, our communities?" If these needs are truly *outside* ourselves, how can we possibly deal with them? And how can we trust in the future when it took until 1976 to "find the confidence" needed to persevere: "Two hundred years later, we know God has [favored our undertaking]." With a heavenly time lag of this magnitude, can this really be called a speech of hope?

Given these flights of fancy, what are we to make of such criticism? Can it be valid, useful, and important? Or only an amusing diversion? Any message, after all, could be "destroyed" as we have destroyed Mr. Ford's speech. That is a crucial fact, the deconstructionists would reply. After all, if a carefully crafted, simple speech like Ford's can be shown to be pessimistic, reactionary, materialistic, isolationistic, and hierarchical rather than their opposites, should we not be especially on guard when presented with vastly more subtle rhetorical materials?

Perhaps, but was our deconstruction really fair? Did it not put words into Mr. Ford's mouth? Not really, for Ford's vacuums of meaning came from *his own remarks.* Admittedly, we did not interpret the President's words as he would have preferred. But why should we help Ford fashion his message? Aren't critics free agents? Must they slavishly conform to the author's rhetorical directions? Besides, is Gerald Ford not a grown man? If he could not make his words stand still, why should the critic compensate for him?

It is rather important, after all, that Ford's language could not obviate problems that have plagued American democracy throughout its history: poverty in a land of opportunity, peace in a land of militarism, godlessness in a land of churches. If these inconsistencies have not been resolved in two centuries, how could Gerry Ford resolve them in one five-minute speech? Ultimately, then, there is nothing magical about deconstruction except that it forces a text to be honest with itself.

Perhaps the sharpest challenge to deconstruction is that, as in the example above, President Ford's *actual audience* probably never noticed what Johnson [1981:166] has called the "warring forces of signification" in a text. Indeed,

Mr. Ford's audience was probably charmed by his oration. Do not such real-life responses give the lie to deconstruction? Only if the critic wishes to become an audience member and not a critic. In deconstruction, it is the critic who must highlight the conflicts inside texts, thereby making those texts problematic for the wider community. The deconstructionist is essentially a consciousness-raiser, spotting trouble in a text where there seems to be none. Ultimately, the question becomes, who will have the last word—Gerry Ford or the critic? It is not to Mr. Ford's advantage to have his speeches deconstructed. But it may be to society's advantage, which is why the critic does criticism.

Obviously, we have purposely misunderstood Ford's intentions here, in order to illustrate the instability of meaning—as well as the deconstructionist's trademark playfulness. But many contemporary critics inspect the same five "trouble spots" we isolated here (without always taking them to the same extremes). Reed [2000], for example, traced the sometimes comical cultural discourse used in the second half of the twentieth century to "domesticate" computers. She found that, like other media before it (telegraph, telephone, radio, TV), the computer was at first met with scattered enthusiasm and more widespread fear and resistance. So how did the technology become accepted? Reed says that popular magazine rhetoric helped to adjust (or in Foucault's terms, "normalize") society's designations of what counts as "normal" and "abnormal" [p. 181]. Both the pleasures and dangers of computer use were depicted through abstract language like "cyberphobia," "addiction," and "the joys of word processing," along with figurative language that depicted the computer-as-rival (competing for the spouse's attention), and eventually, as friend or even family, hierarchically making life better: "Who would have thought that a machine would make us feel closer? [M]y computer is now like family" [pp. 175, 177, 178].

The most devastating critique of deconstruction is that of the Marxists, who find it too gamelike. It produces an "infinite regression" in texts, warns Barney [1987:199], a kind of "textual fiddling while Rome burns," says Norris [1982:131]. While "millions have been killed because they were Marxists," observes Ryan [1982:1], "no one will be obliged to die because s/he is a deconstructionist."

Not surprisingly, the Marxist focus on physical, material reality lends itself to a more serious concern with implications: What social policies does this critique put in place? How will people's lives be improved because of it? But the deconstructionist and the Marxist have much in common: Both expose "the complicity between rhetoric, power, and authority" [Cain, 1984:241] and can therefore be liberating.

MARXIST CRITIQUE

The Marxist critic takes a very old story—a story of exploitation—and tells it again and again. What is its plot? It is this: The ruling classes use rhetoric to justify their exalted positions, rationalize the meager existences of the down-trodden, and inhibit insurrection. How do they do so? Through education, religion, political patronage, banking systems, nationalism, bureaucracies, and manufacturing processes. Why does rhetoric enter the picture? Because each system of exploitation needs an attractive public face. So what does the critic do? Expose the constantly changing disguises of repression.

Even in this simplistic rendering, the appeal of Marxist thought is clear. In the scholarly world, it especially captivates those tired of traditional criticism and, more recently, of deconstruction. According to the Marxist, traditional critics "appreciate" rather than critique discourse, thereby making criticism a decadent, socially irresponsible activity, like collecting Beanie Babies or reading *People* magazine.

In short, Marxists aim to make a difference in the world of politics by making a row in the world of criticism. Unlike deconstructionists, Marxists will risk being both repetitious and tendentious if it will open people's eyes to the political manipulations surrounding (and suppressing) them. For Marxists, a text is worth studying not for itself but because it signals such manipulation. Marxist criticism relies on the following premises:

1. *Economic factors determine rhetoric.* There is no plainer way of stating the most fundamental presupposition of Marxist, or Materialist, criticism. And the word "determine" is key: not only does Matter matter, but the possibilities for communication are set by society's structural and economic mechanisms. These mechanisms make only certain thoughts thinkable and, hence, only certain messages sayable. Although this "vulgar" form of Marxism has become less popular as Marxist theory has matured, Marx's fundamental dictum still informs most such criticism: "Consciousness does not determine life; life determines consciousness" [Eagleton, 1976:4].

Why is this true? Because society needs to reproduce itself from age to age and therefore needs a rhetoric capable of making its favored institutions compelling and dynamic. Aune [2001] points out that the very phrase "*free* market" is one such rhetorical tactic: it takes a treasured value—freedom—and asserts it as a feature of the economic system in question (i.e., U.S. capitalism). But if a politico-economic "base" is to remain viable, it must also produce "superstructures" (e.g., religious, social, cultural, and educational systems) capable of sustaining that base. Thus, it is not enough for a capitalistic system to produce goods (its economic base), but it must also find a rhetoric to make such production continuingly necessary. So, says King [1987:73], "Americans have been told to feel that their bodies are filthy, rotting masses of chemicals and that their odors and body faults must be constantly disguised, or they will be found out and ridiculed. [Marxist] theorists point to the enormous sales of soaps and deodorants as proof that the engineered insecurity of the masses is a fact of life."

2. *Messages are produced, not created.* This proposition proceeds logically from the first: If the base dominates the superstructure, then human texts are fashioned automatically. (In her pithy paraphrase of Marx, Cloud [2002:343]

writes, "People make history, but not under conditions of their own making.") The implications of this proposition are stark and unsettling: People's most unique thoughts are little more than the thoughts "granted" them by the larger social system. So, for example, a high school sophomore who thinks herself dressed distinctively when wearing her Tommy Hilfiger jeans is not just deluded but trebly deluded: (1) she is wearing jeans because that is what the powerful cotton industry in the United States has made available for her to wear; (2) she has chosen the Tommy Hilfiger brand because it can be purchased locally, meaning that in comparison to its competitors Hilfiger, Inc., has best managed to keep wages low and profits high, and (3) she feels distinctive because the Hilfiger ads have depicted independent women doing independent things.

Our high school sophomore would naturally be outraged by this analysis, believing that her choice of clothing was, in fact, *her choice.* She must embrace this delusion, the Marxist says, for without such "false consciousness" the social and economic system would fail. Delusions like these result from what Williams [1977] and others have called **hegemony,** an all-encompassing Master Text so broadly based in society that it usually goes unseen by both rhetor and audience. "The author does not make the materials with which he works," claims Eagleton [1976:29], just as "the worker in a car-assembly plant fashions his product from already-processed materials."

So, says Eagleton [1975:52], the three-volume novel became popular in Victorian England not because writers wished to write them or readers read them but because publishers found them profitable to produce and formed a cartel with the newly emerging circulating libraries for their distribution. In short, while we may wish to believe that ideas spring from Nothingness, the Marxist finds this a silly notion.

3. *Ideologies leave textual evidence.* Generally speaking, Marxist critics treat an individual message as a fragment of a larger, coherent cultural experience. They differ with one another about how easy it is to find such coherence but few doubt it can be found. The basic critical operation for the Marxist is thus one of "rewriting" a text so that its ideological imprintings can be observed. For the Marxist, true critical consciousness is being able to know even "yourself as the product of a historical process that has deposited its traces in you" [Lentricchia, 1983:11]. This is similar to the cultural critic's challenge (as seen in Chapter 11) and the deconstructionist's intertextuality, but Marxism adds a new dimension—the State—by looking for the political and economic truths a text honors.

But it is often hard to find ideology within texts because it hides inside "natural" phenomena. For example, Triece [2001] found that the nineteenth-century ideology of "true womanhood"—that women should be pious, pure, domestic, and submissive—was ordinarily hidden from the middle-class women at whom it was targeted, women who could afford to stay in their "natural" (private) sphere, unsullied by work in the (public) "man's world."

This ideology became visible to working-class women only because of the collisions between their own experiences and those of the "natural" woman.

4. *Established institutions need rhetoric.* While rhetoric can be the tool of the downtrodden, a way of changing the status quo, Marxist critics have shown that the Establishment also depends on public discourse, even if it does so less colorfully. Religious leaders attend political gatherings, CEOs appear on the nightly news, and Hollywood personalities, well-paid athletes, and military leaders move about constantly in each other's company, forming what Hart [1994b] has called a "rhetorical establishment." Their persuasive skills make for what Thompson [1984:68] calls "cultural capital" which, when combined with having an education, gaining access to the media, and learning bureaucratic routines, makes some people very powerful indeed.

This shower of Establishment rhetoric often makes us forget what we know. We know, for example, that individuals have different amounts of money. But in capitalistic societies, rhetorics develop to make these differences seem both natural and necessary. Still other rhetorics develop to prove that these inequalities need not be permanent (the Rags-to-Riches tale, the Lottery Millionaire myth). Cultural rituals, political oratory, and television dramas cooperate to make what we see with our eyes (disparity) different from what we come to accept (justifiable disparity).

At times, these differential allocations are even made to seem *attractive* (e.g., the fluffy Goldie Hawn/Susan Sarandon movie *The Banger Sisters* in which a poor-but-lively rock groupy rescues a long-lost friend from wealthy, beige boredom). These messages bombard us so constantly and so unobtrusively that we are not just awakened to Establishment values but deadened to all competing values as well.

Given these assumptions about rhetoric, what do Marxist critics do? At the risk of generalizing about a diverse group, it seems that they do two main things. The first goal of Marxist criticism is to reestablish the history that produced the text. Marxists remind us constantly that rhetoric is crafted by particular people for particular people. They steer clear of what Tony Bennett [1979:147] calls the "metaphysic of the text" (a text in pure form) by repopulating it. So, for example, a Marxist critic would never treat a documentary on Central America as a mere example of its genre. Rather, the critic would want to know *who* financed the film, *whom* the director studied under, why *this* political figure and not *that* political figure was profiled, *who* was made to seem a devil and *who* an angel, *to whom* the documentary was distributed and through *whose* agency.

Naturally, one need not be a Marxist to be interested in such questions. But Marxists take special pains to remember (1) that each piece of rhetoric contains the marks of its unique historical situation and (2) that rhetoric has a powerful (and dangerous) capacity to make the world abstract. This is why Marxists are interested in a rhetorical image's **material conditions** (e.g., who lives and dies in the documentary, what sorts of food people eat in the restaurant scenes, what type of work they perform in the fields, etc.). According to the Marxist, traditional criticism too often overlooks such facts by "aestheticizing" a text. So, for example, the Marxist critic would discover whether peasant rituals were treated paternalistically, whether the film accurately depicted the reality of prostitution in Central America, and whether a rock beat or a Latin beat was featured in the nightclub scenes. In other words, a Marxist critic would never forget that the Central American documentary ultimately dealt with Central Americans.

The second goal of Marxist criticism is to comfort the afflicted and afflict the comfortable, often by amplifying voices that have been previously muted. So, for example, Jameson [1981] urged examination of the oral epics of tribal society, the fairy tales developed by the European underclasses, and the melodramas written for pennies by paupers. Similarly, Genovese [1976] studied how African slaves transformed their oppressors' Christianity into a religious style better suited to their own cultural patterns. Yet another brand of Marxist criticism studies the "symbolic violence" done to oppressed groups by mainstream messages (e.g., how ghetto residents watching *Joe Millionaire* decode its obscene consumerism).

But how do Marxists do their criticism? As with all critics, they ask questions. Specifically, they look for rhetorical features that have been "overdetermined," which is a way of saying that dominant ideological norms are practically enforced by multiple messages from different sources in a culture. Marxists pay special attention to the role of socio-economic conditions in thus overdetermining, or guaranteeing, an ideology's acceptance. We shall consider five common ways of isolating these features. Phrased as critical probes, they are:

- What structural strategies appear in the artifact?
- What homogenizing strategies appear in the artifact?
- What utopian strategies appear in the artifact?
- What dialectical strategies appear in the artifact?
- What strategies of omission does the artifact employ?

Our sample for analysis will be a poor, unsuspecting guide to student parking regulations at the University of Texas. Like so many bureaucratic tomes, this document is almost comically dense. Among its highlights are the following:

> (1) PERMITS REQUIRED FOR ACCESS & PARKING: Only vehicles conspicuously displaying proper University permits (as specified in Section VI, infra) may enter or park on the main campus Monday through Friday from 7:30 A.M. to 5:00 P.M. Purchase of a permit does not guarantee a parking place on campus. (Section II, infra). . . .
>
> (5) OWNERSHIP OF PERMIT: Ownership of the parking permit remains with The University. Purchase of a parking permit signifies that an individual has been granted the privilege of parking a motor vehicle on University property. (Section VI, infra). . . .

(14) BICYCLES AND SKATES: Bicycles must be operated in accordance with the ordinances of the City of Austin, the specific applicable provisions of these regulations, all provisions of these regulations concerning parking restrictions and traffic and applicable state laws. Rollerskating (including skate boards) is not permitted on any part of the campus. (Section IV, infra). . . .

(20) REGISTRATION OF TWO VEHICLES: Holders of Class D, F or O permits may register an alternate vehicle at no extra cost. Holders of Class A, C or G permits may register one additional motorcycle, or moped. (Section VI, infra).

(21) ENFORCEMENT AND IMPOUNDMENTS: Failure to abide by these regulations may be the basis for disciplinary action against students, and faculty/staff (Section V, infra). Upon notice, violators may subject their vehicle(s) to impoundment pending payment of overdue charges (Section VIII, infra). Students may also be barred from readmission and have grades, degree, refunds or official transcripts withheld pending payment of overdue charges. (Section VIII, infra). Vehicles may also be impounded for specific violations. (Section VII, infra). . . .

(23) VISITORS: All visitors need permits to park on campus UNLESS parked at a paid parking meter or at the University Visitor Center or in the parking garage. OFFICIAL VISITORS are those who conduct important business with the University or who are not otherwise eligible for annual parking permits. Official Visitors may obtain temporary visitor parking permits from the guards at the traffic control stations. These permits entitle the holder to park *only* in a space designated "Official Visitor." Permits must be clearly visible and hanging from the rear view mirror support. (Section VI, infra).

(24) PEDESTRIANS-RIGHTS AND DUTIES: Pedestrians are subject to all official traffic control devices. They have the right-of-way at marked crosswalks, in intersections and on sidewalks extending across a service drive, building entrance or driveway. Pedestrians crossing a street at any point other than within a marked crosswalk or within an unmarked crosswalk at an intersection shall yield the right-of-way to all vehicles on said street. Pedestrians shall not leave curb or other place of safety and walk or run into the path of a vehicle which is so close that it is impossible for the driver to yield. They may cross an intersection diagonally only where permitted by special pavement marking.

(25) INOPERABLE VEHICLES: If a vehicle becomes inoperable, a telephone call shall be placed to the University Police Department (471-4441). The police will either render assistance or authorize temporary parking. Temporary parking shall not exceed 24 hours and must not create an obstruction or hazard. Vehicles shall not be left without written permission from UTPD. Hand written notes are NOT acceptable. [Quick Reference, 1986]

Documents like this abound in any bureaucracy, where they are defended as necessary for carrying out mundane affairs. If people were allowed to park conversion vans backward in the reflection pool at dusk, bureaucrats would argue, all order would disappear from a parking infrastructure that is fragile at best with 50,000 students descending on the campus daily. To make interdependence possible on such a campus, bureaucrats continue, rules-of-the-road must be formulated and then shared widely in a society prizing informed consent.

But why do such documents sound the way they do? Do they keep the "extant modes of production" in force, as the Marxists argue? Are students' consciousnesses "colonized" when they passively accept such reading materials?

To answer such questions, Marxist critics might first consider **structural strategies,** given their interest in the ideology of form. Eagleton [1975:56] notes, for example, that John Milton's decision to write *Paradise Lost* in his native tongue, to use the vernacular *form,* was a thunderous rejection of the aristocratic values of his day. In contrast, our list of parking regulations is mainstream. It is highly ordered (note the numbered paragraphs), thereby warning students that any response they might make to it must also be orthodox in form (and hence in content).

The document's voice is muted, discouraging all thought of personal interchange with its author. Moreover, it is a document-within-a-document (note the cross-references), thus threatening students with an endless welter of paperwork should they become obstreperous. It is streamlined in appearance (note the simple, declarative sentences), suggesting that it exhausts all knowledge on the subject. In short, the document's overall form suggests that *the University* knows all and that it knows best. In thereby "reproducing authority," the document maintains the traditional administrator/student power imbalance found on any college campus.

Marxists are also interested in **homogenizing strategies,** which (1) downplay individual desires, (2) simulate a collective consciousness not based on fact, and (3) posit uniform models for appropriate behavior. Clearly, our parking document works hard at homogenization. It issues common permits to all University personnel (paragraph 1); it creates a kind of Grand Overseer out of University and city authorities (paragraph 14); and it affixes its *own* labels to everyone (paragraph 23). Moreover, the document specifies public norms and excoriates countercultural behavior—especially free-spirited skateboarders (paragraph 14). Paragraph 25 forbids handwritten notes of apology. And paragraph 24 even specifies proper walking behavior!

While Marxists are interested in **utopian strategies,** our prosaic parking document has few of them. Still, there is a constant invocation of what McGee [1980] called ideographs, Ultimate Terms that point toward the operating social consensus. Terms like "ownership," "privileges," "regulations," "eligibility" and "the University" reflect an ideal world where matters of authority have been long since settled, where orderliness reigns supreme, where one knows one's place. But there is no real delineation of this ideal state here, perhaps because bureaucrats must guard against preachment. Marxists would therefore be of two minds about this document: They might appreciate its austerity, but worry that by not arguing explicitly for its utopian ideals, it removes them from public scrutiny, thereby instantiating them in the audience's minds.

Marxists note that utopianism typically serves the interests of the exploiters rather than the exploited. As Eagleton [1976:45] reports, Marx's own tastes in literature tended to the "realist, satirical, radical writers" who were hostile to Romanticism, a movement that Marx thought "concealed the sordid prose of bourgeois life." In other words, because utopian visions are so rich and yet so malleable, they can be used to sanctify the unsanctifiable, something evidenced in the early 1990s by Afrikaners who used the Christian vision to defend apartheid in South Africa. (It was for such reasons that Marx called religion, in his famous phrase, "the opiate of the masses," for it has often been used to direct attention to the Eternal Reward, rather than the ways in which working people can organize to improve the conditions of their lives while on earth.)

Marxists are particularly sensitive to the **dialectical strategies** of rhetoric. They believe that each text contains evidence of the oppositions facing its creator (and its creator's culture) and that good criticism "reads the code" of these oppositions. Although our parking document tries to put its best foot forward, even it betrays stresses and strains: University versus city jurisdiction (paragraph 14), drivers versus pedestrians (paragraph 24), visitors with "important business" versus informal visitors (paragraph 23). Often, these dialectical themes quietly "reproduce the hierarchy" of the University community, with faculty members, but not students, able to "register an alternate vehicle at no extra cost" (paragraph 20) and with penalties specified for students but not for faculty (paragraph 21). The job of rhetoric, then, is to explain, justify, and ultimately resolve such dialectical tensions. As Marxists show, these resolutions typically favor established sources of power. It is clear, after all, that even though the parking document deals with student life on campus, it was *not* written by students.

Rhetorically speaking, one of the most remarkable things about the parking document is that it is so unremarkable. Its words tumble from on high—sensible, rational, drained of emotion. And yet look what happens: It establishes a park-for-pay system with differential allocations of resources, with career-threatening sanctions for untoward behavior, with governance vested in a small number of unnamed persons, and with all signs of student individuality punished severely. The Marxist would quickly draw a parallel between this minisociety (this textual fragment) and the larger society of which it is a part (the Master Text).

And their case would be strongest when focusing on the **strategies of omission** it employs. Like the deconstructionist, the Marxist examines the not-said because it often speaks the unspeakable: that which cannot be argued clearly because it cannot be argued at all. Imagine the rhetoric required, for example, to justify the following propositions: a parking permit is a privilege, not a right (paragraph 5); a student-purchased decal belongs to the University (paragraph 5); economic penalties for parking misbehavior are legitimate (paragraph 21).

Naturally, an experienced bureaucrat could eventually generate enough words to justify these nonarguments. But ideology obviates the need to do so, functioning like a "linguistic legislature which defines what is available for public discussion and what is not" [Thompson, 1984:85]. Reacting against such trends, Marxist critics try to make rhetoric work harder by exploring what it wishes to conceal: its unargued premises. Unless required to do so, rhetoric will follow the path of least resistance, tapping values rooted in the political and economic priorities a society has already established.

Marxist critics study such things as parking regulations because their ordinariness allows them to deliver ideology to our doorsteps daily, along with the morning news. Early reportage of the first Gulf War in 1991, argues Cloud [1998], covered a range of viewpoints, including opposition to the war, but was soon overtaken by stories about brave soldiers and the families they left behind, a troubling turn that Cloud calls "therapeutic" discourse designed to provide comfort to those left at home. Such rhetorics reverse the feminist slogan "the personal is political" so that what could be seen as political is again personalized, and hence removed from consideration for political action. As we noted in Chapter 9, news rhetoric is especially likely to bill itself as nonrhetorical, and hence deserves our careful critical attention. (Of course critical probes from Chapter 9 may be used in conjunction with Marxist criticism of various media.)

Studies like these show how dependent on the mass media political leaders are for keeping ideological beliefs available, relevant, and powerful for their citizens. Another study by Thomas [1985] also traced ideology in the media, finding that religious programs designed for the working class (e.g., Rex Humbard) differed considerably from programs pitched to the upwardly mobile (e.g., *The 700 Club*). The former minimized worldly achievements (concentrating instead on piety and spiritual devotion) while the latter found God's hand at work in their viewers' economic successes. A similar study by Butsch [1992] found that lower-class fathers on TV sitcoms were consistently portrayed as less competent and less responsible than middle-class dads, while a study by Illouz [1991] found that the language of the marketplace has now penetrated even the advice women receive in popular magazines on how to tend a relationship: Organize it, strategize it, measure it, in short, manage it. Indeed, the economic benefits of a good education are even reinforced on TV quiz shows which "demonstrate symbolically that the rewards a society offers really *are* available for all, that the free-enterprise, equal-opportunity systems *works*. All you need is a bit more luck than the next bloke and the bedroom suite falls into your lap" [Fiske, 1983:143].

A central theme in Marxist criticism is that ideology operates most powerfully when audiences are relaxed. Popular films such as *Boyz N the Hood*, *South Central*, and *Menace II Society*, says Cloud [1998], could serve as powerful portraits of the systemic violence inflicted on African American residents of urban ghettos (through inferior housing, education, health care, and employment), but instead provide audiences with visions of a better life through the strengthening of the family, especially the reinstatement of a father figure. Thus such dramas, while emotionally moving, serve to reinscribe rather than challenge Establishment values.

But not all popular rhetoric does so. Kendrick [1999], for example, found countercultural values in the films of James Cameron (*Titanic, The Termina-*

tor, The Abyss). In each case, Kendrick argues, the dramatic struggle is between the forces of wealth and power and "upstanding, headstrong members of the proletariat" [p. 44]. Thus the American ideal of a classless society is revealed to be a myth, capitalistic excess is condemned, and the feisty, heroic worker manages to upset the better-organized, better-funded elite.

Marxist criticism has its detractors, such as Felperin [1985], who object to what they see as its circularity: Exploitation is posited; the marks of exploitation are sought in a text; the text is then used to prove the exploitation. While some accuse Marxists of applying their model too forcefully, others question the model itself. Deconstructionists, for example, reject the notion of base/superstructure relationships. Economic forces, historical events, and political entanglements come to people *through texts*, they say, so the "the firm and privileged ground of marxist history as the basis for a scientific study of literature turns out to be not only firm or privileged, but not even a ground at all; it is more like an abyss" [Felperin, 1985:68].

Certainly class oppression exists, and awareness of its appearance in rhetorical artifacts is an important tool for the critic. The Marxist approach provides an important way into such critical reflections. In the last decades, some scholars have begun to interrogate the principles of classical Marxism, in what has been called post-Marxism, which finds value as well as problems in Marx's original approach. Just as poststructuralists questioned the values and systems of the structural analysis of texts, and postmodernists argue that the modern worldview represented a stable ideal that no longer (if it ever) existed, post-Marxists attempt to take into consideration factors that Marx did not sufficiently account for, factors that have recently received more critical and societal attention: race, gender, sexuality, nationality, education, language fluency, and so on, which work together with class to advantage and disadvantage citizens.

POSTCOLONIAL CRITIQUE

Postcolonial criticism takes up these multicultural concerns, which is no surprise, since it is an intellectual heir—as well as a reaction—to the likes of deconstruction and Marxism. Shome and Hegde [2002:250] locate it within cultural studies, noting that "In its best work, it theorizes not just colonial conditions but *why* those conditions are what they are, and how they can be undone and redone." Like feminism and Marxism, then, postcolonial scholarship concerns itself with issues of **power** and **agency** and carries an activist presumption. So what makes it different? Postcolonial critics practice resistance to Western ideals, emphasizing the ways in which established forms of thought and action have colonized people's minds long after their bodies were ostensibly freed. Sim [1999:336] offers a concise summary:

> "Colonialism" is the conquest and direct control of another people's land, a phase
> in the history of imperialism, which in turn is the globalization of the capitalist

mode of production from the sixteenth century onwards. In the context of cultural production, "postcolonialism" is "writing after empire," the analysis of both colonial discourse and the writings of the ex-colonized. . . . The field . . . [uses] a variety of postmodern theories concerning language, gender, subjectivity and race.

As Shome and Hegde [2002:252] say, "postcolonial scholarship provides a historical and international depth to the understanding of cultural power." Like "feminism," "postcolonial" is a contested term, and postcolonial theory and criticism are complex and varied phenomena. Therefore, rather than seeking to present a full portrait of the breadth of the field, we will content ourselves with a few common principles.

1. *West is not necessarily best.* Postcolonial critics seek to expose the insidious influence of colonialism on the minds of colonizer and colonized, alike. They argue that Western Enlightenment values (such as rationality, order, conquest, and a belief in the perfectability of human systems), have become **naturalized,** or taken for granted, but are not the only possible values. Like Marxists, then, postcolonial critics are sensitive to the ways in which capitalism has become **globalized.** They seek to make visible—in order to critique—that which has presented itself as **universal,** such as the God Term of economic "progress," and the sense that it must take the form of industrial development and "modernization" (with the "third world" becoming more like the West). As Grossberg [2002:368] emphasizes, context is always active, rather than inert, and structure is never politically neutral.

Zacharias [2003] found a fascinating example of this in her study of the introduction of consumer television to India in the late 1980s. She describes a 1988 newspaper advertisement for Crown TV (even the name is Imperial!) that depicted the Mona Lisa on a television screen, with text that claimed "classics are . . . appreciated by only those who have been gifted with the luxury of good taste" [p. 388]. Asking, "Why is an Indian television set advertising itself with the image of a white woman?" Zacharias finds,

> It would appear that the subtext of the advertisement is the promise of whitening, of racial transformation through the consumption of television. Wearing Mona Lisa's mask, a new colonizing force has now emerged, a class that is in the permanent process of racial passage from brown to white, and which may be unwilling, or even helpless, to reverse the material destiny of this upwardly mobile trajectory of signification. Using the seductive form of a white woman, the advertisement also allays the anxieties that the image of the white male colonizer may evoke. [p. 389]

Thus, to become classy and modern meant to identify with the Western consumer of art, perhaps the object of art herself, and to imbibe Western standards of beauty and success. Postcolonial critics are highly skeptical of such claims.

2. *Binaries are seductive but dangerous.* Postcolonialism as a time period began in the mid-twentieth century, when European powers formally acknowledged the independence of their former colonies in Africa, Asia, and the Caribbean, but its critical roots as a practice trace back to a specific work: Ed-

ward Said's 1978 publication of *Orientalism*. In his book, Said argued that the Western world's **representation** of the East (the Orient) created the East (in the Western imagination) as exotic, dark, mysterious, the exact opposite of Western rationality—in other words, as **Other.** (Postcolonial critics use the term **alterity** to refer to this quality of "otherness.") But such imaginative creations (stereotypes) impact their creators as well. Said observed that this allowed the Western world to define itself in particular ways, since (as Kenneth Burke and the deconstructionists tell us) we define things by what they are not.

At times, postcolonial critics study the discourse of Western democracies to discern how colonialism has been justified. Hasian [2002] investigated the impeachment trial of Warren Hastings, one-time British Governor of Bengal, who was accused (and eventually acquitted) of misdeeds against the Indian people. "This was not just a trial that involved the guilt or innocence of a single individual," Hasian writes:

> it was a proceeding that brought into question both the role of the East India Company and the legitimacy of coercive rules of conquest. . . . The defendant . . . may not have been convicted, but he had figuratively stood in the place of all magistrates and governors who were going to be entrusted with colonial power. . . . Both [the prosecution and the defense] were simply advocating different types of colonial power, and neither could contemplate the possibility that *all* forms of colonialism were problematic. [2002:236,246,248]

The issue in the Hastings trial was thus not whether a man had the right to such power over others, but whether he had misused his power—a question of degree, not of kind. In postcolonial criticism, the legitimacy of who is deciding and speaking about, and for, whom, is always at issue.

3. *Identities are not stable.* Postcolonial critiques often seek to **interrogate,** or take apart by careful questioning, the ways in which the **subaltern** (those subordinated because of gender, class, race, or culture [Mongia, 1997:17]) have been represented. Thus, an important task becomes recovering their voices and perspectives, including those living in the former colonies, as well as the **diaspora** (the geographically dispersed former residents of those colonies). When colonization officially ended, many colonial "natives" chose to emigrate to the former colonial power—and hence they, and their descendents, are often possessed of a sense of multiple (sometimes contradictory) cultural identities that postcolonial critics call **hybridity** [Bhabha, 1990].

But this complexity is not often represented in mainstream portrayals. In her analysis of the popular 1994 documentary *Hoop Dreams,* about two young, Black, aspiring basketball players from inner-city Chicago, bell hooks [1996:77,78] calls the film a "neo-colonial fantasy of conquest" that simply "show[s] us the 'dark other' from the standpoint of whiteness." Rather than a textured portrayal of the full lives of its subjects, hooks says, the film promotes competitive values (and male sports success) as a universally American Dream, thus disguising the "institutionalized racism and white supremacist attitudes in everyday American life [which] actively prohibit black male participation in diverse cultural arenas and spheres of employment while presenting sports as the 'one' location where recognition, success, and material reward can be obtained" [p. 79]. Postcolonial critics examine such naturalized assumptions, often from the perspective of the colonized, with the double goal of exposing the ways such assumptions support the status quo, and subverting that arrangement of power.

With these principles in mind, we offer the following critical probes as a starting point for postcolonial criticism.

- How do the West and the Other constitute one another in this artifact?
- How do the West and the Other comply with and resist these mutual constitutions?
- How do these constitutions invite audiences to respond?

Consider, for example, the 2000 film *Finding Forrester,* about Jamal Wallace, an African American high school student in the Bronx with two passions: writing and basketball. He chances to meet William Forrester, a reclusive but great European novelist, who becomes his mentor in letters. A postcolonial critique of this film might note how the "West," in the form of Forrester himself, and the literary canon and the "rules" of writing he embodies, are not only unquestioned, but reinforced through the enthusiastic embrace of Jamal, the "Other." (He has been reading, practically memorizing, Western "classics" on his own initiative.) In one scene, William answers a *Jeopardy* question without putting it into the proper form. Jamal corrects him impatiently, intoning, "Gotta know the rules if ya wanna play the game." Viewers know that this is meant to apply not only to "success" in *Jeopardy,* but to basketball, writing, and American life itself. Hearing these words come out of Jamal's mouth assuages white liberal guilt, the conscience of the colonizer, and disciplines the Other, requiring that African American viewers command "standard" English in order to excel.

At times, the differences between the two characters are played for laughs, and at times, their similarities are presented as surprising. At times this reveals, and at other times, it reinforces the ways in which we have been taught to expect them to constitute one another (as opposites). Because they are individuals, the ways in which the characters learn from one another are presented as heartwarming (personal) rather than overtly political. The only message about the lessons young men can teach older men ("don't give up on your dreams") disregards race and ethnicity as factors. When Jamal does make a contribution to the intellectual life of his school through his writing, his success is measured by the fact that his writing is indistinguishable from that of his white mentor.

If audience members question the idea that a sixteen-year-old Black kid from the Bronx would see great value in nineteenth-century (white) British poetry, there is an implicit invitation to judge such responses as conditioned racism. True, his intellectual brilliance (by Western standards) does make

Jamal stand out as worthy of attending a swanky (white) private school on scholarship. (He is "a credit to his race"? his neighborhood?) But without William's tutelage, the odds against him would have been difficult to overcome. At the end of the film, Jamal and his family have been saved, by William's intervention, from a life of poverty. White viewers are not motivated to go forth and change any of their beliefs or practices, because they have been assured that the cream really does rise to the top. And subaltern viewers have received yet another message that in order to make a valued contribution to society, they must excel according to the established rules, rather than questioning the universality of those rules.

Granted, resisting Western patterns of thought is difficult. It is difficult even for members of the diaspora who may be well aware of both the devastations of colonialism on their ancestral culture and the prejudice they face in the West. Postcolonial critics often write from within Western academia, trained in Western institutions. While some (e.g. Kavoori, 1998) see this as hypocritical, Shome [1998:209] responds with passionate eloquence, "Isn't that the very predicament that is the postcolonial subject position? That the 'knowledge structure' in which many postcolonial intellectuals are/were trained was *itself* an effect of colonialism to which they were and are 'subject'?. . . . Pure spaces and pure identities do not exist anymore; that itself is an effect of colonialism." Ideological critics thus call into question the *assumptions* we make about rhetoric, about criticism, and about life itself. No self-respecting critic could resist such an important call for introspection.

CONCLUSION

Ideological criticism asks constantly if we know what we are doing and, if we know, how we know. It requires us to examine where we go for our premises and why we go there and not elsewhere. It asks whether our critical practices are of benefit to anyone in particular and, if not, why not.

Ideological critics sense a certain, systematic unfairness in the world. And they see rhetoric as a tool for turning such unfairness into social routines and thenceforth into public policy. Thus, they offer a critique. In doing so, they operate as critics always have, reminding us that criticism itself is a minority business. There are powerful people in the world. There always have been. They use rhetoric to maintain their power. They always will. Somebody, therefore, must call attention to how they do what they do and ask if it is right that they do so. This challenge is challenge enough for legions of rhetorical critics since the odds so heavily favor the producers of rhetoric and, hence, the producers of power. So for reasons both conceptual and practical, we urge critics to aspire to the skepticism and playful imagination of the deconstructionist; the class-consciousness and material focus of the Marxist; and the self-reflexivity and constant interrogation of the postcolonial critic.

TIPS FOR THE PRACTICING CRITIC

1. If it feels awkward at first, think of ideological criticism as perspective-taking, method acting, or empathizing with the concerns of an oppressed group. Picture yourself as the committed representative of those who feel frustration with the reverent attitude toward the dominant culture, workers who have been prevented from enjoying the wealth they have produced, or citizens whose religious or cultural practices have been first outlawed, then marketed as folk art to members of a more privileged group.

2. Strive for boldness in ideological criticism. Try to minimize qualifiers (e.g., sometimes, often, probably). Ideological critics fight repression in order to accomplish important social, cultural, and political goals. Justifiable anger can be channeled into productive, consciousness-raising criticism.

3. Training and practice in rhetorical criticism encourages the examination of critical assumptions (our own and others'), sharpening our perceptions of what happens when people use symbols to influence one another. And in a world increasingly shaped by "information" and "communication," those are very useful skills indeed.

REFERENCES

POPULAR REFERENCES

"All That. *Savoy* Hall of Fame: Dick Gregory." (December 2001–January 2002). *Savoy:* 34.

Amdahl Corporation. (1994). "Mission Statement," in J. W. Graham and W. C. Havlick (eds.), *Mission Statements: A Guide to the Corporate and Nonprofit Sectors* (New York: Garland). 40–41.

Austen, J. (1993). *Pride and Prejudice* (New York: Barnes and Noble Classics).

BBC. [2003]. "POW Coverage Shows Bias in Favor of Beauty," retrieved 12/29/03 from http://indymedia.org.uk/en/2003/04/63602.html.

Bird, C. (November, 1971). "Myths That Keep Women Down," *Ladies' Home Journal:* 68, 70.

Boone, P. et al. (1970). *The Solution to Crisis-America* (Van Nuys, CA: Bible Voice, Inc.).

Bulworth. (1998). Dir. Warren Beatty. Twentieth Century Fox.

Bush, G. H. W. (October 16, 1992). "Remarks During the Second Presidential Debate," *Washington Post:* A35–36.

Dalai Lama. (December 2001–February 2002). "World Peace," *Mandala: Buddhism in Our Time:* 10–11.

Dallek, R. (February 24, 1991). Quoted in P. Applebome, "Sense of Pride Outweighs Fears of War," *New York Times,* p. 1.

Ehrenreich, B., and D. English. (1973). *Witches, Midwives, and Nurses: A History of Women Healers*. New York: CUNY/Feminist Press.

Eisenhower, D. (July 26, 1953). "The Korean Armistice," *Vital Speeches of the Day*, 19: 21, 642.

Eisenhower, D. (April 7, 1958). "Remarks to the Easter Egg Rollers on the White House Lawn," *Public Papers of the Presidents, 1958*, 65.

Erlich, P. (1972). "Eco-Catastrophe!" June 9, 1970, in K. K. Campbell (ed.), *Critiques of Contemporary Rhetoric*. Belmont, CA: Wadsworth. 111–123.

Fairlie, H. (July 13, 1980). "TV's Conventions will be a Lie," *Washington Post:* E1.

Faludi, S. (1991). *Backlash: The Undeclared War against American Women* (New York: Anchor/Doubleday).

Feldmann, L., and L. Marlantes. (December 17, 2003). "Dean vs. Bush: Would it be close?" *Christian Science Monitor:* 11+.

Findlen, B. (2001). "Introduction," in *Listen Up: Voices from the Next Feminist Generation*, ed. Barbara Findlen, (New York: Seal Press). xiii–xvii.

Ford, G. (July 1, 1976a). "Remarks at the Centennial Safe Opening at the Capitol," *Public Papers of the Presidents, 1976:2*, 1941–1943.

Ford, G. (April 29, 1976b). "Remarks at the Waco Suspension Bridge in Waco, Texas," *Public Papers of the Presidents, 1976:2*, 1335–1336.

"Fox and Jacobs Fetes Grand Opening in Ember Oaks." (August 21, 1988). *Dallas Times Herald:* J5.

Gallagher, W. N. (August, 1984). "Throw This Away" (Publicly Circulated Letter).

Gibbs, N. (2002) "Summer of Mistrust." *CNN.com/Inside Politics.* http://www.cnn.com/2002/ALLPOLITICS/07/15/time.mistrust/.

Goldwater, B. (October 21, 1964). "Foreign Policy," *Vital Speeches of the Day*, 31: 2, 36–38.

Gould, F. *Funeral Services without Theology* (Girard, Ks.: Haldeman-Julius Publ., n.d.).

Hitler, A. (November 10, 1933). "Speech at Siemensstadt, Berlin," Fugitive translation. Partially translated in A. Hitler, *My New Order*, ed. R. DeSales (New York: Reynal and Htchcock, 1941) as well as in N. Baynes (ed.), *The Speeches of Adolf Hitler, April 1922–August, 1939* (London: Oxford University Press, 1942) and F. Prange (ed.), *Hitler's Words* (Washington: American Council on Public Affairs, 1944).

"In *kabary*, the point is to avoid the point." (May 9, 2002). *Christian Science Monitor:* 11+.

Ivins, M. (February 20, 2003). "The French Try to Tell Us What They Have Learned from History." http://www.sltrib.com/2003/Feb/02202003/commenta/commenta.asp.

Johnson, J. H. *Religion is a Gigantic Fraud* (No publisher cited, n.d.).

Johnson, L. (August 24, 1960). "Address at the 10th District Rally," Special Files, Box #4, Lyndon Baines Johnson Presidential Library, Austin, TX.

Johnson, L. (May 17, 1966). "Remarks at a Party Rally in Chicago," *Weekly Compilations of Presidential Documents,* 2:20, 657–660.

Kampfner, J. (2003). "Saving Private Lynch story 'flawed,'" retrieved 12/29/03. http://news.bbc.co.uk/2/hi/programmes/correspondent/3028585.stm

Kennedy, J. (1961a). "Remarks to the Greater Houston Ministerial Association, September 12, 1960," in T. H. White, *The Making of the President, 1960* (New York: Atheneum). 427–430.

Kennedy, J. (January 21, 1961b). "Remarks at a Meeting of the Democratic National Committee," *Public Papers of the Presidents, 1961b:* 4–5.

King, L. (1994). "The Father of 'Talk Show Democracy': On the Line with Larry King," *Media Studies Journal* 8: 123–137.

King, M. L. (1964). "I Have a Dream," in R. Hill (ed.), *The Rhetoric of Racial Revolt* (Denver: Golden Bell Press [1963]). 371–375.

"Kiss Someone You Love When You Get This Letter and Make Magic." (1985). (Publicly circulated letter, Austin, TX.)

"Legend Oaks: Live a Legendary Lifestyle." (August 21, 1988). *Austin American-Statesman:* F12.

"Love's Reflections." (November, 1971). *Ladies' Home Journal:* 14–15.

Macdonald, C. (1985). "Two Brothers in a Field of Absence," in *Alternate Means of Transport: Poems* (New York: Knopf), 75–6.

Meltzer, M. (Winter 2002). "Hollywood's Big New Minstrel Show," *Bitch: Feminist Response to Pop Culture* 15: 19–20.

Muñoz, N. (December 2002–January 2003). "Women of the Year 2002: Cristina Saralegui," *Ms.:* 59–60.

Neuborne, E. (2001). "Imagine My Surprise," in *Listen Up: Voices from the Next Feminist Generation,* ed. Barbara Findlen (New York: Seal Press). 182–187.

Nixon, R. (1970). "Letter to Pat Boone." Reprinted in P. Boone, et al., *The Solution to Crisis-America* (Van Nuys, CA: Bible Voice, Inc.). 18.

Nixon, R. (January 20, 1973). "Second Inaugural Address," *Public Papers of the Presidents, 1973:* 12–5.

Noonan, P. (1998). *On Speaking Well: How to Give a Speech With Style, Substance, and Clarity* (New York: Harper Collins).

"One oil rig, 14 showers and the soapy scum of 127 sweaty men, for over a month." (June 2003). Tilex advertisement, *more:* 80.

Orwell, G. (1960). *Animal Farm* (New York: Harcourt [1946]).

Patton, G. (1946). "Speech to the Troops in July, 1944," in W. B. Mellor, *Patton: Fighting Man* (New York: Putnam). 2–5.

Pershing, J. (February 28, 1919). "My Fellow Soldiers," General Orders No. 38A, G.H.Q. American Expeditionary Forces.

"Prayer at the Funeral Service." (1979). *Book of Common Prayer: According to the Uses of the Episcopal Church* (New York: Church Hymnal Corp., [1789]). 482–485.

Prinz, J. (August 28, 1963). "Speech at the March on Washington." Original recording.

"Quayle Attacks Unfounded." (August 29, 1988). By J. H., Letter-to-the-editor in the *Provo Daily Herald:* 6.

"Quick Reference to Parking and Traffic Regulations." (1986). University of Texas at Austin.

Reagan, R. (March 5, 1987). "Address to the Nation on the Iran Arms Controversy," *New York Times:* 12.

Rostand, E. (1898). *Cyrano de Bergerac (*New York: Doubleday & McClure Co.)

Shakespeare in Love. (1996). Dir. John Madden. Miramax Films.

Shelton, R. *Ideals of a Klansman* (Denham Springs, LA: Invisible Empire Knights of the Ku Klux Klan, n.d.)

Sinclair, G. (1973). "Americans." (Detroit: Westbound Records).

"Supporter Ousted." (September 9, 1988). *New York Times:* 1.

Truman, H. (May 15, 1950). "Democratic Aims and Achievements," *Vital Speeches of the Day.* 16:16, 496–498.

U.S. Army. (April, 1972). "Eleven Point Checklist for Job Hunters." Flyer circulated nationally.

Vail Resort Association. "Ski, Mix, Meet," (Nationally circulated advertisement, n.d.).

von Hoffman, N. (January 24, 1973). "Andy Jackson's Boy," *Washington Post:* B1.

Webelos Scout Book. (1979). (Boy Scouts of America).

"Weston Lakes Has Superlative Golf, Swimming, Tennis, Croquet." (August 21, 1988). *Houston Post (Homefinder):* 5.

Willson, M. (1958). *The Music Man* (New York: Putnam).

"Wimbledon Country." (August 21, 1988). *Houston Post (Homefinder):* 3.

SCHOLARLY REFERENCES

Abraham L. et al. (June, 1995). "The Effects of MTV-Style Editing on Viewers' Comprehension of a PSA." Paper presented at the 9th annual Visual Communication Conference.

Adams, W. C. (1986). "Whose Lives Count?: TV Coverage of Natural Disasters," *Journal of Communication* 36:2, 113–122.

Anderson, K. V. (2002). "Hillary Clinton as 'Madonna': The Role of Metaphor and Oxymoron in Image Restoration," *Women's Studies in Communication* 25: 1–24.

Appel, E. (1987). "The Perfected Drama of Reverend Jerry Falwell," *Communication Quarterly* 35: 26–38.

Arendt, H. (1963). *Eichmann in Jerusalem: A Report on the Banality of Evil* (New York: Viking).

Aristotle. (2001/1924). *Rhetoric.* Trans. W. Rhys Roberts. In *The Rhetorical Tradition: Readings from Classical Times to the Present*, eds. Patricia Bizzell and Bruce Herzberg. (Boston: Bedford/St. Martin's [circa 350 BCE]). 179–240.

Armstrong, G. B., K. A. Neuendorf, & J. E. Brentar. (1992). "TV Entertainment, News, and Racial Perceptions of College Students," *Journal of Communication* 42: 153–176.

Arnold, C. (1968). "Oral Rhetoric, Rhetoric, and Literature," *Philosophy and Rhetoric* 1: 191–210.

Arnold, C. (1972). "*Inventio* and *Pronuntiatio* in a 'New Rhetoric.'" Paper presented at the annual convention of the Central States Speech Association.

Arnold, C. (1974). *Criticism of Oral Rhetoric* (Columbus: Merrill).

Arnold, C. (1977). "Reflections on American Public Discourse," *Central States Speech Journal* 28: 73–85.

Aune, J. (1983). "Beyond Deconstruction: The Symbol and Social Reality," *Southern Speech Communication Journal* 48: 255–268.

Aune, J. A. (2001). *Selling the Free Market: The Rhetoric of Economic Correctness* (New York: Guilford).

Austin, J. L. (1970). *How to Do Things with Words* (New York: Oxford University Press).

Barbatsis, G., M. R. Wong, & G. M. Herek. (1983). "A Struggle for Dominance: Relational Communication Patterns in Television Drama," *Communication Quarterly* 31: 148–155.

Barney, R. (1987). "Uncanny Criticism in the United States," in J. Natoli (ed.), *Tracing Literary Theory* (Urbana: University of Illinois Press). 177–212.

Barreca, R. (1991). *They Used to Call Me Snow White . . . But I Drifted: Women's Strategic Use of Humor* (New York: Penguin).

Barthes, R. (1981). "Theory of the Text," in R. Young (ed.), *Untying the Text: A Post-Structuralist Reader* (London: Routledge and Kegan Paul). 31–47.

Barthes, R. (1985). *The Responsibility of Forms: Critical Essays on Music, Art, and Representation* (New York: Hill and Wang).

Battles, K., and W. Hilton-Morrow. (2002). "Gay Characters in Conventional Spaces: *Will and Grace* and the Situation Comedy Genre," *Critical Studies in Media Communication* 19: 87–105.

Beasley, V. B. (1994). "The Logic of Power in the Hill-Thomas Hearings: A Rhetorical Analysis," *Political Communication* 11: 287–297.

Beasley, V. B. (2001). "Making Diversity Safe for Democracy: American Pluralism and the Presidential Local Address, 1885–1992," *Quarterly Journal of Speech* 87: 25–40.

Belsey, C. (1980). *Critical Practice* (London: Methuen).

Benjamin, J. (1976). "Performatives as a Rhetorical Construct," *Philosophy and Rhetoric* 9: 84–95.

Benjamin, W. (1969). "The Work of Art in the Age of Mechanical Reproduction," in H. Arendt (ed.), *Illuminations* (New York: Schocken Books). 217–51.

Bennett, T. (1979). *Formalism and Marxism* (London: Methuen).

Benson, T. (1968). "Poisoned Minds," *Southern Speech Communication Journal* 34: 54–60.

Bettinghaus, E., and M. Cody. (1994). *Persuasive Communication* (Fort Worth: Harcourt).

Berthold, C. (1976). "Kenneth Burke's Cluster-Agon Method: Its Development and Application," *Central States Speech Journal* 27: 302–9.

Bhabha, H. (1990). "The Third Space," in J. Rutherford (ed.), *Identity: Community, Culture, Difference* (London: Lawrence & Wishart). 90–118.

Bitzer, L. (1968). "The Rhetorical Situation," *Philosophy and Rhetoric*, 1, 1–14.

Bizzell, P., and B. Herzberg. (2001). *The Rhetorical Tradition: Readings from Classical Times to the Present* (Boston: Bedford/St. Martin's).

Black, E. (1970). "The Second Persona," *Quarterly Journal of Speech* 56: 109–119.

Black, E. (1978a). *Rhetorical Criticism: A Study in Method* (Madison: University of Wisconsin Press [1965]).

Black, E. (1978b). "The Sentimental Style as Escapism, or the Devil with Dan'l. Webster," in K. Campbell and K. Jamieson (eds.), *Form and Genre: Shaping Rhetorical Action* (Falls Church, VA: Speech Communication Association). 75–86.

Black, E. (1992). *Rhetorical Questions: Studies of Public Discourse* (Chicago: University of Chicago Press).

Black, E. (2000). "On Objectivity and Politics in Criticism," *American Communication Journal* 4.1. Retrieved February 17, 2002 on the World Wide Web at http://acjournal.org/holdings/vol4/iss1/special/black/html.

Blair, C. (1999). "Contemporary U.S. Memorial Sites as Exemplars of Rhetoric's Materiality," in J. Selzer and S. Crowley (eds.), *Rhetorical Bodies* (Madison: University of Wisconsin Press). 16–57.

Blair, C., J. Brown, and L. Baxter. (1994). "Disciplining the Feminine," *Quarterly Journal of Speech* 80: 383–409.

Blankenship, J. (1968). *A Sense of Style: An Introduction to Style for the Public Speaker* (Belmont, CA: Wadsworth).

Bloch, M. (ed.) (1975). *Political Language and Oratory in Traditional Society* (London: Academic Press).

Booth, W. C. (1961). *The Rhetoric of Fiction* (Chicago: University of Chicago Press).

Bordo, S. (1993). *Unbearable Weight: Feminism, Western Culture, and the Body* (Berkeley: University of California Press).

Bordo, S. (December 19, 2003). "The Empire of Images in Our World of Bodies," *The Chronicle of Higher Education:* B6–9.

Bormann, E. G. (1972). "Fantasy and Rhetorical Vision: The Rhetorical Criticism of Social Reality," *Quarterly Journal of Speech* 58: 396–407.

Bormann, E., J. Cragan, and D. Shields. (1994). "In Defense of Symbolic Convergence Theory: A Look at the Theory and its Criticisms after Two Decades," *Communication Theory* 4: 259–294.

Bosmajian, H. (1974). "The Sources and Nature of Adolph Hitler's Techniques of Persuasion," *Central States Speech Journal* 25: 240–248.

Bostdorff, D. (1987). "Making Light of James Watt: A Burkean Approach to the Form and Attitude of Political Cartoons," *Quarterly Journal of Speech* 73: 43–59.

Brinton, C. (1938). *The Anatomy of Revolution* (New York: Vintage).

Brock, B. (1985). "Epistemology and Ontology in Kenneth Burke's Dramatism," *Communication Quarterly* 33: 94–104.

Brockriede, W. (1974). "Rhetorical Criticism as Argument," *Quarterly Journal of Speech* 60: 165–174.

Brownmiller, S. (1975). *Against Our Will: Men, Women, and Rape* (New York: Bantam).

Brownmiller, S. (1984). *Femininity* (New York: Fawcett Columbine).

Brummett, B. (1984). "Burkean Comedy and Tragedy, Illustrated in Reactions to the Arrest of John DeLorean," *Central States Speech Journal* 35: 217–227.

Brummett, B., and M. Duncan. (1992). "Toward a Discursive Ontology of Media," *Critical Studies in Mass Communication* 9: 229–249.

Bryant, D. (1972). "Rhetoric: Its Functions and Its Scope," in D. Ehninger (ed.), *Contemporary Rhetoric: A Coursebook* (Glenview: Scott, Foresman [1953]). 15–38.

Brydon, S. (1985). "The Two Faces of Jimmy Carter: The Transformation of a Presidential Debater, 1976 and 1980," *Central States Speech Journal* 36: 138–151.

Burgin, V. (1983). "Seeing Sense," in H. Davis and P. Walton (eds.), *Language, Image and Media* (New York: St. Martins). 226–244.

Burke, K. (1962). *A Grammar of Motives* (Cleveland: World Publishing Co.).

Burke, K. (1964). "Antony in Behalf of the Play," in S. E. Hyman (ed.). *Perspectives by Incongruity* (Bloomington: Indiana University Press). 64–75.

Burke, K. (1968). *Counter-Statement* (Berkeley: University of California Press, [1931]).

Burke, K. (1969). *A Rhetoric of Motives.* (Berkeley: University of California Press).

Burke, K. (1973). *The Philosophy of Literary Form* (Berkeley: University of California Press, [1941]).

Burke, K. (1984). *Permanence and Change* (Berkeley: University of California Press, [1935]).

Butler, J. (1990). "Performative Acts and Gender Constitution: An Essay in Phenomenology and Feminist Theory," in S. E. Case (ed.), *Performing Feminisms: Feminist Critical Theory and Theatre* (Baltimore: Johns Hopkins University Press). 270–283.

Butsch, R. (1992). "Class and Gender in Four Decades of Television Situation Comedy: *Plus ça change…*," *Critical Studies in Mass Communication* 9: 387–399.

Cain, W. E. (1984). *The Crisis in Criticism: Theory, Literature and Reform* (Baltimore: Johns Hopkins University Press).

Campbell, K. K. (1989). *Man Cannot Speak for Her: A Critical Study of Early Feminist Rhetoric,* Vol. I. (New York: Greenwood Press).

Campbell, K. K. (2002). "Consciousness-Raising: Linking Theory, Criticism, and Practice," *Rhetoric Society Quarterly* 32: 45–64.

Carlson, A. C. (1991). "The Role of Character in Public Moral Argument: Henry Ward Beecher and the Brooklyn Scandal," *Quarterly Journal of Speech* 77: 38–52.

Carlson, A. C. (1994). "Defining Womanhood: Lucretia Coffin Mott and theTransformation of Femininity," *Western Journal of Communication* 58: 85–97.

Carpignano, P., R. Andersen, S. Aronowitz, & W. Difazio. (1990). "Chatter in the Age of Electronic Reproduction: Talk, Television, and the 'Public Mind,'" *Social Text* 25–26: 93–120.

Chapman, S. and G. Eggar. (1983). "Myth in Advertising and Health Promotion," in H. Davies and P. Walton (eds.), *Language, Image Media* (London: Blackwell). 166–186.

Charlesworth, D. (Spring, 2003). "Transmitters, Caregivers, and Flowerpots: Rhetorical Constructions of Women's Early Identities in the AIDS Pandemic," *Women's Studies in Communication* 26.1: 60–87.

Cherwitz, R. and T. Darwin. (1995). "Toward a Relational Theory of Meaning," *Philosophy and Rhetoric* 28: 17–29.

Cherwitz, R. and K. Zagacki. (1986). "Consummatory Versus Justificatory Crisis Rhetoric," *Western Journal of Speech Communication* 50: 307–324.

Chesebro, J. (1994). "Extending the Burkean System: A Response to Tompkins and Cheney," *Quarterly Journal of Speech* 80: 83–90.

Clark, K. (1999). "Pink Water: The Archetype of Blood and the Pool of Infinite Contagion," in W. N. Elwood (ed.), *Power in the Blood: A Handbook on Aids, Politics, and Communication* (Mahwah, NJ: Lawrence Erlbaum). 9–24.

Clark, T. (1977). "An Exploration of Generic Aspects of Contemporary American Christian Sermons," *Quarterly Journal of Speech* 63: 384–394.

Cloud, D. L. (1998). *Control and Consolation in American Culture and Politics: Rhetorics of Therapy* (Thousand Oaks, CA: Sage).

Cloud, D. L. (2001). "The Affirmative Masquerade," *American Journal of Communication* 4.3. Retrieved 2/17/02 from http://acjournal.org/holdings/vol4/iss3/special/cloud.html.

Cloud, D. L. (2002). "Rhetoric and Economics: Or, How Rhetoricians Can Get a Little Class," *Quarterly Journal of Speech* 88: 342–358.

Coles, R. L. (2001). "Building the Clinton Legacy Through Frame Alignment," *Cultural Studies ↔ Critical Methodologies* 1: 459–487.

Collins, P. H. (2000). *Black Feminist Thought: Knowledge, Consciousness, and the Politics of Empowerment,* 2nd ed. (New York: Routledge).

Condit, C. M. (1997). "In Praise of Eloquent Diversity: Gender and Rhetoric as Public Persuasion," *Women's Studies in Communication* 20: 91–116.

Condit, C. and J. Lucaites. (1993). *Crafting Equality: America's Anglo-African Word* (Chicago: University of Chicago Press).

Cooper, M. (1988). "Rhetorical Criticism and Foucault's Philosophy of Discursive Events," *Central States Speech Journal* 39: 1–17.

Crane, J. (1988). "Terror and Everyday Life," *Communication* 10: 367–382.

Culler, J. (1982). *On Deconstruction: Theory and Criticism after Structuralism* (Ithaca: Cornell University Press).

Darsey, J. (1991). "From 'Gay is Good' to the Scourge of AIDS: The Evolution of Gay Liberation Rhetoric, 1977–1990," *Communication Studies* 42: 43–66.

Darsey, J. (1994). "Must We All Be Rhetorical Theorists?: An Anti-Democratic Inquiry," *Western Journal of Communication* 58: 164–181.

Darsey, J. (1995). "Joe McCarthy's Fantastic Moment," *Communication Monographs* 62: 65–86.

Daughton, S. (1991). "The Rhetorical Nature and Function of First-Person Narrative." (Diss., University of Texas at Austin).

Daughton, S. (1993). "Metaphoric Transcendence: Images of the Holy War in Franklin Roosevelt's First Inaugural," *Quarterly Journal of Speech* 79: 427–446.

Daughton, S. (1995). "The Fine Texture of Enactment: Iconicity as Empowerment in Angelina Grimké's Pennsylvania Hall Address," *Women's Studies in Communication* 18: 19–43.

Davis, O. I. (1998). "A Black Woman as Rhetorical Critic: Validating Self and Violating the Space of Otherness," *Women's Studies in Communication* 21: 77–89.

Delgado, F. P. (1998). "Chicano Ideology Revisited: Rap Music and the (Re)articulation of Chicanismo," *Western Journal of Communication* 62: 95–113.

DeLuca, K. M., and J. Peeples. (2002). "From Public Sphere to Public Screen: Democracy, Activism, and the 'Violence' of Seattle," *Critical Studies in Media Communication* 19: 125–151.

Dickinson, G. (1997). "Memories for Sale: Nostalgia and the Construction of Identity in Old Pasadena," *Quarterly Journal of Speech* 83: 1–27.

Doane, M. A. (1984). "The Woman's Film: Possession and Address," In M. A. Doane, P. Mellencamp, and L. Williams (Eds.), *Re-vision: Essays in Feminist Film Criticism* (Los Angeles: University Publications of America). 67–83.

Donovan, J. (1980). "The Silence is Broken," in S. McConnell-Ginet et al. (eds.), *Women and Language in Literature and Society* (New York: Praeger). 205–218.

Donsbach, W., H. B. Brosius, and A. Mattenklott. (May, 1992). "Second-Hand Reality: A Field Experiment on the Perception of a Campaign Event by Participants and Television Viewers." Paper delivered at the annual convention of the International Communication Association.

Douglas, S. (1994). *Where the Girls Are: Growing Up Female with the Mass Media* (New York: Random House).

Douglass, R. and C. Arnold. (1970). "On Analysis of *Logos:* A Methodological Inquiry," *Quarterly Journal of Speech* 56: 22–32.

Dow, B. J., and M. B. Tonn. (1993). "Feminine Style and Political Judgment in the Rhetoric of Ann Richards," *Quarterly Journal of Speech* 79: 286–302.

Dow, B. J. (1996). *Prime-Time Feminism: Television, Media Culture, and the Women's Movement Since 1970* (Philadelphia: University of Pennsylvania Press).

Dow, B. J. "*Ellen,* Television, and the Politics of Gay and Lesbian Visibility," *Critical Studies in Media Communication* 18 (2001): 123–140.

Downey, S. D. (1997). "Rhetoric as Balance: A Dialectical Feminist Perspective," Women's Studies in Communication 20: 137–150.

Eagleton, T. (1975). *Criticism and Ideology: A Study in Marxist Literary Theory* (London: Verso).

Eagleton, T. (1976). *Marxism and Literary Criticism* (Berkeley: University of California Press).

Eagleton, T. (1983). *Literary Theory: An Introduction* (Minneapolis: University of Minnesota Press).

Edelman, M. (1964). *The Symbolic Uses of Politics* (Urbana: University of Illinois Press).

Edelman, M. (1971). *Politics as Symbolic Action: Mass Arousal and Quiescence* (Chicago: Markham).

Edelman, M. (1977). *Political Language: Words that Succeed and Policies that Fail* (New York: Academic Press).

Ehninger, D., and W. Brockriede. (1963). *Decision by Debate* (New York: Dodd, Mead).

Einhorn, L. (1981). "Basic Assumptions in the Virginia Ratification Debate: Patrick Henry vs. James Madison on the Nature of Man and Reason," *Southern Speech Communication Journal* 46: 327–340.

Engell, R. A. (2001). "Toward an Ethic of Evocative Language: Contemporary Uses of Holocaust-Related Terminology," *Southern Communication Journal* 66: 312–322.

Enkvist, N. (1971). "On the Place of Style in Some Linguistic Theories," in S. Chatman (ed.), *Literary Style: A Symposium* (London: Oxford). 47–64.

Enos, R. L. (2002) "The Archaeology of Women in Rhetoric: Rhetorical Sequencing as a Research Method for Historical Scholarship," *Rhetoric Society Quarterly* 32: 65–79.

Entman, R. (1991). "Framing U.S. Coverage of International News: Contrasts in Narratives of the KAL and Iran Air Incidents," *Journal of Communication* 41: 6–27.

Erickson, K. and C. Fleuriet. (1991). "Presidential Anonymity: Rhetorical Identity Management and the Mystification of Political Reality," *Communication Quarterly* 39: 272–289.

Espy, W. (1983). *The Garden of Eloquence: A Rhetorical Bestiary* (New York: Dutton).

Farrell, T. (1980). "Critical Modes in the Analysis of Discourse," *Western Journal of Speech Communication* 44: 300–314.

Feder, A. M. (1994). "'A Radiant Smile from the Lovely Lady': Overdetermined Femininity in 'Ladies' Figure Skating," *The Drama Review* 38: 62–78.

Ferris, S. P., and S. Roper. (2002). "Same and Mixed Gender Intimacy in a Virtual Environment," *Qualitative Research Reports in Communication* 3: 47–55.

Fetterly, J. (1978). *The Resisting Reader* (Bloomington: Indiana University Press).

Fetterly, J. (1991). "Introduction: On the Politics of Literature," in R. R. Warhol, & D. P. Herndl (eds.), *Feminisms: An Anthology of Literary Theory and Criticism* (New Brunswick: Rutgers University Press). 492–502.

Fisher, W. (1982). "Romantic Democracy, Ronald Reagan, and Presidential Heroes," *Western Journal of Speech Communication* 46: 299–310.

Fisher, W. (1987). *Human Communication as Narration: Toward a Philosophy of Reason, Value and Action* (Columbia: University of South Carolina Press).

Fisher, W. (1989). "Clarifying the Narrative Paradigm," *Communication Monographs* 56: 55–58.

Fiske, J. (1983). "The Discourses of TV Quiz Shows or, School + Luck = Success + Sex," *Central States Speech Journal* 34: 139–150.

Foss, S. (1986). "Ambiguity as Persuasion: The Vietnam Veterans Memorial," *Communication Quarterly* 34: 326–340.

Foss, S., and K. Foss. (1994). "The Construction of Feminine Spectatorship in Garrison Keillor's Radio Monologues," *Quarterly Journal of Speech* 80: 410–426.

Foss, S. K., and C. Griffin. (1992). "A Feminist Perspective on Rhetorical Theory: Toward a Clarification of Boundaries," *Western Journal of Communication* 56: 330–349.

Foss, S. K., C. L. Griffin, and K. A. Foss (1997). "Transforming Rhetoric Through Feminist Reconstruction: A Response to the Gender Diversity Perspective," *Women's Studies in Communication* 20: 117–135.

Foster, D. (2000). *Author Unknown: On the Trail of Anonymous* (New York: Henry Holt).

Foucault, M. (1981). "The Order of Discourse," in R. Young (ed.), *Untying the Text: A Post-Structuralist Reader* (London: Routledge and Kegan Paul). 48–78.

Fox-Genovese, E. (1991). *Feminism without Illusions: A Critique of Individualism* (Chapel Hill, NC: University of North Carolina Press).

Frank, J. (1969). "Symbols and Civilization," in W. Rueckert (Ed.), *Critical Responses to Kenneth Burke* (Minneapolis: University of Minnesota Press). 401–6.

Fraser, N. (1992). "Sex, Lies, and the Public Sphere: Some Reflections on the Confirmation of Clarence Thomas," *Critical Inquiry* 18: 595–613.

Fürsich, E., and M. B. Robins. (2002). "Africa.com: The Self-Representation of Sub-Saharan Nations on the World Wide Web," *Critical Studies in Media Communication* 19: 190–211.

Gaines, R. (1979). "Doing by Saying: Toward a Theory of Perlocution," *Quarterly Journal of Speech* 65: 207–217.

Gallagher, V. (1995). "Remembering Together: Rhetorical Integration and the Case of the Martin Luther King, Jr. Memorial," *Southern Communication Journal* 60: 109–119.

Gastil, J. (1992). "Undemocratic Discourse: A Review of Theory and Research on Political Discourse," *Discourse and Society* 3: 469–500.

Geis, M. (1982). *The Language of Television Advertising* (New York: Academic Press).

Genovese, E. (1976). *Roll Jordan Roll* (New York: Vintage).

Gerland, O. (1994). "Brecht and the Courtroom: Alienating Evidence in the 'Rodney King' Trials," *Text and Performance Quarterly* 14: 305–318.

Gibson, W. (1966). *Tough, Sweet and Stuffy: An Essay on Modern Prose Styles* (Bloomington: Indiana University Press).

Gilberg, S., C. Eyal, M. McCombs, & D. Nicholas. (1980). "The State of the Union Address and the Press Agenda," *Journalism Quarterly* 57: 584–588.

Gilbert, J. R. (2004). *Performing Marginality: Humor, Gender, and Cultural Critique* (Detroit: Wayne State University Press).

Giroux, H. A. (2001). "Breaking Into the Movies: Pedagogy and the Politics of Film," *JAC* 21: 583–598.

Gitlin, T. (1980). *The Whole World Is Watching: Mass Media in the Making and Unmaking of the New Left* (Berkeley: University of California Press).

Gitlin, T. (1987). "Car Commercials and *Miami Vice:* 'We Build Excitement,'" in T. Gitlin (ed.), *Watching Television* (New York: Pantheon). 136–161.

Goffman, E. (1959). *Presentation of Self in Everyday Life* (New York: Anchor Books).

Goldman, R., D. Heath, & S. L. Smith. (1991). "Commodity Feminism," *Critical Studies in Mass Communication,* 8, 333–351.

Goodall, H. L. (1994). "Living in the Rock 'n Roll Campaign: Or Mystery, Media, and the American Public Imagination," in S. Smith (ed.), *Bill Clinton on Stump, State and Stage: The Rhetorical Road to the White House* (Fayetteville: University of Arkansas Press). 365–416.

Grabe, M. E. (2002). "Maintaining the Moral Order: A Functional Analysis of '*The Jerry Springer Show,*'" *Critical Studies in Media Communication* 19: 311–328.

Gregg, R. (1971). "The Ego-Function of the Rhetoric of Protest," *Philosophy and Rhetoric* 4: 71–91.

Griffin, C. (1990). "The Rhetoric of Form in Conversion Narratives," *Quarterly Journal of Speech* 76: 152–163.

Griffin, C. (1994). "Rhetoricalizing Alienation: Mary Wollstonecraft and the Rhetorical Construction of Women's Oppression," *Quarterly Journal of Speech* 8: 293–312.

Griffin, L. (1969). "A Dramatistic Theory of the Rhetoric of Movements," in W. Rueckert (ed.), *Critical Responses to Kenneth Burke* (Minneapolis: University of Minnesota Press). 456–478.

Griffin, L. (1984). "When Dreams Collide: Rhetorical Trajectories in the Assassination of President Kennedy," *Quarterly Journal of Speech* 70: 111–131.

Griffin, M. (1992). "Looking at TV News: Strategies for Research," *Communication,* 13: 121–141.

Gronbeck, B. (1974). "Rhetorical Timing in Public Communication," *Central States Speech Journal* 25: 84–94.

Grossberg, L. (1984). "Strategies of Marxist Cultural Interpretation," *Central States Speech Journal* 1: 392–421.

Grossberg, L. (2002). "Postscript," *Communication Theory* 12: 367–370.

Gumpert, G., and R. Cathcart. (1985). "Media Grammars, Generations and Media Gaps," *Critical Studies in Mass Communication* 2: 23–35.

Gumpert, G. and S. Drucker. (1992). "From the Agora to the Electronic Shopping Mall: Shopping as a Form of Interpersonal Communication," *Journal of Communication* 9: 186–198.

Hall, S. (1992). "Cultural Studies and its Theoretical Legacies," in L. Grossberg, C. Nelson, and P. Treichler (eds.), *Cultural Studies* (New York: Routledge). 277–286.

Halliday, J., S. Curry Jansen, and J. Schneider. (October, 1990). "After the Wall: Myth, Metaphor and Articulation in U.S. Media Representations of Events in Eastern Europe," Dept. of Communication Studies, Muhlenberg College.

Harari, J. (1979). "Critical Factions/Critical Fictions" in J. Harari (ed.), *Textual Strategies: Perspectives in Post-Structuralist Criticism* (Ithaca: Cornell University Press). 17–72.

Harrell, J., et al. (1975). "Failure of Apology in American Politics: Nixon on Watergate," *Communication Monographs* 42: 245–261.

Harris, R. A. (2003). *Writing with Clarity and Style: A Guide to Rhetorical Devices for Contemporary Writers* (Los Angeles: Pyrczak Publishing).

Hart, R. (1971). "The Rhetoric of the True Believer," *Speech Monographs* 38: 249–261.

Hart, R. (1973). "On Applying Toulmin: The Analysis of Practical Discourse," in G. P. Mohrmann et al. (eds.), *Explorations in Rhetorical Criticism* (University Park, PA: Pennsylvania State University Press). 75–95.

Hart, R. (1977). *The Political Pulpit* (W. Lafayette, IN: Purdue University Press).

Hart, R. (1978). "An Unquiet Desperation: Rhetorical Aspects of Popular Atheism in the United States," *Quarterly Journal of Speech* 64: 33–46.

Hart, R. (1984a). "The Functions of Human Communication in the Maintenance of Public Values," in C. Arnold and J. Bowers (eds.), *Handbook of Rhetorical and Communication Theory* (Boston: Allyn and Bacon). 749–791.

Hart, R. (1984b). "The Language of the Modern Presidency," *Presidential Studies Quarterly* 14: 249–264.

Hart, R. (1984c). *Verbal Style and the Presidency* (New York: Academic Press).

Hart, R. (1985). "Systematic Analysis of Political Discourse: The Development of DICTION," in K. Sanders et al. (eds.), *Political Communication Yearbook, 1984* (Carbondale, Il.: Southern Illinois University Press).

Hart, R. (1986). "Of Genre, Computers, and the Reagan Inaugural," in H. Simons and A. Aghazarian (eds.), *Form, Genre, and the Study of Political Discourse* (Columbia: University of South Carolina Press). 278–298.

Hart, R. (1987). *The Sound of Leadership: Presidential Communication in the Modern Age* (Chicago: University of Chicago Press).

Hart, R. (1994a). "Doing Criticism My Way: A Reply to Darsey," *Western Journal of Communication* 58: 308–312.

Hart, R. (1994b). *Seducing America: How Television Charms the Modern Voter* (New York: Oxford University Press).

Hart, R. (2000). *Campaign Talk: Why Elections Are Good for Us* (Princeton: Princeton University Press).

Hart, R. and D. Burks. (1972). "Rhetorical Sensitivity and Social Interaction," *Speech Monographs* 39: 75–91.

Hart, R., G. W. Friedrich, and W. D. Brooks. (1983). *Public Communication* (New York: Harper).

Hart, R., and S. Jarvis. (1997). "Political Debate: Forms, Styles, and Media," *American Behavioral Scientist* 40: 1095–1122.

Hart, R., P. Jerome, and K. McComb. (1984). "Rhetorical Features of Newscasts about the President," *Critical Studies in Mass Communication* 1: 260–286.

Hart, R., D. Smith-Howell, and J. Llewellyn. (1990). "Evolution of Presidential News Coverage," *Political Communication* 7: 213–230.

Hart, R., K. J. Turner, and R. E. Knupp. (1980). "Religion and the Rhetoric of the Mass Media," *Review of Religious Research* 21: 256–275.

Hasian, M., Jr. (2002). "Nostalgic Longings and Imaginary Indias: Postcolonial Analysis, Collective Memories, and the Impeachment Trial of Warren Hastings," *Western Journal of Communication* 66: 229–255.

Hayden, S. (2001). "Teenage Bodies, Teenage Selves: Tracing the Implications of Bio-Power in Contemporary Sexuality Education Texts," *Women's Studies in Communication* 24.1: 30–61.

Hayes, J. (1976). "Gayspeak," *Quarterly Journal of Speech* 62: 255–266.

Heath, R. (1986). *Realism and Relativism: A Perspective on Kenneth Burke* (Macon: Mercer University Press).

Helmers, M. (2001). "Painting as Rhetorical Performance: Joseph Wright's An Experiment on a Bird in the Air Pump," *JAC* 21: 71–95.

Hetherington, M. (1996). "The Media's Role in Forming Voters' National Economic Evaluations in 1992," *American Journal of Political Science* 40.

Hillbruner, A. (1960). "Inequality, the Great Chain of Being, and Ante-Bellum Southern Oratory," *Southern Speech Communication Journal* 25: 172–189.

Hillbruner, A. (1974). "Archetype and Signature: Nixon and the 1973 Inaugural," *Central States Speech Journal* 25: 169–181.

Himelstein, J. (1983). "Rhetorical Continuities in the Politics of Race: The Closed Society Revisited," *Southern Speech Communication Journal,* 48, 153–166.

Hirsch, E. D. (1967). *Validity in Interpretation* (New Haven: Yale University Press).

Hitchon, J. C., and J. O. Jura. (1997). "Allegorically Speaking: Intertextuality of the Postmodern Culture and Its Impact on Print and Television Advertising," *Communication Studies* 48: 142–158.

hooks, b. (1984). *Feminist Theory: From Margin to Center* (Boston: South End Press).

hooks, b. (1991). "Writing Autobiography," in R. R. Warhol and D. P. Herndl (eds.), *Feminisms: An Anthology of Literary Theory and Criticism* (New Brunswick: Rutgers University Press). 1036–1040.

hooks, b. (1996). *Reel to Real: Race, Sex, and Class at the Movies* (New York: Routledge).

Horton, D. and R. Wohl. (1986). "Mass Communication and Para-Social Interaction: Observation on Intimacy at a Distance," in G. Gumpert and R. Cathcart (eds.), *Inter/Media: Interpersonal Communication in a Media World,* 3rd ed. (New York: Oxford University Press). 185–206.

Hubbard, R. C. (1985). "Relationship Styles in Popular Romance Novels, 1950 to 1983," *Communication Quarterly* 33:2: 113–125.

Hughey, J. et al. (1987). "Insidious Metaphors and the Changing Meaning of AIDS," Paper Presented at the Annual Convention of the Speech Communication Association.

Huspek, M. and K. Kendall. (1991). "On Withholding Political Voice: An Analysis of the Political Vocabulary of a 'Non-Political' Speech Community," *Quarterly Journal of Speech* 77: 1–19.

Huxman, S. S. (1997). "The Tragi-Comic Rhetorical 'Dance' of Marginalized Groups: The Case of Mennonites in the Great War," *The Southern Communication Journal* 4: 305–318.

Hyde, M. (1993). "Medicine, Rhetoric and Euthanasia: A Case Study in the Workings of a Postmodern Discourse," *Quarterly Journal of Speech* 79: 201–224.

Illouz, E. (1991). "Reason within Passion: Love in Women's Magazines," *Critical Studies in Mass Communication* 8: 231–248.

Ivie, R. (1980). "Images of Savagery in American Justifications for War," *Communication Monographs* 47: 279–294.

Jablonski, C. (1979a). "Institutional Rhetoric and Radical Change: The Case of the Contemporary Roman Catholic Church in America, 1947–1977." Diss., Purdue University.

Jablonski, C. (1979b). "Richard Nixon's Irish Wake: A Case of Generic Transference," *Central States Speech Journal* 30: 164–173.

Jablonski, C. (1980). "Promoting Radical Change in the Roman Catholic Church: Rhetorical Requirements, Problems, and Strategies of the American Bishops," *Central States Speech Journal* 31: 282–289.

Jameson, F. (1981). *The Political Unconscious: Narrative as a Socially Symbolic Act* (Ithaca: Cornell University Press).

Jamieson, K. (1973). "Generic Constraints and the Rhetorical Situation," *Philosophy and Rhetoric* 6: 162–170.

Jamieson, K. (1975). "Antecedent Genre as Rhetorical Constraint," *Quarterly Journal of Speech* 61: 406–415.

Jamieson, K. (1980). "The Metaphoric Cluster in the Rhetoric of Pope Paul VI and Edmund G. Brown, Jr.," *Quarterly Journal of Speech* 66: 51–72.

Jamieson, K. (1984). *Packaging the Presidency: A History and Criticism of Presidential Campaign Advertising* (New York: Oxford University Press).

Jamieson, K. (1988a). *Eloquence in an Electronic Age* (New York: Oxford University Press).

Jamieson, K. (1988b). "Television, Presidential Campaigns and Debates," in J. Swerdlow (ed.), *Presidential Debates: 1988 and Beyond* (Washington, DC: Congressional Quarterly Press). 27–33.

Jamieson, K. and K. Campbell. (1982). "Rhetorical Hybrids: Fusions of Generic Elements," *Quarterly Journal of Speech* 68: 146–157.

Jamieson, K. and J. Cappella. (1996). *Spirals of Cynicism* (New York: Oxford).

Japp, P. (1985). "Esther or Ishiah? The Abolitionist-Feminist Rhetoric of Angelina Grimké," *Quarterly Journal of Speech* 71: 335–348.

Jewett, R. (1973). *The Captain America Complex: The Dilemma of Zealous Nationalism* (Philadelphia: Westminister Press).

Johannesen, R. (1985). "The Jeremiad and Jenkin Lloyd Jones," *Communication Monographs* 52: 156–172.

Johnson, B. (1981). "The Critical Difference: Balzac's *Sarrasine* and Barthes's *S/Z*," in R. Young (ed.), *Untying the Text: A Post-Structuralist Reader* (London: Routledge/Kegan Paul). 162–174.

Johnstone, H. (1969). "Truth, Communication, and Rhetoric in Philosophy," *Revue Internationale de Philosophie* 90:404–409.

Jones, A. R. (1991). "Writing the Body: Toward an Understanding of *l'Ecriture Féminine*," in R. R. Warhol and D. P. Herndl (eds.), *Feminisms: An Anthology of Literary Theory and Criticism* (New Brunswick: Rutgers University Press). 357–371

Jorgensen-Earp, C. R. (1990). "The Lady, the Whore, and the Spinster: The Rhetorical Use of Victorian Images of Women," *Western Journal of Speech Communication* 54: 82–98.

Katriel, T. (1994). "Sites of Memory: Discourses of the Past in Israeli Pioneering Settlement Museums," *Quarterly Journal of Speech* 80: 1–20.

Katz, J., narr. (2000). [video] *Tough Guise: Masculinity and Violence* (Amherst, MA: Media Education Foundation). Dir. Sut Jhally.

Kaufer, D. (1981). "Ironic Evaluations," *Communication Monographs* 48: 25–38.

Kavoori, A. P. (1998). "Getting Past the Latest 'Post': Assessing the Term 'Post-Colonial,'" *Critical Studies in Mass Communication* 15: 195–203.

Kendrick, J. (1999). "Marxist Overtones in Three Films by James Cameron," *Journal of Popular Film and Television* 27: 36–44.

Kenski, H. C. (1996). "From Agenda-Setting to Priming and Framing," in M. E. Stuckey (ed.), *The Theory and Practice of Political Communication Research* (Albany: State University of New York Press). 67–83.

Kerbel, M. (1994). "Covering the Coverage: The Self-Referential Nature of Television Reporting of the 1992 Presidential Campaign." Paper presented at the annual meeting of the American Political Science Association.

Kidd, V. (1975). "Happily Ever After and Other Relationship Styles: Advice on Interpersonal Relations in Popular Magazines, 1951–1973," *Quarterly Journal of Speech* 61: 31–39.

King, A. (1987). *Power and Communication* (Prospect Heights, IL: Waveland).

Kirkwood, W. (1983). "Storytelling and Self-Confrontation: Parables as Communication Strategies," *Quarterly Journal of Speech* 69: 58–74.

Klaus, C. (1969). "Reflections on Prose Style," in G. Love and M. Payne (Eds.), *Contemporary Essays on Style* (Glenview, IL: Scott, Foresman). 52–62.

Knapp, M., R. P. Hart, and H. S. Dennis. (1974). "Deception as a Communication Construct," *Human Communication Research* 1: 15–29.

Knight, J. P. (1990). "Literature as Equipment for Killing: Performance as Rhetoric in Military Training Camps," *Text and Performance Quarterly* 10: 157–168.

Koerber, A. (2001). "Postmodernism, Resistance, and Cyberspace: Making Rhetorical Spaces for Feminist Mothers on the Web," *Women's Studies in Communication* 24: 218–240.

Kolata, G. (1975). "Communicating Mathematics: Is It Possible?", *Science* 187: 732.

Kristol, I. (1972). *On the Democratic Idea in America* (New York: Harper and Row).

Kuypers, J. A. (2000a). "From Science, Moral-Poetics: Dr. James Dobson's Response to the Fetal Tissue Research Initiative," *Quarterly Journal of Speech* 86: 146–167.

Kuypers, J. A. (2000b). "Must We All Be Political Activists?," *American Communication Journal* 4.1. Retrieved 2/17/2002 from http://acjournal.org/holdings/vol4/iss1/special/kuypers.html.

Lacy, M. (1992). "Toward a Rhetorical Conception of Civil Racism." Diss., University of Texas at Austin.

Langer, J. (1981). "Television's 'Personality System,'" *Media, Culture and Society* 4: 351–365.

Lake, R. (1983). "Enacting Red Power: The Consummatory Function in Native American Protest Rhetoric," *Quarterly Journal of Speech* 69: 127–142.

Lakoff, G. and M. Johnson. (1980). *Metaphors We Live By* (Chicago: University of Chicago Press).

Lanham, R. (1983). *Analyzing Prose* (New York: Scribners).

Lee, R., and K. Lee. (1998). Multicultural Education in the Red Schoolhouse: A Rhetorical Exploration of Ideological Justification and Mythic Repair," *Communication Studies* 49: 1–17.

Leff, M. (1992). "Things Made By Words: Reflections on Textual Criticism," *Quarterly Journal of Speech* 78: 223–231.

Leiss, W., S. Kline, & S. Jhally. (1990). *Social Communication in Advertising: Advertising, Persons, Products and Images of Well-being* (New York: Routledge).

Lentricchia, F. (1983). *Criticism and Social Change* (Chicago: University of Chicago Press).

Lester, P. (1994). "African American Photo Coverage in Four U.S. Newspapers, 1937–1990," *Journalism Quarterly* 71: 129–136.

Lévi-Strauss, C. (1955). "The Structural Study of Myth," *Journal of American Folklore* 68: 428–444.

Lewis, L. (1972). "On the Genesis of Gray-Flanneled Puritans," *A.A.U.P. Bulletin* Spring: 21–29.

Lipari, L. (1994). "As the Word Turns: Drama, Rhetoric, and Press Coverage of the Hill-Thomas Hearings," *Political Communication* 11: 299–308.

Logue, C. and E. Miller. (1995). "Rhetorical Status: A Study of its Origins, Functions and Consequences," *Quarterly Journal of Speech* 81: 20–47.

Lorde, A. (1981). "The Master's Tools Will Never Dismantle the Master's House," in C. Moraga and G. Anzaldua (eds.), *This Bridge Called My Back: Writings by Radical Women of Color* (New York: Kitchen Table, Women of Color Press). 98–102.

Lowry, D. and D. Towles. (1989). "Soap Opera Portrayals of Sex, Contraception, and Sexually Transmitted Diseases," *Journal of Communication* 39: 76–83.

Lucaites, J. L., and C. M. Condit. (1995). "Reconstructing <Equality>: Culturetypal and Counter-Cultural Rhetorics in the Martyred Black Vision," in C. R. Burgchardt (ed.), *Readings in Rhetorical Criticism* (State College, PA: Strata). 457–477.

Mackin, J. (1991). "Schismogenesis and Community: Pericles Funeral Oration," *Quarterly Journal of Speech* 77: 251–262.

Mader, T. (1973). "On Presence in Rhetoric," *College Composition and Communication* 24: 375–381.

Maranhão, T. (1990). "Psychoanalysis: Science or Rhetoric," in H. Simons (ed.), *The Rhetorical Turn: Invention and Persuasion in the Conduct of Inquiry* (Chicago: University of Chicago Press). 116–144.

Marback, R. (2001). "Ebonics: Theorizing in Public Our Attitudes toward Literacy," *College Composition and Communication* 53: 11–32.

Mattingly, C. "Telling Evidence: Rethinking What Counts in Rhetoric," *Rhetoric Society Quarterly* 32 (2002): 99–108.

Mayne, J. (1984). "The Woman at the Keyhole: Women's Cinema and Feminist Film Criticism," in M. A. Doane, P. Mellencamp, and L. Williams (eds.), *Re-vision: Essays in Feminist Film Criticism* (Los Angeles: University Publications of America). 49–67.

McCombs, M. and D. Shaw. (1972). "The Agenda-Setting Function of the Mass Media," *Public Opinion Quarterly* 36: 176–187.

McDonald, L. (1969). "Myth, Politics, and Political Science," *Western Political Quarterly* 22: 141–150.

McGee, B. R. (1998). "Witnessing and *Ethos*: The Evangelical Conversion of David Duke," *Western Journal of Communication* 62: 217–243.

McGee, M. (1975). "In Search of 'The People': A Rhetorical Alternative," *Quarterly Journal of Speech* 61: 235–249.

McGee, M. (1980). "The 'Ideograph': A Link Between Rhetoric and Ideology," *Quarterly Journal of Speech* 66: 1–16.

McGee, M. C. (2001). "On Objectivity and Politics in Rhetoric," *American Communication Journal* 4. Retrieved 3/21/02 http://acjournal.org/holdings/vol4/iss3/special/mcgee.htm.

McGuire, M. D. (1977). "Mythic Rhetoric in *Mein Kampf*: A Structuralist Critique," *Quarterly Journal of Speech* 63: 1–13.

McIntosh, P. (1998). "White Privilege and Male Privilege: A Personal Account of Coming to See Correspondences through Work in Women's Studies," in M. L. Andersen and P. H. Collins (eds.), *Race, Class, and Gender: An Anthology* (3rd ed.) (Belmont, CA: Wadsworth). 94–105.

McMullen, W., and M. Solomon. (1994). "The Politics of Adaptation: Steven Spielberg's Appropriation of *The Color Purple*," *Text and Performance Quarterly* 14: 158–174.

Mechling, E. Walker, and J. Mechling. (1992). "Hot Pacifism and Cold War: The American Friends Service Committee's Witness for Peace in 1950s America," *Quarterly Journal of Speech* 78: 173–196.

Merritt, R. (1966). *Symbols of American Community, 1735–1775* (New Haven: Yale University Press).

Messner, B. A. (1996). "'Sizing Up' Codependency Recovery," *Western Journal of Communication* 60: 101–123.

Meyer, D. (1995). "Framing National Security: Elite Public Discourse on Nuclear Weapons During the Cold War," *Political Communication* 12: 173–192.

Meyers, R., T. L. Newhouse, and D. E. Garrett. (1978). "Political Momentum: Television News Treatment," *Communication Monographs* 45: 382–388.

Mikell, G. (1995). "African Feminism: Toward a New Politics of Representation," *Feminist Studies* 21: 405–424.

Milburn, M. and A. McGrail. (1992). "The Dramatic Presentation of News and Its Effects on Cognitive Complexity," *Political Psychology* 13: 613–632.

Milic, L. (1971). "Rhetorical Choice and Stylistic Option: The Conscious and Unconscious Poles," in S. Chatman (ed.), *Literary Style: A Symposium* (London: Oxford University Press). 77–94.

Miller, C. R. (2002). "Foreword," in P. Sipiora and J. S. Baumlin (eds.), *Rhetoric and Kairos: Essays in History, Theory, and Praxis* (Albany: SUNY). xi–xiii.

Miller, J. B. (1999). "'Indians,' 'Braves,' and 'Redskins': A Performative Struggle for Control of an Image," *Quarterly Journal of Speech* 85: 188–202.

Miller, M. C. (1987). "Prime Time: Deride and Conquer," in T. Gitlin (ed.), *Watching Television* (New York: Pantheon). 183–228.

Millett, K. (1970/1990). *Sexual Politics*. 2nd. ed. (New York: Touchstone/Simon & Schuster).

Minnick, W. (1968). *The Art of Persuasion* (Boston: Houghton-Mifflin [1957]).

Moi, T. (1985). *Sexual/Textual Politics: Feminist Literary Theory* (London: Methuen).

Mongia, P. (1997). "Introduction," in P. Mongia (ed.), *Contemporary Postcolonial Theory: A Reader* (New York: Oxford). 1–18.

Morris, C. E., III. (1996). "Contextual Twilight/Critical Liminality: J. M. Barrie's *Courage* at St. Andrew's, 1922," *Quarterly Journal of Speech* 82: 207–227.

Morrison, M. (Fall–Winter 1992). "Laughing with Queers in My Eyes: Proposing 'Queer Rhetorics' and Introducing a Queer Issue," *Pre/Text* 13: 11–36.

Motion, J. (1999). "Politics as Destiny, Duty, and Devotion," *Political Communication* 16: 61–76.

Mulvey, L. (1991). "Visual Pleasure and Narrative Cinema," in R. R. Warhol and D. P. Herndl (eds.) *Feminisms: An Anthology of Literary Theory and Criticism* (New Brunswick: Rutgers University Press). 432–443.

Murphy, J. M. (1997). "Inventing Authority: Bill Clinton, Martin Luther King, Jr., and the Orchestration of Rhetorical Traditions," *Quarterly Journal of Speech* 83: 71–89.

Murphy, J. M. (1998). "Knowing the President: The Dialogic Evolution of the Campaign History," *Quarterly Journal of Speech* 84: 23–40.

Nelson, M. B. (1994). *The Stronger Women Get, The More Men Love Football: Sexism and the American Culture of Sports* (New York: Harcourt Brace Jovanovich).

Newton, J. (1998). "White Guys," *Feminist Studies* 24: 572–598.

Nichols, M. H. (1969). "Kenneth Burke and the 'New Rhetoric,'" in W. Rueckert (ed.), *Critical Responses to Kenneth Burke* (Minneapolis: University of Minnesota Press). 270–287.

Norris, C. (1982). *Deconstruction: Theory and Practice* (London: Methuen).

Nothstine, W., C. Blair, and G. Copeland. (1994). "Professionalization and the Eclipse of Critical Invention," in W. Nothstine et al. (eds.), *Critical Questions: Invention, Creativity and the Criticism of Discourse and Media* (New York: St. Martins). 15–70.

Olds, S. (1984). *The Dead and the Living* (New York: Alfred A. Knopf).

Olsen, T. (1978). *Silences* (New York: Delacorte Press/Seymour Lawrence).

Olson, K., and T. Goodnight. (1994). "Entanglements of Consumption, Cruelty, Privacy, and Fashion: The Social Controversy over Fur," *Quarterly Journal of Speech* 80: 249–276.

Olson, L. (1987). "Benjamin Franklin's Pictorial Representations of the British Colonies in America: A Study in Rhetorical Iconography," *Quarterly Journal of Speech* 73: 18–42.

Osborn, M. (1976). *Orientations to Rhetorical Style* (Chicago: Science Research Associates).

Osborn, M. (1977). "The Evolution of the Archetypal Sea in Rhetoric and Poetic," *Quarterly Journal of Speech* 63: 347–363.

Parry-Giles, S. J., and T. P. Parry-Giles. (1999). "Meta-Imaging, *The War Room*, and the Hyperreality of U.S. Politics," *Journal of Communication* 49: 28–45.

Patterson, T. (1993). *Out of Order* (New York: Knopf).

Pauley, J. L., II. (1998). "Reshaping Public Persona and the Prophetic *Ethos*: Louis Farrakhan at the Million Man March," *Western Journal of Communication* 62: 512–536.

Payne, D. (1989). *Coping with Failure: The Therapeutic Uses of Rhetoric* (Columbia: University of South Carolina Press).

Payne, D. (1992). "Political Vertigo in 'Dead Poets Society,'" *Southern Communication Journal* 58: 13–21.

Pearce, K. C. (1995). "The Radical Feminist Manifesto as Generic Appropriation: Gender, Genre, and Second Wave Resistance," in C. R. Burgchardt (ed.), *Readings in Rhetorical Criticism* (State College, PA: Strata). 307–315.

Pineau, E. L. (2000). "*Nursing Mother* and Articulating Absence," *Text and Performance Quarterly* 20: 1–19.

Pittman, R. "How TV Babies Learn," *New York Times,* September 30, 1990: 19.

Pocock, J. (1971). *Politics, Language and Time: Essays on Political Thought and History* (New York: Atheneum).

Poirot, K. (Spring, 2004). "Mediating a Movement, Authorizing Discourse: Kate Millett, *Sexual Politics,* and Feminism's Second Wave," *Women's Studies in Communication* 27: 204–235.

Powell, M. (2002). "Rhetorics of Survivance: How American Indians Use Writing," *College Composition and Communication* 53: 396–434.

Projansky, S. (2001). *Watching Rape: Film and Television in Postfeminist Culture* (New York: NYU Press).

Radway, J. (1984). *Reading the Romance: Women, Patriarchy and Popular Literature* (Chapel Hill: University of North Carolina Press).

Rainville, R. E., and E. McCormick. (1977). "Extent of Covert Racial Prejudice in Pro Football Announcers' Speech," *Journalism Quarterly* 54: 20–26.

Rangel, M. C. (2001). "Knowledge Is Power," in B. Finlen (ed.), *Listen Up: Voices from the Next Feminist Generation* (New York: Seal Press). 188–196.

Rasmussen, K., and S. Downey. (1991). "Dialectical Disorientation in Vietnam War Films: Subversion of the Mythology of War," *Quarterly Journal of Speech* 77: 176–195.

Rawlence, C. (1979). "Political Theatre and the Working Class," in C. Gardner (ed.), *Media, Politics and Culture: A Socialist View* (London: Macmillan). 61–70.

Reed, L. (2000). "Domesticating the Personal Computer: The Mainstreaming of a New Technology and the Cultural Management of a Widespread Technophobia, 1964–," *Critical Studies in Media Communication* 17: 159–185.

Reeves, C. (1998). "Rhetoric and the AIDS Virus Hunt," *Quarterly Journal of Speech* 84: 1–22.

Regan, A. (1994). "Rhetoric and Political Process in the Hill-Thomas Hearings," *Political Communication* 11: 277–285.

Rich, A. (1972). "When We Dead Awaken: Writing as Re-Vision," *College English* 33: 18–30.

Richardson, G. W., Jr. (2000). "Pulp Politics: Popular Culture and Political Advertising." *Rhetoric & Public Affairs* 3: 603–626.

Rosenfield, L. (1968). "A Case Study in Speech Criticism: The Nixon-Truman Analog," *Communication Monographs* 35: 435–450.

Rosenfield, L. (1972). "The Anatomy of Critical Discourse," in R. Scott and B. Brock (eds.), *Methods of Rhetorical Criticism: A Twentieth Century Perspective* (New York: Harper and Row, [1968]). 131–157.

Rosteck, T. (1994). "The Intertextuality of 'The Man from Hope,'" in S. Smith (ed.), *Bill Clinton on Stump, State and Stage: The Rhetorical Road to the White House* (Fayetteville, AR: University of Arkansas Press). 223–247.

Rueckert, W. (1963). *Kenneth Burke and the Drama of Human Relations* (Minneapolis: University of Minnesota Press).

Rueckert, W. (1982). "Some of the Many Kenneth Burkes," in H. White and M. Brose (eds.), *Representing Kenneth Burke* (Baltimore: Johns Hopkins University Press). 1–30.

Rushing, J. H. (1989). "Evolution of 'The New Frontier' in Alien and Aliens: Patriarchal Co-Optation of the Feminine Archetype," *Quarterly Journal of Speech* 75: 1–24.

Ruthven, K. K. (1984). *Feminist Literary Studies: An Introduction* (Cambridge: Cambridge University Press).

Ryan, M. (1982). *Marxism and Deconstruction: A Critical Articulation* (Baltimore: Johns Hopkins University Press).

Said, E. (1978). *Orientalism* (New York: Vintage).

Samp, J. A., E. M. Wittenberg, and D. L. Gillett. (2003). "Presenting and Monitoring a Gender-Defined Self on the Internet," *Communication Research Reports* 20: 1–12.

Saporta, S. (1988–89). "Linguistic Taboos, Code-Words and Women's Use of Sexist Language: A Double Bind," *Maledicta* 10: 163–166.

Sarch, A. (1997). "Those Dirty Ads! Birth Control Advertising in the 1920s and 1930s," *Critical Studies in Mass Communication* 14: 31–48.

Satterfield, J. M. (1998). "Cognitive-Affective States Predict Military and Political Aggression and Risk Taking: A Content Analysis of Churchill, Hitler, Roosevelt, and Stalin," *Journal of Conflict Resolution* 42: 667–690.

Savage, K. (1994). "The Politics of Memory: Black Emancipation and the Civil War Monument," in J. Gillis (ed.), *Commemorations: The Politics of National Identity* (Princeton: Princeton University Press). 127–149.

Schlenker, J. A., S. L. Caron, and W. A. Halteman. (1998). "A Feminist Analysis of *Seventeen* Magazine: Content Analysis from 1945 to 1995," *Sex Roles* 38: 135–149.

Schmuhl, R. (1990). *Statecraft and Stagecraft: American Political Life in the Age of Personality* (Notre Dame: Notre Dame University Press).

Schweickart, P. (1991). "Reading Ourselves: Toward a Feminist Theory of Reading," in R. R. Warhol and D. P. Herndl (eds.), *Feminisms: An Anthology of Literary Theory and Criticism* (New Brunswick: Rutgers University Press). 525–551.

Scott, R. (1987). "Argument as a Critical Art: Re-Forming Understanding," *Argumentation* 1: 57–71.

Sedelow, S., and W. Sedelow. (1966). "A Preface to Computational Stylistics," in J. Leed (ed.), *The Computer and Literary Style* (Kent, OH: Kent State University Press). 1–13.

Shome, R. (1998). "Caught in the Term 'Post-Colonial': Why the 'Post-Colonial' Still Matters," *Critical Studies in Mass Communication* 15, 203–212.

Shome, R., and R. Hegde. (2002). "Postcolonial Approaches to Communication: Charting the Terrain, Engaging the Intersections," *Communication Theory* 12: 249–270.

Showalter, E. (1985). "Toward a Feminist Politics," in E. Showalter (ed.), *The New Feminist Criticism: Essays on Women, Literature and Theory* (New York: Pantheon). 125–143.

Sigelman, L. (2001). "The Presentation of Self in Presidential Life: Onstage and Backstage with Johnson and Nixon," *Political Communication* 18: 1–22.

Silverstone, R. (1986). "The Agonistic Narratives of Television Science," in J. Corner (ed.), *Documentary and The Mass Media* (London: Edwin Arnold): 81–106.

Sim, S. (1999). "Postcolonialism," in S. Sim (ed.), *Routledge Critical Dictionary of Postmodern Thought* (New York: Routledge). 336–337.

Simons, H. (1986). *Persuasion: Understanding, Practice, and Analysis* (2nd ed.) (New York: Random House).

Sloop, J. (1994). "'Apology Made to Whoever Pleases': Cultural Discipline and the Grounds of Interpretation," *Communication Quarterly* 42: 345–362.

Smith, S. (1980). "Sounds of the South: The Rhetorical Saga of Country Music Lyrics," *Southern Speech Communication Journal* 45: 164–172.

Snitow, A. (1986). "Mass Market Romance: Pornography for Women is Different," in M. Eagleton (ed.), *Feminist Literary Theory: A Reader* (London: Blackwell). 134–139.

Spurling, L. (1977). *Phenomenology and the Social World: The Philosophy of Merleau-Ponty and Its Relations to the Social Sciences* (London: Routledge).

Steuter, E. (1990). "Understanding the Media/Terrorism Relationship: An Analysis of Ideology and the News in *Time* Magazine," *Political Communication* 7: 257–278.

Strine, M., and M. Pacanowsky. (1985). "How To Read Interpretive Accounts of Organizational Life: Narrative Bases of Textual Authority," *Southern Speech Communication Journal* 50: 283–297.

Sumner, C. (1979). *Reading Ideologies: An Investigation into the Marxist Theory of Ideology and Law* (London: Academic Press).

Tavris, C. (1992). *The Mismeasure of Woman* (New York: Simon & Schuster).

Taylor, B. (1992). "The Politics of the Nuclear Text: Reading Robert Oppenheimer's *Letters and Recollections*," *Quarterly Journal of Speech* 78: 429–449.

Thomas, S. (1985). "The Route to Redemption: Religion and Social Class," *Journal of Communication* 35:1: 111–122.

Thompson, J. B. (1984). *Studies in the Theory of Ideology* (London: Polity).

Tonn, M. B., V. Endress, and J. Diamond. (1993). "Hunting and Heritage on Trial: A Dramatistic Debate over Tragedy, Tradition, and Territory," *Quarterly Journal of Speech* 79: 165–181.

Topf, M. A. (1992). "Communicating Legitimacy in U.S. Supreme Court Opinions," *Language & Communication* 12: 17–29.

Toulmin, S. (1958). *The Uses of Argument* (Cambridge: Cambridge University Press).

Triece, M. E. (1999). "The Practical True Woman: Reconciling Women and Work in Popular Mail-Order Magazines, 1900–1920," *Critical Studies in Mass Communication* 16: 42–62.

Triece, M. E. (2001). *Protest and Popular Culture: Women in the U.S. Labor Movement, 1894–1917* (Boulder: Westview).

Tucker, D. L. (2001). "A Gender Drama in American Football Culture: The Case of the Coach's Wife." *Football Studies* 42: 58–76.

Tucker, L., and H. Shah. (1992). "Race and the Transformation of Culture: The Making of the Television Miniseries *Roots*," *Critical Studies in Mass Communication* 9: 325–336.

Turner, G. (1973). *Stylistics* (Baltimore: Penguin).

Vartabedian, R. (1985). "Nixon's Vietnam Rhetoric: A Case Study of Apologia as Generic Paradox," *Southern Speech Communication Journal* 50: 366–381.

Vavrus, M. D. (2000). "Putting Ally on Trial: Contesting Postfeminism in Popular Culture," *Women's Studies in Communication* 23: 413–428.

Wallman, S. (1981). "Refractions of Rhetoric: Evidence for the Meaning of 'Race' in England," in R. Paine (ed.), *Politically Speaking: Cross-Cultural Studies of Rhetoric* (Philadelphia: Institute for the Study of Human Issues). 143–164.

Walzer, M. (1988). *The Company of Critics: Social Criticism and Political Commitment in the Twentieth Century* (New York: Basic Books).

Wander, P. (1983). "The Ideological Turn in Criticism," *Central States Speech Journal* 34: 1–18.

Wander, P. (1984). "The Rhetoric of American Foreign Policy," *Quarterly Journal of Speech* 70: 339–361.

Ware, B., and W. Linkugel. (1973). "They Spoke in Defense of Themselves: On the Generic Criticism of Apologia," *Quarterly Journal of Speech* 54: 273–283.

Warner, W. L. (1976). "The Ritualization of the Past," in J. Combs and M. Mansfield (eds.), *Drama in Life: The Uses of Communication in Society* (New York: Hastings House). 371–388.

Warnick, B. (1979). "Structuralism vs. Phenomenology: Implications for Rhetorical Criticism," *Quarterly Journal of Speech* 65: 260–261.

Weaver, R. (1953). *The Ethics of Rhetoric* (Chicago, Henry Regnery).

Weaver, R. (2001). "Language Is Sermonic," in P. Bizzell and B. Herzberg (eds.), *The Rhetorical Tradition: Readings from Classical Times to the Present* (Boston: Bedford/St. Martin's [1963]). 1351–1360.

Weisman, E. (1980). "The Rhetoric of Holocaust Survivors: A Dramatistic Perspective." Diss., Temple University.

Weldon, R. A. (2001). "The Rhetorical Construction of the Predatorial Virus: A Burkian Analysis of Nonfiction Accounts of the Ebola Virus," *Qualitative Health Research* 11: 5–25.

Whedbee, K. (2001). "Perspective by Incongruity in Norman Thomas's 'Some Wrong Roads to Peace,'" *Western Journal of Communication* 65: 45–64.

White, R. (1949). "Hitler, Roosevelt, and the Nature of War Propaganda," *Journal of Abnormal and Social Psychology* 44: 157–174.

Whittenberger-Keith, K. (1989). "Paradox and Communication: The Case of Etiquette Manuals." Diss., University of Texas at Austin.

Wichelns, H. (1972). "The Literary Criticism of Oratory," in R. Scott and B. Brock (eds.), *Methods of Rhetorical Criticism: A Twentieth Century Perspective* (New York: Harper and Row [1925]). 27–60.

Williams, L. (1984). "When the Woman Looks," in M. A. Doane, P. Mellencamp, and L. Williams (eds.), *Re-vision: Essays in Feminist Film Criticism* (Los Angeles: University Publications of America). 83–100.

Williams, R. (1977). *Marxism and Literature* (London: Oxford).

Wilson, A. (1996). "Death and the Mainstream: Lesbian Detective Fiction and the Killing of the Coming-out Story," *Feminist Studies* 22: 251–278.

Wilson, J., and C. Arnold. (1974). *Public Speaking as a Liberal Art* (3rd ed.) (Boston: Allyn and Bacon).

Wolf, N. (November, 1993). "Excerpts from *Fire with Fire*," *Glamour:* 221+.

Woolf, V. (1929). *A Room of One's Own* (New York: Harcourt).

Worth, S. (1981). *Studying Visual Communication* (Philadelphia: University of Pennsylvania Press).

Zacharias, U. (2003). "The Smile of Mona Lisa: Postcolonial Desires, Nationalist Families, and the Birth of Consumer Television in India," *Critical Studies in Mass Communication* 20: 388–406.

Zelizer, B. (1992). *Covering the Body: The Kennedy Assassination, the Media, and the Shaping of Collective Memory* (Chicago: University of Chicago Press).

Zyskind, H. (1968). "A Case Study in Philosophic Rhetoric: Theodore Roosevelt," *Philosophy and Rhetoric* 1: 228–254.

INDEX

Credits